T0211193

Lecture Notes in Computer Science 10141

Commenced Publication in 1973
Founding and Former Series Editors:
Gerhard Goos, Juris Hartmanis, and Jan van Leeuwen

More information about this series at http://www.springer.com/series/7410

Robert Krimmer · Melanie Volkamer
Jordi Barrat · Josh Benaloh
Nicole Goodman · Peter Y.A. Ryan
Vanessa Teague (Eds.)

Electronic Voting

First International Joint Conference, E-Vote-ID 2016
Bregenz, Austria, October 18–21, 2016
Proceedings

 Springer

Editors

Robert Krimmer
Tallinn University of Technology
Tallinn
Estonia

Nicole Goodman
University of Toronto
Toronto
Canada

Melanie Volkamer
Karlstad University
Karlstad
Sweden

Peter Y.A. Ryan
Université du Luxembourg
Luxembourg
Luxembourg

Jordi Barrat
EVOL2-eVoting Research Lab
Tarragona
Spain

Vanessa Teague
University of Melbourne
Parkville, VIC
Australia

Josh Benaloh
Microsoft Research
Seattle
USA

ISSN 0302-9743   ISSN 1611-3349   (electronic)
Lecture Notes in Computer Science
ISBN 978-3-319-52239-5   ISBN 978-3-319-52240-1   (eBook)
DOI 10.1007/978-3-319-52240-1

Library of Congress Control Number: 2016963155

LNCS Sublibrary: SL4 – Security and Cryptology

Printed on acid-free paper

This Springer imprint is published by Springer Nature
The registered company is Springer International Publishing AG
The registered company address is: Gewerbestrasse 11, 6330 Cham, Switzerland

Preface

This volume contains papers presented at E-Vote-ID 2016: the International Joint Conference on Electronic Voting held October 18–21, 2016, in Bregenz, Austria.

E-Vote-ID is a combination of EVOTE and Vote-ID. The EVOTE conference started in 2004. Since then, the biannual EVOTE conference has become a central meeting place for electronic voting researchers, election management boards, election observers, practitioners, and vendors. Electronic voting experts with varied backgrounds and from various disciplines come to discuss the current research in this subject area. An intellectual electronic voting conference counterpart, with the same target group, is Vote-ID, which also took place biannually starting in 2007. The two conferences conjointly attracted more than 700 experts from over 35 countries over the last 12 years. Hence, they developed into the major events in the field of electronic voting. One of the major objectives of both conferences was to provide a forum for interdisciplinary and open discussion of all issues relating to electronic voting, with three tracks introduced.

E-VOTE-ID had 57 submissions. Each submission was reviewed by an average of 3.5 Program Committee members using a double-blind review process. The Program Committee decided to accept 14 papers for this issue.

The accepted papers represent a wide range of technological proposals for different voting settings (be it in polling stations, remote voting, or even mobile voting) and case studies from different countries already using electronic voting or having conducted their first trial elections.

Special thanks go to the members of the international Program Committee for their hard work in reviewing, discussing, and shepherding papers. They ensured the high quality of these proceedings with their knowledge and experience.

We would also like to thank the German Informatics Society (Gesellschaft für Informatik) and its ECOM working group for their partnership over several years. A big thank you goes to the Austrian Federal Ministry of the Interior, the Regional Government of Vorarlberg, the Swiss Federal Chancellery, the Secretary General of the Council of Europe, Thorbjørn Jagland, and the Estonian Presidency of the Council of Europe for their continued support.

October 2016

Robert Krimmer
Melanie Volkamer
Jordi Barrat
Josh Benaloh
Nicole Goodman
Peter Y.A. Ryan
Vanessa Teague

Organization

Program Committee

Jussi Aaltonen	Ministry of Justice, Finland
Roberto Araujo	Universidade Federal do Pará, Brazil
Nicolas Arni-Bloch	State Chancellery of Geneva, Switzerland
Frank Bannister	Trinity College Dublin, Ireland
Jordi Barrat	EVOL2 – eVoting Research Lab, Spain
Josh Benaloh	Microsoft Research, USA
Konstantin Beznosov	University of British Columbia, Canada
David Bismark	Votato, Sweden
Nadja Braun Binder	German Research Institute for Public Administration Speyer, Germany
Thomas Buchsbaum	Ministry for European and International Affairs, Austria
Christian Bull	Telenor, Norway
Craig Burton	Victorian Election Commission, Australia
Susanne Caarls	Election Expert
Gianpierro Catozzi	EC-UNDP, Belgium
Veronique Cortier	CNRS, France
Paul Degregorio	A-Web, USA
Chakrapani Dittakavi	CIPS, India
Wolfgang Drechsler	Tallinn University of Technology, Estonia
Ardita Driza Maurer	Election Expert
Eric Dubuis	Bern University of Applied Sciences, Switzerland
Paul Gibson	Telecom SudParis, France
Kristian Gjosteen	NTNU Trondheim, Norway
Nicole Goodman	University of Toronto, Canada
Rajeev Gore	Australian National University, Australia
Rüdiger Grimm	University of Koblenz, Germany
Paul Gronke	Reed College, USA
Rolf Haenni	Bern University of Applied Sciences, Switzerland
Thad Hall	University of Utah, USA
Tarmo Kalvet	Tallinn University of Technology, Estonia
Norbert Kersting	University of Münster, Germany
Aggelos Kiayias	University of Athens, Greece
Shin Dong Kim	Hallym University, South Korea
Reto Koenig	Bern University of Applied Sciences, Switzerland
Steven Kremer	LORIA, France
Robert Krimmer	Tallinn University of Technology, Estonia
Ralf Kuesters	University of Trier, Germany

Steven Martin	OSCE/ODIHR, Poland
Ronan McDermott	Election Expert
Juan Manuel Mecinas	CIDE, Mexico
Hannu Nurmi	University of Turku, Finland
Jon Pammett	Carleton University, Canada
Oliver Pereira	Université Catholique de Louvain, Belgium
Julia Pomares	CIPPEC, Argentina
Marco Prandini	DISI, Università di Bologna, Italy
Josep Reniu	University of Barcelona, Spain
Ron Rivest	MIT, USA
Mark Ryan	University of Birmingham, UK
Peter Ryan	University of Luxembourg, Luxembourg
Steve Schneider	University of Surrey, UK
Berry Schoenmakers	Eindhoven University of Technology, The Netherlands
Carsten Schuermann	IT University of Copenhagen, Denmark
Uwe Serdült	Centre for Research on Direct Democracy, Switzerland
Oliver Spycher	Federal Chancellery, Switzerland
Philip B. Stark	University of California, Berkeley, USA
Robert Stein	Federal Ministry of the Interior, Austria
Vanessa Teague	The University of Melbourne, Australia
Alexander Trechsel	EUI, Florence, Italy
Priit Vinkel	National Electoral Committee, Estonia
Melanie Volkamer	Technische Universität Darmstadt, Germany
Kare Vollan	Quality AS, Norway
Gregor Wenda	Federal Ministry of the Interior, Austria
Peter Wolf	International IDEA, Stockholm, Sweden
Filip Zagorski	Wroclaw University of Technology, Poland
Dimitris Zissis	University of the Aegean, Greece

Contents

Preventing Coercion in E-Voting: Be Open and Commit

Wojciech Jamroga[1] and Masoud Tabatabaei[2(✉)]

[1] Institute of Computer Science, Polish Academy of Sciences, Warszawa, Poland
w.jamroga@ipipan.waw.pl
[2] Interdisciplinary Centre for Security and Trust,
University of Luxembourg, Esch-sur-alzette, Luxembourg
masoud.tabatabaei@uni.lu

Abstract. We present a game-theoretic approach to coercion-resistance from the point of view of an honest election authority that chooses between various protection methods with different levels of resistance and different implementation costs. We give a simple game model of the election and propose a preliminary analysis. It turns out that, in the games that we look at, Stackelberg equilibrium for the society does not coincide with maxmin, and it is always more attractive to the society than Nash equilibrium. This suggests that the society is better off if the security policy is publicly announced, and the authorities commit to it.

1 Introduction

It was recognised early on in the history of voting that *ballot privacy* is an essential property of voting systems to counter threats of coercion or vote buying. More recently, cryptographers and security experts have been looking at using cryptographic mechanisms to provide *voter-verifiability*, i.e. the ability of voters to confirm that their votes are correctly registered and counted. This strengthens to integrity properties, but, if it is not done carefully, new threats to ballot secrecy can be introduced. The observation lead to the introduction of more sophisticated privacy-style notions: *receipt-freeness* and *coercion-resistance*. The latter is the strongest property and can be defined informally as: a voting system provides coercion-resistance if the voter always has a strategy to vote as they intend while appearing to comply with all the coercer's requirements. The coercer is assumed to be able to interact with the voter throughout the voting process: before, during and after.

Achieving coercion-resistance is extremely challenging, especially in the context of internet and remote voting (e.g. postal). A number of schemes have been proposed that provide it, but typically this comes at a cost, in particular in terms of usability. In this paper, we take a game theoretic approach to analyse the trade-offs between the costs of implementing coercion-resistance mechanisms on the one hand, and on the other hand the cost the to society regarding the threats to the legitimacy of the outcome due to coercion attacks.

© Springer International Publishing AG 2017
R. Krimmer et al. (Eds.): E-Vote-ID 2016, LNCS 10141, pp. 1–17, 2017.
DOI: 10.1007/978-3-319-52240-1_1

Unlike most existing papers, we neither propose a new coercion-resistant voting scheme nor prove that a scheme is secure in that respect. Instead, we focus on the context of coercion attempts in e-voting, namely costs and benefits of involved parties. The main question is: *Should the society invest in protection against coercion attempts, and if so, in what way?*. We do not aim at devising a secure voting procedure, but rather at exposing conditions under which security of a procedure is relevant at all.

Our game models rely on several simplifying assumptions. We do not represent ballot privacy explicitly, and we do not investigate its relation to coercion. Furthermore, we do not differentiate on different coercion scenarios. Instead, we model the level of coercion attempts and coercion-resistance as simple scalars. The former refers to how many voters the coercer(s) attempt to coerce, i.e., indicates the scale of coercion in the election. The latter indicates how much effort/cost is needed to break the protection measures. Although an actual voting system might consist of a set of authorities with possibly different interests, we assume a single agent that we call the "election authority" whose interests are in line with what we consider "the common good of the society". This agent's interests might or might not represent the preferences of the actual authorities of the election. But by modelling it this way we can study the question of what strategy should the authorities collectively choose, *if* they want to benefit the society as a whole. Finally, we assume that all the potential coercers fully cooperate so that they can be represented by a single "coercer" player. Thus, the scenario can be modelled as a two-player game with largely conflicting incentives.

Related Work on Preventing Coercion in Elections. The related work can be roughly divided into three strands: definitions of coercion-resistance and its relation to privacy, proposals of coercion-resistant voting procedures, and studies of the context of coercion-resistance. The notion of coercion-resistance was first introduced in [10]. In [5], a formalization of coercion-resistance was proposed, and its relation to receipt-freeness and privacy was studied. [7] gave a formal definition of coercion-resistance for the end-to-end voting schemes. In [14], a game-based cryptographic definition of coercion-resistance was proposed.[1] The same authors added a game-based cryptographic definition of privacy in [15], and showed that the relationship between privacy and coercion-resistance can be more subtle than it is normally assumed. [6] provided formal definitions of various privacy notions in applied pi calculus, and showed how they are related to each other. Finally, [9] used CSP to fit a wide range of definitions and properties given in the literature for coercion-resistance.

The second strand overlaps with the first: [7,10] all propose voting protocols that satisfy their definitions of coercion-resistance while [14] proves coercion-resistance of two previously existing protocols. Another coercion-resistant voting scheme was introduced in [2]. Several other papers proposed voting schemes

---

[1] The definition was game-based in the technical sense, i.e., the security property was defined as the outcome of an abstract game between the "verifier" and the "adversary". In this paper, we use game models to study the interaction between the actual participants of the protocol.

which provably satisfy privacy as an intuitive argument for coercion-resistance, cf. e.g. [23]. Several works such as [1,2,13,16,17,20,24,27] have developed weaker, more practical or more efficient ways to realize coercion-resistance.

Putting coercion-resistance in a broader economic or social context has been, to our best knowledge, largely left untouched. The only paper in this strand that we are aware of is [4]. The authors compare two voting systems using game models, more precisely zero-sum two-player games based on attack trees. Two actions are available for the attacker (performing the attack or not); the authority is presumably choosing one of the two voting systems. The utility of the attacker is the expected probability of successful coercion minus the expected probability of being caught. The value is computed for the two systems using empirical data. In contrast, we consider a more general game where coercion – and resistance measures – come at a *cost* (instead of simply assuming probability distributions for the possible events), and we look for the rational choices of the players using game-theoretic solution concepts. We also argue that the coercion game is not zero-sum, with important consequences for the best policy to be chosen.

Game-Based Analysis of Similar Application Domains. Our analysis is based on two game-theoretic solution concepts: Nash equilibrium and Stackelberg equilibrium. Nash equilibrium corresponds to the behaviour of players that should emerge "organically" when they adapt to the behaviour observed from the other players over a period of time. It is often used to analyse how the policies of multiple interacting users are likely to converge in the long run. The typical application is to so called *energy games* where dynamic pricing schemes are proposed and studied in order to balance the supply and demand of electrical energy in a small-scale distributed market, cf. e.g. [19,22,25,30].

Stackelberg equilibrium corresponds to a scenario where a designated "leader" commits openly to a selected strategy and thus forces the response from the other players. Stackelberg games have become very popular in design and analysis anti-terrorist policies [11,12,26,28]. Our study comes close to that line of research, but differs in two important ways. First, anti-terrorist games focus on protection of multiple tangible resources (planes, airport buildings, etc.), while our coercion games address protection of "the good of the society" as a whole. Secondly, because of the inherent differences between the two application domains, we only use Stackelberg equilibria in pure (deterministic) strategies, whereas the main solutions in the research on strategic prevention of terrorism are based on mixed (randomised) Stackelberg strategies.

Finally, we mention [29] that applies Stackelberg games to prevent manipulation of elections, but its focus is on the computational complexity of preventing Denial of Service type attacks.

2   Game-Theoretic Preliminaries

In this paper, we propose a preliminary game-theoretic analysis of coercion prevention in an election. The main idea is to model the election as a simple strategic game between the society and coercer(s). We begin by a gentle introduction to

Bob \ Sue	Bar	Home	Theater
Bar	3, 2	2, 1	1, 0
Theater	4, 0	0, 0	2, 3

Fig. 1. Example two-player strategic game. The only Nash equilibrium is indicated by the black frame, maxmin for Bob is highlighted in bold, and Stackelberg equilibrium for Bob is set on yellow background. The players' best responses to the other player's strategies are underlined. (Color figure online)

the basic concepts of noncooperative game theory. A more detailed exposition can be found in numerous textbooks, cf. e.g. [3,18,21].

2.1 Strategic Games

Definition 1 (Strategic game). *A strategic game (called also normal form game) is a tuple* $\Gamma = (N, \Sigma, u)$, *consisting of:*

1. *a finite set of agents or players* $N = \{A_1, \ldots, A_{|N|}\}$,
2. *a set of strategy profiles* $\Sigma = \Sigma_{A_1} \times \cdots \times \Sigma_{A_{|N|}}$, *where* Σ_{A_i} *collects the available strategies of player* $A_i \in N$,
3. *a utility profile* $u = \{u_1, \ldots, u_{|N|}\}$ *with* $u_i : \Sigma \to \mathbb{R}$ *being the utility function of player* A_i *that assigns the "payoffs" of* A_i *to strategy profiles.*

When needed, we will refer to A_i's *part of strategy profile* σ *by* σ_i, *and to the other players' part of the profile by* σ_{-i}.

A strategic game captures a "bird's-eye view" of interaction, where A_i's strategies represent her possible behaviours in a game. Strategies are treated as atomic: we are not interested in their internal structure, and can as well view them as simple actions. The combined behaviour of all the players is represented by a strategy profile, i.e., a tuple of individual strategies. Given a strategy profile σ, $u_i(\sigma)$ defines how much the outcome of the game is "worth" to player A_i. Thus, the utility profile is meant to represent the incentives (or preferences) of each player. An example strategic game – a slightly modified variant of the "Battle of the Sexes" – is shown in Fig. 1. Two players (Bob and Sue) are choosing in parallel whether to go to the local bar, or to the theater. The strategies and utilities of Sue are set in grey font for better readability.

When modelling interaction by a strategic game, we implicitly assume *complete information*, i.e., that the structure of the game is common knowledge among the players. In particular, players know each others' preferences and the available actions of the opponents. Especially the former assumption is often unrealistic. We will come back to this issue and relax the assumption in Sect. 4.

2.2   Solution Concepts

In game theory, *solution concepts* are used to define which collective behaviours are "rational" and should (or may) be selected by players in the game. Formally, a solution concept maps each game to a subset of strategy profiles. Different solution concepts encode different assumptions about the deliberation process that leads to selecting one or another strategy. In this paper, we compare the predictions obtained by three solution concepts: Nash equilibrium, maxmin, and Stackelberg equilibrium, presented briefly below.

Nash Equilibrium. A strategy profile σ is a *Nash equilibrium* if it is stable under unilateral deviations of players, i.e., if player A_i changed her part of σ (and the other players stuck to their strategies) then the payoff of A_i would decrease or stay the same. Formally, for every $A_i \in N$ and $\sigma_i' \in \Sigma_i$, it must hold that $u_i(\sigma) \geq u_i(\sigma_i', \sigma_{-i})$. Equivalently, σ is a Nash equilibrium if each σ_i is the best response to σ_{-i}. As an example, consider the game in Fig. 1. The strategy profile (*Theater, Bar*) is not stable because Sue can improve her payoff from 0 to 3 by changing her strategy to *Theater*. On the other hand, (*Theater, Theater*) is stable because both players can only lose when the change their minds: Bob would then decrease his utility from 2 to 1, and Sue analogously from 3 to 0.

Intuitively, Nash equilibrium represents a collective behaviour that can emerge when players play the game multiple times, and adapt their choices to what they expect from the other players. Thus, it captures the "organic" emergence of behaviour through a sequence of strategy adjustments from different players that leads to a point when nobody is tempted to change their strategy anymore.

Maxmin. *Maxmin for player A_i* aims at the largest value that the player can ensure regardless of what the other players do. Formally, it is the strategy profile σ^* such that $\sigma_i^* = \mathrm{argmax}_{\sigma_i} \min_{\sigma_{-i}} u_i(\sigma_i, \sigma_{-i})$ and $\sigma_{-i}^* = \mathrm{argmin}_{\sigma_{-i}} u_i(\sigma_i^*, \sigma_{-i})$. Intuitively, maxmin captures decision making of "paranoid" agents who always look at the worst possible outcome of their choices.

The maxmin for Bob in Fig. 1 is (*Bar, Theater*), since playing *Bar* guarantees the payoff of at least 1 to Bob, while playing *Theater* may obtain 0.

Stackelberg Equilibrium. Finally, *Stackelberg equilibrium for player A_i* represents rational play in 2-player games where a designated player (the *leader*) makes her choice first. Formally, it is the strategy profile σ^* for which $\sigma_i^* = \mathrm{argmax}_{\sigma_i} u_i(\sigma_i, \mathrm{argmax}_{\sigma_{-i}} u_{-i}(\sigma_i, \sigma_{-i}))$ and $\sigma_{-i}^* = \mathrm{argmax}_{\sigma_{-i}} u_{-i}(\sigma_i^*, \sigma_{-i})$. That is, for every strategy σ_i of the leader we find the response $resp(\sigma_i)$ that maximizes the utility of the opponent; then, we select the σ_i which maximizes $u_i(\sigma_i, resp(\sigma_i))$. In our example, *Bar* is Sue's best response to Bob's strategy *Bar*, and *Theater* is Sue's best response to Bob's *Theater*. Thus, the Stackelberg equilibrium is (*Bar, Bar*) because it obtains 3 for Bob, whereas (*Theater, Theater*) obtains only 2.

Intuitively, analysis based on Stackelberg equilibrium assumes that the leader can either execute her strategy before the other player, or irrevocably commit to her choice. Moreover, the choice of σ_i becomes common knowledge before the opponent chooses his strategy. Such commitment is typically possible in case of public institutions and agencies that can commit to a chosen policy through suitable legislation. Note that, when Stackelberg equilibrium coincides with maxmin, it is actually irrelevant for the leader whether her choice will be known to the opponent or not. Conversely, when Stackelberg equilibrium is different from maxmin, the leader is better off *publicly committing to her policy*, because this way she forces the other player to respond in a desirable way.

2.3 Pure Vs. Mixed Strategies

So far, we have mentioned only *pure strategies* of players, i.e., the choices explicitly given in sets Σ_{A_i} of the game model. More sophisticated behaviour of players can be represented by so called *mixed strategies* that model randomized play. Formally, a mixed strategy for player A_i is a probability distribution over Σ_{A_i}, with the idea that the player will randomize her choice according to that distribution. A *mixed strategy profile* is a combination of mixed strategies, one per player. Note that such a strategy profile uniquely determines a joint probability distribution over Σ (assuming that individual probability distributions are independent), and hence also the expected utility of each player. Thus, each normal form game induces an infinite payoff table where the rows and columns are given by the mixed strategies, and the cells contain vectors of the expected utility values. This way, solution concepts like Nash equilibrium, maxmin, and Stackelberg equilibrium are easily extended to analysis of randomized play.

Randomization makes it harder for the opponents to predict the player's next action, and to exploit the prediction. Moreover, the importance of randomized strategies in game theory stems from the fact that Nash equilibrium is guaranteed to exist in mixed strategies, whereas no such guarantee applies to pure strategies. We notice that Stackelberg equilibrium in mixed strategies, while theoretically elegant, is often questionable in practice. This is because the leader's commitment to her strategy must be believable to the opponent. However, commitment to a randomized strategy is hard to verify unless the game is played very frequently. This condition is satisfied, e.g., in case of anti-terrorist policies for deployment of air marshals on domestic flights [11], with multiple flights every day. On the other hand, elections are run way too infrequently to achieve the same effect. Thus, we will limit our analysis of Stackelberg equilibrium to pure strategies of the leader.

We also note that all but one of our coercion models have Nash equilibria and maxmins in pure strategies.

3 A Simple Game Model of Coercion

Consider an election with a set of candidates $\Omega = \{\omega_1, ..., \omega_g\}$ and a set of n voters. We model the election as a strategic game $\langle \{A, C\}, \Sigma, (u_A, u_C) \rangle$, where $\Sigma = \Sigma_A \times \Sigma_C$ with the ingredients defined below.

3.1   Players, Strategies, Utilities

Players. A and C are the players. Player A is an honest election authority who acts on behalf of the society. We assume that the goal of A is in line with "the good of the society" as a whole. A has no preference for any of the candidates, and tries to make the result of the election as close as possible to the result when no coercion occurs, i.e., when the voters vote according to their own preferences.

Player C represents the coercer. The coercer tries to change the result of the election by threatening or bribing voters in order to make them vote according to his plan, rather than to the voters' own preferences over the candidates. In general, several coercers can try to change the result of the election simultaneously. We adopt the worst case assumption that they all collude, and hence may be represented by actions and preferences of a single player C.

Note that we do not consider candidates and voters as players in the game, but rather as parameters of the model.

Strategies. $\Sigma_A = \{\alpha_0, \ldots, \alpha_{\text{Max}}\}$ is the set of protection methods that can be implemented by the election authority A. These represent the protection measures that can prevent, or make it harder for the coercer to discover the actual values of votes. It is assumed that α_0 represents the case of no protection.

$\Sigma_C = \{0, \ldots, n^*, \ldots, n\}$ is the set of strategies for C, indicating the number of voters that the coercer attempts to bribe or threaten to bribe according to his wish. The minimal number of voters that the coercer needs to coerce in order to change the result of the election in his favor is n^*. We assume that the value of n^* is common knowledge; we will relax the assumption in Sect. 4.

Preferences. Preferences are represented by utility functions over possible combinations of strategies. We define the utility of the election authority A as $u_A(\alpha_j, k) = v_A(out(\alpha_j, k)) - imp(\alpha_j)$ where:

- $imp(\alpha_j)$ is the cost of implementing the protection method α_j. We assume that $imp(\alpha_0) = 0$, and $t < t'$ implies $imp(\alpha_t) \leq imp(\alpha_{t'})$.
- $out(\alpha_j, k)$ is the outcome of the election when A implements α_j and C attempts to coerce k voters.
- $v_A(\omega)$ is the social value of the election outcome ω. We assume that $v_A(\omega) = v_A^*$ if the outcome of the election is the same as it would be without coercion, and $v_A(\omega) = v_A^* - \epsilon_A$ otherwise.
  Moreover, $\epsilon_A > imp(\alpha_i)$ for all $\alpha_i \in \Sigma_A$.

The utility of the coercer is $u_C(\alpha_j, k) = v_C(out(\alpha_j, k)) - k \cdot cost_C(\alpha_j)$ where:

- $v_C(\omega)$ is the value of the election outcome ω from the coercer's point of view. We assume that $v_C(\omega) = v_C^*$ if the outcome of the election is in favor of the coercer, and $v_C(\omega) = v_C^* - \epsilon_C$ otherwise, for some $\epsilon_C > 0$.
- $cost_C(\alpha_j) = d_C(\alpha_j) + \beta_C$ is the total cost that the coercer must bear when coercing one voter, where $d_C(\alpha_j)$ is the cost of overcoming the protection method, and β_C is the bribing cost. We assume that $d_C(\alpha_0) = 0$ and $d_C(\alpha_j)$ increases with j. Moreover, β_C is constant.

$A \setminus C$	0	n^*
α_0	$\underline{v_A^*}, v_C^* - \epsilon_C$	$v_A^* - \epsilon_A, \underline{v_C^*} - \beta_C \cdot n^*$
α_1	$\mathbf{v_A^* - imp(\alpha_1)}, \underline{v_C^* - \epsilon_C}$	$\mathbf{v_A^* - imp(\alpha_1)}, \underline{v_C^* - \epsilon_C} - \beta_C \cdot \mathbf{n}^*$

Fig. 2. Game model for perfect protection. The maxmin profiles and the Stackelberg equilibrium for A are shown. The game has no Nash equilibrium in pure strategies. (Color figure online)

We also assume that at least the strongest protection method α_{Max} induces so high costs of coercion that effective coercing becomes unprofitable, formally: $cost_C(\alpha_{\mathrm{Max}}) \cdot n^* > \epsilon_C$.

We will consider two possible settings for the coercion game. In Sect. 3.2, we assume that a perfect protection method is available to A, and if it is used then any coercion attempt will inevitably fail. In Sect. 3.3, we analyze the other variant where any protection method can be broken if the coercer invests enough money and effort.

3.2 Coercion Against Perfect Protection

We first study the case where the election authority has a choice between no protection (strategy α_0) and perfect protection against coercion (α_1). When A plays α_1 then the coercer cannot change the result of the election no matter how many voters he attempts to bribe, as there is no way for him to verify the values of the votes. Therefore the utility of the coercer in this case is $v_C^* - \epsilon_C - k \cdot \beta_C$, where k is the number of voters he attempts to bribe. We assume that a coercion attempt is successful only if the coercer can verify the votes.

Note that, for player C, the strategies 1 to $n^* - 1$ are all dominated by strategy 0. That is, C gets a higher payoff playing 0 no matter what the other player chooses. In consequence, they never belong to any rational solution, and can be omitted from the game table. Similarly, the coercer's strategies from n^*+1 to n are dominated by strategy n^*. Thus, it suffices to consider only choices 0 and n^*. The resulting game table is shown in Fig. 2. In all the strategic games from now on, we will underline the best response strategies of both players', indicate Nash equilibria by putting them in black frames, highlight the maxmin for A by bold font, and point out the Stackelberg equilibrium for A by the yellow background.

The game has no Nash equilibrium in pure strategies. The unique Nash equilibrium in randomized strategies is as follows: the authority chooses "no protection" with probability $p = \frac{\beta_C \cdot n^*}{\epsilon_C}$ and "perfect protection" with probability $1 - p$, whereas the coercer attempts to coerce n^* voters with probability $q = \frac{imp(\alpha_1)}{\epsilon_A}$ and 0 voters with probability $1 - q$. This yields the expected utility of $v_A^* - imp(\alpha_1)$ for the society. The maxmin for A is strategy α_1 which provides exactly the same payoff for the society, and the same holds for the Stackelberg equilibrium. Thus, it does not matter whether A adapts to the coercer's strategy

$A \setminus C$	0	n^*
α_0	$\underline{v_A^*}, v_C^* - \epsilon_C$	$\mathbf{v_A^* - \epsilon_A}, v_C^* - \mathrm{cost}_C(\alpha_0) \cdot \mathbf{n^*}$
α_{m^*-1}	$v_A^* - imp(\alpha_{m^*-1}), v_C^* - \epsilon_C$	$v_A^* - imp(\alpha_{m^*-1}) - \epsilon_A, \underline{v_C^*} - \mathrm{cost}_C(\alpha_{m^*-1}) \cdot n^*$
α_{m^*}	$v_A^* - imp(\alpha_{m^*}), v_C^* - \epsilon_C$	$v_A^* - imp(\alpha_{m^*}) - \epsilon_A, v_C^* - \mathrm{cost}_C(\alpha_{m^*}) \cdot n^*$
α_{Max}	$v_A^* - imp(\alpha_{\mathrm{Max}}), \underline{v_C^*} - \epsilon_C$	$v_A^* - imp(\alpha_{\mathrm{Max}}) - \epsilon_A, v_C^* - \mathrm{cost}_C(\alpha_{\mathrm{Max}}) \cdot n^*$

Fig. 3. Game model for breakable protection (Color figure online)

(i.e., plays the Nash equilibrium), publicly commits to strategy α_1 of maximal protection method (i.e., plays the Stackelberg equilibrium), or simply chooses α_1 and sticks to it (i.e., follows the maxmin).

3.3   Coercion Game for Breakable Protection

The analysis in Sect. 3.2 did not bring very interesting conclusions, but the assumption of a perfect protection method was not very realistic either. From now on, we will assume that the election authority can implement several alternative protection methods, none of them fully coercion-proof. In other words, the coercer can successfully coerce against any protection method. The costs of both A and C increase with implementation of (resp. coercion against) more advanced methods. As before, we assume that the structure of the game is common knowledge, in particular, the value of n^* (the amount of voters needed to be coerced in order to change the result of the election in favour of the coercer) is known to both players. The resulting strategic game is depicted in Fig. 3. Similarly to Fig. 2, we omit dominated strategies from the table for better readability. Best responses, maxmin, Nash equilibrium, and Stackelberg equilibrium are indicated in the same way as before.

Like in the previous game model, the only undominated strategies for C are 0 and n^*, i.e., it makes only sense to coerce either 0 or n^* voters. Moreover, as the authority changes the protection method from α_0 to α_{Max}, the difficulty of coercing for the coercer increases. For a given α, if $v_C^* - \mathrm{cost}_C(\alpha) \cdot n^*$ is larger than $v_C^* - \epsilon_C$ then C prefers coercing over not coercing. Note that, from some protection method α_m on, the cost of coercing for the coercer is more than ϵ_C. In that case the coercer, although being able to coerce successfully, prefers not to tamper with the election. It is easy to observe the following.

Theorem 1. *For the coercion game with breakable protection, the Nash equilibrium and the maxmin for A is (α_0, n^*), whereas the Stackelberg equilibrium for A is $(\alpha_m, 0)$. Moreover, $u_A(\alpha_0, n^*) < u_A(\alpha_m, 0)$.*

The unique Nash equilibrium in pure strategies is (α_0, n^*): the coercer attempts to coerce sufficiently many voters, and the authority chooses the cheapest protection method, leaving the election open to manipulation. Thus, when the players mutually adapt to each other's play, the outcome is clearly undesirable for the society. The Stackelberg equilibrium $(\alpha_m, 0)$ is much better in this respect: the authority invests in the minimal sufficient protection that makes coercion unprofitable, and the coercer gives up coercion. Thus, A should choose its strategy in advance and stick to it, without adapting to C's play. Moreover, the maxmin for A in the game coincides with the Nash equilibrium and not the Stackelberg equilibrium, so in order to end up in the latter, the authority must publicly and believable commit to strategy α_m.

4   Coercion with Incomplete Information

In the previous section, we assumed that the players have complete information about the structure of the game. In many scenarios the assumption is not realistic, as players are not certain about some aspects of the game they are playing. For example, they may be uncertain about the available strategies of other players, their preferences, etc. We have deliberately defined the utility functions u_A, u_C based on several basic parameters instead of fixing concrete utility values, and specified as few constraints as possible about the relationships between the parameters. Since our results hold for *all* the admissible values of the parameters, our conclusions are valid even if the players do not know the exact numerical values.[2] By and large, this seems a justifiable level of abstraction except for one point: typically, neither the election authority nor the coercer will know the *precise* number of voters that need to be coerced in order to swing the outcome of the election. The coercer is also unlikely to know exactly which voters are the right targets of coercion (for instance, it makes little sense to coerce voters that plan to vote for the coercer's favourite candidate). What the players know instead is some probabilistic information, obtained e.g. from pre-election polls. We incorporate the observation in this section and extend our game model to include probabilistic uncertainty of the players about the n^* parameter.

Formally, we will model the uncertainty by assuming that the players take into account not one, but a set Γ of strategic games for different possible values of n^*. The current belief of each player is represented by a probability distribution over Γ, and possibly also over the probability distributions held as beliefs by the other players. Such models are known as *Bayesian games*. Again, we refer the interested reader to [3,18] for details.

In what follows, we assume that the coercer and the election authority hold the same beliefs about n^* (represented by the same probability distribution). In general, this may not be true, but in the case of an election the players' beliefs are usually based on public opinion polls which are equally accessible to everyone. Thus, the assumption seems acceptable in our application domain. At the same time, it greatly simplifies the analysis, as we will only need to take into account the players' factual beliefs, and not their beliefs about each others' beliefs, beliefs about beliefs about beliefs, and so on.

---

[2] It suffices that the constraints are common knowledge among the players.

4.1 Bayesian Game for Coercion

We consider the Bayesian game $\langle \{A, C\}, \Omega, \Sigma, T, \tau, p, (\hat{u}_A, \hat{u}_C) \rangle$ with the following elements:

Players and Strategies. The sets of players and their available strategies are defined as before (cf. Sect. 3).

States of the World. $\Omega = \{1, \ldots, n\}$ is the set of possible *states of the world* (sometimes also called *states of nature*). In our scenario, each state of the world corresponds to one possible value of n^*, i.e., the number of voters needed to be coerced to swing the outcome of the election. Note that the same strategies are available to players in all states of the world.

Preferences. $\hat{u}_A, \hat{u}_C : \Omega \times \Sigma \to \mathbb{R}$ are utility functions of the players. The only difference to the complete information setting is that $\hat{u}_{A_i}(n^*, \alpha_j, k)$ depends not only on the strategy profile (α_j, k), but also on the actual value of n^*.

Player Types and Signaling. In Bayesian games, the set of *type profiles* $T = T_A \times T_C$ is used to construct higher-order beliefs of players, i.e., beliefs about beliefs etc. We define $T_A = \{t_A\}$ and $T_C = \{t_C\}$. That is, players' uncertainty about each others' beliefs is irrelevant. The *signaling functions* $\tau_A : \Omega \to T_A$ and $\tau_C : \Omega \to T_C$ are trivial and can be also omitted from our analysis.

Players' Beliefs. The probabilistic beliefs of A and C are represented by a single probability distribution $p \in \Delta(\Omega)$ over the states of nature. In this work, we consider two cases of such probabilistic beliefs, based on the uniform distribution (Sect. 4.2) and the normal distribution (Sect. 4.3). Although the values of n^* are discrete, when the number of voters is large we can use continuous probability distributions to estimate the probability of different intervals of n^*.

Solution Concepts. In order to apply solution concepts to Bayesian games, we use the standard transformation into strategic games [8]. That is, we transform the Bayesian game $\langle \{A, C\}, \Omega, \Sigma, T, \tau, p, (\hat{u}_A, \hat{u}_C) \rangle$ into a strategic game $\langle \{A, C\}, \Sigma, (u_A, u_C) \rangle$ such that, for every strategy profile $s \in \Sigma$,

$$u_A(s) = \mathbf{E}_{\omega \in \Omega}[\hat{u}_A(\omega, s)] \quad \text{and} \quad u_C(s) = \mathbf{E}_{\omega \in \Omega}[\hat{u}_C(\omega, s)].$$

4.2 Uniform Probabilistic Beliefs

Our first approach is to assume the players' beliefs in the form of a uniform probability distribution in range $[n_a, n_b]$, where $0 \le a \le b \le n$. Thus, we assume that A and C can rule out some values of n^*, but apart from that they consider all the possible states of nature equally likely. In order to transform the model to a strategic game, we need to compute $u_A(\alpha, n)$ and $u_C(\alpha, n)$ for a protection method α and the number of voters to coerce k.

Utility of the Coercer. We consider three ranges for k and compute $u_C(\alpha, k)$ in each range separately:

– If $k < a$ then in all states of the nature $k < n^*$, therefore:

$$u_C(\alpha, k) = v_C^* - \epsilon_C - k \cdot cost_C(\alpha).$$

In this range the strategy 0 is the best response of player C. By choosing this strategy the utility of the coercer is $v_C^* - \epsilon_C$.

– If $k \geq b$ then in all states of the nature $k \geq n^*$, therefore:

$$u_C(\alpha, k) = v_C^* - k \cdot cost_C(\alpha).$$

In this range the strategy b is the best response of the player C, which corresponds to the utility $v_C^* - b \cdot cost_C(\alpha)$ for the coercer.

– If $a \leq k < b$ then

$$u_C(\alpha, k) = \mathbf{E}_{\omega \in \Omega}[\hat{u}_C(\omega, (\alpha, k))] = v_C^* - k \cdot cost_C(\alpha) - \frac{b-k}{b-a} \cdot \epsilon_C$$

$$= v_C^* - \frac{b}{b-a} \cdot \epsilon_C + k \cdot (\frac{\epsilon_C}{b-a} - cost_C(\alpha)).$$

If $\frac{\epsilon_C}{b-a} - cost_C(\alpha)$ is positive then $u_C(\alpha, k)$ is increasing in k and otherwise it is decreasing in k.

Utility of A. Again, we consider three possible ranges of k:

– If $k < a$ then in all states of the nature $k < n^*$, therefore:

$$u_A(\alpha, k) = v_A^* - imp(\alpha).$$

– If $k \geq b$ then in all states of the nature $k \geq n^*$, therefore:

$$u_A(\alpha, k) = v_A^* - imp(\alpha) - \epsilon_A.$$

– If $a \leq k < b$ then

$$u_A(\alpha, k) = \mathbf{E}_{\omega \in \Omega}[\hat{u}_A(\omega, (\alpha, k))] = v_A^* - imp(\alpha) - \frac{k-a}{b-a} \cdot \epsilon_A.$$

Best Responses and Equilibria. By observing the values of u_C, we can see that in the range $[0, a]$, and also when $k > b$, $u_C(\alpha, k)$ is decreasing in k. In the range $[a, b]$, based on the sign of $(\frac{\epsilon_C}{b-a} - cost_C(\alpha))$ it can be increasing or decreasing in k. So the best response of the coercer is always one of the strategies 0 or b (strategy a is always dominated by 0). Therefore we need only to consider these two strategies for player C. We have that $u_C(\alpha, 0) = v_C^* - \epsilon_C$ and $u_C(\alpha, b) = v_C^* - b \cdot cost_C(\alpha)$. The coercer profits more by coercing b voters when $cost_C(\alpha) < \frac{\epsilon_C}{b}$, and otherwise would prefer to not to coerce. We assume that from α_0 to α_{m^*-1}, it holds that $cost_C(\alpha) < \frac{\epsilon_C}{b}$ and from α_{m^*} on, it holds that $cost_C(\alpha) > \frac{\epsilon_C}{b}$. Figure 4 shows the resulting strategic game for the uniform distribution of n^*.

Theorem 2. *For the coercion game with uniform beliefs, the Nash equilibrium and the maxmin for A is (α_0, b), while the Stackelberg equilibrium for A is $(\alpha_{m^*}, 0)$. Moreover, $u_A(\alpha_0, b) < u_A(\alpha_{m^*}, 0)$.*

Thus, similar to the game in Sect. 3.3, this game has a unique pure Nash equilibrium (α_0, b). Again, the equilibrium is undesirable, and the authority should instead prefer the Stackelberg equilibrium which is at $(\alpha_{m^*}, 0)$. As the Stackelberg equilibrium is different from the maxmin for A, player A needs to commit to strategy α_m, and to make this commitment public.

$A \setminus C$	0	b
α_0	$\underline{v_A^*}, v_C^* - \epsilon_C$	$\boxed{\mathbf{v_A^* - \epsilon_A}, \mathbf{v_C^* - \beta_C \cdot b}}$
α_{m^*-1}	$v_A^* - imp(\alpha_{m^*-1}), \underline{v_C^* - \epsilon_C}$	$v_A^* - imp(\alpha_{m^*-1}) - \epsilon_A, v_C^* - b \cdot cost_C(\alpha_{m^*-1})$
α_{m^*}	$\boxed{v_A^* - imp(\alpha_{m^*}), v_C^* - \epsilon_C}$	$v_A^* - imp(\alpha_{m^*}) - \epsilon_A, v_C^* - b \cdot cost_C(\alpha_{m^*})$
α_{Max}	$v_A^* - imp(\alpha_{\text{Max}}), \underline{v_C^* - \epsilon_C}$	$v_A^* - imp(\alpha_{\text{Max}}) - \epsilon_A, v_C^* - b \cdot cost_C(\alpha_{\text{Max}})$

Fig. 4. Coercion game with incomplete information, where the number of voters needed to coerce is estimated by a uniform probability distribution (Color figure online)

4.3   Normal Probabilistic Beliefs

In our second approach, we assume that the players' beliefs about the value of n^* are represented by a normal probability distribution with mean μ and standard deviation σ.

Utility of the Coercer. When n^* has a normal distribution with mean μ and standard deviation σ, the probability of a chosen k being more than n^* is:

$$Pr[n^* \leq k] = \frac{1}{2}[1 + \text{erf}(\frac{k - \mu}{\sigma\sqrt{2}})]$$

where:

$$\text{erf}(x) = \frac{1}{\sqrt{\pi}} \int_{-x}^{x} e^{-t^2} \cdot dt.$$

Therefore $u_C(\alpha, k)$ can be calculated as:

$$u_C(\alpha, k) = \mathbf{E}_{\omega \in \Omega}[\hat{u}_C(\omega, (\alpha, k))] = v_C^* - k \cdot cost_C(\alpha) - \frac{1}{2}[1 - \text{erf}(\frac{k - \mu}{\sigma\sqrt{2}})] \cdot \epsilon_C$$

$$= v_C^* - \mu \cdot cost_C(\alpha) - \frac{\epsilon_C}{2} + \gamma(k).$$

where:

$$\gamma(k) = \frac{\epsilon_C}{2} \cdot \text{erf}(\frac{k - \mu}{\sigma\sqrt{2}}) - (k - \mu) \cdot cost_C(\alpha).$$

Analysing the changes of function $\gamma(k)$ shows that if $cost_C(\alpha) > \frac{\epsilon_C}{\sigma\sqrt{2}}$ then $\gamma(k)$ is decreasing in k. In this case $u_c(\alpha, k)$ has its maximum at $k = 0$. If $cost_C(\alpha) < \frac{\epsilon_C}{\sigma\sqrt{2}}$ then $\gamma(k)$, and hence $u_C(\alpha, k)$, has a maximum at

$$k_\alpha^{max} = \mu + \sqrt{2\sigma^2 ln(\frac{\epsilon_C}{\sqrt{2\pi} \cdot cost_C(\alpha) \cdot \sigma})}.$$

Notice that this number is decreasing in $cost_C(\alpha)$. We denote the value of $u_C(\alpha, k)$ at this point by $u_C^{max,\alpha}$, where:

$$u_C^{max,\alpha} = v_C^* - k_\alpha^{max} \cdot cost_C(\alpha) - \frac{1}{2}[1 - \text{erf}(\frac{k_\alpha^{max} - \mu}{\sigma\sqrt{2}})] \cdot \epsilon_C$$

$u_C^{max,\alpha}$ is positive and is increasing in σ and decreasing in $cost_C(\alpha)$.

$A \setminus C$	0	k^{max}_{m*-1}	k^{max}_0
α_0	$\underline{v_A^*}, v_C^* - \epsilon_C$	$u_A(\alpha_0, k^{max}_{m*-1}), u_C(\alpha_0, k^{max}_{m*-1})$	$\boxed{u_A(\alpha_0, k^{max}_0)}, u_C^{max, \alpha_0}$
α_{m*-1}	$v_A^* - imp(\alpha_{m*-1}), v_C^* - \epsilon_C$	$u_A(\alpha_{m*-1}, k^{max}_{m*-1}), u_C^{max, \alpha_{m*-1}}$	$u_A(\alpha_{m*-1}, k^{max}_0), u_C(\alpha_{m*-1}, k^{max}_0)$
α_{m*}	$\boxed{v_A^* - imp(\alpha_{m*}), v_C^* - \epsilon_C}$	$u_A(\alpha_{m*}, k^{max}_{m*-1}), u_C(\alpha_{m*}, k^{max}_{m*-1})$	$u_A(\alpha_{m*}, k^{max}_0), u_C(\alpha_{m*}, k^{max}_0)$
α_{Max}	$v_A^* - imp(\alpha_{Max}), v_C^* - \epsilon_C$	$u_A(\alpha_{Max}, k^{max}_{m*-1}), u_C(\alpha_{Max}, k^{max}_{m*-1})$	$u_A(\alpha_{Max}, k^{max}_0), u_C(\alpha_{Max}, k^{max}_0)$

Fig. 5. Coercion game with incomplete information, where the number of voters needed to coerce is estimated by a normal probability distribution (Color figure online)

Utility of A. The utility of the society in the transformed game is:

$$u_A(\alpha, k) = v_A^* - imp(\alpha) - \frac{1}{2}[1 + \text{erf}(\frac{k - \mu}{\sigma\sqrt{2}})] \cdot \epsilon_A.$$

Notice that if we fix k, this function is decreasing in $imp(\alpha)$.

Best Responses and Equilibria. We can consider two cases: If $cost_C(\alpha) > \frac{\epsilon_C}{\sigma\sqrt{2}}$ then the best response for the coercer is 0, and otherwise his best response is k^{max}_α. We assume that from α_0 to α_{m*-1}, it holds that $cost_C(\alpha) < \frac{\epsilon_C}{\sigma\sqrt{2}}$ and from α_{m*} on, it holds that $cost_C(\alpha) > \frac{\epsilon_C}{\sigma\sqrt{2}}$.

Figure 5 shows the strategic game for the normal distribution of n^*. For the choices of the authority, we have only shown four protection measures: α_0, α_{m*-1}, α_{m*} and α_{Max}. For the choices of the coercer, we only included the ones that are the best responses to one of the depicted choices of the authority. The choice 0 is the best response for the coercer when authority chooses any protection method from α_{m*} on. The choice k^{max}_0 is the best response when authority chooses α_0, and the choice k^{max}_{m*-1} is the best response when authority's choice is α_{m*-1}.

The game has a unique pure Nash equilibrium at (α_0, k^{max}_0), which is clearly a bad outcome for the society. However, if the implementation cost of the protection method α_{m*} is less than the expected damage that player A gets from the coercion at the Nash equilibrium, i.e., if $imp(\alpha_{m*}) < \frac{1}{2}[1 + \text{erf}(\frac{k^{max}_0 - \mu}{\sigma\sqrt{2}})] \cdot \epsilon_A$, then the authority can use the Stackelberg equilibrium at $(\alpha_{m*}, 0)$ by committing itself to choose the method α_{m*} and to make this commitment public.

Now consider that the authority cannot, or does not prefer to implement α_{m*} or more secure protection methods (for example because of the high cost of it) and the strongest protection method that can be implemented is a suboptimal protection method α_{m*-1}. By announcing its choice and committing to it, the authority can achieve an equilibrium at $(\alpha_{m*-1}, b_{k^{max}_{m*-1}})$. In this equilibrium the estimated cost of a successfully coerced election for the authority ($\frac{1}{2}[1 + \text{erf}(\frac{k - k_\mu}{\sigma\sqrt{2}})] \cdot \epsilon_A$) is lower than ones in the pure Nash equilibrium of the game. If this reduction of cost is worthwhile for the authority (in comparison to the extra implementation cost of α_{m*-1} comparing to α_0), the authority can benefit from announcing and committing to its strategy even in a suboptimal protection method.

Notice that by increasing the uncertainty about the number of needed votes to buy, i.e. by increasing σ, the value of m^* decreases. It means that the Stackelberg equilibrium can be moved to a one with lower implementation cost for the authority. This may suggest that the authority can in fact benefit from making very accurate polls *unavailable* to the public before the election.

5 Conclusions

In this work, we look at simple game models of protection against coercion in voting procedures. The models are two-person nonzero-sum noncooperative games, where one player represents the society and the other a potential coercer in the election. Our modelling relies on a number of abstractions and simplifying assumptions. Still, even at this level of abstraction some interesting patterns can be observed. Most importantly, we show that in all games that we consider, Stackelberg equilibrium is different from Nash equilibrium. In other words, it is in the interest of the society *not* to adapt to the expected strategy of the coercer. Instead of that, the society should decide on its coercion-resistance policy in advance.

Moreover, for almost all of our models, the Stackelberg equilibrium does not coincide with maxmin. Translating the formal result to intuitive terms, the society will benefit from *announcing its anti-coercion policy openly*. This way, the rational coercer is forced to refraining from coercion altogether. Paraphrasing the well-known slogan, the advice is *not to seek coercion-resistance through obscurity*.

Acknowledgements. Wojciech Jamroga acknowledges the support of the National Research Fund (FNR), Luxembourg, under the project GALOT (INTER/DFG/12/06), the support of the 7th Framework Programme of the European Union under the Marie Curie IEF project ReVINK (PIEF-GA-2012-626398), and the support of the National Centre for Research and Development (NCBR), Poland, under the PolLux project VoteVerif (POLLUX-IV/1/2016). Masoud Tabatabaei acknowledges the support of the National Research Fund Luxembourg under project GAIVS (AFR Code: 5884506).

References

1. Aditya, R., Lee, B., Boyd, C., Dawson, E.: An efficient mixnet-based voting scheme providing receipt-freeness. In: Katsikas, S., Lopez, J., Pernul, G. (eds.) TrustBus 2004. LNCS, vol. 3184, pp. 152–161. Springer, Heidelberg (2004). doi:10.1007/978-3-540-30079-3_16

2. Araújo, R., Rajeb, N., Robbana, R., Traoré, J., Youssfi, S.: Towards practical and secure coercion-resistant electronic elections. In: Heng, S.-H., Wright, R.N., Goi, B.-M. (eds.) CANS 2010. LNCS, vol. 6467, pp. 278–297. Springer, Heidelberg (2010). doi:10.1007/978-3-642-17619-7_20

3. Bonanno, G.: Game Theory (open access textbook with 165 solved exercises). CoRR, abs/1512.06808, 2015

4. Buldas, A., Mägi, T.: Practical security analysis of e-voting systems. In: Miyaji, A., Kikuchi, H., Rannenberg, K. (eds.) IWSEC 2007. LNCS, vol. 4752, pp. 320–335. Springer, Heidelberg (2007). doi:10.1007/978-3-540-75651-4_22

5. Delaune, S., Kremer, S., Ryan. M.: Coercion-resistance and receipt-freeness in electronic voting. In: 19th IEEE Computer Security Foundations Workshop, p. 12. IEEE (2006)
6. Dreier, J., Lafourcade, P., Lakhnec, Y.: A formal taxonomy of privacy in voting protocols. In: 2012 IEEE International Conference on Communications (ICC), pp. 6710–6715. IEEE (2012)
7. Gardner, R.W., Garera, S., Rubin, A.D.: Coercion resistant end-to-end voting. In: Dingledine, R., Golle, P. (eds.) FC 2009. LNCS, vol. 5628, pp. 344–361. Springer, Heidelberg (2009). doi:10.1007/978-3-642-03549-4_21
8. Harsanyi, J.C., Selten, R.: A generalized Nash solution for two-person bargaining games with incomplete information. Manag. Sci. 18(5–part–2), 80–106 (1972)
9. Heather, J., Schneider, S.: A formal framework for modelling coercion resistance and receipt freeness. In: Giannakopoulou, D., Méry, D. (eds.) FM 2012. LNCS, vol. 7436, pp. 217–231. Springer, Heidelberg (2012). doi:10.1007/978-3-642-32759-9_19
10. Juels, A., Catalano, D., Jakobsson, M.: Coercion-resistant electronic elections. In: Proceedings of the 2005 ACM Workshop on Privacy in the Electronic Society, pp. 61–70. ACM (2005)
11. Kiekintveld, C., Jain, M., Tsai, J., Pita, J., Tambe, M., Ordonez, F.: Computing optimal randomized resource allocations for massive security games. In: Proceedings of AAMAS, pp. 689–696. IFAAMAS (2009)
12. Korzhyk, D., Yin, Z., Kiekintveld, C., Conitzer, V., Tambe, M.: Stackelberg vs. Nash in security games: an extended investigation of interchangeability, equivalence, and uniqueness. J. Artif. Intell. Res. 41, 297–327 (2011)
13. Ku, W.-C., Ho, C.-M.: An e-voting scheme against bribe and coercion. In: 2004 IEEE International Conference on e-Technology, e-Commerce and e-Service EEE 2004, pp. 113–116. IEEE (2004)
14. Küsters, R., Truderung, T., Vogt, A.: A game-based definition of coercion-resistance and its applications. In: Proceedings of the 2010 23rd IEEE Computer Security Foundations Symposium, pp. 122–136. IEEE Computer Society (2010)
15. Küsters, R., Truderung, T., Vogt, A.: Verifiability, privacy, and coercion-resistance: new insights from a case study. In: 2011 IEEE Symposium on Security and Privacy (SP), pp. 538–553. IEEE (2011)
16. Lee, B., Boyd, C., Dawson, E., Kim, K., Yang, J., Yoo, S.: Providing receipt-freeness in mixnet-based voting protocols. In: Lim, J.-I., Lee, D.-H. (eds.) ICISC 2003. LNCS, vol. 2971, pp. 245–258. Springer, Heidelberg (2004). doi:10.1007/978-3-540-24691-6_19
17. Lee, B., Kim, K.: Receipt-free electronic voting scheme with a tamper-resistant randomizer. In: Lee, P.J., Lim, C.H. (eds.) ICISC 2002. LNCS, vol. 2587, pp. 389–406. Springer, Heidelberg (2003)
18. Leyton-Brown, K., Shoham, Y.: Essentials of Game Theory: A Concise, Multidisciplinary Introduction. Morgan and Claypool, San Rafael (2008)
19. Li, N., Chen, L., Low, S.H.: Optimal Demand Response based on Utility Maximization in Power Networks. IEEE (2011)
20. Magkos, E., Burmester, M., Chrissikopoulos, V.: Receipt-freeness in large-scale elections without untappable channels. In: Schmid, B., Stanoevska-Slabeva, K., Tschammer, V. (eds.) Towards the E-Society, pp. 683–693. Springer, New york (2001)
21. Osborne, M., Rubinstein, A.: A Course in Game Theory. MIT Press, Cambridge (1994)

22. Pedrasa, M., Spooner, T., MacGill, I.: Coordinated scheduling of residential distributed energy resources to optimize smart home energy services. IEEE Trans. Smart Grid 1(2), 134–143 (2010)
23. Peter, Y., Ryan, A.: The computer ate my vote. In: Boca, P., Bowen, J.P., Siddiqi, J. (eds.) Formal Methods: State of the Art and New Directions, pp. 147–184. Springer, London (2010)
24. Schläpfer, M., Haenni, R., Koenig, R., Spycher, O.: Efficient vote authorization in coercion-resistant internet voting. In: Kiayias, A., Lipmaa, H. (eds.) Vote-ID 2011. LNCS, vol. 7187, pp. 71–88. Springer, Heidelberg (2012). doi:10.1007/978-3-642-32747-6_5
25. Su, C.L., Kirschen, D.: Quantifying the effect of demand response on electricity markets. IEEE Trans. Power Syst. **24**(3), 1199–1207 (2009)
26. Tambe, M.: Security and Game Theory: Algorithms, Deployed Systems, Lessons Learned. Cambridge University Press, Cambridge (2011)
27. Weber, S.G., Araujo, R., Buchmann, J.: On coercion-resistant electronic elections with linear work. In: The Second International Conference on Availability, Reliability and Security, ARES 2007, pp. 908–916. IEEE (2007)
28. Xu, H.: The mysteries of security games: equilibrium computation becomes combinatorial algorithm design. In: Proceedings of SECMAS. IFAAMAS (2016)
29. Yin, Y., Vorobeychik, Y., An, B., Hazon, N.: Optimally protecting elections. In: Proceedings of SECMAS. IFAAMAS (2016)
30. Zhang, J., Fuller, J.D., Elhedhli, S.: A stochastic programming model for a day-ahead electricity market with real-time reserve shortage pricing. IEEE Trans. Power Syst. **25**(2), 703–713 (2010)

Automatic Margin Computation for Risk-Limiting Audits

Bernhard Beckert[1], Michael Kirsten[1(✉)], Vladimir Klebanov[1], and Carsten Schürmann[2]

[1] Institute of Theoretical Informatics,
Am Fasanengarten 5, 76131 Karlsruhe, Germany
{beckert,kirsten,klebanov}@kit.edu
[2] IT University of Copenhagen (ITU),
Rued Langgaards Vej 7, 2300 Copenhagen, Denmark
carsten@itu.dk

Abstract. A risk-limiting audit is a statistical method to create confidence in the correctness of an election result by checking samples of paper ballots. In order to perform an audit, one usually needs to know what the election margin is, i.e., the number of votes that would need to be changed in order to change the election outcome.

In this paper, we present a fully automatic method for computing election margins. It is based on the program analysis technique of bounded model checking to analyse the implementation of the election function. The method can be applied to arbitrary election functions without understanding the actual computation of the election result or without even intuitively knowing how the election function works.

We have implemented our method based on the model checker CBMC; and we present a case study demonstrating that it can be applied to real-world elections.

Keywords: Risk-limiting audit · Margin computation · Software bounded model checking · Static analysis

1 Introduction

One reliable method to create confidence in the outcome of an election among the electorate is to audit the election result against the physical evidence, i.e., the ballots. Different methods for auditing elections exist, some of them require the computation of a margin, that is the minimal number of ballots to be changed, misfiled, etc. to affect the election outcome. For those methods, the precise definition of the margin is often hidden inside the theory, as it depends on the election function—or social choice function—and the particular auditing methodology. This means, that (1) for many election functions, including Ranked Choice Voting (RCV) and Single Transferable Vote (STV), or election functions that combine different electoral systems, for example on state and federal level, it is difficult if not impossible to give closed forms for how to compute a margin, and

© Springer International Publishing AG 2017
R. Krimmer et al. (Eds.): E-Vote-ID 2016, LNCS 10141, pp. 18–35, 2017.
DOI: 10.1007/978-3-319-52240-1_2

(2) even if one manages to find a closed form for how to compute the margin, the implementations of election function and margin computation differ, for example in the way ambiguities are resolved, when and how to which precision to round, how tie-breaking rules are implemented, etc.

In this paper, we focus on auditing methods that require the margins to be known before they can be applied. Examples of these methods are, e.g., risk-limiting audits that draw a random sample of paper ballots [14] whose size is computed from (a) a risk-limit, i.e., how confident we wish to be in the election result, and (b) the margin. For a *comparision audit*, the margin of a risk-limiting audit is defined as the minimal number of votes that would need to be misfiled in order to change the election outcome. The margin is identical to the number of votes that would have had to be miscounted or tampered with during tabulation. If the election margin is large, only a small sample needs to be drawn and audited. The smaller the margin, the larger the sample. In the worst case, the audit will trigger a full manual recount.

We describe a way to compute the margins that does not presuppose the existence of a closed form for the margin and works directly on the source code (e.g., written in C/C++). Our technique can be applied to any election function, but it will perform best on those that are conceptually simple, such as D'Hondt and Sainte-Laguë. The technique can in principle also be applied to more complex election functions, such as instant-runoff voting (IRV), but only for small elections with a small number of seats and candidates. For bigger elections, such as the national elections in Australia, our technique does not scale – yet.

Our technique takes advantage of the state-of-the-art in program analysis, in particular software bounded model checking (SBMC). We compute the margin directly from the implementation of the election function. The trick is to use software bounded model checking for determining whether tampering with (at most) n votes can lead to a change in the election result. If yes, we have found an upper bound for the margin; and, if no, we have found a lower bound. The model checker is then called iteratively with different values for n, using binary search to determine the exact value of the margin. Our method is agnostic to the mathematics behind the election function, and the statistics behind the audit sample size computations. It can be applied to arbitrary C/C++ implementations of election functions without understanding the actual computation of the election result or without even intuitively knowing how the election function works.

Contents of this Paper. In Sect. 2, we recapitulate the idea of risk-limiting audits and describe how election margins influence the audit; and in Sect. 3, we give an introduction to software bounded model checking. Then, in Sect. 4, we introduce our method that, based on SBMC, allows to automatically compute election margins for arbitrary election functions. In Sect. 5, we illustrate our approach using an election function based on the D'Hondt method. An extension that leads to increased efficiency is described in Sect. 6. In Sect. 7, we present a case study where we apply our method to compute the election margin for the main part of the 2015 Danish national parliamentary elections. Finally, in Sect. 8, we draw conclusions and discuss future work.

Related Work. The contribution of our paper is a *generic* method that infers election margins for any election function, for which an implementation is available. In contrast to our work, there has been a lot of research on how to compute margins for *specific* election functions, for which that problem is particularly hard. The most prominent example is Instant-Runoff Voting (IRV) where margin computation is NP-hard [2]. Methods for computing lower bounds on margins for IRV have been developed by Cary [6] and Sarwate et al. [16]; and methods for computing the exact margin have been presented by Magrino et al. [15] and, recently, by Blom et al. [5].

To compute the margin of an election is an instance of the general problem of inverting a function for which an implementation is given, i.e., to ask for an input to the implementation that leads to a particular kind of output. The idea of using model checkers for solving such problems has also been applied in the field of test-case generation, where one is looking for input values leading to some specific program behaviour [20]. For example, the software model checker CBMC has been integrated into the extensive test-suite FShell [12]. Similar techniques have been used for generating high-quality game content, such as well-designed puzzles that are hard to solve [17].

In the context of elections, SBMC with SAT/SMT solvers can furthermore be used for analysing, whether the given election function does indeed compute the correct result with respect to some given formal criteria [3].

2   Risk-Limiting Audits and Election Margins

A risk-limiting audit is a statistical method to create confidence in the correctness of an election result by checking samples of paper ballots. Lindeman and Stark [14] distinguish *ballot-polling audits*, where they draw a carefully chosen random sample of ballots to check whether the sample gives sufficiently strong evidence for the correctness of the published election result. In contrast, a *comparison audit* checks the ballot interpretation for a random sample during the audit against the ballot's respective interpretation in a vote-tabulation system.

Both auditing techniques, ballot-polling and comparison audits, rely on the availability of the ballot manifest which describes in detail how the ballots are organised and stored, including how many stacks there are and how many ballots can be found in each stack. This information is needed for drawing the sample.

In addition, one needs to know what the *election margin* is, i.e., the number of votes that would need to be changed in order to change the election outcome. This is also the number of votes that would have had to be miscounted or tampered with in order to change the election outcome. If the election margin is large, only a small ballot sample needs to be audited. If it is small, the required sample size increases.

We assume that the election function we consider has the anonymity property, i.e., identical ballots have the same effect on the election outcome. Then, for a given election with TOTAL votes, during the counting process, the votes are accumulated into stacks $S_1, \ldots, S_k$, where each stack holds p_i identical votes

($p_i \geq 0$ is the size of S_i) and TOTAL $= \sum_i p_i$. This allows us to use $\langle p_1, \ldots, p_k \rangle$ as input to the election function. In the following, we assume that each stack is associated with a political party and that PARTIES is the number of the running parties, i.e., $k =$ PARTIES (there can also be stacks for special cases such as invalid votes). We call $\langle p_1, \ldots, p_k \rangle$ the vote table for the election.

The election margin is the smallest number of votes that need to be put on stacks different from where they are in order to change the outcome of the election.

Definition 1. *The* election margin *for an election function E and a vote table $\langle p_1, \ldots, p_k \rangle$ is the smallest number* MARGIN *such that there is a vote table $\langle p'_1, \ldots, p'_k \rangle$ with*

$$E(\langle p_1, \ldots, p_k \rangle) \neq E(\langle p'_1, \ldots, p'_k \rangle)$$

and

1. MARGIN $= \sum_{i=1}^{k} d_i$ *where $d_i = p'_i - p_i$ if $p'_i > p_i$ and $d_i = 0$ otherwise.*
2. $\sum_{i=1}^{k} p'_i - p_i = 0$.

The first condition in the above definition ensures that the total number of votes that are moved between stacks is of size MARGIN. Furthermore, the second condition ensures that a vote is moved from one stack to the other and is not created or removed.

Besides the (global) margin defined above, our approach allows as well to compute other margins that are defined by different types of changes in the vote table or by particular effects on the election result. For example, one may compute the margin for increasing the number of mandates allocated to a particular party.

It is important to note that our technique is a *generic* one, and is hence also applicable to different kinds of margins and types of changes in the votes, than the ones defined in Definition 1. Instead of distinguishing between different types, in the following we focus on *two-vote overstatements* of the margin, as these are suitable for a variety of election functions. An audited ballot is a *two-vote overstatement* if it witnesses simultaneously two mistakes, namely that it was counted wrongly towards someone who won, while it should have been counted towards someone who lost. In contrast, a *one-vote overstatement* refers to a ballot that was erroneously not counted towards the loser, but neither was it counted towards the winner. For the purposes of this paper, both one-vote and two-vote overstatements are counted as one change in the vote tabulation. Our methods can be extended to distinguish between the two types of error, but as we want our method for margin computation to be general and the distinction between one-vote and two-vote overstatements does not exist for all election functions (e.g., approval voting), we do not address it within this paper.

Next, we review the statistics underlying margin-based risk-limiting audits following [18]. Risk-limiting audits are performed in stages. At every stage, the theory requires that we audit at least $n = \rho/\mu$ ballots, which is also called the *sample size.* The value ρ is called the *sample-size multiplier* and defined below. Each ballot is randomly chosen among all the ballots, and the audit verifies that they were each counted for the correct stack S_i. The fraction μ refers to the *diluted margin*, i.e., the percentage of votes that would have to be changed to change the election outcome. It is computed as $\mu = $ MARGIN$/$TOTAL, where MARGIN is the election margin (Definition 1), and TOTAL is the total number of ballots cast.

Before the audit can start, a set of auditing parameters needs to be determined, which allows us to calculate the size of the sample to be drawn. The *auditing parameters* include

- the *risk-limit* α, which determines the largest chance that an incorrect outcome will not be corrected by the audit (if we want to be 99% sure that the election outcome is correct, then we choose $\alpha = 0.01$);
- the *error inflation factor* γ, which controls the trade-off between initial sample size and the additional counting required if the audit finds too many errors;
- and lastly the *tolerance factor* λ, which describes the tolerance towards errors; it is the number of detected errors that is tolerated, expressed as a fraction of the election margin (i.e., $\lambda = 0.1$ means that 5 errors are tolerated when MARGIN $= 50$).

Finally, we have everything in place needed to define the sample-size multiplier ρ, which only needs to be computed once for each audit, as follows:

$$\rho = \frac{-\log\alpha}{\frac{1}{2\gamma} + \lambda\log(1 - \frac{1}{2\gamma})}.$$

In summary, the auditing process as described by Stark [18] adheres to the following steps:

First, the auditor commits values for α, γ, and λ and computes the value ρ as shown above. Then, the diluted margin μ is computed, which explicitly depends on the election margin MARGIN. Next, the real audit commences by drawing the sample of size $n = \rho/\mu$ at random. If the audit encounters too many errors (more than $\lambda * $ MARGIN), a new stage is triggered, with a sample size that is increased by the factor γ; otherwise the audit is successfully concluded. In the worst case, the technique proceeds to a full hand-count when the sample size exceeds TOTAL. For a more detailed description on by how to compute by how much the sample must grow from stage to stage, consult [18].

In all of this, the true challenge is to compute the correct election margin. Different election functions require different margin computations, and for many an algorithm to compute the margin is unknown. This is the challenge that we are going to solve with this paper.

3   Software Bounded Model Checking

The technique of *software bounded model checking* (SBMC) statically analyses programs. The method is static in the sense that programs are analysed without executing them on concrete values. Instead, programs are symbolically executed and exhaustively checked for errors up to a certain bound, restricting the number of loop iterations.

Even though this check is bounded, SBMC also checks whether the chosen bound is sufficiently large to cover all possible program executions. Therefore, if firstly the analysed program is shown to be correct up to the specified bound and, secondly, SBMC verifies that this bound is sufficiently large, we obtain a full proof which says there does not exist any counterexample—neither for the specified nor any other bound. In case there exists no counterexample within the bound, but there may exist one for a larger bound, SBMC outputs that a larger bound is needed. Theoretically, we can always choose a sufficiently high bound to be sure we compute the correct margin. As, however, the analysis for very large bounds may require a considerable amount of computation time and memory resources, the feasibility of SBMC generally relies on the small-scope hypothesis [13], which argues that a high proportion of bugs can be found for inputs within some small scope [1]. For our purposes, moreover, the search for a sufficiently large bound is usually very simple, because we apply the method for concrete elections. Here, the numbers of parties, mandates, etc., affecting the number of required loop iterations, are known at the time when we compute the election margin.

SBMC is a fully automatic technique and provides full verification covering all possible inputs (within the scope of the given bound), including a verification that the specified bound is sufficiently large. An SBMC tool unrolls the control-flow graph of the program observing the bound for loop iterations and then checks whether an assertion can be violated (leading to a counterexample) [4]. Other than generating a counterexample or proving the assertion, an SBMC tool may also run into a timeout, or indicate that the specified bounds may need to be increased for the assertion to be proven. Hence, one can simply increase the specified bound until the assertion is fully proven. Additionally, SBMC analyses the program beforehand, and—if no bound is specified by the user—infers a sufficiently large bound if the program is simple enough, as it is the case for the experiments within this paper. The graph resulting from symbolic execution is transformed into a formula in a decidable logic (in our case propositional) that is satisfiable if and only if a counterexample exists, reducing the verification problem to a decidable satisfiability problem. Then, modern SAT/SMT-solving technology is used to check whether such a counterexample exists. Furthermore, SBMC tools support features of common complex programming languages such as complex memory models or standard data types in order to check a wider range of correctness properties, e.g., correct memory allocation.

In contrast to more heavy-weight verification techniques, SBMC does not aim to establish universal correctness guarantees or full reliability for all possible input parameters. It is usually being used to find general low-level bugs in programs, such as memory access errors or other sources of non-deterministic behaviour. Nevertheless, SBMC can also be used to check more complex functional properties – as we do for the purposes of this paper. SBMC considers only a finite state space by cutting off program execution paths at a certain length. Thus, it is comparable to systematic exhaustive testing up to a certain boundary of input size. However, SBMC provides means of symbolic representation for a state space and thus generally outperforms exhaustive testing by far.

Within this work, we use the model checker CBMC [7], which takes C/C++ or Java programs as input. The programs are annotated with specifications in the form of assumptions and assertions. Since universal and existential quantifiers are not supported by CBMC using the SAT back end, quantified expressions need to be expressed as assumptions/assertions within a loop. CBMC internally models all data structures as bit vectors. The symbolically executed programs are translated into equations over bit vectors, which are then processed by a powerful SAT solver modulo theories.

For our experiments, we use CBMC 5.3 with the built-in solver based on the SAT solver MiniSat 2.2.0 [9]. All experiments are performed on an Intel(R) Core(TM) i5-3360M CPU at 2.80 GHz with 4 cores and 16 GB of RAM.

4   Automated Margin Computation Using SBMC

We assume that an election function is given as an imperative program (a C function called `election_function` in our case) as well as a concrete input (denoted as `vote_table`) for that election function. The `vote_table` is the result of vote counting and tabulation. We model `vote_table` as an integer array of size `PARTIES`, where `PARTIES` is the number of different stacks into which identical votes are accumulated during counting.

The idea of our approach is to use an SBMC tool to check an assertion claiming that, when `vote_table` is changed by putting at most a certain number m of votes on other stacks than they were on, the outcome of the election is *not* changed. If that assertion is provable, we know that the actual election margin is greater than m. If the assertion is not provable, we know that the actual election margin is less than or equal to m. In the latter case, the SBMC tool generates a counterexample to the assertion demonstrating that the election outcome can be changed by changing m votes. Having this proof obligation as a basis, we can use binary search to find a value for m such that the assertion holds for $m - 1$ but fails for m, i.e., m is exactly the election margin.

The check for a particular prospective margin m can be executed by running the SBMC tool CBMC on the program shown in Listing 1, where the variables written in capital letters are given as concrete input values, and the method `nondet_int()` is a CBMC feature in order to denote non-deterministic, i.e., potentially different for each function call, and symbolic, i.e., unknown, integer values.

The changes in the sizes of the vote stacks are non-deterministically chosen (Line 4) in such a way that the total difference is zero (assumption in Line 15), i.e., votes can be moved from one stack to the other but not removed or created, and such that the number of votes in each stack cannot become negative (Line 6). Other types of margins for other kinds of changes to the vote table can be computed using different assumptions on the chosen values for `diff`.

```
1  void verify() {
2      int new_votes[PARTIES], diff[PARTIES], total_diff, pos_diff;
3      for (int i = 0; i < PARTIES; i++) {
4          diff[i] = nondet_int();
5          __CPROVER_assume (-1 * MARGIN ≤ diff[i] ≤ MARGIN);
6          __CPROVER_assume (0 ≤ ORIG_VOTES[i] + diff[i]);
7      }
8
9      for (int i = 0, total_diff = 0, pos_diff = 0; i < PARTIES; i++) {
10         new_votes[i] = ORIG_VOTES[i] + diff[i];
11         if (0 < diff[i]) pos_diff += diff[i];
12         total_diff += diff[i];
13     }
14     __CPROVER_assume (pos_diff ≤ MARGIN);
15     __CPROVER_assume (total_diff == 0);
16
17     int *result = election_function(new_votes);
18     assert (equals(result, ORIG_RESULT));
19 }
```

Listing 1. Implementation of the margin computation for CBMC.

The changes are added to the original vote table for computing the new table (Line 10). And the election result for the new vote table is computed by calling the method election_function (Line 17).

Finally, the program contains the assertion to be checked by CBMC (Line 18), expressing that the new election result is equal to the original one. Intuitively, we have encoded any difference between the original election outcome and the new one as a bug to be found by the model checker. This also means that our approach gives us a concrete redistribution of votes for the computed margin, as CBMC encodes detected bugs as concrete paths through the program, which lead to the assertion violation, i.e., the changed outcome.

The algorithm performing a binary search for the exact election margin is shown in Table 1 (for our experiments we use a shell script implementation of this algorithm). The algorithm takes as input the implementation of an election function and a concrete vote table. Its output is the exact election margin.

The algorithm first calls election_function to obtain the original election result (Line 3). The left and right bounds of the binary search are initialised to zero resp. the total number of votes (Lines 5 to 6). Then, a while loop (Lines 9 to 17) performs the binary search and calls CBMC on the program from Listing 1 with different values for MARGIN, i.e., different candidate margins, until the solution is found. If the result of CBMC indicates that MARGIN is too low, the left bound is increased (Line 13), and if CBMC indicates that MARGIN is either the correct margin or is too high, then the right bound is decreased (Line 15). To be more precise, if the result of calling CBMC reads SUCCESS, we know that the assertion in the program in Listing 1 holds, i.e., the election outcome cannot be

Table 1. Binary search for election margin using SBMC.

Input:
    `election_function`: implementation of the election function
    `ORIG_VOTES`: array with the size of each of the stacks of identical votes,
                i.e., the input for the election function
    `PARTIES`: size of the vote table array
Output:
    `MARGIN`: computed election margin

```
 1  function SEARCHMARGIN
 2      // initialisation
 3      ORIG_RESULT ← election_function(ORIG_VOTES)
 4      MARGIN ← 0
 5      left ← 0
 6      right ← ∑_{i=1,...,PARTIES} ORIG_VOTES[i]  // total number of votes
 7
 8      // search for margin
 9      while left < right do
10          MARGIN ← left + ⌈(right−left)/2⌉
11          result ← cbmc(verify(), MARGIN, PARTIES, ORIG_VOTES, ORIG_RESULT)
12          if result = SUCCESS then
13              left ← MARGIN + 1, MARGIN ← MARGIN + 1
14          else
15              right ← MARGIN
16          end if
17      end while
18
19      return MARGIN
20  end function
```

---

affected and the speculative margin `MARGIN` is too low; otherwise `MARGIN` either is the correct election margin or it is too high.

Note that neither the algorithm in Table 1 nor the program in Listing 1 make any further assumptions regarding the election function. Our method can be applied to arbitrary implementations of `election_function` without making any changes, only influencing the computation time needed by the satisfiability solver used as a back end, e.g., for more complex mathematical operations. The approach can also be adapted to more complex ballot structures. And, as said above, margins for different notions of vote changes can be computed by using different assumptions on the array `diff` in Listing 1, and margins for different notions of changes in the election outcome can be computed by using different versions of the function `equal` called in Line 18 from Listing 1.

5   Margin Computation for the D'Hondt Method

Margin computation also plays a central role for risk-limiting audits regarding the results after performing seat allocation methods such as the D'Hondt or Saint-Laguë method [19]. In this section, we exemplarily apply our technique to the D'Hondt method, which allocates mandates to a number of parties based on the votes cast for these parties. Before the D'Hondt election function is applied, vote counting and tabulation sorts the votes into stacks where each stack contains votes for a single party. The input for the election function then is the number of votes for each party (i.e., the number of votes in the corresponding stack).

The D'Hondt method proportionally allocates mandates to parties in such a way that the number of votes represented by mandates is maximised, i.e., the votes-per-seats ratio—intuitively the price in number of votes to be paid by a party to get one seat—is made as high as possible while still allocating all seats in parliament. By this means, D'Hondt achieves an—as far as possible—proportional representation in parliament [11].

D'Hondt can be implemented as a *highest averages* method: the number of votes for each party is divided successively by a series of divisors, which produces a table of quotients (or averages). In that table, there is a row for each divisor and a column for each party. For the D'Hondt method, these divisors are the natural numbers $1, 2, \ldots,$ MANDATES, where MANDATES is the total number of mandates to be distributed. Then, the highest numbers in the quotient table—resp. the parties in whose columns these numbers are—are each allocated one seat. The "final" seat goes to the MANDATES'th highest number. Hence, the threshold level of the votes-per-seats-ratio lies in the interval between the MANDATES'th highest number and the (MANDATES + 1)'st highest number of all computed averages in the quotient table.

An efficient C implementation of D'Hondt is shown in Listing 2. There, the constants PARTIES and MANDATES encode the numbers of parties and the number of mandates to be allocated, respectively. The input is given in the array vote_table, which holds the numbers of votes cast for each individual party. This implementation avoids constructing the complete quotient table. Instead, it stops as soon as the MANDATES'th highest quotient has been found. For this purpose, the divisors currently under consideration for finding the next highest value are stored in the array divisor for each party. Note that in case of a tie, the order in vote_table is the tie-breaker, i.e., the first party in vote_table which is tied with the current maximum divisor takes the seat.

After initialising the arrays mandates and divisor (Lines 5 and 6), we execute the outer loop (Lines 9 to 15) MANDATES times. Each time, it uses the inner loop (Lines 10 to 12) to find the maximum

$$\text{elected} = \max_{i=1,\ldots\text{PARTIES}} \frac{\text{vote\_table}[i]}{\text{divisor}[i]}$$

and then assigns one seat to the elected'th party (Line 13), and increases the divisor for that party (Line 14). To find the maximum, the comparison

```
 1 int *election_function(int vote_table[PARTIES]) {
 2     int *mandates = malloc(PARTIES * sizeof(int));
 3     int divisor[PARTIES];
 4
 5     for (int i = 0; i < PARTIES; i++) mandates[i] = 0;
 6     for (int i = 0; i < PARTIES; i++) divisor[i] = 1;
 7
 8     int elected = 0;
 9     for (int j = 0, j < MANDATES; j++) {
10         for (int i = 0; i < PARTIES; i++)
11             if (divisor[i] * vote_table[elected]
12                     < divisor[elected] * vote_table[i]) elected = i;
13         mandates[elected]++;
14         divisor[elected]++;
15     }
16     return mandates;
17 }
```

Listing 2. Implementation of the D'Hondt method as a C program.

$vote\_table[elected]/divisor[elected] < vote\_table[i]/divisor[i]$ is replaced by $divisor[i] *$ $vote\_table[elected] < divisor[elected] * vote\_table[i]$, which is equivalent as the divisors are positive numbers. The advantage of using the latter form for the comparison is to avoid dealing with fractional numbers and rounding effects in C. This is a sensible choice for any implementation of D'Hondt as, depending on the programming language and hardware, rounding may both show unexpected behaviour and potentially lead to faulty election results.

In order to test our margin computation for D'Hondt, we used the preliminary official results of the Schleswig-Holstein state elections in 2005[1]. In that election, $1,367,095$ votes were cast and 69 mandates were to be allocated. Out of the 13 parties running, four parties received the necessary quota of 5% to be eligible for the mandate allocation. The fifth party to receive seats, the South Schleswig Voter Federation, represents the Danish minority and is exempted from the quota rule for reasons of minority protection. The mandates (seats in parliament) were allocated using the D'Hondt method. The parties, their votes, and the allocated mandates are shown in Table 2.

We applied our approach to the vote numbers (i.e., the vote_table) of the Schleswig-Holstein election for various values of MANDATES. In doing so, we were able to compute the margin of the election with the runtime increasing for higher values of MANDATES as shown in Fig. 1a and b. The runtime for the final check is shown in Fig. 1a. This check requires showing that the election result can be changed by changing m votes (counterexample generation) but cannot be changed by changing $m - 1$ votes (margin verification), implying that m is the

---

[1] The results of that election are also used as an example in the German Wikipedia article on the D'Hondt method (http://de.wikipedia.org/wiki/D'Hondt-Verfahren).

Table 2. Preliminary official results for the 2005 Schleswig-Holstein elections.

Party	Votes	%	Mandates	%
Christian Democratic Union (CDU)	576 100	42.1	30	43.4
Social Democratic Party (SPD)	554 844	40.6	29	42.0
Free Democratic Party (FDP)	94 920	6.9	4	5.8
Alliance '90/The Greens	89 330	6.5	4	5.8
South Schleswig Voter Federation (SSW)	51 901	3.7	2	2.9
Totals	1 367 095		69	

true margin. Figure 1a shows the accumulated time for the complete binary search that computes m. For values of MANDATES between 2 and 45, the computed margins range from only 433 (for MANDATES $= 23$) to 177, 863 (for MANDATES $= 2$). Note that, with only two mandates, the CDU and the SPD each get a seat; the margin of 177, 863 then is the number of votes that have to be moved from the SPD to the CDU so that the CDU gets both mandates instead of only one, which is smaller than the number of votes that would have to be moved from the SPD to the FDP so that the FDP gets a seat instead of the SPD.

The runtimes shown in the figure do not form a smooth curve because they depend on the margin that is computed, which is, e.g., smaller for 40 mandates than for 35. But the numbers increase with the value of MANDATES. And as can be seen from the figure, they get prohibitively large for more than about 45 mandates.

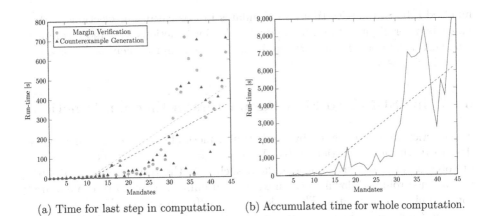

(a) Time for last step in computation.   (b) Accumulated time for whole computation.

Fig. 1. Runtimes of automatic margin computation for the D'Hondt method with various values for MANDATES.

Thus, our approach can be applied to real implementations of real election functions, but only if the number of loop iterations does not go beyond a few

```
1  int *election_function(int votes[PARTIES]) {
2      int *mandates = malloc(PARTIES*sizeof(int));
3      for (int i = 0; i < PARTIES; i++) mandates[i] = 0;
4
5      int quotaNumerator   = nondet_int();
6      int quotaDenominator = nondet_int();
7
8      __CPROVER_assume (0 < quotaNumerator   ≤ INT_MAX);
9      __CPROVER_assume (0 < quotaDenominator ≤ MANDATES);
10     __CPROVER_assume (quotaDenominator < quotaNumerator);
11
12     for (int i = 0; i < PARTIES; i++) {
13         __CPROVER_assume (0 ≤ quotaDenominator * votes[i] ≤ INT_MAX);
14         mandates[i] = ((quotaDenominator * votes[i]) / quotaNumerator);
15         __CPROVER_assume (0 ≤ mandates[i] ≤ MANDATES);
16     }
17
18     int total_mand = 0;
19     for (int i = 0, total_mand = 0; i < PARTIES; i++)
20         total_mand += mandates[i];
21     __CPROVER_assume (total_mand == MANDATES);
22
23     return mandates;
24 }
```

Listing 3. Implementation of the Jefferson method as a symbolic C program.

hundred (about 5 parties times 45 mandates in this case). For elections with a larger number of parties and mandates or election functions with more complex loop nestings, improvements are required. One such improvement is discussed in the following section.

6   Using SBMC to Find Parameters in Election Function

The election function defined by the D'Hondt method can also, equivalently, be described without a quotient table. Instead, a quota is chosen, i.e., a number of votes needed to "buy" one mandate, such that the resulting mandates per party, when rounded down to the next natural number, sum up to the required total number of mandates. This is known as Jefferson's method and is similar to *largest-remainder* methods such as the Hare-Niemeyer method. The quota corresponds to the lowest quotient in the D'Hondt table for which a mandate is allocated.

If the implementation of an election function is based on choosing or searching for some parameter (here the quota), then the margin computation can be made much more efficient by replacing the search for the parameter by a non-deterministic choice to be resolved by the SBMC tool.

An implementation of the Jefferson method in C is shown in Listing 3. It uses a non-deterministic choice of `quota` $=$ `quotaNumerator`/`quotaDenominator` (Lines 5 to 6). Assumptions are made to limit the range of the quota (Lines 8 to 10 and Line 13). The number of mandates for each party is computed (Line 14), as well as the total number of mandates (Lines 18 to 20). Then, the assumption is checked that the total number of mandates for the chosen quota is the correct one (Line 21). This final check is an assumption and not an assertion, i.e., we want to consider only the case(s) where the total number of mandates is correct; other cases are irrelevant. An assertion, on the other hand, would have to be true for all cases where the (other) assumptions are fulfilled. Note that this implementation does not deal with tie-breaking, as in this case no such quota can be found, and no program execution path can satisfy the assumption in Line 21. However, tie-breaking mechanisms can easily be integrated in the program.

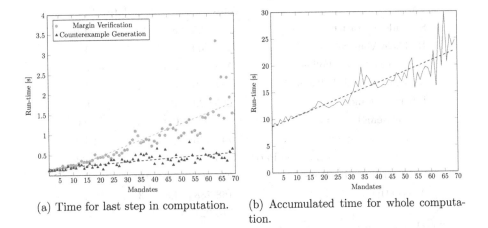

(a) Time for last step in computation.   (b) Accumulated time for whole computation.

Fig. 2. Runtimes of automatic margin computation for the Jefferson method with various values for `MANDATES`.

The runtimes of the automatic margin computation for the 2005 Schleswig-Holstein state elections with various values for `MANDATES`, i.e., the total number mandates to be allocated, are shown in Fig. 2a and b. Note that these runtimes are much lower than those for the D'Hondt method in Fig. 1a and b. Now, all computations stay well below the time-out of $9,000$ s (i.e., 2.5 h), even below 30 s. And the computation of the election margin for the original number of mandates in the election, which is 69, is now easily possible; that margin is 634. The computed margins range from only 42 (for `MANDATES` $= 62$) to $177,863$ (for `MANDATES` $= 2$). Performing our method for various values for `MANDATES` scales well on the Jefferson method, as we got rid of the loop depending on the value of `MANDATES`. However, further experiments also indicated a non-exponential dependency on the value for `PARTIES`. For example, an allocation of 69 mandates to 10 parties takes about 55 s, whereas for 20 parties, the analysis runs in ca. 300 s.

Naturally, the implementation in Listing 3 cannot be compiled and executed to produce a binary file using standard C compilers, because it contains constructs only understood by the model checker CBMC. However, it can nevertheless be compiled and executed using CBMC, which also allows for performing tests and similar measures in order to generate confidence in the implementation. Furthermore, when any C implementation of the Jefferson method is given, it is easy to construct a CBMC version in a uniform way by replacing the search for `quota` by a non-deterministic choice. The same principle for making margin computations more efficient can uniformly be applied to any election function where parameters such as quotas are chosen or computed within the election function.

Table 3. Official results for the 2015 national Danish elections [8].

Party	Votes	%	Mandates	%
Socialdemokratiet	924 940	26.3	43	31.9
Radikale Venstre	161 009	4.6	2	1.5
Det Konservative Folkeparti	118 003	3.4	0	0.0
SF – Socialistisk Folkeparti	147 578	4.2	2	1.5
Liberal Alliance	265 129	7.5	9	6.7
Kristendemokraterne	29 077	0.8	0	0.0
Dansk Folkeparti	741 746	21.1	33	24.4
Venstre, Danmarks Liberale Parti	685 188	19.5	33	24.4
Enhedslisten – De Rød-Grønne	274 463	7.8	10	7.4
Alternativet	168 788	4.8	3	2.2
Totals[a]	3 515 921		135	

[a]Excluding non-party votes.

7   Computing the Margin for National Danish Elections

In this section, we demonstrate the applicability of our approach to a further, more complex real-world election, namely the Danish parliamentary elections in 2015. The Danish elections use a two-tier system, further classified as an *adjustment-seat system*, where the main part of the seats (135 mandates) is allocated using the D'Hondt method for each of the lower-tier electoral districts (so-called constituencies) separately [10]. The remaining seats (40 mandates) are used for adjusting the proportionality with respect to the three higher-tier districts using the Saint-Laguë method (which is also a *highest averages method*, bounded by the Hare quota).

The aggregated results for the 2015 election are shown in Table 3. For the sake of readability, the table only contains the total numbers of votes, not the numbers for each constituency. In the following, we perform our analysis on the first tier, i.e., the distribution of the 135 mandates which are allocated separately within each constituency.

Using the Jefferson-version of D'Hondt, we compute a margin of 10 votes within 7,815 s, i.e., around 2 h and 10 min. The final verification (proving that a change in 9 votes cannot change the election outcome) takes 53 s and a counterexample for 10 votes (i.e., an example ballot box that does change the election outcome) can be found within 27 s. The generated counterexample shows that shifting – only – 10 votes from *SF – Socialistisk Folkeparti* to *Venstre, Danmarks Liberale Parti* in the constituency of Sjællands Storkreds results in a different election outcome where one mandate goes the same way as the 10 votes. That is, SF loses its single seat, and Venstre then has five seats. The vote table and election results for the constituency of Sjællands Storkreds are shown in Table 4.

Table 4. Results for the Danish constituency Sjællands Storkreds [8].

Party	Votes	%	Mandates	%
Socialdemokratiet	146 464	27.9	7	35.0
Radikale Venstre	16 906	3.2	0	0.0
Det Konservative Folkeparti	15 083	2.9	0	0.0
SF - Socialistisk Folkeparti	20 575	3.9	1	5.0
Liberal Alliance	32 598	6.2	1	5.0
Kristendemokraterne	1 996	0.4	0	0.0
Dansk Folkeparti	134 195	25.6	6	30.0
Venstre, Danmarks Liberale Parti	102 818	19.6	4	20.0
Enhedslisten - De Rød-Grønne	35 374	6.7	1	5.0
Alternativet	18 202	3.5	0	0.0
Totals[a]	524 211		20	

[a]Excluding non-party votes.

With the table-based D'Hondt method as a basis (Listing 2), the margin computation takes 16,860 s (around 4 h and 40 min). The final verification takes 659 s and a counterexample can be found within 652 s. Using the table-based D'Hondt implementation, for which margin computation is less efficient, is possible in this case because the number of mandates for each constituency is sufficiently low (around 20).

8 Conclusion and Future Work

In this paper, we have presented a method that computes election margins fully automatically. It can be applied to arbitrary implementations of election functions without understanding or even knowing how the election result is computed. Our approach can be applied to real implementations of real election functions if the number of loop iterations in the election function does not go beyond a few hundred. With the improvement from Sect. 6 for guessing parameters needed in the computation, the method scales up to larger and more complex elections.

Future work includes the computation of different types of election margins and an integration with software for supporting real-world risk-limiting audits. Further, we plan to apply our method to election functions for which margin computation is notoriously hard (such as instant-runoff voting). First experiments indicate that such functions are hard for our method as well. But it will be possible to adapt our method to computing lower bounds for margins in IRV elections using techniques described in the literature [6,16].

Acknowledgements. This work has been partly supported by COST Action IC1205 on Computational Social Choice. This publication was made possible in part by the DemTech grant 10-092309 from the Danish Council for Strategic Research, Program Commission on Strategic Growth Technologies and in part by NPRP Grant #7-988-1-178 from the Qatar National Research Fund (a member of Qatar Foundation). The statements made herein are solely the responsibility of the authors.

References

1. Andoni, A., Daniliuc, D., Khurshid, S.: Evaluating the "small scope hypothesis". Technical report, MIT Laboratory for Computer Science, Cambridge, MA (2003)
2. Bartholdi, J.J., Orlin, J.: Single transferable vote resists strategic voting. Soc. Choice Welf. **8**, 341–354 (1991)
3. Beckert, B., Goré, R., Schürmann, C., Bormer, T., Wang, J.: Verifying voting schemes. J. Inf. Secur. Appl. **19**(2), 115–129 (2014)
4. Biere, A., Cimatti, A., Clarke, E., Zhu, Y.: Symbolic model checking without BDDs. In: Cleaveland, W.R. (ed.) TACAS 1999. LNCS, vol. 1579, pp. 193–207. Springer, Heidelberg (1999). doi:10.1007/3-540-49059-0_14
5. Blom, M.L., Stuckey, P.J., Teague, V., Tidhar, R.: Efficient computation of exact IRV margins. Computing Research Repository (CoRR) abs/1508.04885 (2015)
6. Cary, D.: Estimating the margin of victory for instant-runoff voting. In: Conference on Electronic Voting Technology/Workshop on Trustworthy Elections (EVT/-WOTE). USENIX Association (2011)
7. Clarke, E., Kroening, D., Lerda, F.: A tool for checking ANSI-C programs. In: Jensen, K., Podelski, A. (eds.) TACAS 2004. LNCS, vol. 2988, pp. 168–176. Springer, Heidelberg (2004). doi:10.1007/978-3-540-24730-2_15
8. Statistik, D.: Befolkning og valg (2015). http://www.dst.dk/valg/Valg1487635/other/2015-Folketingsvalg.pdf. Accessed 23 August 2016
9. Eén, N., Sörensson, N.: An extensible SAT-solver. In: International Conference on Theory and Applications of Satisfiability Testing (SAT), Selected Revised Papers, pp. 502–518 (2003)
10. Elklit, J., Pade, A.B., Nyholm Miller, N.: The parliamentary electoral system in Denmark (2011). http://www.ft.dk/Dokumenter/Publikationer/Engelsk/The_Parliamentary_Electorial_System_Denmark.aspx. Accessed 23 August 2016
11. Gallagher, M.: Proportionality, disproportionality and electoral systems. Elect. Stud. **10**(1), 33–51 (1991)

12. Holzer, A., Schallhart, C., Tautschnig, M., Veith, H.: FSHELL: systematic test case generation for dynamic analysis and measurement. In: Gupta, A., Malik, S. (eds.) CAV 2008. LNCS, vol. 5123, pp. 209–213. Springer, Heidelberg (2008). doi:10.1007/978-3-540-70545-1_20
13. Jackson, D.: Software Abstractions: Logic, Language, and Analysis. MIT Press, Cambridge (2006)
14. Lindeman, M., Stark, P.B.: A gentle introduction to risk-limiting audits. IEEE Secur. Priv. 10(5), 42–49 (2012)
15. Magrino, T.R., Rivest, R.L., Shen, E., Wagner, D.: Computing the margin of victory in IRV elections. In: Conference on Electronic Voting Technology/Workshop on Trustworthy Elections (EVT/WOTE). USENIX Association (2011)
16. Sarwate, A., Checkoway, S., Shacham, H.: Risk-limiting audits and the margin of victory in nonplurality elections. Stat. Polit. Policy 4(1), 29–64 (2013)
17. Smith, A.M., Butler, E., Popovic, Z.: Quantifying over play: constraining undesirable solutions in puzzle design. In: International Conference on the Foundations of Digital Games (FDG), pp. 221–228 (2013)
18. Stark, P.B.: Super-simple simultaneous single-ballot risk-limiting audits. In: Conference on Electronic Voting Technology/Workshop on Trustworthy Elections (EVT/WOTE), pp. 1–16 (2010)
19. Stark, P.B., Teague, V.: Verifiable european elections: risk-limiting audits for D'Hondt and its relatives. USENIX J. Elect. Technol. Syst. (JETS) 1, 18–39 (2014)
20. Vorobyov, K., Krishnan, P.: Combining static analysis and constraint solving for automatic test case generation. In: Fifth IEEE International Conference on Software Testing, Verification and Validation (ICST), pp. 915–920 (2012)

E-Voting in Developing Countries

Current Landscape and Future Research Agenda

Manik Hapsara(✉), Ahmed Imran, and Timothy Turner

University of New South Wales, Canberra, Australia
evotingindonesia@gmail.com,
{a.imran, t.turner}@adfa.edu.au

Abstract. The rate of e-voting implementation in developing countries is too significant to ignore, yet the lack of theoretical common ground has resulted in dispersed ways of perceiving the technology. The objectives of this paper, therefore, are twofold: (1) providing a thematic landscape and defining the state of the current research on e-voting in developing countries, and (2) propounding courses for future research on e-voting which emphasize social, organizational and technological accounts of the technology. Following a systematic examination of sixty seven articles, this work found that the current studies have inclined towards technological centrism and that the question is no longer 'why' but 'how' to fit e-voting concepts and theoretical constructs into the various contexts of developing democracy. There is also evidence to suggest that system design studies have often been conducted without sufficient effort allocated for the strategic design of e-voting initiatives. This paper thus argues that future research on e-voting in developing countries should be focused on drawing the holistic image of reciprocal relationships between social and technical aspects of the technology. As a consequence, future studies must perceive e-voting not as a mere technological means but rather as a complex socio-technical agent that plays an important role in social and political reforms. They need to be more critical of the motives behind e-voting initiatives and conservative in following established development frameworks.

Keywords: E-voting in developing countries · Socio-technical aspects · Technological centrism

1 Introduction

The developing world has been reported to have significant interests in voting technology [1] and the rate of e-voting implementation has been faster therein than in developed countries [2]. In countries such as Nigeria, e-voting has been considered a necessity [3] and as the only solution for credible elections [4]. Nigeria has set its eyes on e-voting since 2011 [3, 5] and, undeterred by the problems found during its implementation [4, 6], seems determined to proceed with the technology. In Nigeria, the traditional voting system was believed to have allowed significant irregularities and a lower level of probity, accountability and transparency [6], and have overseen corruptions, oppressive acts and administrative failures [3, 4, 7]. Similar enthusiasm has

© Springer International Publishing AG 2017
R. Krimmer et al. (Eds.): E-Vote-ID 2016, LNCS 10141, pp. 36–55, 2017.
DOI: 10.1007/978-3-319-52240-1_3

been shown in India, where e-voting was assumed to be significantly more reliable than paper ballot [8]. In contrast, e-voting in Brazil is often seen from a different perspective, placing more concerns in the social aspects of its implementation. Although Brazil's e-voting election in 2000 was considered a success [9], issues of the lack of public trust and confidence in the system have been raised [10]. E-voting has failed to improve public involvement in politics and the delivery of public services despite the vast investments made to generate public trust in the system [11]. Critiques have also been raised over the government decision to employ the technology, given that millions of Brazilians still suffered from poverty and illiteracy [12]. The decision has been seen as market-driven and lacked adequacy in terms of information and communication technologies strategy [13].

Such a dispersed way of perceiving the technology might have been caused by a lack of theoretical common ground, departing from an insufficient literature review that focused specifically on e-voting in developing countries. This study aims to fill this gap by providing a landscape of current themes of research on the subject, underpinned by rigor and transparency. The result of this study is expected to endorse theoretical progress [14] and serves as a solid ground for academic communities [15], as well as to help practitioners developing a more grounded protocol [16] for e-voting initiatives in developing countries. This present study systematically examined sixty seven academic articles to answer the following questions: (1) what is the thematic landscape of the current research on e-voting in developing countries?; and (2) how should future research on e-voting in developing countries be conducted, taking into account the associated social, organizational, and technological aspects? This paper provides empirical evidence of the current state of the research and generates a summary of the existing research gaps, presented in the following structure. Firstly, Sect. 2 presents the arguments on the needs to view e-voting as an intricate interrelatedness of social, organizational, and technological actors. Subsequently how this present study was conducted and the definition of the classification methods employed are introduced in Sect. 3. Next, Sect. 4 identifies existing research gaps and discusses the findings. Note that, due to the limitation of space, the full list of articles included in the final dataset is only available in the appendix. Finally, recommendations for future e-voting inquiries are developed based on these gaps and presented in Sect. 5.

2   The Need for an Ecological View in E-Voting Research

Khan et al. [17] suggested that the success of computer-based systems implementations should be attributed to the simultaneous configuration of technical, organizational, and social aspects of the systems. The technical aspect concerns how technology and business processes transform inputs to outputs; while the organizational and social system emphasizes the needs for understanding people's attitudes, skills and values, as well as the relationships among them within an organizational structure [18]. This conception sees information technology not as a mere tool which is readily, un-problematically applicable in any given context for any specific purpose [19], but rather as a complex socio-technical agent whose correlative interactions with other social agents are significant in order to understand how the technology works.

Technology has only a small effect in shaping human intention and choices, hence the impacts associated with e-voting initiatives, for instance, can be attributed to human agency shaped by social context [20]. It does not mean that technical solutions for e-voting systems can be ignored, rather the emphasis is on how social and organizational aspects should be seen just as decisive [21], if not more, to e-voting success.

It has been reported that the use of technology in elections might have failed to improve public participation due to socio-technical gaps. Al Shammari et al. [22] identified three dimensions of disparities lingering in e-voting implementations. First is the technological gap caused by incompatibility between systems components – both hardware and software. Next is the social gap occurring between social policies and human behavior which represents moral discrepancies among users, between users and social values, and between democratic culture and election protocols. E-voting indeed conveys different significance for different actors, and their use of the technology may depart from different agendas [23]. The last dimension is the socio-technical gap caused by disparities between social and computer policies. For e-voting systems therefore, the social world and the technology used therein cannot be seen as separate, rather, they co-constitute each other [24].

The causes of failures to implement electoral information technology are associated not only with the technological aspects of the systems, but also with the organizational context in which they are used [21, 25]. Although one of the main objectives of utilizing technology in elections is to improve democracy through increases in voter turnouts [26], in practice e-voting is seldom seen as a social utility. Adoptions are often driven simply by over-acknowledgement of technological possibilities and for the sake of bureaucratic convenience [27], as a result of unsatisfactory experiences from the use of traditional paper-based systems. In some cases, failures may originate from the scarcity of resources [28, 29] and the overreliance of governments on the private sector [27, 29] due to the lack of IT expertise.

The decision on whether or not a country should implement e-voting can never be detached from the political implications that precede and may follow. The question is what drives governments to initiate the adoption of a system that arguably is not better than the one it replaces? What motivates government to tolerate "social trade-offs" [23] to ensure public acceptance of the technology even though it may put democratic practices in the hands of near-monopolist private sectors [27]? E-voting, therefore, needs to be seen from a broader, ecological point-of-view that goes beyond the technology and includes social and organizational perspectives and interrelationships amongst them [22, 23].

3 Research Method

3.1 Literature Sampling

The approach for performing rigorous literature reviews [14–16, 30–32] was employed in this study. This present work examined a saturated set of literature which fell within the following criteria. Firstly, the main object of discussion of the reviewed papers was electronic voting or e-voting - a system, device, machine that records, stores, and processes election data electronically – as illustrated by [33], among others. This present study agrees with the thematic characterization of e-participation wherein e-voting is defined as an instance of e-participation activities [34–36], and also with the view in which e-voting is considered an artefact of e-government [37]. Echoing [20], this paper took into account only sources associated specifically with e-voting, henceforth articles concerned with other closely related technologies, i.e. e-government, e-governance, e-polling, e-participation, e-democracy, e-inclusion, e-petition, e-politics, e-consultation, e-decision making, e-rule making, e-deliberation, e-campaign, and e-community were excluded even if they referred to e-voting as an instance. Secondly, this present study looked only at e-voting systems used in either presidential or parliamentary elections where they were considered safety-critical, thus those used for purposes otherwise, e.g. e-voting for entertainment [38], were not included. Thirdly, the context to which the research applies was of developing countries, or countries with a developing economy as indicated by the International Monetary Fund [39]. Finally, this study was interested only in papers published between January 2000 and January 2015 and discarded papers written in non-English language.

This study performed searches over several publication databases, rather than concentrating only on a limited number of journals. The reason for this was to include articles available across disciplines, hence enriching the dataset [31]. The databases used in the sampling were: IEEEXplore, ScienceDirect, EbscoHost, ACM Digital Library, Springer Link, ProQuest, Emerald, Web of Science, SCOPUS, and Google Scholar. It is realized that the term "electronic voting" – despite being widely used since 1970s [40] – was not the only form, and that other phrases have been used to name or refer to the same instance. Moreover, this present study was interested in e-voting conducted at voting kiosks, through the internet and/or using mobile devices, and therefore it also searched for terms beyond "electronic voting" and "e-voting" (see Table 1). The sampling process was composed of episodes performed from March 2015 to September 2015 and was iterative in nature. This approach was preferred as it enabled the examination of the result of earlier set sampling, as well as provided chances to revisit the criteria and make necessary adjustments. Indeed, along the process several phrases which might have considerable similarities in their properties to e-voting, such as tele-voting [38, 41] and mobile referendum or m-referendum [42] had

Table 1. List of search terms

Search Terms					
Developing country	Internet voting	Online voting	Digital ballot	Virtual voting	e-voting
Developing countries	Internet election	Online election	Remote voting	Virtual election	e-election
Electronic voting	Internet ballot	Online ballot	Remote election	Virtual ballot	e-ballot
Electronic election	Mobile voting	Digital voting	Remote ballot	Voting machine	i-voting
Electronic ballot	Mobile ballot	Digital election	Voting device	Voting technology	m-voting

been identified. However, since they were used mainly for public polling and petition, they were taken out of the dataset. Furthermore, for the purpose of sampling, this present study adopted the selection algorithm proposed by [30] where the final dataset was the result of the following cyclic sampling-sequence: (1) After the first search, duplicates were identified and excluded from the sample; (2) Next, more papers that did not fit the criteria were left out after careful examination of the titles, abstracts and full texts; (3) Finally, to enhance the quality of the search, backward and forward citations checks were performed and the sequence was reiterated if new articles came up. This present work agrees with [30] that a literature review is never complete and that new articles will always appear, however, the sampling process was terminated when the data was exhausted, i.e. when there was no new result after the repeated search that fitted the criteria [15]. At the end, sixty-seven selected articles were included in the final dataset.

3.2   Research Themes Classification

Very few observers have contributed to the mapping of theoretical advancement in e-voting. Some of the most recent work offering a conceptual framework to perceive the trend of e-voting studies [22] have effectively categorized the current development and catered a clearly defined foundation for future inquiries. Despite their contributions, however, such studies have focused on technological aspects of e-voting and left little space for social, cultural and political variables. This study, therefore, looked further into the field of e-government and primarily adopted the themes classification of [17] for the following reasons. Firstly, their work emphasized framing e-government studies within socio-technical systems theory which enables the definition of the current state of research on e-voting aligned with social, organizational and technological aspects of e-voting implementations. Secondly, the context of their study was developing countries. Therefore, owing to this similarity, both studies are expected to enhance each other and set down a more resolute foundation for future work on e-government and e-voting in developing democracy.

The framework consists of four topic-clusters or themes: society-related, organization-related, technology-related, and combined issues. The society category encompasses issues from a society point-of-view where e-government initiatives are questioned over their effectiveness and impact on citizens, and how social behavior may, in return, determine government policies, strategies and practices. Topics of digital divide, e-readiness, public acceptance and attitude, trustworthiness, as well as socio-economic aspects were included in this class.

For e-voting, however, the mechanisms of public reviews and assessments needed to be further included for a design specification better resembling the reality [43] and the improvement of public awareness on e-voting implementation strategy [44]. Public debates, for example, foster public trust and confidence in the system, provide transparency over the decision-making process, and reveal if potential voters are willing to use the technology. This study further imposed that voters' education is an important factor to enhance people's intention to use the system [45], and hence also needs to be included. Next, the organization cluster includes topics related to organizational arrangements, processes and performance, among others. Research that looks at public-sector innovation, public-sector performance assessments, institutional arrangements – e.g. organizational structures, managerial processes, bureaucracy – organization e-readiness, public sector reforms and open governments were classified into this group. Then, there is the technology class where discussions on e-government technologies and systems are grouped together. This category forms a circle around information security, information and telecommunications infrastructure, mobile government, e-government model, et cetera. Borrowing from Ngai and Wat's classification of e-commerce [46], this category was further expanded to include topics on network technology and infrastructure, algorithms, technological components, and system security. It also accommodates formal methods, such as model checking and theorem proving, to support un-biased assessment of voting protocols and to impose transparency during the process [22]. Finally, the combined category incorporates research which is a compound of social, organizational and/or technical issues; such as those on the effects of e-government system on public sector, the problems with digitization and access to cultural heritage, as well as the existing reality-design gaps in e-government systems. Table 2 presents the themes classification used in this review.

Table 2. Themes classification (adapted from [17])

Society	Organization	Technology	Combined
E-voting social outcomes; Culture issues and e-voting adoption; E-voting success factors; E-voting and political, economic and social development; E-voting socialization (education and campaign) Industry-enabled e-voting; Digital divide (access, awareness, infrastructure, cost); Service localization; Public infrastructure (internet); Demographics (gender, education); User satisfaction, socio-economic and socio-political context; Citizen's acceptance and attitude; E-skills; Citizens e-readiness; Public reviews and assessments	Leadership; Project management; IS competencies development; IT Change Management; E-voting and intellectual capital; Public servant training; Perception of public servants; Work performance assessment (CSFs, KPIs); Cross-agency collaboration, inter-organizational information integration; Institutional arrangements (structures, bureaucracy); Inter-organizational connectivity agreements (Service Level Agreements); Standardization; Organization e-readiness; Public sector reforms; Open government; IT law (regulations, legal infrastructures); Organizational performance framework; Inter-operability framework and standards; Certification and audit	Information security (data security, system security: secure transactions, VPN, internal/external attacks); Information security management; Service quality (information/system quality); Multi-platform approach; Technological components (DRE, EVM); Network technology and infrastructure (inter-platform connectivity and compatibility, security); Algorithm and protocols; Mobile voting; Voter's systems requirements; ICT infrastructure; E-voting risk management; E-voting models and prototypes; E-voting infrastructure; E-voting technology evaluation framework; E-voting standards and compliance; E-voting governance; Open systems model and safety-critical systems approach; Formal design analysis and specifications	E-voting assessment framework (strategic, technological, organizational, economic, operational, and service); E-voting technology adoption and diffusion (system characteristics, user characteristics, external variables); Effects of e-voting on public sector (public servant ethics and attitude, organizational changes and restructuring, organizational policies, other organizational, technological, managerial, political legal and human aspects); Effects of e-voting on society (alterations in political paradigm, culture and uses of democratic apparatus); E-society readiness (technological, social, organizational, political, cultural and legal aspects); Digitization and access to political traditions and cultural heritage; Reality-design gaps in e-voting systems

4 Findings and Discussion

4.1 Descriptive Overview of the Result

It is apparent from Fig. 1 that, even though interests in research on e-voting in developing countries did not start until late 2003, there has been a significant increase in the number of publications during the last fifteen years. The numbers of articles in 2013 and 2014 make up a total of 38.8 percent of the reviewed papers and have more than doubled the number of the previous years. Since some countries, such as India in 2009 [8, 47], had initiated and been considered successful in implementing e-voting [48]; it is interesting to further inquire if this might have excited e-voting initiatives in other developing countries and motivated researchers in the field. Nigerian e-voting, for instance, had a considerable effect upon research on e-voting in other African countries (see for example [49]). Interestingly, it was not until Nigeria planned to employ the technology in 2011 [3, 5] that there was a sudden, significant growth in the number of publications. This suggests that nation's agenda might have been another factor leading to more productive inquiries on the topic. Indeed, countries such as Lebanon and Thailand, who apparently had never exhibited strong interest in the technology, had only one publication each [50, 51]. Similarly, although e-voting in South Africa had drawn researchers' interest as early as Nigeria [52], it has been scarcely discussed since.

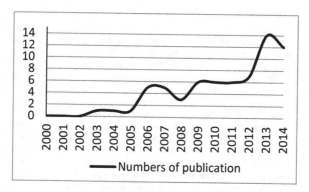

Fig. 1. Numbers of publications by year

Next, in order to understand the state of research on e-voting in developing countries, the articles under review were categorized according to the context in which the research was applied and were not associated with the country of the authors' origin or where their affiliation resided (see Table 3). This approach was favorable for two reasons: (1) the result can be used to depict the global interests in e-voting in a particular country, and (2) it enriched and improved the accuracy of the dataset. For example, the articles on e-voting in Nigeria were associated not only with Nigerian institutions but also with Malaysian [4, 7] and British [53] universities, among others. On the other hand, research on Brazilian e-voting was more society-centric and was, to a large extent, driven by only two prominent groups, namely Filho [11–13], and Avgerou [10, 54, 55].

Table 3. Distribution of articles by subject country

Country	n	%	Country	n	%	Country	n	%	Country	n	%
Nigeria	19	27.54	Iran	3	4.35	Tanzania	2	2.90	Mauritius	1	1.45
Brazil	7	10.14	Jordan	3	4.35	UAE	2	2.90	Mexico	1	1.45
Indonesia	5	7.25	S. Africa	3	4.35	Ghana	2	2.90	Thailand	1	1.45
Argentine	4	5.80	Colombia	2	2.90	Ecuador	1	1.45	Turkey	1	1.45
India	3	4.35	Pakistan	2	2.90	Lebanon	1	1.45	Uganda	1	1.45
									Others	5	7.25

This study further inquire on whether e-voting initiatives in developing countries have been preceded by a firm research foundation or otherwise. Indonesia, for instance, despite having only recently experienced several e-voting simulations at village and district level elections [56–58], contributed to 23.8 percent of the number of publications on e-voting in Asia. India, on the other hand, whose full e-voting elections had been referred to by many [9, 59, 60], was subject to fewer publications. Indeed several developing countries had conducted e-voting, such as Philippines in 2010 and 2013 respectively [61], and yet scientific articles that put significant effort into discussing them could hardly be found.

4.2 The Thematic Landscape of the Current Research

This study found that forty six percent of the reviewed articles saw e-voting from technological perspectives, where Nigeria topped the list with fourteen technology-related papers (see Table 4). That body of work mostly involved the development of e-voting models and prototypes, security analysis of the current systems [62] and assessment of mobile voting [63]. Topics looking into technology standards and compliance, governance, evaluation frameworks, and service quality have not been discussed anywhere during the last fifteen years. Understandably, emphasizing the provision of cutting-edge voting technology would likely speed up the

Table 4. Distribution of articles (Theme vs Country)

Theme	Nigeria	Brazil	Indonesia	Argentine	India	Iran	Jordan	S. Africa	Colombia	Pakistan	Tanzania	UAE	Ghana	Ecuador	Lebanon	Mauritius	Mexico	Thailand	Turkey	Uganda	Others
Society	1	3	1	0	0	0	2	2	1	0	1	0	0	1	0	0	0	0	0	1	0
Organization	0	0	0	0	0	0	0	0	0	0	0	0	0	0	0	0	0	0	0	0	0
Technology	14	1	1	0	3	1	1	0	0	1	0	0	2	0	1	1	0	1	0	0	4
Combined	4	3	3	4	0	2	0	1	1	1	1	2	0	0	0	0	0	1	0	1	1

technological advancement of e-voting, which might have been considered as a major factor to further improve its adoptability. This emphasis is endorsed in the society theme which saw public acceptance of e-voting as the major issue to address, making up 76.9% of the number of articles in this class. As much as this topic would encourage better understanding of system requirements from voters' points of view, it might have overlooked e-voting social outcomes and its relationship with political and economic development. Topics on the digital divide [64], the socio-economic context of e-voting [11, 65, 66] and culture-related issues [52] have been scarcely discussed. The absence of society discussion suggests that current studies are technology-centric, reinforced by the lack of interest shown towards solely organization-related topics. The literature appears to show a growing focus on technology as the only solution for credible elections and for eliminating election irregularities, and that there exists no disparities between social/organizational agents and e-voting. That might have led to deficiencies of theoretical and conceptual advancement in the institutionalization of e-voting initiatives, which may, ironically, further jeopardize its implementation in developing countries. On a positive note, however, there have been attempts to combine organization with other themes, e.g. a look at security issues from organizational perspective [67], which contributed to thirty four percent of the total number of papers. Researchers have seen interrelationships among themes and acknowledged the complex nature of the context of e-voting implementations. The papers on combined issues discussed mainly topics of e-voting assessment framework, technology adoption and diffusion, and e-society readiness. Issues of how voting technology may affect public servants' ethics and attitude, how to narrow the reality-design gaps, as well as how e-voting impacts organizational changes and policies therefore still need attention.

Although technology-related research has had a positive trend, it showed an average growth-rate of only 0.3 publications per year. It seems that despite displaying sudden increases in some places, there were scattered swift declines and plateaux in publications (see Fig. 2), which might have come from a lack of research continuity on

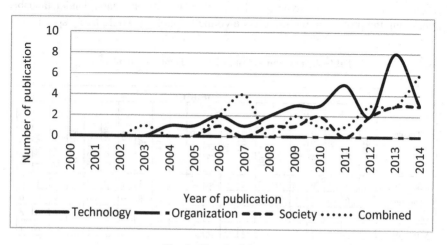

Fig. 2. Trend of themes

countries such as Lebanon and Thailand (see Table 4). The same situation also occurred in society-related themes (for example, Uganda and Ecuador) and combined studies (for example, Mexico and Turkey). With regard to technology-related theme, only Nigeria has demonstrated continuity since 2006 when the first end-to-end e-election model was proposed [68]. The trend continued with half of the publications afterwards addressing the prospect [63, 69] and promoting some models [5, 70] of mobile voting systems.

Other technology-related topics, such as service quality, multi-platform approaches, technology components, network technology and infrastructure, as well as formal design analysis and specifications have not drawn any interest. Articles of non-technological nature were first published in 2012 [71] and the later period has seen combined issues emerging in the field. Research on Nigerian e-voting, therefore, seems to have shifted towards more holistic inquiries such as on technology adoption [1, 4] and on critical factors of e-voting implementations [53] during recent years. The characteristics shown by Brazil, on the other hand, were considerably different. It is apparent that since its first full utilization of e-voting in 2000, Brazil has found researchers mostly interested in issues related to finding answers to electoral fraud problems [72], assessing the risks that come with implementing the system [13], and examining its social impacts [10, 11, 55, 65]. There are topics, nevertheless, that have never been visited, e.g. voter education, readiness of national industries, effects of e-voting on public sectors, reality-design gaps, and those under technology and organization-related themes, which require more attention in the future.

5 Recommendations

Society-related studies of e-voting in developing countries have put a greater emphasize on looking at citizens' acceptance of and their attitude towards the technology. Researchers have been trying to identify the applicability of e-voting concepts and theoretical constructs within the various contexts of developing democracies. These investigations can be understood as an attempt to answer challenges arising during several instances of e-voting implementation in, most notably, Latin America where election technology is seen as a social agent that interacts and reciprocally modifies political, economic, and other social agents. Concerns over the decision making process and public trust have been brought into attention by highlighting the correlations between e-voting and the citizens, for instance. There was a supposition that election technology contributes to changes in social, economic and political structures, whether positively or negatively, which need to be properly addressed to ensure smooth transitions as the consequence of e-voting adoption initiatives. Encouragement should be given to specific studies on how healthy domestic industries would have enabled developing countries' self-provision of e-voting infrastructures to eliminate their technological and political dependencies on foreign power and preserve their control over democracy. E-voting, hence, must not be seen as a mere technological means but a complex socio-technical agent that contributes to social and political reforms. In addition, there also needs to be more inquiries highlighting public education to improve voters' e-skills and invite substantial feedback for e-voting arrangements more suited to voters' demographic characteristics.

Such supposition, that technologies play important roles in developing countries, was even more apparent in technology-related studies. The shortcomings experienced during previous democratic practices might have resulted in technological determinism shown by countries such as Nigeria and India. Research in this theme has focused on equipping democracy with technological advancement, but it exhibited a significant void in coping with issues associated with the increasing technological intricacies. While topics of mobile voting and information security were popular among researchers, there was an absence of studies on e-voting technology standards, compliance and governance, for instance, which may later cause setbacks to the progress of e-voting development. Moreover, technological centrism should be limited to allow a state of parity among the themes. Indeed organization-related issues have been largely neglected during the last fifteen years, which may result in government having difficulties defining the relevance of posing technological advantages against the expected implementation model – an instance of design-reality gaps. Future inquiries on e-voting in developing countries, therefore, are expected to look further into the complex nature of e-voting implementations and their impacts within public sector organizations. They need to closely examine the motives behind e-voting initiatives, clearly define system ownership, and distinctly specify all institutional arrangements necessary. There are also issues of public sector reforms and public servant training that need addressing in order to make sure that there will not be any discontinuity issues found further down the road. Nevertheless, research on some countries such as Nigeria has started to shift towards a more holistic approach addressing the topics under combined issues.

Failures to sustainably run e-voting projects in most developing countries mainly come down to the lack of political commitment and the lower level of resources available. Such states of affairs will likely induce changes in the countries' political and strategic agendas, creating a condition unsuitable for large and long-term investments in ICT development. E-voting researchers may further find it difficult to keep their interests in the field as their research will at the end have little practical impact. This is apparent in the reviewed studies, shown by a very small number of articles early on which were then followed by an absence of publication for a considerably long period of time. The government of developing countries and the academic world, for these reasons, need to work towards a common goal and incorporate a holistic view while perceiving e-voting development in order to benefit from the technology. Furthermore, another form of discontinuity is where studies on particular themes by a particular research group were ceased in the interest of pursuing knowledge categorized under different themes. This is not by any means a bad practice, however, it meant the earlier studies were left incomplete and hence might only contribute to providing partial representation of the overall picture. Comprehensiveness, on the other hand, will likely add to a more thorough assessment necessary for authorities to make decisions on whether or not to initiate e-voting projects.

6 Conclusion

The contribution of this present study is twofold. Firstly, it provides the thematic landscape and defines the state of the current research on e-voting in developing countries. The study systematically examined sixty-seven articles and found that the current literature was in favor of the technology-related theme. There are signs of technological centrism in the literature and there is a growing belief that technology is the only solution for credible elections and for eliminating election irregularities. The current studies seemed to focus on how to practically put the technology into effect by fitting e-voting concepts and theoretical constructs into the various contexts of developing democracy. They tended to solve problems associated with the technology, which were not necessarily election problems, while paying little attention to the issues of increasing technological intricacies and navigating away from socio-cultural, organizational and political aspects of e-voting implementations. There is also evidence to suggest that the current research was vested at socio-technical system design without sufficient effort allocated for strategic design of e-voting initiatives, which might result in poor decision on whether or not a developing country should use e-voting technology. Secondly, this present study propounds courses for future research on e-voting in developing countries. Despite the strong inclination towards the technology-related theme identified in the current studies, for instance, topics on e-voting standards and compliance, election technology evaluation frameworks and service quality still require more attention. This technological advancement should further be rooted in theoretical fluency in social aspects of e-voting. E-voting must be seen as a complex socio-technical agent that plays an important role in social and political reforms and future research on the subject should be focused on drawing the holistic image of reciprocal relationships between social and technical aspects of the technology. Future studies on e-voting in developing countries should also consider the complex nature of its implementations and its impacts within public sector organizations. They need to constantly question the motives behind e-voting initiatives and look further into other organizational issues such as public sector reforms and institutional arrangements. Further inquiries on system ownership, following investigations on problems lingering in traditional voting, are also encouraged.

Finally, the authors realize that a number of limitations of the approach used in this study needs to be taken into consideration. First, this paper includes only literature written in English. This might have allowed a relevant portion of e-voting inquiries at national and local level, which are published in national language other than English, to be excluded from the final dataset. Second, the search process has focused on academic publishing outlets and, thus, might have ignored other types of literature, such as government reports, which may be decisively relevant to directing future e-voting research. The authors welcome all comments, critiques, and recommendations.

Acknowledgement. This research has been funded by Lembaga Pengelola Dana Pendidikan (LPDP), Ministry of Finance of the Republic of Indonesia.

Appendix: List of Articles Included in the Final Dataset

Papers discussing more than one country of interest are listed under each country, respectively.

Country of interest	Title
Nigeria	Ayo, C., Daramola, J., Grabriel, O. & Sofoluwe, A. An End-to-End e-Election System based on Multimodal Identification and Authentication. In: 6th International Conference on E-Government, 2006 Cape Town, South Africa
	Ekong, U. & Ayo, C. 2007. The Prospects of M-Voting Implementation in Nigeria. 3GSM & Mobile Computing: An emerging growth engine for national development, 172-179
	Ayo, C., Adebiyi, A. & Fatudimu, I. 2008. E-Democracy: A requirement for a successful e-voting and e-government implementation in Nigeria. International Journal of Natural and Applied Sciences, 4, 310-318
	Ayo, C., Adebiyi, A. & Sofoluwe, A. 2009. E-Voting Implementation in Nigeria: the success factors. In: Curbing Political Violence in Nigeria: The role of security profession. Nigeria: Institute of Security, Mukagamu and Brothers Ent.
	Ayo, C. & Azeta, A. A Framework for Voice-Enabled m-Voting System: Nigeria a case study. In: 9th European Conference on E-Government, 2009 London, UK
	Ekong, U. & Ekong, V. 2010. M-Voting: A panacea for enhanced e-participation. Asian Journal of Information Technology, 9, 111-116
	Olaniyi, O., Adewumi, D., Oluwatosin, E., Bashorun, M. & Arulogun, O. 2011. Framework for Multilingual Mobile E-Voting Service Infrastructure for Democratic Governance. African Journal of Computing & ICT, 4, 23-32
	Faniran, S. & Olaniyan, K. Strengthening Democratic Practice in Nigeria: A case for e-voting. In: 5th International Conference on Theory and Practice of Electronic Governance, 2011 Tallin, Estonia. 337-340
	Adeyinka, T. & Olasina, G. 2012. Voter's Perception of the Adequacy and Suitability of e-Voting in the Nigeria Polity. In: Handbook of Research on E-Government in Emerging Economies: Adoption, e-participation, and legal frameworks. IGI Global
	Kuye, C., Coker, J., Ogundeinde, I. & Coker, C. 2013. Design and Analysis of Electronic Voting System in Nigeria. International Archive of Applied Sciences and Technology, 4, 15-20
	Ishaq, S., Osman, W., Shittu, A. & Jimoh, R. 2013. Adoption of E-Voting System in Nigeria: A conceptual framework. International Journal of Applied Information Systems, 5, 8-14
	Musa, M. & Aliyu, F. 2013. Design of Electronic Voting Systems for Reducing Election Process. International Journal of Recent Technology and Engineering, 2, 183-186
	Olaniyi, O., Arulogun, O. & Omidiora, E. 2013. Design of Secure Electronic Voting System using Multifactor Authentication and Cryptographic Hash Function. International Journal of Computer and Information Technology, 2, 1122-1130
	Adeshina, S. Towards Improved Adoption of e-Voting - Analysis of the case of Nigeria. 8th International Conference on Theory and Practice of Electronic Governance, 2014 Portugal
	Brooks, L. & Mohammed, A. eVoting in Nigeria: The case of the Independent National Electoral Commission. EGOSE '14, 2014 St. Petersburg, Russian Federation. 127-136

(continued)

(continued)

Country of interest	Title
	Folarin, S., Ayo, C., Oni, A. & Gberevbie, D. Challenges and Prospects of e-Elections in Nigeria. European Conference on eGovernment, 2014 Brasov, Romania Akeem, B., Salihu, S. & Nuradeen, I. 2014. Electronic Process in Africa: A proposed general e-voting model (Case study - Nigeria). International Journal of Scientific & Engineering Research, 5, 920-927 Iromini, N., Onawola, H. & Ajao, A. 2014. Electronic Voting System for Student Election Process. International Journal of Computer & Communication Engineering Research, 2, 183-192 Olaniyi, O., Arulogun, O., Omidiora, E. & Okediran, O. 2014. Performance Assessment of an Imperceptible and Robust Secured E-Voting Model. International Journal of Scientific & Technology Research, 3, 127-132
Brazil	Rezende, P. 2004. Electronic Voting Systems, Is Brazil ahead of its time? RSA Laboratories, 7 Filho, J., Alexander, C. & Batista, L. E-Voting in Brazil - the risks to democracy. In: Electronic Voting, 2006 Bonn, Germany. Bregenz, 85-94 Avgerou, C., Ganzaroli, A., Poulymenakou, A. & Reinhard, N. ICT and Citizens' Trust in Government: Lessons from electronic voting in Brazil. In: 9th International Conference on Social Implications of Computers in Developing Countries, 2007 Sao Paulo, Brazil Filho, J. E-Voting in Brazil - Reinforcing institutions while diminishing citizenship. In: 3rd International Conference on Electronic Voting, 2008 Castle Hofen, Bregenz, Austria. 239-248 Avgerou, C., Ganzaroli, A., Poulymenakou, A. & Reinhard, N. 2009. Interpreting the Trustworthiness of Government Mediated by Information and Communication Technology: Lessons from electronic voting in Brazil. IT for Development, 15, 133-148 Filho, J. R. 2010. E-Voting and the Creation of Trust for Socially Marginalized Citizens in Brazil. eJournal of eDemocracy & Open Government, 2, 184-193 Avgerou, C. 2013. Explaining Trust in IT-Mediated Elections: A case study of e-voting in Brazil. Journal of the Association for Information Systems, 14, 420-451
Indonesia	Jillbert, J. & Musaruddin, M. Online Voting for E-Democracy in Developing Countries: Is it possible? 5th International Conference on Information Technology in Regional Areas, 2003 Queensland, Australia Hapsara, M. Imposing Transparency in Indonesia's E-Voting System through Security by Design. E-Indonesia Initiative, 2011 Bandung, Indonesia Hapsara, M. E-Voting Indonesia: A safety-critical-systems model towards standard and framework for Indonesia's presidential election. In: International Conference on Information Technology, 2013 Bali, Indonesia. 81-86 Hapsara, M. Electronic Voting for the People of Mount Merapi, Really? In: IEEE International Symposium on Technology Management and Emerging Technology, 2014 Bandung, Indonesia Hapsara, M. E-Voting Indonesia: Framing the Research. In: 9a Conferencia Iberica de Sistemas y Tecnologias de Informacion, 2014 Barcelona Spain
Argentine	Vilamala, J. 2007. E-Voting: An analysis of sociopolitical acceptance. 21st IPSA World Congress. Chile Alvarez, R., Katz, G. & Pomares, J. 2011. The Impact of New Technologies on Voter Confidence in Latin America: Evidence from E-Voting Experiments in Argentina and Colombia. Journal of Information Technology and Politics, 8, 199-217

(continued)

(continued)

Country of interest	Title
	Alvarez, R., Levin, I., Pomares, J. & Leiras, M. 2013. Voting Made Safe and Easy: The impact of e-voting on citizen perception. Political Science Research and Methods, 1, 117-137
	Pomares, J., Levin, I., Alvarez, R., Mirau, G. & Overejo, T. From Piloting to Roll-Out: voting experience and trust in the first full e-election in Argentina. In: 6th International Conference on Electronic Voting, 2014 Lochau/Bregenz. Austria
India	Wolchok, S., Wustrow, E., Halderman, J., Prasad, H., Kankipati, A., Sakhamuri, S., Yagati, V. & Gonggrijp, R. Security Analysis of India's Electronic Voting Machines. 17th ACM Conference on Computer and Communications Security, 2010 Chicago, USA
	Kumar, D. & Begum, T. Electronic Voting Machine - A review. International Conference on Pattern Recognition, Informatics and Medical Engineering, 2012
	Yadav, S. & Singh, A. 2013. A Biometric Traits-based Authentication System for Indian Voting System. International Journal of Computer Applications, 65, 28-32
Iran	Kahani, M. 2005. Experiencing Small-Scale E-Democracy in Iran. The electronic Journal on Information Systems in Developing Countries, 22, 1-9
	Isaai, M., Firoozi, F. & Hemyari, M. E-Election in Digital Society. Third International Conference on Digital Society, 2009 Cancun
	Basirat, P. 2012. The Relationship between the National Culture and the Implementation of the E-Voting System. International Journal of Innovation, Management and Technology, 3, 811-815
Jordan	Abu-Shanab, E., Knight, M. & Refai, H. 2010. E-Voting Systems: A tool for e-democracy. Management Research and Practice, 2, 264-274
	Nu'man, A. 2012. A Framework for Adopting E-Voting in Jordan. Electronic Journal of e-Government, 10, 133-146
	Abandah, G., Darabkh, K., Ammari, T. & Qunsul, O. 2013. Secure National Electronic Voting System. Journal of Information Science and Engineering, 30, 1339-1364
South Africa	Gefen, D., Rose, G., Warketin, M. & Pavlou, P. 2006. Culture and Trust in the Adoption of Electronic Voting: A look at the USA and South Africa. Advanced Topics in Global Information Management, 5
	Swanepoel, E., Thomson, K. & Vanniekerk, J. E-Voting: A South African perspective. In: First International ICST Conference, 2010 Maputo, Mozambique. 70-77
	Achieng, M. & Ruhode, E. 2013. The Adoption and Challenges of Electronic Voting Technologies within The South African Context. International Journal of Managing Information Technology, 5, 1-12
Colombia	Alvarez, R., Katz, G., Llamosa, R. & Martinez, H. Assessing Voters' Attitudes towards Electronic Voting in Latin Amerika: Evidence from Colombia's e-voting pilot. In: VOTE-ID, 2009
	Alvarez, R., Katz, G. & Pomares, J. 2011. The Impact of New Technologies on Voter Confidence in Latin America: Evidence from E-Voting Experiments in Argentina and Colombia. Journal of Information Technology and Politics, 8, 199-217
Pakistan	Bokhari, H. & Khan, M. Digitisation of Electoral Rolls: Analysis of multi-agency e-government project in Pakistan. In: 6th International Conference on Theory and Practice of Electronic Government, 2012 Albany, USA. 158-165
	Ullah, M., Umar, A., Amin, N. & Nizamuddin. An Efficient and Secure Mobile Phone Voting System. Eight International Conference on Digital Information Management, 2013 Islamabad. 332-336

(continued)

(continued)

Country of interest	Title
Tanzania	Kimbi, S., Nkansah-Gyekye, Y. & Michael, K. 2014. Towards a Secure Remote Electronic Voting in Tanzania - Organizational challenges. Advances in Computer Science: an International Journal, 3, 122-131 Kimbi, S. & Zlotnikova, I. 2014. Citizens' Readiness for Remote Electronic Voting in Tanzania. Advances in Computer Science: an International Journal, 3, 150-159
UAE	Salem, F. 2007. Enhancing Trust in e-Voting through Knowledge Management: The case of UAE. In: Managing Knowledge to Build Trust in Government. New York: United Nations Department of Economic and Social Affairs (UNDESA) Al-Khouri, A. 2012. E-Voting in UAE FNC Elections: A case study. Information and Knowledge Management, 2, 25-84
Ghana	Ofori-Dwumfuo, G. & Paatey, E. 2011. The Design of An Electronic Voting System. Research Journal of Information Technology, 3, 91-98 Yinyeh, M. O. & Gbolagade, K. 2013. Overview of Biometric Electronic Voting System in Ghana. International Journal of Advanced Research in Computer Science and Software Engineering, 3, 624-628
Ecuador	Pozo, J. Implementation Project Electronic Voting Azuay 2014 - Ecuador. In: 6th International Conference on Electronic Voting, 2014 Lochau/Bregenz, Austria. 47-58
Lebanon	Hajjar, M., Daya, B., Ismail, A. & Hajjar, H. 2006. An E-Voting System for Lebanese Elections. Journal of Theoretical and Applied Information Technology, 2, 21-29
Mauritius	Sheeba, A., Vinaye, A., Sameer, S. & Yatin, D. Comparative Study of Electronic Voting Models and A Proposed Security Framework for the Implementation in Mauritius. IEEE Symposium on Humanities, Science and Engineering Research, 2012 Kuala Lumpur, Malaysia
Mexico	Vilamala, J. 2007. E-Voting: An analysis of sociopolitical acceptance. 21st IPSA World Congress. Chile
Thailand	Thammawaja, S. & Lertwatechakul, M. Design a Secure Electronic Voting System for Thailand's Election. International Symposium on Communication and Information Technologies, 2008 Lao
Turkey	Cetinkaya, O. & Cetinkaya, D. Towards Secure E-elections in Turkey: Requirements and principles. The Second International Conference on Availability, Reliability and Security, 2007 Vienna
Uganda	Eilu, E. & Baguma, R. Designing Reality Fit m-Voting. 7th International Conference on Theory and Practice of Electronic Governance, 2013 Seoul, Korea. 326-329
Others	Ojo, A., Adeshina, A. & Ayo, C. Electronic Voting: Lessons and guide for developing countries. In: 6th European Conference on e-Government, 2006 Marburg, Germany Jegede, A., Aimufua, G. & Akosu, N. 2009. Electronic Voting: A panacea for electoral irregularities in developing countries. Journal of Mobile Communication, 3, 22-33 Essex, A., Clark, J. & Adams, C. 2010. Aperio: High integrity elections for developing countries. In: Towards Trustworthy Elections Kumar, S. & Walia, E. 2011. Analysis of Electronic Voting System in Various Countries. International Journal on Computer Science and Engineering, 3, 1825-1830 Al-Ameen, A. & Talab, S. 2013. The Technical Feasibility and Security of E-Voting. The International Arab Journal of Information Technology, 10, 397–404

References

1. Adeshina, S.A.: Towards improved adoption of e-voting - analysis of the case of Nigeria. In: 8th ACM International Conference on Theory and Practice of Electronic Governance, Portugal (2014)
2. Pomares, J., et al.: From piloting to roll-out: voting experience and trust in the first full e-election in Argentina. In: IEEE 6th International Conference on Electronic Voting. Lochau/Bregenz, Austria (2014)
3. Kuye, C.O., et al.: Design and analysis of electronic voting system in Nigeria. Int. Arch. Appl. Sci. Technol. 4(2), 15–20 (2013)
4. Ishaq, S.R., et al.: Adoption of e-voting system in Nigeria: a conceptual framework. Int. J. Appl. Inf. Syst. 5(5), 8–14 (2013)
5. Olaniyi, O.M., et al.: Framework for multilingual mobile e-voting service infrastructure for democratic governance. Afr. J. Comput. ICT 4(3), 23–32 (2011)
6. Ayo, C., Adebiyi, A., Sofoluwe, A.B.: E-voting implementation in Nigeria: the success factors, In: Salawu, R.I. (ed.) Curbing Political Violence in Nigeria: The Role of Security Profession, Institute of Security, pp. 50–60. Mukagamu and Brothers Ent., Nigeria (2009)
7. Musa, M., Aliyu, F.: Design of electronic voting systems for reducing election process. Int. J. Recent Technol. Eng. 2(1), 183–186 (2013)
8. Yadav, S., Singh, A.: A biometric traits-based authentication system for Indian voting system. Int. J. Comput. Appl. 65(15), 28–32 (2013)
9. Faniran, S., Olaniyan, K.: Strengthening democratic practice in Nigeria: a case for e-voting. In: 5th ACM International Conference on Theory and Practice of Electronic Governance, Tallin, Estonia (2011)
10. Avgerou, C., et al.: ICT and Citizens' trust in government: lessons from electronic voting in Brazil. In: 9th International Conference on Social Implications of Computers in Developing Countries, Sao Paulo, Brazil (2007)
11. Filho, J.R.: E-Voting and the creation of trust for socially marginalized citizens in Brazil. eJ. eDemocr. Open Govern. 2(2), 184–193 (2016)
12. Filho, J.R.: E-Voting in Brazil - Reinforcing institutions while diminishing citizenship. In: Electronic Voting 2008, Caste Hofen, Bregenz, Austria (2008)
13. Filho, J.R., Alexander, C.J., Batista, L.C.: E-voting in Brazil - the risks to democracy. In: Electronic Voting 2006. Bregenz, Bonn, Germany (2006)
14. Birks, D.F., et al.: Grounded theory method in information systems research: its nature, diversity and opportunities. Eur. J. Inf. Syst. 22, 1–8 (2013)
15. Okoli, C., Schabram, K.: A guide to conducting a systematic literature review of information systems research. Sprouts: Work. Papers Inf. Syst. 10, 1–26 (2010)
16. Kitchenham, B., et al.: Systematic literature reviews in software engineering - a systematic literature review. Inf. Softw. Technol. 51, 7–15 (2009)
17. Khan, G.F., et al.: A Socio-technical perspective on e-government issues in developing countries: a scientometrics approach. Scientometrics 87, 267–286 (2011)
18. Bostrom, R.P., Heinen, J.S.: MIS problems and failures: a socio-technical perspective part I: the causes. MIS Q. 1(3), 17–32 (1977)
19. Kling, R., Lamb, R.: IT and organizational change in digital economies: a socio-technical approach. Comput. Soc. 29(3), 17–25 (1999)
20. Heeks, R., Bailur, S.: Analyzing E-government research: perspectives, philosophies, theories, methods, and practice. Gov. Inf. Q. 24, 243–265 (2007)
21. Oostveen, A.-M.: Users' experiences with e-voting: a comparative case study. Int. J. Electron. Gov. 2(4), 357–377 (2009)

22. Al-Shammari, A., Villafiorita, A., Weldemariam, K.: Understanding the development trends of electronic voting systems. In: Seventh International Conference on Availability, Reliability and Security (2012)

23. Prandini, M., Sartori, L., Oostveen, A.-M.: Why electronic voting? In: Conference for eDemocracy and open Government (2014)

24. Kling, R.: Learning about information technologies and social change: the contribution of social informatics. Inf. Soc. Int. J. 16(3), 217–232 (2000)

25. Gauld, R., Goldfinch, S.: Dangerous Enthusiasms: E-government, computer failure and information systems development. Otago University Press, Dunedin (2006)

26. Benoist, E., Anrig, B., Jaquet-Chiffelle, D.-O.: Internet-voting: opportunity or threat for democracy? In: Alkassar, A., Volkamer, M. (eds.) Vote-ID 2007. LNCS, vol. 4896, pp. 29–37. Springer, Heidelberg (2007). doi:10.1007/978-3-540-77493-8_3

27. Oostveen, A.-M.: Outsourcing democracy: losing control of e-voting in the Netherlands. Policy Internet 2(4), 201–220 (2010)

28. Liptrott, M.: e-Voting: Same pilots, same problems, different agendas. Electron. J. E-Gov. 5(2), 205–212 (2007)

29. Moynihan, D.P.: Building secure elections: e-voting, security, and systems theory. Pub. Adm. Rev. 64(5), 515–528 (2004)

30. Wolfswinkel, J., Furtmueller, E., Wilderom, C.: Using grounded theory as a method for rigorously reviewing literature. Eur. J. Inf. Syst. 22, 45–55 (2013)

31. Webster, J., Watson, R.T.: Analyzing the past to prepare for the future writing a literature review. MIS Q. 26(2), 13–23 (2002)

32. Kitchenham, B., et al.: Systematic literature reviews in software engineering - a tertiary study. Inf. Softw. Technol. 52, 792–805 (2010)

33. Pieters, W.: Internet Voting: A Conceptual Challenge to Democracy. In: Trauth, E.M., Howcroft, D., Butler, T., Fitzgerald, B., DeGross, J.I. (eds.). IIFIP, vol. 208, pp. 89–103. Springer, Heidelberg (2006). doi:10.1007/0-387-34588-4_7

34. Sanford, C., Rose, J.: Characterizing eParticipation. Int. J. Inf. Manag. 27, 406–421 (2007)

35. Saebo, O., Rose, J., Flak, L.S.: The shape of eParticipation: characterizing an emerging research area. Gov. Inf. Q. 25, 400–428 (2008)

36. Medaglia, R.: eParticipation research: moving characterization forward (2006-2011). Gov. Inf. Q. 29, 346–360 (2012)

37. Wahid, F.: Themes of research on egovernment in developing countries: current map and future roadmap. In: IEEE 46th International Conference on System Sciences, Hawaii (2013)

38. Blangiardo, M., Baio, G.: Evidence of Bias in the eurovision song contest: modelling the votes using Bayesian hierarchical model. J. Appl. Stat. 41(10), 2312–2322 (2014)

39. IMF: World Economic Outlook. Database - WEO groups and aggregates information. World Economic and Financial Surveys (2014). http://www.imf.org/external/pubs/ft/weo/2014/01/weodata/groups.htm#eom. Cited 31 Mar 2015

40. Stiefel, R.C.: Electronic voting system. Soc.-Econ. Plann. Sci. 4(1), 33–39 (1970)

41. Tambouris, E.: An integrated platform for tele-voting and tele-consulting within and across european cities: the EURO-CITI project. In: Traunmüller, R., Lenk, K. (eds.) EGOV 2002. LNCS, vol. 2456, pp. 350–357. Springer, Heidelberg (2002). doi:10.1007/978-3-540-46138-8_57

42. Dukic, B., Mesaric, J., Katic, M.: Conceptual model of public opinion monitoring system using mobile phones (m-Referendum). In: IEEE 30th International Conference on Information Technology Interfaces, Dubrovnik (2008)

43. Caarls, S.: E-Voting handbook: key steps in the implementation of e-enabled elections. Council of European Publishing, Strasbourg (2010)

44. DCLG: Implementing Electronic Voting in the UK. Department for Communities and Local Government, London (2006)
45. Belanger, F., Carter, L.: The impacts of the digital divide on citizens' intentions to use internet voting. Int. J. Adv. Internet Technol. **3**(3, 4), 203–211 (2010)
46. Ngai, E.W.T., Wat, F.K.T.: A literature review and classification of electronic commerce research. Inf. Manag. **39**, 415–429 (2002)
47. Wolchok, S., et al. Security Analysis of India's Electronic Voting Machines. In: 17th ACM Conference on Computer and Communications Security Chicago, USA (2010)
48. Kalvet, T.: Innovation: a factor explaining e-government success in Estonia. Electron. Gov. Int. J. **9**(2), 142–157 (2012)
49. Eilu, E., Baguma, R.: Designing reality fit m-voting. In: 7th ACM International Conference on Theory and Practice of Electronic Governance, Seoul, Republic of Korea (2013)
50. Hajjar, M., et al.: An e-voting system for Lebanese elections. J. Theoret. Appl. Inf. Technol. **2**(1), 21–29 (2006)
51. Thammawaja, S., Lertwatechakul, M.: Design a secure electronic voting system for Thailand's election. In: IEEE International Symposium on Communication and Information Technologies, Lao (2008)
52. Gefen, D., et al.: Culture and trust in the adoption of electronic voting: a look at the USA and South Africa. Adv. Topics Glob. Inf. Manag. **5**, 102–127 (2006)
53. Brooks, L., Mohammed, A.B.: ACM eVoting in Nigeria: the case of the independent national electoral commission. In: EGOSE 2014, St. Petersburg, Russian Federation (2014)
54. Avgerou, C.: Explaining trust in IT-mediated elections: a case study of e-voting in Brazil. J. Assoc. Inf. Syst. **14**(8), 420–451 (2013)
55. Avgerou, C., et al.: Interpreting the trustworthiness of government mediated by information and communication technology: lessons from electronic voting in Brazil. Inf. Technol. Dev. **15**(2), 133–148 (2009)
56. BPPT: Rekomendasi Hasil Simulasi e-Voting Pemilukada Kabupaten Bantaeng Provinsi Sulawesi Selatan. Pusat Teknologi Informasi dan Komunikasi, Jakarta, Badan Pengkajian dan Penerapan Teknologi (2013)
57. BPPT: Rekomendasi Hasil Alih Teknologi Pemilihan Kepala Desa menggunakan e-Voting di Kabupaten Boyolali. Pusat Teknologi Informasi dan Komunikasi, Jakarta, Badan Pengkajian dan Penerapan Teknologi (2013)
58. Hapsara, M.: E-voting Indonesia: framing the research. In: 9a Conferencia Iberica de Sistemas y Tecnologias de Informacion. AISTI, Barcelona, Spain (2014)
59. Bokhari, H., Khan, M.: Digitisation of electoral rolls: analysis of multi-agency e-government project in Pakistan. In: 6th ACM International Conference on Theory and Practice of Electronic Government, Albany, USA (2012)
60. Achieng, M., Ruhode, E.: The Adoption and challenges of electronic voting technologies within the South African context. Int. J. Manag. Inf. Technol. **5**(4), 1–12 (2013)
61. Reyes, M.A.L.: World Leader in e-Voting. Business (2013). http://www.philstar.com/business/2013/09/25/1237748/world-leader-e-voting. Cited 31 Aug 2015
62. Olaniyi, O.M., Arulogun, O.T., Omidiora, E.O.: Design of secure electronic voting system using multifactor authentication and cryptographic hash function. Int. J. Comput. Inf. Technol. **2**(6), 1122–1131 (2013)
63. Ekong, U.O., Ayo, C.K.: The prospects of M-voting implementation in Nigeria. In: 3GSM & Mobile Computing: An Emerging Growth Engine for National Development, pp. 172–179 (2007)
64. Hapsara, M.: Electronic voting for the people of Mount Merapi, really? In: International Symposium on Technology Management and Emerging Technology Bandung, IEEE, Indonesia (2014)

65. Filho, J.R.: E-Voting in Brazil - reinforcing institutions while diminishing citizenship. In: 3rd International Conference on Electronic Voting, Gesellschaft fur Informatik, Castle Hofen, Bregenz, Austria (2008)

66. Pozo, J.: Implementation project electronic voting Azuay 2014 - Ecuador. In: 6th International Conference on Electronic Voting Lochau/Bregenz, IEEE, Austria

67. Kimbi, S., Nkansah-Gyekye, Y., Michael, K.: Towards a secure remote electronic voting in tanzania - organizational challenges. Adv. Comput. Sci. Int. J. 3(5), 122–131 (2014)

68. Ayo, C., et al.: An end-to-end e-election system based on multimodal identification and authentication. In: 6th International Conference on E-Government. Academic Publishing Ltd, Cape Town, South Africa (2006)

69. Ekong, U.O., Ekong, V.E.: M-voting: a panacea for enhanced e-participation. Asian J. Inf. Technol. 9(2), 111–116 (2010)

70. Ayo, C., Azeta, A.: A framework for voice-enabled m-Voting system: Nigeria a case study. In: 9th European Conference on E-Government. Academic Publishing Ltd., London, UK (2009)

71. Adeyinka, T., Olasina, G.: Voter's perception of the adequacy and suitability of e-Voting in the Nigeria polity. In: Bwalya, K.J. (ed.) Handbook of Research on E-Government in Emerging Economies: Adoption, e-Participation, and Legal Frameworks, pp. 123–140. IGI Global, Hershey (2012)

72. Rezende, P.A.D.: Electronic voting systems, is Brazil ahead of its time? RSA Lab. 7(2), 2–8 (2004)

Truly Multi-authority *'Prêt-à-Voter'*

Thomas Haines[✉] and Xavier Boyen

Queensland University of Technology, Brisbane, Australia
t1.haines@qut.edu.au

Abstract. In-polling-booth electronic voting schemes are being implemented in government binding elections to enable fast tallying with end-
to-end verification of the election result. One of the most significant issues
with these schemes is how to print or display the ballot without jeopar-
dising privacy. In several of these schemes, freshly generated unmarked
ballots contain critical information which combined with public "bulletin
board" information breaks ballot secrecy. We present a practical solution
which uses re-encryption inside the polling booth to print ballot papers
in a privacy-preserving manner. This makes practical, at a user rather
than computer level, multi-authority voting.

We apply this solution to *Prêt à Voter*, a state-of-the-art electronic
voting system trialled in a recent Victorian state election. We propose two
approaches: one with higher security and another with stricter usability
constraints. The primary benefit is that ballot papers no longer pose a
privacy risk. The solution has the major benefit of resolving the conflict
between auditability and forward secrecy of printers, a problem left open
by the most recent work in this area. Additional benefits include practical privacy from compromised polling-place devices, while preserving
receipt-freeness against a more general adversary. Although we do not
provide privacy against a wholly compromised authority, a voter needs
honesty from only one of the machines at the polling site for secrecy.

1 Introduction

Cryptographic voting schemes in the literature can be categorised into three
areas: those using mixnets [1,7,11,28,32,33]; those using homomorphic encryption [3,13,14,21]; and those using blind signatures [8,18,26,27].

- Mixnet-based schemes in general allow arbitrarily expressive voting at a relatively fixed cost, since tallying is done on the mixed votes in plaintext; however
  there is a delay in tallying due to the necessity of applying verifiable mixes
  after the election. Our proposals fall into this category.
- Homomorphic schemes facilitate a higher possible level of privacy since individual votes are not revealed, only the final tally with suitable proofs, but
  expressiveness suffers and tallying is an even more expensive proposition.

X. Boyen—Supported by ARC Future Fellowship FT1401185. All opinions are the
authors' only.

R. Krimmer et al. (Eds.): E-Vote-ID 2016, LNCS 10141, pp. 56–72, 2017.
DOI: 10.1007/978-3-319-52240-1_4

- Blind-signature-based schemes require different implementations of anonymous channels than mixnet-based schemes, and shift much of the cryptographic work from the authority onto the voter, which can be more efficient.

We present two new variants of Prêt à Voter [31], based on re-encryption. Our variants achieve threshold device privacy without relying on prior secrets.

In Prêt à Voter, the voter is required to receive some secret information (a permutation of candidates) in order to fill and cast their ballot. Similarly, in Scantegrity II (another major electronic voting system) [6], the voter must receive secret confirmation codes. The requirement that this information must be kept secret creates difficulties in the generation and transportation of ballot papers. The tamper-evident ballot papers of Scantegrity II should provide strong evidence to the voter that the information has been transported securely but provides no guarantees about privacy against the printing authority. There has been work on secure printing [17], nevertheless in that instance the voter receiving the ballot paper is unable to readily verify the privacy of their ballot.

1.1 Background

The central issue which dominates the security of voting is how, simultaneously, to achieve integrity and privacy. An untappable channel in at least one direction, between voter and authority, seems necessary for receipt-freeness [21]. Polling-booths are often kept in schemes designed for government binding elections to realise this constraint.

The issue of privacy against the adversary is further complicated when we consider the election authority itself as an adversary. To mitigate and control this issue, the role of the election authority is often divided among a collection of parties whose interests are in conflict. The preferred mechanism for this is threshold cryptography. However, this does not defend privacy from the machine that encrypts the vote (as in Wombat [20], StarVote [4], or the Moran-Naor scheme [24]) or prints the ballot (as in Prêt à Voter and Scantegrity II).[1]

Dividing "trust" amongst multiple entities creates a strong difference between privacy against the election tellers (those holding the threshold key parts) and privacy against the poll-site machines or printers. We show how to defend against a compromise of all but one of the machines that a voter uses in a polling place. This does not protect against a completely corrupt election authority who sets up the polling-booth and hence controls all of its computational device(s). It does, however, protect against *ad hoc* compromises of individual poll-site devices.

Three of the prominent in-polling-booth voting systems are Prêt à Voter [31], Scantegrity II [10] and STAR-Vote [4]. Each represents a very different approach to in-polling-booth computer-assisted voting. Each of these approaches has a largely disjoint set of possible solutions to achieving privacy against corrupt devices. We review these briefly.

---

[1] Threshold cryptography is further complicated by requiring an additional trusted computational device, in the absence of human-computable threshold schemes.

STAR-Vote uses a device to encrypt votes directly from human input. Such a device necessarily learns the votes, so any solution attempting to achieve privacy against corrupt devices in STAR-Vote would seem to require the use of multiple devices to encrypt votes.

Scantegrity II relies on optical scan systems and provides end-to-end verifiability of election results. It does this through printing confirmation codes on the ballot which the voter uncovers as a part of voting. These confirmation codes later appear on the Bulletin Board allowing voters to confirm their vote. In Scantegrity II, the use of static (non-randomised) confirmation codes prevents re-encryption. Since re-encryption is not possible, cast ballots cannot be further anonymising through mixing.

Prêt à Voter uses hybrid human-computer cryptography to achieve a high level of practicality and privacy. The issue of privacy against corrupted devices in Prêt à Voter exists primarily in the way ballots are generated. Ballots cannot be generated directly due to issues of privacy breaches and kleptographic [19] attacks. The kleptographic problem is generally resolved by distributing ballot generation information across a set of tellers, as in [15]. However, solutions of this sort still use a single physical printer which must be trusted for privacy.

So, while it is possible to divide the authority among election tellers and to suggest constructions of secure channels, all of these solutions currently require some single device (printer or ballot marker) to be trusted. That device presents sufficient information to the voter to enable them to vote, and in doing so, that device learns sufficient information to recover the voter's selection (at least once verification information appears on the Bulletin Board). In the context of Prêt à Voter, a solution was proposed in [17] to make use of visual cryptography to allow multiple printers to construct a ballot. Another approach involving the use of multiple re-encryption clerks was suggested in [30], but this was later shown to be broken in [29] because the large permutations leaked are likely to be unique. While Ryan and Teague in the same paper [29] presented a fix, their solution is of partial applicability and the current literature around implementing voting schemes has not incorporated it.

1.2   Our Solution

The core idea behind the solution in our paper is to allow optional re-encryption on *separated*[2] ballots to provide privacy against corrupted devices. Our variants are similar to the theoretical voting system of Hirt and Sako [21], however, Hirt and Sako do not make the distinction between the voter and their computational device. It is precisely the challenge of practically unraveling how to achieve security to the voter, without trusting the device, which is our primary contribution. In both of our variants it constructs an anonymous channel using a set of tellers, much like a mixnet. However, in contrast to mixnets, the re-encryption occurs on individual ballots, and is driven by voter action. The scheme has some features

---

[2] In a nutshell, a Prêt-à-Voter separated ballot is the one half of the paper ballot that is about to be cast; see Sect. 2 for details.

in common with the trusted (re)randomisers of Lee *et al.* [23] and Aditya *et al.* [2], but we use no trusted components or authorities for the randomisation, and we preserve cast-as-intended verification.

The most important property we aim to achieve with our system(s) is to require **no prior secrets**. It aims to capture an adversary's power to control all items and data that the voter brings into the polling booth.

Definition 1 *No prior secrets: The adversary has full knowledge and control over all the information handed to the voter before entering the polling booth.*

We note that other end-to-end schemes such as STAR-Vote, and Prêt à Voter as implemented in Victoria (Australia), do not require prior secrets to be passed to the voter. Instead, they contain single devices which are only procedurally prevented from breaking privacy. We define the **full threshold device privacy** property to reflect a scheme which holds against single-device attacks.

Definition 2 *Full threshold device privacy: A voting system has full threshold device privacy, if, provided that at least one device is honest, the voter's privacy is assured.*

We also add the additional constraint that the devices should not be networked. This allows procedural measures against kleptographic and other attacks targeting and originating from the devices to be more readily implemented.

Definition 3 *No networks: No device inside the polling-booth requires network access to any other device, local or remote, to function during the election.*

We make the assumption that the receipts that the voters receive are publicly known and linked to them. Since voters are encouraged in most proposals to share their receipts with as many interested parties as possible, this assumption seems reasonable.

Assumption 1 *Public Receipts: The information provided on the Bulletin Board, and on receipts, to enable vote verification, is publicly available, and the links to voters are known.*

Our first variant relies upon a human mental calculation assumption very similar to that of Prêt à Voter. In standard Prêt à Voter, it is assumed that a voter given a permutation of candidates can apply the mental permutation of their preferences and create a ranking. This is a reasonable assumption[3] is slightly modified for our variant, we assume the voter can take two listed permutations and compose them.

Assumption 2 *Mental Calculation: Voters can compose two permutations.*[4]

---

[3] It is reasonable for small permutations. Nevertheless, the Victorian Prêt-à-Voter variant used a machine to assist voters with this task because computing a permutation of its 50 candidates was deemed too difficult.

[4] The composition of two permutations resulting in their product is a basic algebraic operation. This operation is a special case of the pointwise sequential evaluation of two enumerated functions.

We also define a second variant that does not rely on the mental calculation assumption, making it more suited for the less complicated Single Transferable Vote or Instant-Runoff Voting contests. To achieve **threshold device privacy** and **no prior secrets** without using voter **mental calculations**, we require a slightly stronger polling-booth assumption which we call **device anonymous polling-booth**. This assumption means that the devices have no means to identify the voter other than from the information that passes between them.

Assumption 3 *Device Anonymous Polling-Booth:* *A voter interacting with devices in a polling booth does so over an anonymous untappable channel.*

No new information is revealed to general adversaries since the **separated** ballots, now to become re-encrypted and mixed, were public information in the original Prêt à Voter. A completely corrupt authority, or an external attacker, may still compromise privacy, but only if all the machines that the voter uses in the polling place are corrupt. We stress that since in-booth mixing is optional, it cannot guarantee coercion resistance against the election authority.

1.3   Motivation and Contribution

Motivation. The bottleneck of the single device able to break privacy in the polling booth is of great concern and largely unaddressed. We propose to allow concerned voters to interact with the set of tellers inside the polling booth, thus removing their reliance on a single device. Our scheme provides no privacy against a fully corrupt set of tellers; it does however provide privacy against a partial compromise of the poll-site devices.

None of the current voting schemes being implemented in government-binding elections [4–6] offers privacy against a compromised printing or voting device. While this may be acceptable in some situations, there is certainly a need for solutions that do not require this trust assumption.

Contribution. We make practical, at a user rather than computer level, multi-authority voting. We do this through a process of re-encryption by mixers which act on individual paper ballots, possibly after marking, but before scanning, to prevent information learned in printing from being readily used to reveal votes. This is our primary contribution.

This approach has the following advantages over previous work:

1. A lack of prior secrets on the ballot papers allows them to be printed, transported and distributed without additional complication.
2. All devices with which the voters interact must collude to break their privacy (barring an active voter coercion attack by the authority itself).
3. No scheme which would have otherwise achieved receipt-freeness or coercion resistance will lose those properties through the use of our extension.[5]

---

[5] This is because all information the in-booth mixers see, used to be public in the original scheme.

4. In the context of the Victorian election system vVote [16], our approach would mitigate the lack of printer forward secrecy because a re-encrypted receipt keeps the vote secret even if the printer's data is later exposed.

Practically, our improvements would directly provide higher levels of privacy, e.g., to the version of Prêt à Voter recently used in a parliamentary election in the Australian state of Victoria [16]. The white papers by the vVote team have always described a networked printer or electronic ballot marker with access to enough information to break ballot secrecy. Our solution allows a voter to interact with re-encryption mixers and remove this trust in the privacy of those devices, as long as not all of them collude.

Limitations. If the election authority can observe the voter in the polling booth, there is no privacy, however this is true of all schemes discussed. Indeed, even in the remote setting, JCJ [22] and Civitas [12], among others, assume that the voter cannot be observed at key points of the process. The more interesting and controversial assumption we make is that the voter will not subject themself to coercion and provide the proofs of correct mixing to the election authority, although he or she would be able to do so.

2   Prêt à Voter

Before entering into the details of the scheme we provide an overview of Prêt à Voter, with particular emphasis on the elements that allow re-encryption.

Prêt à Voter was introduced by Ryan [31] based on Chaum's "Visual Cryptography" [9]. The key innovation, which is at the heart of Prêt à Voter, is to vary the candidate order. Prêt à Voter provides privacy equivalent to the cryptosystem, used to encrypt the candidate order, unless the trusted devices are corrupt.

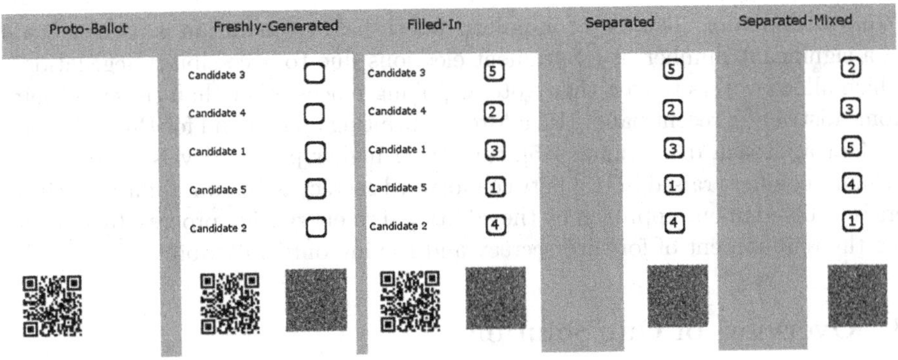

Fig. 1. Summary of Prêt à voter ballot states.

A Prêt à Voter ballot, ready to be filled in, is shown in Fig. 1, under the description *freshly-generated*. It consists of a left hand side (LHS) and a right hand side (RHS). The LHS contains the list of candidates in a certain ranking in both human and computer readable forms. The RHS contains boxes in which the selection (or ranking) can be marked and an encryption of the candidate order under a threshold-cryptographic key of the election tellers (encoded as a high-density QR code).

"Conventional" Prêt à Voter ballots can be thought of as existing in three distinct states: *freshly-generated*, *filled-in* and *separated*. For Prêt à Voter to be receipt-free, it is clear that the *separated* ballots should not reveal the votes. In addition, it is clear that *filled-in* ballots will reveal votes. *Freshly-generated* ballots are interesting, since they do not reveal votes on their own; however, they contain the relationship between the permutation and the ciphertext/serial. Since this serial/ciphertext will later appear on the Bulletin Board next to a ranking, *freshly-generated* ballots *do* reveal votes, as noted by Ryan in [30]. The fact that an unmarked *freshly-generated* ballot reveals votes in Prêt à Voter runs contrary to expectation provided by current voting schemes, which only serves to exacerbate this security issue.

The addition of printing on demand and re-encryption before scanning increases the distinct states into which Prêt-à-Voter ballots fall. There are two new states: *proto-ballots* and *separated-mixed*. *Proto-ballots* contain only a seed which will be used to deterministically generate the ballot. The process by which this ballot generation occurs uses trapdoor information; without this trapdoor, the *proto-ballots* leak no information. *Separated-mixed* ballots are the result of applying *separated* ballots to one or more re-encryption mixers. The *separated-mixed* have the same receipt-freeness property as *separated* ballots; they also have the additional property that the ciphertext containing the candidate order does not match that generated by the printer, since the ciphertext has been re-encrypted. This prevents deanonymisation of the voters by the printer and its trapdoor without the assistance of all re-encryption mixers.

Print-on-Demand. The use of in-polling-booth ballot generation is necessitated in a significant number of government elections due to accessibility legislation, which allows voters to cast their vote at polling places other than those in their home district. A recent paper [15] addresses printing on demand for Prêt à Voter.

Our approach draws upon [15], targetting higher privacy levels. One of the primary conflicts raised in [15] between forward secrecy and auditability of printers is resolved in our approach by the additional re-encryption process, by removing the requirement of forward secrecy and leaving only auditability.

3   Overview of Our Solution

Our primary technique is to re-encrypt a *separated* ballot, either before or after marking, inside the polling-booth to prevent single points of failure for privacy.

We can do this because Prêt à Voter, among others, has a ballot paper which contains a plaintext list of candidates, an encrypted component (for which the plaintext list could be re-constructed) and a space for voter input. The reason we need to re-encrypt is that an attacker who compromises the printer could otherwise use the unchanged encrypted component to correlate the plaintext list of candidates learned through printing and the voter's selection that will later appear on the Bulletin Board, to break privacy.

Throughout the rest of the paper, we will describe the encrypted component as $E(p, r)$, the encryption of the permutation p using the randomness r. The permutation p here is the order in which the candidates appear on the ballot. Additionally, we denote the input component as R, the ranking of the candidates according to permutation p. For concreteness, we focus on Single Transferable Vote (STV) and Instant Runoff Voting (IRV), although to the best of our knowledge there is no standard voting method to which our method would not apply.

The goal of our mixing technique is simple: it attempts to take two sets, representing a ballot appearing to the adversary at two different stages (first through the printer, and second through the scanner or Bulletin Board), and make them un-connectable. The sets are $(E(p, r), p)$ and $(E(p, r'), R)$ where any change must preserve the relation between R and p. The commonality between the sets is $E(p, .)$ which provides the intuition that it is this data that must be mixed (re-encrypted). Indeed, both our variants primarily function by re-encrypting $E(p, r)$, albeit composed to achieve security in significantly different ways.

First Variant. The first variant uses re-encryption to distribute the ballot generation and the entropy therein. Once the re-encryption has occurred the voter fills in their ballot. The difficulty of the filling process is captured by the mental calculation assumption. Privacy here is provided since no number of devices, less than the threshold, can learn the value of p; this directly implies information-theoretic privacy.

Second Variant. The second variant targets the situation where an Electronic Ballot Marker (EBM) is provided for accessibility reasons. Re-encryption will seek to disconnect the identity of the voter from the information collected by the EBM, after the user has interacted with the EBM to fill their vote. Privacy here is provided because the EBM cannot connect any vote to any voter with better success than a generic passive Italian attack[6], without controlling all mixers. The nature of a polling booth that prevents the trivial revelation of the voters' identity to the EBM is captured by the assumption of a device-anonymous polling booth.

3.1 Differences Compared to a Mixnet

Our proposal has a strong similarity to a standard re-encryption mixnet; for that reason, we will in this section discuss some key differences.

---

[6] The Italian attacks works in systems where the set of all ballots cast is known; the attacker gets the voter to cast an unusual vote and then checks to see if this vote occurs in the set of ballots cast.

In a standard mixnet the ballots are collected then processed as a series of batches, re-encrypting and permuting the ballots within each batch. In comparison, in both of our variants the voter directly takes their individual ballot to some or all of the re-encryption mixers, to permute the order of candidates within the ballot. If a standard method of mixing was used, the last mixer would have full knowledge of which ballot belonged to whom.

The possibility of timing attacks opened by the individual rather than batch processing has no effect on our first variant. In the second variant, a timing attack may allow a complete or partial identification of the voter, based on three-way collusion between EBM, scanner, and polling-station attendants in charge of ushering in the voters (or an onlooker with a facial recognition database), which would violate our Assumption 3 of a device-anonymous polling booth. This attack works on all schemes that rely on a device-anonymous polling booth.

4   Variant 1: Human-Computable Permutation

In this section we detail the human-permutation variant, and the common parts with the EBM variant. The in-booth flows for both are depicted on Fig. 2.

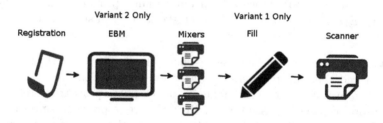

Fig. 2. Overview of the in-booth voting flow. The EBM step occurs only in Variant 2; the Fill step occurs only in Variant 1.

In our first variant we avoid providing the ranking R to any of the mixers. In a sense we use them in a similar way to the re-encryption clerks proposed by Ryan [30]. In Ryan's solution, two separate ciphertexts, called *onions*, $E(p, r)$, are constructed: one is used with the cast ballot and another is extracted in the polling booth. In our variant the one onion is constantly updated with a new permutation. This update to the permutation is reported to the voter who then uses this knowledge to vote. In both cases the clerks or mixers are used to distribute the generation of the ballot which the voter will then fill in.

Ryan's solution does not provide privacy in variant 1's model, because the device which makes the decrypted onion available to the voter learns the permutation under which the voter will cast their ballot. It can then match this information with the ranking that will later appear publicly, to break privacy.[7]

---

[7] While Ryan's solution would work in variant 2's EBM model, it may still allow an adversary knowing the initial permutation to trace votes, and it would require a device capable of *decrypting* the onions inside every polling booth: a risky proposition.

The various agents and components of our system are:

1. **An Election Authority (EA)**, tasked to run the election, and controlling:
   (a) **Printers**, to print freshly generated ballots,
   (b) (in Variant 2 only) **Electronic Ballot Markers (EBMs)**,
   (c) **Scanners**, to record the final separated-mixed ballots;
2. **Election Tellers**, typically interested parties such as political parties, and here used as members of the privacy threshold, controlling:
   (a) **Mixers**, for mixing single ballots inside the polling booth,
   (b) **Mixnets**, for anonymising batches of ballots on the BB before tallying;
3. **A Bulletin Board (BB)**, realising a broadcast channel with memory;
4. **Ballot Generators**, generating (the randomness used for) fresh ballots.

It is expected that ballot generators and election tellers will be the same entities, and that the printer will print ballots as generated (easy to verify, see below).

Ballot Construction. For convenience we assume that ballots are generated in the form suggested in [5]. That is to say, the onion (or encrypted ballot) is a tuple of encrypted candidate-IDs; for example, in an election for parties $\mathcal{A}, \mathcal{B}, \mathcal{C}$ the onion will be the concatenation of $E(\mathcal{A}), E(\mathcal{B}), E(\mathcal{C})$.

Audit 1: Checking Ballot Construction. The most common suggestion to realise in-booth ballot construction is to use a trapdoor Verifiable Pseudo-Random Number Generator (VPRNG). The output of VPRNG can be used as input to a function which generates ballots. Once ballots are generated they can be printed on paper. Verification of correctness of the VPRNG, the correct running of the ballot generation function, and the correct printing of this information forms a valid proof of ballot construction. A simple case to consider is when a non-randomised signature scheme is used as a VPRNG. The auditor checks the validity of the signature, then runs the public function on the signature and checks that the ballot printed matches the output of the function. The audit can be conducted on any machine, since there are no privacy implications. To perform an audit the voter checks the following:

1. The public key printed is as expected, namely valid for the printer.
2. The signature is valid on the serial for that public key.
3. The rest of the content of the ballot is the correct output of the publicly known function on that signature.

Check-in with Election Officials. The voter enters the polling station and registers with officials. At this point the voter is given a ballot by the official. This is similar in process to that provided by the printer in [5], with the notable difference that we require the entire ciphertext to be printed on the ballot to enable mixing and re-encryption, rather than a mere serial number. The voter can optionally choose to audit the ballot paper, as detailed in Audit 1, without invalidating it.

Third-Party Mixing (Optional). The voter physically separates the Left Hand Side (LHS) from the Right Hand Side. The voter is then allowed to have their RHS re-permuted and re-encrypted by any sequence of the mixers provided. If the voter chooses to have their ballot mixed, they input their ballot into the mixer. The mixer reads the ballot, permutes and re-encrypts the onion. Upon completion the mixer outputs its change to the permutation and a new RHS, which the voter can either further mix or cast their vote on. In addition, the mixer outputs a receipt which the voter takes home to verify that the mix was done correctly, see Audit 2.

Audit 2: Correct Mixing. As previously mentioned, the mixer prints an audit paper with the new permutation and randomness values revealed. The voter can take this paper home to verify the correctness of the mix. This audit paper should be signed by the mixer to provide non-repudiation.

To verify the i-th round mix, the voter checks the following:

- The ciphertext candidate-IDs output by the mix are equal to the candidate-IDs re-encrypted with the randomness and permutation claimed;
- The ranking output is equal to the ranking input permuted with the claimed permutation.

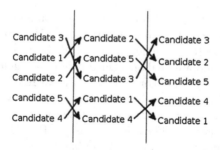

Fig. 3. Visually composing a sequence of permutations, from (3,1,2,5,4) to (2,5,3,1,4) then (3,2,5,4,1).

Filling. The voter composes the LHS of the original ballot with the permutations of each subsequent mix, in sequence. This can be done by placing the printouts next to each other and updating the permutation as shown in Fig. 3. Once the final permutation is calculated, the RHS can be filled in. The voter must then discard the LHS of the original ballot.

Scanning. With the final ballot suitably re-mixed to the desired "privacy threshold" now filled in, the voter then goes to the scanner. The scanner submits the ballot to the Bulletin Board (BB), which sends back a signature on the hash of the ballot. The scanner prints out this signed hash which the voter can check later on. If the ballots used were not kept private before the election, the scanner should perform an additional mix before scanning and uploading.

Audit 4: Mix Correctness.[8] To verify the i-th round of mixing, the voter checks the following:

– The ciphertext candidate-IDs outputted by the mix are equal to the candidate-IDs re-encrypted with the randomness and permutation claimed.

Audit 5: Signature Correctness. The signature can be checked by an external computation device. The voter would be permitted to use these devices outside the polling booth only.

Audit 6: Receipt on Bulletin Board. If the receipt does not appear on the BB then the voter can produce their RHS. The presence of a valid signature on the receipt is considered proof that it should have appeared on the BB.

Mixing and Tallying. Since, from the viewpoint of the authority, our ballots are constructed in the same way as in the Victorian elections using Prêt à Voter [16] (albeit without vote packing), the methods presented in that paper, and indeed any appropriate method from literature.

5 Variant 2: EBM Assisted Variant

Fig. 4. Ballot ready to be voted on.

In our second variant we include an Electronic Ballot Marker (EBM) to assist the voter in filling their ballot, and which in doing so necessarily learns the votes. Under the Device-Anonymous Polling Booth assumption, the EBM however will not directly learn the identity of the voters casting those votes. Unfortunately, if the ballots were then immediately scanned and posted without further mixing, the $E(p, r)$ value seen by the EBM would become public and linkable to a specific voter, under the Public Receipts assumption. The process of re-encryption mixing in variant 2 follows almost directly from standard mixnets.

Election Official. The voter enters the polling station and registers with officials. At this point the voter is given a ballot by the official which is similar to that provided by the printer in [5]. The voter can undertake Audit 1 to check that the ballot is correct. An example ballot is shown in Fig. 4.

Filling. The voter takes the ballot to the Electronic Ballot Marker (EBM). This ballot contains a plaintext version of the candidate list, a machine readable candidate list in the bottom left and an encrypted candidate list in the bottom right.

---

[8] Audit 3 is temporarily omitted; it will be needed in the second variant of the scheme.

The EBM transforms the candidate list into the standard order and displays the result on its touch screen. The voter can then enter their preferences in the standard manner. Once the voter has entered and confirmed their choices the EBM overprints them on the ballot paper.

Audit 3: EBM Printing. The voter should check that the selection printed on the ballot reflects their choices. At this point the voter is required to place their LHS into a disposal bin, to ensure receipt-freeness.

Party Mixing (Optional). The voter is then allowed to have their ballot mixed by any subset of the mixers provided in-booth, in any order. If the voter chooses to have their ballot mixed, they input their ballot into the mixer. The mixer permutes and re-encrypts the onion (encrypted preferences), and effects the corresponding permutation on the ranking. Upon completion, the mixer outputs a new RHS, which the voter can either further mix or take to the scanner. In addition, the mixer outputs a receipt which the voter takes home to verify that the mix was done correctly.

Scanning. As before, once the ballot has been sufficiently remixed to the desired privacy threshold against the election authority, the voter goes to the scanner which performs its own final mix. The scanner then submits the ballot to the Bulletin Board, which responds with a signature on the hash of the ballot. The scanner prints out this signed hash which the voter can check later.

6   Practical Matters

One of the primary concerns with our improvement is an increase in time and complexity of the voting process, which has a cost. We argue that in general the cost of this improvement is less than the amount spent on printers, EBMs and scanners already. Since there are normally only a few major parties across a country and several smaller relevant parties in each electorate, the time spent at an EBM is orders of magnitude higher than that required to scan and mix a few times, even if all major parties were to offer a mixer. Since the number of mixers is small and the number of EBMs required is high, the relative cost seems reasonable.

6.1   Auditing

The system provides 5 or 6 personal audits, depending on the variant, in order to ensure integrity. We summarise the overall audit flow as follows.

Audit 1: Correct Ballot Construction. This first audit ensures that the original ballot correctly captures the voter input, i.e., that the claimed printed permutation of the ballot is the same as the actual encrypted permutation.

Audit 3: Correct EBM. This audit step, only used in variant 2, ensures that the EBM correctly records the voter selection on the ballot.

Audits 2 and 4: Correct Mixing (Individual). Audits 2 and 4 verify the mixes before and after marking. The two are virtually identical, the one difference being that Audit 4 further requires that the ranking has been correctly updated.

Audit 5: Signature Correctness. This audit involves checking that the scanner has read the ballot correctly and properly committed to its receipt.

Audit 6: Ballots Collected. This audit ensures that the ballot has actually been collected and will be counted.

The cumulative effect of this set of audits is to ascertain that the ballot correctly captures the voter's input (1,3); the ballot will not be changed (2,4,5); and the ballot will be collected and input to counting (5,6).

There are also two universal audits. We require each in-booth mixer to also provide a universal proof of shuffle. This can be achieved by using a [25] style proof.

Audit 7: Correct In-Booth Mixing Universal. This audit ensures that all in-booth mixers acted correctly on all inputs.[9]

Audit 8: Correct General Mixing Universal. This audit ensures that all mix servers acted correctly on all inputs.

6.2   What Do We Do in Case of Failure?

The question of what to do when an audit fails is known to be non-trivial; we make some brief suggestions here. We first note that failure of an audit may fall into one of three general categories: 'spoof-able', 'manageable' and 'delayed'. We will explain these categories as we come to them.

One of the major issues with audits in electronic voting is the desire of disgruntled voters to cast false aspersions on the integrity of the election. Our scheme, along with many others, counters this issue by digitally signing all the receipts. This means that a disgruntled voter cannot produce a valid fake receipt without breaking the underlying signature scheme. However, this does not entirely resolve the issue, since a malicious device can now produce a receipt with an incorrect signature which when the voter complains would not be believed. This brings us to Audit 5 in our scheme where the voter checks the signature on their receipts. This audit can be spoofed by voters wishing to cast doubt on the election result, albeit with significant difficulty. This makes the response to failures of this audit particularly difficult. The easiest solution is likely to be physical, complicating the receipt (by using non-standard paper, watermarking, among many other methods), which would make it harder for voters to spoof.

Having dealt with the issue of false aspersions, it is no longer possible for election trustees to avoid culpability for their negligence or deliberate attacks. This provides a significant disincentive for parties to attack the system. The remaining audits fall into two further categories. Failure of Audit 3 is 'manageable'

---

[9] This audit is required to prevent a Pfitzmann malleability attack which would break privacy.

since it is detected before the voter has continued with their vote. The voter should then spoil their current ballot and vote again.

Audits 1, 2, 4 and 6 are in the 'delayed' category; that is, the results of delayed audits has the potential to be known only after the election has concluded. Failures in these categories are problematic for election organisers. On one hand, it is possible to correctly ascribe which party caused the issue. On the other hand, by the time these results arrive the election may already have ended.

7 Conclusion

We propose a refinement of Prêt-à-Voter in-polling-booth end-to-end verifiable electronic voting schemes, which provides privacy against *ad hoc* compromises of individual poll-site devices without dependence on prior secrets or personal trusted devices. In addition, our improvement alleviates the privacy issues of ballot generation and storage since their contents are no longer required to be secret, greatly simplifying the pre-election logistics, while also solving the problem of forward secrecy and auditability of printers. Our solution relies on the use of autonomous individual-ballot third-party mixing and re-encryption inside the polling booth.

While the need for additional in-booth hardware may make it unsuitable for some voting scenarios, we contend that the benefits outweigh the costs, particularly in situations where the voters are unwilling to trust the election authority, or fear reprisal for voting their conscience—an increasing concern worldwide. The method we present seems inapplicable to STAR-Vote or any scheme which uses direct encryption. It is an issue of on-going investigation whether Scantegrity II can be adjusted to have re-mixable confirmation codes, which would make it eligible for the privacy enchantment of our technique.

Acknowledgements. The authors would like to thank Vanessa Teague for stimulating discussions on this and related subjects. We would also like to thank Douglas Wikström and the reviewers for their helpful comments.

References

1. Abe, M.: Mix-networks on permutation networks. In: Lam, K.-Y., Okamoto, E., Xing, C. (eds.) ASIACRYPT 1999. LNCS, vol. 1716, pp. 258–273. Springer, Heidelberg (1999). doi:10.1007/978-3-540-48000-6_21
2. Aditya, R., Lee, B., Boyd, C., Dawson, E.: An efficient mixnet-based voting scheme providing receipt-freeness. In: Katsikas, S., Lopez, J., Pernul, G. (eds.) TrustBus 2004. LNCS, vol. 3184, pp. 152–161. Springer, Heidelberg (2004). doi:10.1007/978-3-540-30079-3_16
3. Benaloh, J.: Verifiable secret-ballot elections. Ph.D. thesis, Yale University (1987)
4. Benaloh, J., Byrne, M., Kortum, P.T., McBurnett, N., Pereira, O., Stark, P.B., Wallach, D.S.: Star-vote: a secure, transparent, auditable, and reliable voting system. CoRR abs/1211.1904 (2012)

5. Burton, C., Culnane, C., Heather, J., Peacock, T., Ryan, P.Y., Schneider, S., Srinivasan, S., Teague, V., Wen, R., Xia, Z.: Using Prêt à voter in Victorian state elections. In: Proceedings of USENIX EVT/WoTE (2012)

6. Carback, R., Chaum, D., abd John Conwaym, J.C., Essex, A., Hernson, P.S., Mayberry, T., Popoveniuc, S., Rivest, R.L., Shen, E., Sherman, A.T., Vora, P.L.: Scantegrity II municipal election at Takoma Park: the first E2E binding governmental election with ballot privacy. In: Proceedings of USENIX Accurate Electronic Voting Technology Workshop (2010)

7. Chaum, D.: Untraceable mail, return addresses and digital pseudonyms. Commun. ACM **24**(2), 84–88 (1981)

8. Chaum, D.: Elections with unconditionally-secret ballots and disruption equivalent to breaking RSA. In: Barstow, D., et al. (eds.) EUROCRYPT 1988. LNCS, vol. 330, pp. 177–182. Springer, Heidelberg (1988). doi:10.1007/3-540-45961-8_15

9. Chaum, D.: Secret-ballot receipts: true voter-verifiable elections. IEEE Secur. Priv. **2**(1), 38–47 (2004)

10. Chaum, D., Carback, R., Clark, J., Essex, A., Popoveniuc, S., Rivest, R.L., Ryan, P.Y.A., Shen, E., Sherman, A.T.: Scantegrity ii: end-to-end verifiability for optical scan election systems using invisible ink confirmation codes. In: EVT. USENIX Association (2008)

11. Chaum, D., Ryan, P.Y.A., Schneider, S.: A practical voter-verifiable election scheme. In: Vimercati, S.C., Syverson, P., Gollmann, D. (eds.) ESORICS 2005. LNCS, vol. 3679, pp. 118–139. Springer, Heidelberg (2005). doi:10.1007/11555827_8

12. Clarkson, M.R., Chong, S., Myers, A.C.: Civitas: toward a secure voting system. In: Proceedings of IEEE Symposium on Security and Privacy (2008)

13. Cohen, J.D., Fischer, M.J.: A robust and verifiable cryptographically secure election scheme. In: FOCS, pp. 372–382 (1985)

14. Cramer, R., Franklin, M., Schoenmakers, B., Yung, M.: Multi-authority secret-ballot elections with linear work. In: Maurer, U. (ed.) EUROCRYPT 1996. LNCS, vol. 1070, pp. 72–83. Springer, Heidelberg (1996). doi:10.1007/3-540-68339-9_7

15. Culnane, C., Heather, J., Joaquim, R., Ryan, P.Y.A., Schneider, S., Teague, V.: Faster print on demand for prêt à voter. J. Election Technol. Sys. **2**(1), 1–14 (2013)

16. Culnane, C., Ryan, P.Y.A., Schneider, S.A., Teague, V.: vVote: a verifiable voting system. ACM Trans. Inf. Syst. Secur. **18**(1), 3 (2015)

17. Essex, A., Clark, J., Hengartner, U., Adams, C.: How to print a secret. In: Proceedings of USENIX Hot Topics in Security (2009)

18. Fujioka, A., Okamoto, T., Ohta, K.: A practical secret voting scheme for large scale elections. In: Seberry, J., Zheng, Y. (eds.) AUSCRYPT 1992. LNCS, vol. 718, pp. 244–251. Springer, Heidelberg (1993). doi:10.1007/3-540-57220-1_66

19. Gogolewski, M., Klonowski, M., Kubiak, P., Kutyłowski, M., Lauks, A., Zagórski, F.: Kleptographic attacks on e-voting schemes. In: Müller, G. (ed.) ETRICS 2006. LNCS, vol. 3995, pp. 494–508. Springer, Heidelberg (2006). doi:10.1007/11766155_35

20. Grundland, E.: An analysis of the wombat voting system model (2012)

21. Hirt, M., Sako, K.: Efficient receipt-free voting based on homomorphic encryption. In: Preneel, B. (ed.) EUROCRYPT 2000. LNCS, vol. 1807, pp. 539–556. Springer, Heidelberg (2000). doi:10.1007/3-540-45539-6_38

22. Juels, A., Catalano, D., Jakobsson, M.: Coercion-resistant electronic elections. In: Proceedings of WPES (2005)

23. Lee, B., Boyd, C., Dawson, E., Kim, K., Yang, J., Yoo, S.: Providing receipt-freeness in mixnet-based voting protocols. In: Lim, J.-I., Lee, D.-H. (eds.) ICISC 2003. LNCS, vol. 2971, pp. 245–258. Springer, Heidelberg (2004). doi:10.1007/978-3-540-24691-6_19

24. Moran, T., Naor, M.: Split-ballot voting: everlasting privacy with distributed trust. ACM Trans. Inf. Syst. Secur. **13**(2), 16 (2010)

25. Neff, C.A.: A verifiable secret shuffle and its application to e-voting. In: CCS (2001)

26. Okamoto, T.: An electronic voting scheme. In: Terashima, N., Altman, E. (eds.) Advanced IT Tools, pp. 21–30. Springer, New York (1996)

27. Okamoto, T.: Receipt-free electronic voting schemes for large scale elections. In: Christianson, B., Crispo, B., Lomas, M., Roe, M. (eds.) Security Protocols 1997. LNCS, vol. 1361, pp. 25–35. Springer, Heidelberg (1998). doi:10.1007/BFb0028157

28. Park, C., Itoh, K., Kurosawa, K.: Efficient anonymous channel and all/nothing election scheme. In: Helleseth, T. (ed.) EUROCRYPT 1993. LNCS, vol. 765, pp. 248–259. Springer, Heidelberg (1994). doi:10.1007/3-540-48285-7_21

29. Ryan, P.Y.A., Teague, V.: Ballot permutations in pret a voter. In: Proceedings of Electronic Voting Technology/Workshop on Trustworthy Elections (2009)

30. Ryan, P.: The computer ate my vote. In: Boca, P., Bowen, J.P., Siddiqi, J. (eds.) Formal Methods: State of the Art and New Directions, pp. 147–184. Springer, London (2010)

31. Ryan, P.: A variant of the Chaum voter-verifiable scheme. In: Proceedings of the 2005 Workshop on Issues in the Theory of Security, pp. 81–88. ACM (2005)

32. Sako, K., Kilian, J.: Receipt-free mix-type voting scheme. In: Guillou, L.C., Quisquater, J.-J. (eds.) EUROCRYPT 1995. LNCS, vol. 921, pp. 393–403. Springer, Heidelberg (1995). doi:10.1007/3-540-49264-X_32

33. Wikström, D.: A universally composable mix-net. In: TCC, pp. 317–335 (2004)

Cast-as-Intended Verification in Electronic Elections Based on Oblivious Transfer

Rolf Haenni$^{(\boxtimes)}$, Reto E. Koenig, and Eric Dubuis

Bern University of Applied Sciences, CH-2501 Biel, Switzerland
{rolf.haenni,reto.koenig,eric.dubuis}@bfh.ch

Abstract. In this paper, we propose a new method for cast-as-intended verification in remote electronic voting. We consider a setting, in which voters receive personalized verification code sheets from the authorities over a secure channel. If the codes displayed after submitting a ballot correspond to the codes printed on the code sheet, a correct ballot must have been submitted with high probability. Our approach for generating such codes and transferring them to the voter is based on an existing oblivious transfer protocol. Compared to existing cast-as-intended verification methods, less cryptographic keys are involved and weaker trust and infrastructure assumptions are required. This reduces the complexity of the process and improves the performance of certain tasks. By looking at cast-as-intended verification from the perspective of an oblivious transfer, our approach also contributes to a better understanding of the problem and relates it to a well-studied cryptographic area of research.

1 Introduction

In remote electronic voting, voters may not always have access to a trustworthy platform for creating and casting the ballot. Malware on such a platform may take control over the vote casting process, for example by submitting a ballot containing a vote different from the voter's intention or by not casting a ballot at all. Without any counter-measures, such attacks are difficult to detect and may remain unnoticed even by a large number of affected voters. Since the correct outcome of an election is of great significance for the whole electorate, every infected computer becomes inevitably a problem for everybody. This so-called *secure platform problem* is one of the most critical and challenging obstacles in remote electronic voting [SV12].

Malware attacks against remote electronic voting may aim at violating either the secrecy or the integrity of the vote (or both). Full protection against both types of attacks is very hard to achieve. Some approaches suggest using an out-of-band channel such as regular postal mail as a trust anchor, over which additional information is transmitted securely to the voters. In this paper, we consider a setting, in which each voter receives a *verification code sheet* from the authorities over such a trusted channel. After submitting the ballot, codes for the chosen candidates are displayed by the voting application and voters are instructed to check if the displayed codes match with the codes printed on the verification

© Springer International Publishing AG 2017
R. Krimmer et al. (Eds.): E-Vote-ID 2016, LNCS 10141, pp. 73–91, 2017.
DOI: 10.1007/978-3-319-52240-1_5

code sheet. Matching codes imply with high probability that a correct ballot has been submitted. This step—called *cast-as-intended verification*—is an effective counter-measure against integrity attacks by malware on the voting platform, but obviously not against privacy attacks. Nevertheless, countries such as Norway or Switzerland have approved this as a sufficient solution for conducting elections over the Internet [GB12,BK113c].

1.1   Related Work

The idea of printing verification code sheets and distributing them over a trusted channel to the voters has first been proposed for the Norwegian Internet voting projects *eValg2011* and *eValg2013* [GB12]. From a technical point of view, the cryptographic protocols for the offline generation of the verification code sheets and the online generation of corresponding *return codes* for the chosen candidates have changed slightly in the course of time [Gjø10,Gjø11,Lip11,PG11,PG12], but the general underlying idea remained the same. Upon receiving one or multiple encrypted votes from a voter, two non-colluding servers conduct a series of cryptographic computations to remove the encryption randomizations in such a way that the plaintext votes are not disclosed. For this mechanism to work, the two servers must hold shares of the private key, under which the votes are encrypted. The return codes are then derived from the resulting deterministic values (the same deterministic values have been computed during the election preparation phase to enable the printing of the verification code sheets) and delivered over a separate channel to the voters' mobile phones. In case of non-matching return codes, voters are instructed to submit another ballot from a different platform. The separate channel for delivering the return codes is necessary to prevent the malware-infected voting application from learning the return codes when multiple ballots are submitted by the same voter.

A similar approach has been proposed for the voting system in the canton of Neuchâtel in Switzerland [GGP15]. In the Swiss context, vote updating by submitting multiple ballots is explicitly prohibited. This has two important consequences for the voting process. First, sending the return codes to the voting application is no longer a threat, even if malware has taken full control over the voting process. Second, since voters cannot re-submit the ballot from a different platform in case of non-matching return codes, ballots can only be accepted after receiving a correct *confirmation code* from the voter. In such a case, the server responds by displaying a *finalization code* to the voter for inspection.[1] Both the confirmation and the finalization code are printed on the verification code sheet along with the return codes. In the *Neuchâtel protocol* as presented in [GGP15], a matching finalization code implies that the vote has been cast as intended

---

[1] This extended vote casting process is approved by the Swiss Federal Chancellery as a possible solution for the secure platform problem [BK113a, Appendix 7]. If there is a mismatch between any of the return codes, voters are instructed to abort the online voting process and to submit a paper ballot. In case of mismatched finalization codes, voters are instructed to contact the election administration for an investigation.

by the voting application and recorded as cast by the server. Compared to the Norwegian protocol, the main technical difference is that voters participate in the generation of the return codes. For this, they receive a private key during the registration phase. This key replaces one of the two server-side key shares.

A very different protocol for cast-as-intended verification has been proposed in [HLv10]. To the best of our knowledge, it is the first and only such protocol based on *oblivious transfer* (OT), but it has never been implemented in practice. The idea is to transmit the return codes to the voters via a third party (the proxy) using the 1-*out-of-n proxy oblivious transfer* (POT) protocol from [AIR01]. The choice of using this particular POT protocol has multiple reasons, but most importantly, it enables voters to prove, in zero-knowledge, that the POT query and the encrypted vote contain identical plaintexts. To prove the validity of the encrypted votes, non-interactive *range proofs* are added to the ballots. The protocol is designed for the simple case where voters choose a single candidate from a set of n candidates. Multiple instances of the protocol can be executed in parallel to support general k-out-of-n limited votes, but the protocol is very inefficient for such general cases.

1.2   Contribution and Paper Overview

This paper contains two principal contributions. First, we introduce a new method for cast-as-intended verification, in which the return codes for k candidates are transmitted by an efficient k-out-of-n oblivious transfer [CT05]. This particular protocol requires no additional cryptographic keys and imposes no restrictions with regard to the space of messages that can be transferred. As a consequence, generating the return codes during the preparation of an election and transferring them to the voters during vote casting become two completely independent processes. We provide a description of a cryptographic voting protocol in Sect. 3, which shows how the query for the oblivious transfer can be linked in a natural way to the encrypted vote. Details about the cryptographic setting and the oblivious transfer protocol are given in Sect. 2.

Second, we propose a new technique to guarantee the validity of an encrypted vote without generating expensive zero-knowledge proofs. For this, we derive the return codes from random points of a random polynomial $p(x) \in_R \mathbb{Z}_p[x]$ of degree $k - 1$. This implies that receiving k correct points from the oblivious transfer is sufficient to interpolate the polynomial, whereas receiving $k - 1$ or less points does not provide any information about any other point on the polynomial. As a consequence, provided that p is large enough, knowing the polynomial $p(x)$ for a given verification code sheet entails with high probability that both the original OT query and the encrypted vote contain a valid set of candidates. This allows us to avoid expensive zero-knowledge proofs for proving the validity of the encrypted votes. The details of this technique are also included in the protocol description of Sect. 3. In Sect. 4, we discuss the security properties and performance of our protocol and compare it to existing work. We conclude the paper in Sect. 5.

2   Cryptographic Preliminaries

Let $(\mathcal{G}, \cdot, ^{-1}, 1)$ be a cyclic group of prime order q, for which the decisional Diffie-Hellman (DDH) assumption is believed to hold. Since q is prime, every element $x \in \mathcal{G} \setminus \{1\}$ is a generator. At the moment, we do not restrict ourselves to a particular group, but at some point, we will assume that $\mathcal{G}$ is identical to the set $\mathbb{G}_q \subset \mathbb{Z}_p^*$ of quadratic residues modulo a safe prime $p = 2q + 1$.

2.1   Oblivious Transfer

An oblivious transfer is the execution of a protocol between two parties called *sender* and *receiver*. In a k-out-of-n oblivious transfer, denoted by OT_n^k, the sender holds a list $\mathbf{m} = (m_1, \ldots, m_n)$ of messages $m_i \in \{0, 1\}^\ell$, of which $k \leq n$ can be selected by the receiver. The selected messages are transferred to the receiver such that the sender remains oblivious about the receiver's selections and that the receiver learns nothing about the $n - k$ other messages. Let $\mathbf{s} = (s_1, \ldots, s_k)$ denote the k selections $s_j \in \{1, \ldots, n\}$ of the receiver and $\mathbf{m_s} = (m_{s_1}, \ldots, m_{s_k})$ the k messages to transfer. In the simplest possible case of a two-round protocol, the receiver sends a randomized query $Q \leftarrow \mathsf{Query}(\mathbf{s}, r)$ of size $O(k)$ to the sender, the sender replies with a response $R \leftarrow \mathsf{Response}(Q, \mathbf{m})$ of size $O(n)$, and the receiver obtains $\mathbf{m_s} \leftarrow \mathsf{Open}(R, r)$ by removing the randomization r from R. For the correctness of the protocol, $\mathsf{Open}(\mathsf{Response}(\mathsf{Query}(\mathbf{s}, r), \mathbf{m}), r) = \mathbf{m_s}$ must hold for all possible values of $\mathbf{m}$, $\mathbf{s}$, and r. If a triple $(\mathsf{Query}, \mathsf{Response}, \mathsf{Open})$ of such algorithms satisfies this property, we call it a *(two-round) OT_n^k-scheme*.

An OT_n^k-scheme is called *secure*, if the three algorithms guarantee both *receiver privacy* and *sender privacy*. Usually, receiver privacy is defined in terms of indistinguishability of two selections $\mathbf{s}_1$ and $\mathbf{s}_2$ relative to corresponding queries Q_1 and Q_2, whereas sender privacy is defined in terms of indistinguishable transcripts obtained from executing the real and the ideal protocols in the presence of a malicious receiver (called *simulator*). In the ideal protocol, $\mathbf{s}$ and $\mathbf{m}$ are sent to an incorruptible trusted third party, which forwards $\mathbf{m_s}$ to the simulator.

There are many general ways of constructing OT_n^k-schemes, for example on the basis of less complex OT_n^1 or OT_2^1-schemes, but such general constructions are usually not very efficient. In this paper, we propose to use the second OT_n^k-scheme presented in [CT05], which satisfies our requirements almost perfectly.[2] There are several public parameters: a description of a group $\mathcal{G}$ of prime order q, a generator $g \in \mathcal{G} \setminus \{1\}$, an encoding $\Gamma : \{1, \ldots, n\} \rightarrow \mathcal{G}$ of the possible selections into $\mathcal{G}$, and a collision-resistant hash function $H_\ell : \{0, 1\}^* \rightarrow \{0, 1\}^\ell$ with output length ℓ. In Fig. 1, we provide a detailed formal description of the protocol. The query Q is a vector $\mathbf{a} \in \mathcal{G}^k$ of length k and the response R is a tuple $(\mathbf{b}, \mathbf{c}, d)$

---

[2] The modified protocol as presented in [CT08] is slightly more efficient, but it fits less into the particular context of this paper.

consisting of a vector $\mathbf{b} \in \mathcal{G}^k$ of length k, a vector $\mathbf{c} \in (\{0,1\}^\ell)^n$ of length n, and a single value $d \in \mathcal{G}$. Calls of the algorithms will therefore be denoted by

$$\mathbf{a} \leftarrow \mathsf{Query}(\mathbf{s}, \mathbf{r}),$$
$$(\mathbf{b}, \mathbf{c}, d) \leftarrow \mathsf{Response}(\mathbf{a}, \mathbf{m}, s),$$
$$\mathbf{m_s} \leftarrow \mathsf{Open}(\mathbf{b}, \mathbf{c}, d, \mathbf{r}),$$

where $\mathbf{r} = (r_1, \ldots, r_k) \in_R \mathbb{Z}_q^k$ is the vector of random values used in computing the query and $s \in_R \mathbb{Z}_q$ an additional random value used in computing the response. Both Query and Open require k fixed-base exponentiations in $\mathcal{G}$, whereas Response requires $n + k + 1$ fixed-exponent exponentiations in $\mathcal{G}$. Note that among the $2k$ exponentiations of the receiver, k can be pre-computed, and among the $n + k + 1$ exponentiations of the sender, $n + 1$ can be pre-computed. Therefore, only k online exponentiations remain for both the receiver and the sender, i.e., the protocol is very efficient in terms of computation and communication costs. In the random oracle model, the scheme is provably secure against a malicious receiver and a semi-honest sender.[3] Receiver privacy is unconditional and sender privacy is computational under the *chosen-target computational Diffie-Hellman* (CT-CDH) assumption, which is a weaker assumption than standard CDH [Bol03].

2.2   ElGamal Encryption and Extended Pedersen Commitments

In the case of the ElGamal encryption scheme, a group $\mathcal{G}$ of prime order q and a generator $g \in \mathcal{G} \setminus \{1\}$ are usually fixed as public parameters. If this is the case, the scheme consists of the following three algorithms: (1) a randomized key generation algorithm $(sk, pk) \leftarrow \mathsf{KeyGen}()$, which picks $sk \in_R \mathbb{Z}_q$ uniformly at random and computes $pk = g^{sk}$; (2) a randomized encryption algorithm $e \leftarrow \mathsf{Enc}_{pk}(m)$, which picks $r \in_R \mathbb{Z}_q$ uniformly at random and computes $e = (m \cdot pk^r, g^r)$ for a given plaintext $m \in \mathcal{G}$; (3) a deterministic decryption algorithm $m \leftarrow \mathsf{Dec}_{sk}(e)$, which computes $m = a \cdot b^{-sk}$ for a given ciphertext $e = (a, b) \in \mathcal{G} \times \mathcal{G}$. It is easy to verify that $\mathsf{Dec}_{sk}(\mathsf{Enc}_{pk}(m)) = m$ holds for all $m \in \mathcal{G}$ and all key pairs $(sk, pk) \in \mathbb{Z}_q \times \mathcal{G}$. The ElGamal encryption scheme is provably IND-CPA secure under the decisional Diffie-Hellman assumption.

In an (extended) Pedersen commitment scheme, the public parameters are a group $\mathcal{G}$ of prime order q and independent generators $g, h_1, \ldots, h_s \in \mathcal{G} \setminus \{1\}$. The scheme consists of two deterministic algorithms, one for computing a commitment $c = g^r h_1^{m_1} \cdots h_s^{m_s} \in \mathcal{G}$ to s messages $m_i \in \mathbb{Z}_q$ with randomization $r \in_R \mathbb{Z}_q$, and one for checking the validity of a commitment c when $m_1, \ldots, m_s$ and r are revealed. We denote respective algorithms by $c \leftarrow \mathsf{Commit}(m_1, \ldots, m_s, r)$

---

[3] In the voting protocol presented in Sect. 3, which uses this OT_n^k-scheme to transfer return codes obliviously from the authorities to the voter, sender privacy is only required during vote casting. By revealing all n return codes at the end of the vote casting process, any attempt by malicious authorities to transfer incorrect return codes will be detected.

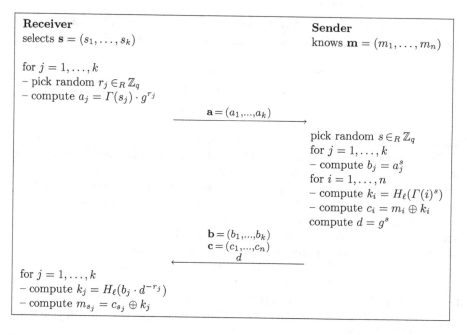

Fig. 1. Two-round OT_n^k-scheme for malicious receiver, where $\mathcal{G}$ is a group of prime order q, $g \in \mathcal{G} \setminus \{1\}$ a generator of $\mathcal{G}$, $\Gamma : \{1, \ldots, n\} \rightarrow \mathcal{G}$ an encoding of the selections into $\mathcal{G}$, and $H_\ell : \{0,1\}^* \rightarrow \{0,1\}^\ell$ a collision-resistant hash function with output length ℓ.

and $d \leftarrow \mathsf{Decommit}(c, m_1, \ldots, m_s, r)$ for $d \in \{0,1\}$. The Pedersen commitment scheme is perfectly hiding and computationally binding under the DL assumption.

2.3 Non-interactive Zero-Knowledge Proofs

Non-interactive zero-knowledge proofs of knowledge are important building blocks in cryptographic protocol design. In a non-interactive *preimage proof* $\mathsf{NIZKP}[(x) : y = \phi(x)]$ for a one-way group homomorphism $\phi : X \rightarrow Y$, the prover proves knowledge of a secret preimage $x = \phi^{-1}(y) \in X$ for a public value $y \in Y$ [Mau09]. The most common construction of a non-interactive preimage proof results from combining the Σ-protocol with the Fiat-Shamir heuristic. Proofs constructed in this way are perfect zero-knowledge in the random oracle model. In practice, the random oracle is implemented with a collision-resistant hash function H.

Generating a preimage proof $(t, c, s) \leftarrow \mathsf{GenNIZKP}_\phi(x, y)$ consists of picking a random value $w \in_R X$ and computing a commitment $t = \phi(w) \in Y$, a challenge $c = H(t, y) \in [0, c_{\max}]$, and a response $s = w + c \cdot x \in X$. Verifying a proof includes checking $c = H(t, y)$ and $\phi(s) = t \times y^c$. Sometimes, the hash function is called with an additional public input z. We denote the inclusion of such an additional input by $(t, c, s) \leftarrow \mathsf{GenNIZKP}_\phi(x, y, z)$ for commitments $c = H(t, y, z)$. This technique, which ties z and (t, c, s) together, is a common practice to prevent copying proofs from one context to another. The verification of a given proof $\pi = (t, c, s)$ is denoted by $v \leftarrow \mathsf{VerifyNIZKP}_\phi(\pi, y, z)$ for $v \in \{0, 1\}$.

An example of a preimage proof results from the ElGamal encryption scheme. The goal of $(t, c, s) \leftarrow \mathsf{GenNIZKP}_{\mathsf{Enc}_{pk}}((m, r), (a, b), z)$ is to prove knowledge of the plaintext m and the randomization r for a given ElGamal ciphertext (a, b) and an additional public input z. Here we understand $\mathsf{Enc}_{pk}(m, r)$ as a deterministic algorithm with two arguments rather than a randomized algorithm $\mathsf{Enc}_{pk}(m)$ with one argument. Since Enc_{pk} is a homomorphism from $\mathcal{G} \times \mathbb{Z}_q$ to $\mathcal{G} \times \mathcal{G}$, both the commitment $t = (t_1, t_2)$ and the response $s = (s_1, s_2)$ are pairs of values. Generating the proof requires two and verifying the proof four exponentiations in $\mathcal{G}$. We will use this proof in the next section.

3   Cryptographic Voting Protocol

The protocol as presented in this section is designed for elections in which submitting multiple ballots is prohibited. Therefore, we assume that someone's right to vote electronically extinguishes with the first submitted ballot. If the vote casting process fails at some point, we assume that voters have an alternative vote casting channel such as postal mail or a local polling station. Note that this scenario corresponds exactly to the particular situation in Switzerland, where postal mail is the most common voting channel and where vote buying and coercion is only a minor security concern. To strengthen the compatibility with the political and legal context in Switzerland, we try to follow the existing technical recommendations as precisely as possible [BK113a, BK113b, BK113c].

3.1   General Setting

The set of *voters* and a small number of *authorities* are the principal parties involved in our protocol. They communicate over different communication channels. To set up an election, the protocol requires a secure channel from the authorities to the voters for the distribution of the verification code sheets. In a real-world setting, like the one described in [BK113a], this channel is implemented by a trusted printing office and a trusted postal service, They print the verification code sheets and deliver them to the voters. Furthermore, a broadcast channel with memory—in the form of a robust append-only *bulletin board*—is needed for collecting the submitted ballots and other election data. We assume that the authorities have their own designated areas on the bulletin board, which they can access for example by signing their messages with a private key. Finally, to emphasize our focus on cast-as-intended verification, we make a distinction between voters and the machines they use for vote casting. We call such a machine *voting platform* and assume that voters can communicate with their voting platform in a secure way (but obviously with limited bandwidth).

Candidate List. We consider elections in which voters can vote for exactly k different candidates from a set $C = \{c_1, \ldots, c_n\}$ of $n \geq 2$ candidates, i.e., no candidate can be selected more than once. Note that this setting is less restrictive than it appears, because C may contain up to k "blank candidates" to allow votes for less than k real candidates. Similarly, C may contain multiple values for each real candidate to allow more than one vote per candidate. We will always refer to the elements of C as *candidates*, but they could as well be parties or any other type of election options. In the simplest case of a yes/no-referendum, we have either $C = \{\text{yes}, \text{no}\}$ or $C = \{\text{yes}, \text{no}, \text{blank}\}$, depending on whether blank votes are allowed or not. We assume that C is defined and published by the election administration prior to an election, so that it is known to everyone.

Verification Code Sheets. If the electorate consists of N eligible voters, we suppose that exactly N verification code sheets are printed, one for each eligible voter. Without loss of generality, we identify both voters and verification code sheets by corresponding indices $i \in \{1, \ldots, N\}$ and assume that code sheet i is sent to voter i prior to an election. Code sheet i contains the list C of candidates along with corresponding *return codes* $R_{ij} \in \{0,1\}^r$ for each candidate $c_j \in C$. It also contains a unique *code sheet identifier* ID_i, a *voting code* $V_i \in \{0,1\}^v$, a *confirmation code* $C_i \in \{0,1\}^c$, and a *finalization code* $F_i \in \{0,1\}^f$. The information printed on code sheet i is therefore a tuple

$$(ID_i, V_i, C_i, F_i, \{(c_j, R_{ij})\}_{j=1}^n).$$

For improved usability, we assume that return codes are printed using $r' = \lceil \frac{r}{\log |A|} \rceil$ characters from an alphabet A, for example $A = \{0, \ldots, 9, A, \ldots, Z\}$. The same holds for the voting, confirmation, and finalization codes. To detect mistyped voting or confirmation codes, we propose the inclusion of checksums.

Voter Authentication. In the remaining of this paper, we assume that someone's right to vote is identical to possessing a valid verification code sheet. With this assumption, we do not disregard the necessity of using additional voter authentication mechanisms based on passwords, biometrics, digital certificates, or physical presence in person, but we do not explicitly include this aspect in our discussion. In other words, we assume that the voter authentication problem is solved, but that eligible voters still require a valid verification code sheet for casting a vote. This implies that the codes printed on a given code sheet must remain secret, especially the voting code V_i and the confirmation code C_i, which the voter enters during vote casting to prove possession of a valid code sheet. These codes should therefore be protected by physical means such as a scratchcard or invisible ink. Note that we do not specify whether code sheets are personal or impersonal, i.e., whether they are tied to a particular voter or not. This aspect is not relevant in this paper.

3.2 Adversary Model and Trust Assumptions

We assume that the general adversarial goal is to break the integrity or secrecy of the votes, but not to influence the election outcome via bribery or coercion. We consider *covert adversaries*, which may arbitrarily interfere with the voting process or deviate from the protocol specification to reach their goals, but only if such attempts are likely to remain undetected [AL10]. Voters and authorities are potential covert adversaries, as well as any external party. This includes adversaries trying to spread dedicated malware to gain control over the voting platforms. For preparing and conducting an election, we assume that a threshold number of non-colluding authorities is available.

All parties are polynomially bounded and thus incapable of solving supposedly hard problems such as the DDH problem or breaking cryptographic primitives such as contemporary hash functions. This implies that adversaries cannot efficiently decrypt ElGamal ciphertexts or generate valid non-interactive zero-knowledge proofs without knowing the secret inputs.

3.3 Detailed Protocol Description

The subsequent description of the cryptographic voting protocol is focused on our new mechanism for cast-as-intended verification, which affects mainly the election preparation and the vote casting phase of the protocol, but not the tallying phase. We are therefore not discussing all the necessary details of the operations executed by the authorities to determine the election result from the list of submitted ballots. This part of an electronic election system is well-documented in the literature. However, we stress that defining an appropriate cryptographic protocol for the tallying phase is crucial for protecting the system against corrupt authorities.

To further simplify the presentation of the protocol, we will look at the group of authorities as a single party called *authorities*. Let $(sk, pk) \leftarrow \mathsf{KeyGen}()$ be their ElGamal key pair, which in reality will be generated in a distributed manner and such that sk is threshold shared among the authorities, for example using the protocol of [Ped91]. We assume that pk is publicly known. In Sect. 3.4, the case of multiple authorities will be discussed in further detail.

Another simplification is to fix the group $\mathbb{G}_q \subseteq \mathbb{Z}_p^*$ of quadratic residues modulo a safe prime $p = 2q + 1$ as the common group for all the cryptographic operations used in this paper. We assume that p (which determines $\mathbb{G}_q$) and independent generators $g, h_1, h_2, h_3, h_4 \in \mathbb{G}_q \setminus \{1\}$ are publicly known. Other public parameters are a second prime number $p' \leq q$, the bit lengths v, c, f, r of the voting, confirmation, finalization, and return codes, respectively, collision-resistant hash functions $H_r : \{0,1\}^* \rightarrow \{0,1\}^r$, $H_f : \{0,1\}^* \rightarrow \{0,1\}^f$, and $H_\ell : \{0,1\}^* \rightarrow \{0,1\}^\ell$ for $\ell = 2 \cdot \lceil \log p' \rceil$, and the list $\mathcal{C} = \{c_1, \ldots, c_n\}$ of candidates.

Election Preparation. As shown by the diagram depicted in Fig. 2, the election preparation consists of two tasks executed by the authorities. They first generate the N verification code sheets and transmit them to the voters. In the second step, they publish commitments to the values contained in the code sheets on the public bulletin board. Under the assumption that possessing a verification code sheet implies eligibility, this list of commitments can be seen as the electoral roll.

To generate verification code sheet i, the authorities pick a random polynomial $p_i(x) = \sum_{j=0}^{k-1} a_{ij} x^j$ of degree $k - 1$ (i.e., $a_{i,k-1} \neq 0$) from the set $\mathbb{Z}_{p'}[x]$ of all such polynomials over the field $\mathbb{Z}_{p'}$ of integers modulo p'. Then they pick n distinct random integers $x_{ij} \in_R \mathbb{Z}_{p'}$, $1 \leq j \leq n$, and compute corresponding points $P_{ij} = (x_{ij}, p_i(x_{ij}))$ on the polynomial. The hash values $R_{ij} = H_r(P_{ij})$ of these points are the return codes for the candidates. The reason for selecting the return codes in this way is to allow the reconstruction of the polynomial when at least k of these points are known. We will use this property to prove the validity of an encrypted vote. Finally, the authorities define an identifier ID_i (e.g., $ID_i = i$), pick random values $V_i \in_R \{0,1\}^v$ and $C_i \in_R \{0,1\}^c$, and compute $F_i = H_f(R_{i,1} \| \cdots \| R_{i,n}) \in \{0,1\}^f$. The resulting tuple $(ID_i, V_i, C_i, F_i, \{(c_j, R_{ij})\}_{j=1}^n)$ is sent to voter i over a secure channel.

After generating verification code sheet i, the authorities select the value $P_i = p_i(0) = a_{i,0} \in \mathbb{Z}_{p'}$. Note that the points P_{ij} can be seen as the n shares obtained from applying Shamir's (k,n)-threshold secret sharing scheme to a secret P_i. Commitments $CV_i \leftarrow \mathsf{Commit}(V_i, \alpha_i)$ and $CC_i \leftarrow \mathsf{Commit}(C_i, P_i, F_i, \beta_i)$ are posted to the public bulletin board for randomizations $\alpha_i, \beta_i \in_R \mathbb{Z}_q$, respectively. The purpose of publishing the set $\{(ID_i, CV_i, CC_i)\}_{i=1}^N$ is to enable the verification that each ballot has been submitted by someone in possession of a valid verification code sheet. This set can therefore be regarded as the electoral roll in a context where possessing a verification code sheet implies eligibility.

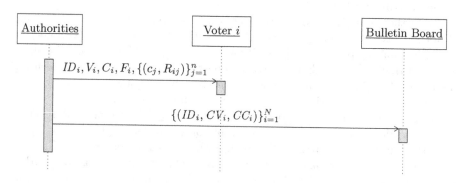

Fig. 2. Sequence diagram of the election preparation phase.

Vote Casting. The vote casting and confirmation phase is the core of the protocol. An overview of the exchanged messages is given in Fig. 3. To initiate the process, the voter enters the code sheet identifier ID_i, the voting code V_i, and the selected candidates $\mathbf{s} = (s_1, \ldots, s_k)$ into the voting platform. The voting platform

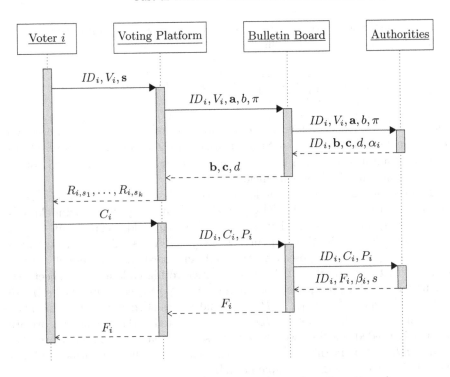

Fig. 3. Sequence diagram of the vote casting and confirmation phase.

then computes a ballot containing an OT_n^k query for the k points $P_{i,s_1}, \ldots, P_{i,s_k}$ (from which the return codes $R_{i,s_1}, \ldots, R_{i,s_k}$ of the k chosen candidates and the value P_i can be derived). For this, the voting platform picks random values $\mathbf{r} \in_R \mathbb{Z}_q^k$ and computes $\mathbf{a} \leftarrow \mathsf{Query}(\mathbf{s}, \mathbf{r})$. There are some important technical details in this step:

- Since we use the OT_n^k protocol to transfer points $P_{ij} \in \mathbb{Z}_{p'} \times \mathbb{Z}_{p'}$, we instantiate the protocol with a message length $\ell = 2 \cdot \lceil \log p' \rceil$. This allows us to encode each of the two coordinates of P_{ij} by $\frac{\ell}{2}$ bits and to concatenate them together.
- The OT_n^k protocol as presented in Sect. 2.1 requires a generator g of $\mathbb{G}_q$. Since $\mathbb{G}_q$ is of prime order, any value in $\mathbb{G}_q \setminus \{1\}$ is admissible. To establish a natural link to the encrypted vote, we require the authorities' public key $pk \in \mathbb{G}_q$ to be used as generator for the oblivious transfer.
- For the encoding $\Gamma : \{1, \ldots, n\} \to \mathbb{G}_q$ used in the OT_n^k protocol, we use the set $\mathbb{P}_n = \{p_1, \ldots, p_n\}$ of the n smallest prime numbers $p_i \in \mathbb{G}_q$, $p_i < p_{i+1}$, and define $\Gamma(i) = p_i$. The purpose of this particular choice is to encode $\mathbf{s}$ as a product $\Gamma(\mathbf{s}) = \prod_{j=1}^k p_{s_j}$, which can then be encrypted using ElGamal. Note that inverting $\Gamma(\mathbf{s})$ by factorization is unique if the product of the largest k primes in $\mathbb{P}_n$ is smaller than q and efficient when n is small [Gjø11].

Since the query $\mathbf{a} = (a_1, \ldots, a_k)$ generated in this way contains values $a_j = \Gamma(s_j) \cdot pk^{r_j}$, we can compute a single value

$$a = \prod_{j=1}^{k} a_j = \prod_{j=1}^{k} \Gamma(s_j) \cdot pk^{r_j} = \Gamma(\mathbf{s}) \cdot pk^r,$$

where $r = \sum_{j=1}^{k} r_j$. Therefore, by computing a second value $b = g^r$, we obtain an ElGamal encryption $(a, b) = \mathsf{Enc}_{pk}(\Gamma(\mathbf{s}), r)$ of the encoded voter's selections $\Gamma(\mathbf{s})$. This simple connection between the OT_n^k query and the encrypted vote is crucial for making the protocol efficient.

The remaining component for forming the ballot is a non-interactive zero-knowledge proof $\pi \leftarrow \mathsf{GenNIZKP}_{\mathsf{Enc}_{pk}}((\Gamma(\mathbf{s}), r), (a, b), V_i)$ for proving knowledge of $\Gamma(\mathbf{s})$ and r. Note that we use V_i as an additional input to the proof generation to disallow copying of encrypted votes. The resulting *ballot* $B = (ID_i, V_i, \mathbf{a}, b, \pi)$ is posted to the bulletin board, from where it can be retrieved by the authorities. If V_i is the correct voting code for code sheet ID_i and if π is a valid proof, they pick a random $s \in_R \mathbb{Z}_q$, compute the response $(\mathbf{b}, \mathbf{c}, d) \leftarrow \mathsf{Response}(\mathbf{a}, (P_{i,1}, \ldots, P_{i,n}), s)$, and return $(\mathbf{b}, \mathbf{c}, d)$ to the voting platform (only if no valid ballot for ID_i has been posted earlier). Since no private channel is needed for this, we propose to send it via the bulletin board. We include ID_i and α_i in this message, which means that the commitment CV_i is opened. The full message is a tuple $(ID_i, \mathbf{b}, \mathbf{c}, d, \alpha_i)$.

Vote Confirmation. Upon receiving the response from the authorities, the voting platform computes the result $(P_{i,s_1}, \ldots, P_{i,s_k}) \leftarrow \mathsf{Open}(\mathbf{b}, \mathbf{c}, d, \mathbf{r})$ of the oblivious transfer. Corresponding return codes $R_{i,s_j} = H_r(P_{i,s_j})$ are displayed to the voter for inspection. If they match with the codes printed on the verification code sheet, the vote must have been cast and recorded as intended with high probability, which the voter confirms by entering the confirmation code C_i into the voting platform. This code is forwarded to the bulletin board together with $P_i = p_i(0)$, which can be computed by interpolating the polynomial $p_i(x)$ from the received points $(P_{i,s_1}, \ldots, P_{i,s_k})$ using Lagrange's method.

If both C_i and P_i are correct, the authorities respond by sending the finalization code F_i to the voter for inspection. If F_i as displayed by the voting platform matches with the finalization code on the code sheet, the vote confirmation must have been successful with high probability. Again, since keeping F_i private is no longer necessary at this point, we propose to send it via the bulletin board to the voter. By including the randomizations β_i, commitment CC_i of code sheet i is opened and can be publicly verified. Similarly, by including the randomization s, the commitment d of the OT_n^k response $(\mathbf{b}, \mathbf{c}, d)$ is opened and all n points P_{ij} are revealed, together with corresponding return codes $R_{ij} = H_r(P_{ij})$ of code sheet i. Public verifiers can then check if $F_i = H_f(R_{i,1} \| \cdots \| R_{i,n})$ holds, which implies that the authorities have responded properly to the OT_n^k query. Public verifiers can also interpolate the polynomial $p_i(x)$ over the points $\{P_{ij}\}_{j=1}^{n}$, check if its degree is $k - 1$, and verify that $p_i(0) = P_i$. This guarantees that the random points P_{ij} and the value P_i have been generated properly during the election preparation.[4]

Tallying. After the election period, the bulletin board contains one or multiple entries for every ID_i. There are several types of entries, depending on whether someone has participated in the election and on whether vote casting and confirmation has been successful:

- (ID_i, CV_i, CC_i): The voter has not participated in the election.
- $(ID_i, CV_i, CC_i, V_i, \mathbf{a}, b, \pi)$: The voter has initiated the vote casting process, but the process stopped after submitting the ballot. Possible causes are an incorrect voting code V_i, an invalid zero-knowledge proof π, or the existence of an earlier valid ballot for ID_i.
- $(ID_i, CV_i, CC_i, V_i, \mathbf{a}, b, \pi, \mathbf{b}, \mathbf{c}, d, \alpha_i)$: The authorities have responded to the OT_n^k query, but either the voter has not entered the confirmation code or the voting platform has not forwarded it to the bulletin board.
- $(ID_i, CV_i, CC_i, V_i, \mathbf{a}, b, \pi, \mathbf{b}, \mathbf{c}, d, \alpha_i, C_i, P_i)$: The voting platform has sent values C_i and P_i to the bulletin board, but then the process has stopped. Possible causes are incorrect values C_i or P_i.
- $(ID_i, CV_i, CC_i, V_i, \mathbf{a}, b, \pi, \mathbf{b}, \mathbf{c}, d, \alpha_i, C_i, P_i, F_i, \beta_i, s)$: This is the success case, in which the authorities have responded to correct values C_i and P_i with the finalization code F_i and randomization s.

It is evident that only ballots from the success case can be considered in the tally. A list of corresponding ElGamal encryptions $(a, b) = (\prod_{j=1}^{k} a_j, b)$ is extracted for further processing. As mentioned earlier, we do not further discuss the tallying part of the protocol, because this is well-studied in the literature of electronic voting protocols. We simply assume that this process reveals—in a publicly verifiable manner—a list of plaintext votes $\Gamma(\mathbf{s})$, which can be decoded into the voter's selections $\mathbf{s} = (s_1, \ldots, s_k)$. Accumulating these selections over all valid votes generates the final election result.

Verification. At the end of an election, a number of verifications can be performed by the public. In Table 1, we list all computations and checks that can be performed for every submitted ballot in the success case. In our setting, in which possessing a verification code sheet implies eligibility, these checks prove

---

[4] Without such checks, malicious authorities could actively attack the vote secrecy of some voters by responding to the OT_n^k query with some incorrect return codes. If the voter then confirms the ballot as cast, the authorities learn that no candidate corresponding to an incorrect return code has been selected. A similar attack could be launched during the election preparation. If some of the random points P_{ij} are not selected from the polynomial, then responding with the correct value P_i tells the authorities that no candidate corresponding to such an incorrect point has been selected. In the covert adversary model, publishing s prevents both variants of this attack (see paragraph on vote secrecy in Sect. 4.1).

that every valid vote has been submitted by an eligible voter and that every eligible voter has voted at most once. To achieve a complete chain of universal verifiability, we assume that the authorities publish cryptographic proofs for the correctness of the election result (corresponding checks are not listed in Table 1).

By performing the computations of Table 1 on their own ballot, participating voters can verify the ballot consistency and the inclusion of their vote in the tally. By checking the validity of the involved commitments, they can verify the consistency of their verification code sheet. It is also possible to check that the return codes have been generated properly and that the authorities responded faithfully to the OT query. Abstaining voters can check that their verification code sheet has not been used by an attacker.

Table 1. List of computations and checks to verify the validity of a ballot in the success case, which corresponds to an entry $(ID_i, CV_i, CC_i, V_i, \mathbf{a}, b, \pi, \mathbf{b}, \mathbf{c}, d, \alpha_i, C_i, P_i, F_i, \beta_i, s)$ on the bulletin board.

Computations	Range	Checks
$d_1 \leftarrow \mathsf{Decommit}(CV_i, V_i, \alpha_i)$		$d_1 = 1$
$d_2 \leftarrow \mathsf{Decommit}(CC_i, C_i, P_i, F_i, \beta_i)$		$d_2 = 1$
$a' = \prod_{j=1}^{k} a_j$		
$v \leftarrow \mathsf{VerifyNIZKP}_{\mathsf{Enc}_{pk}}(\pi, (a', b), V_i)$		$v = 1$
$d' = pk^s$		$d' = d$
$b'_j = a_j^s$	$j = 1, \ldots, k$	$b'_j = b_j$
$P'_{ij} = H_r(c_j \oplus H_\ell(\Gamma(j)^s)) = (x'_{ij}, y'_{ij})$	$j = 1, \ldots, n$	
$R'_{ij} = H_r(P'_{ij})$	$j = 1, \ldots, n$	
$F'_i = H_f(R'_{i,1} \| \cdots \| R'_{i,n})$		$F'_i = F_i$
interpolate $p'_i(x) = \sum_{j=0}^{n-1} a'_{ij} x^j$ over $\{P'_{ij}\}_{j=1}^n$	$j = k, \ldots, n-1$	$a'_{ij} = 0$
		$a'_{i,k-1} \neq 0$
		$a'_{i,0} = P_i$

3.4   Multiple Authorities

The protocol as presented above generalizes naturally to $t \geq 1$ authorities such that no single authority knows the codes of code sheet i. Each authority generates its own verification code sheet exactly as described in Sect. 3.3 and transmits it to voter i over the secure channel. During vote casting, voters send a single OT_n^k query to all authorities, which can respond individually and simultaneously. The actual return codes are $R_{ij} = \oplus_{k=1}^{t} H_r(P_{ijk})$, where P_{ijk} denotes the j-th point on the random polynomial picked by authority k for code sheet i. In a similar way, multiple finalization codes F_{ik} can be merged into a single finalization code

$F_i = \oplus_{k=1}^{t} F_{ik}$. Finally, voting and confirmation codes are concatenated into $V_i = V_{i,1} \| \cdots \| V_{i,t}$ and $C_i = C_{i,1} \| \cdots \| C_{i,t}$, respectively.[5]

4 Discussion

In this section, we will briefly discuss the security properties and the performance of the proposed cryptographic voting protocol and compare it to the existing work in the literature.

4.1 Security

The principal goal of the proposed cast-as-intended verification mechanism is to enable the detection of an attack by malware on the voting platform without compromising vote secrecy on the server side. If an attack—or a defective system—is detected by some voters, it is assumed that they have access to an alternative voting channel such as postal mail.

Correctness. Submitting a ballot that makes it into the final tally requires knowledge of the codes V_i, C_i, and P_i of a valid verification code sheet $i \in \{1, \ldots, N\}$. Any attempt to submit a ballot with incorrect codes will be detected and prohibited by the authorities. Guessing correct codes or an exhaustive search for correct codes can be prevented with high probability by choosing large enough length parameters v and c and a large enough prime p'. Any attempt to submit multiple ballots with the same codes V_i, C_i, and P_i will also be detected and prohibited by the authorities. The authorities themselves can only compute correct codes and use them to submit a ballot if they all collude. A single honest authority is therefore sufficient to prevent ballot stuffing.

If a malicious voting platform tries to submit votes for candidates different from the voter's intention, then the return codes will not match and the voters will abort the voting process. Submitting less than k of the voter's actual selections will be detected as well, because $p_i(x)$ can not be interpolated and P_i can not be computed in this case. Submitting a vote for more than k candidates will be detected and prohibited by the authorities. Submitting an invalid value b along with the OT_n^k query a is prevented by the non-interactive zero-knowledge proof π, i.e., such attempts will be detected by the authorities. Waiting for the voter to enter the confirmation code and then changing the submitted ballot is prevented by the append-only property of the bulletin board. Not submitting the ballot or the values C_i and P_i can not be prevented, but this will be detected by the voter with high probability when a wrong response or no response at all is displayed.

---

[5] Concatenation of voting and confirmation codes is the simplest possible solution to generalize the protocol to multiple authorities. As a consequence, the lengths of F_i and C_i are multiplied by t, which may cause problems from a usability point of view. A discussion of such usability problems and proposals for more sophisticated solutions are beyond the scope of this paper.

Vote Secrecy. Guaranteeing vote secrecy on a malware-infected voting platform is impossible in a system in which voters enter their selections in plaintext. As a consequence, our protocol does not solve this problem. On the server side, provided that a proper privacy-preserving tallying procedure is in place, vote secrecy is guaranteed under the assumptions that the DDH problem is hard (which implies IND-CPA security for ElGamal encryptions) and that a threshold number of authorities holding a share of the private key sk is honest. If this is the case, no information about the voter's selections s is leaked by publishing the ballot $B = (ID_i, V_i, \mathbf{a}, b, \pi)$ on the bulletin board.

Submitting the values C_i and P_i to confirm matching return codes does not reveal anything about the voter's selections to the public, but malicious authorities could break vote secrecy by responding with some incorrect return codes to the OT_n^k query or by sending some incorrect return codes over the secure channel during election preparation. In both cases, confirming the vote reveals to the authorities that no candidate corresponding to an incorrect return code has been selected. In the covert adversary model, our protocol prevents an attack of the first type by requesting the authorities to reveal the randomization s of the OT_n^k response. This permits public verifiers to compute the return codes of all candidates of a given code sheet and to check if these codes match with the finalization code. Any attempt to respond with incorrect return codes would be detected in this way. To detect attacks of the second type and thus to prevent covert adversaries from conducting them, voters could be asked to check if all return codes match with the code sheet and to report to the election administration if this is not the case. Clearly, this is not very practical from usability point of view, especially if n is large, but our protocol does not offer a better solution for this problem.

4.2   Comparison to Existing Work

In Table 2, we present a performance comparison between our approach and the two most relevant approaches from the literature. Since the approach presented in [HLv10] turned out to be much less efficient, we do not further discuss its properties and exclude it from the subsequent comparison.

Compared to the Neuchâtel protocol [GGP15], our approach offers a number of conceptual advantages. First, while the Neuchâtel protocol requires three different types of server-side parties (registrars, code generator, voting server), which are pairwise assumed not to collude, we only require a threshold number of non-colluding authorities performing identical operations. This implies that our protocol offers better flexibility in terms of robustness. Second, while the Neuchâtel protocol requires a private channel to transmit the return codes from the code generator to the voters (otherwise vote secrecy could be violated by the registrars), we can send the OT_n^k response over a public channel. Third, there are two types of private keys in the Neuchâtel protocol, which are used by multiple parties. This creates unnecessary and uncommon trust assumptions, which we do not have in our protocol. Finally, while nN so-called *reference values* need to

Table 2. Performance comparison between the protocol of this paper and existing work in terms of exponentiations in the underlying group. The values given in parentheses indicate the number of exponentiations that can be pre-computed. In the case of [HLv10], which is restricted to 1-out-of-n votes, we assume that k votes are submitted in parallel.

		This paper	[GGP15]	[HLv10]
Election preparation	Authorities	$6N$	$(n+2)N$	nN
Vote casting	Voting platform	$2k+3$	$k+10$	$k(7\log n + 8)$
		$(k+3)$	(7)	$(k(6\log n + 8))$
	Authorities	$n+k+5$	11	$k(5n + 6\log n + 8)$
		$(n+1)$	(0)	$(k(2n + 2\log n))$

be generated and stored in the Neuchâtel protocol for proving vote correctness, we achieve the same in a more elegant way using only N values $P_1, \ldots, P_N$.

In the light of the numbers shown in Table 2, the overall performance of the two protocols is similar. While the election preparation is considerably more efficient in our protocol when n is large, our approach requires more expensive online computations during vote casting. However, if we assume that the voting platform performs pre-computations in the background while the voter is interacting with the voting platform, our approach is slightly more efficient: k versus $k+3$ online exponentiations. If we assume that pre-computations are also performed on the server side, our approach is more efficient for $k < 7$ and less efficient for $k > 7$. Note that server-side pre-computations can be performed well in advance, for example as part of the election preparation. In that case, the overall performance of the election preparation is very similar: $(n+1)N'+6N$ versus $(n+2)N$ exponentiations, where $N' \leq N$ denotes the maximal expected number of participating voters. Nevertheless, by allowing server-side pre-computations at any moment before an election, not necessarily as part of the election preparation, our approach is slightly more flexible.

5 Conclusion

The cryptographic voting protocol presented in this paper introduces a new mechanism for cast-as-intended verification based on oblivious transfer. We believe that the problem of transferring return codes as a response to submitting an encrypted vote *is* an oblivious transfer problem and therefore should be solved as such. The approach presented in this paper is the first efficient solution. Compared to existing cast-as-intended verification methods, our approach is conceptually more elegant and requires less trust assumptions and cryptographic keys. We think that it offers an appropriate solution for countries such as Switzerland, where providing a solution to the secure platform problem is a prerequisite for introducing the next-generation systems. We have been invited by the State of Geneva to participate in implementing this approach for their future system. Formal security proofs will be developed in a separate project.

Acknowledgments. We thank the anonymous reviewers for their reviews and appreciate their comments and suggestions. We are also grateful to Stephan Fischli, Severin Hauser, Thomas Hofer, and Philipp Locher for helpful discussions and proofreading. This research has been supported by the State of Geneva.

References

[AIR01] Aiello, B., Ishai, Y., Reingold, O.: Priced oblivious transfer: how to sell digital goods. In: Pfitzmann, B. (ed.) EUROCRYPT 2001. LNCS, vol. 2045, pp. 119–135. Springer, Heidelberg (2001). doi:10.1007/3-540-44987-6_8

[AL10] Aumann, Y., Lindell, Y.: Security against covert adversaries: efficient protocols for realistic adversaries. J. Cryptol. **23**(2), 281–343 (2010)

[BK113a] Ergänzende Dokumentation zum dritten Bericht des Bundesrates zu Vote électronique. Die Schweizerische Bundeskanzlei (BK) (2013)

[BK113b] Technische und administrative Anforderungen an die elektronischen Stimmabgabe. Die Schweizerische Bundeskanzlei (BK) (2013)

[BK113c] Verordnung der Bundeskanzlei über die elektronische Stimmabgabe (VEleS). Die Schweizerische Bundeskanzlei (BK) (2013)

[Bol03] Boldyreva, A.: Threshold signatures, multisignatures and blind signatures based on the gap-Diffie-Hellman-group signature scheme. In: Desmedt, Y.G. (ed.) PKC 2003. LNCS, vol. 2567, pp. 31–46. Springer, Heidelberg (2003). doi:10.1007/3-540-36288-6_3

[CT05] Chu, C.-K., Tzeng, W.-G.: Efficient k-out-of-n oblivious transfer schemes with adaptive and non-adaptive queries. In: Vaudenay, S. (ed.) PKC 2005. LNCS, vol. 3386, pp. 172–183. Springer, Heidelberg (2005). doi:10.1007/978-3-540-30580-4_12

[CT08] Chu, C.K., Tzeng, W.G.: Efficient k-out-of-n oblivious transfer schemes. J. Univ. Comput. Sci. **14**(3), 397–415 (2008)

[GB12] Gebhardt Stenerud, I.S., Bull, C.: When reality comes knocking - Norwegian experiences with verifiable electronic voting. In: Kripp, M.J., Volkamer, M., Grimm, R. (eds.) EVOTE 2012, 5th International Workshop on Electronic Voting, Bregenz, Austria. Lecture Notes in Informatics, vol. P-205, pp. 21–33 (2012)

[GGP15] Galindo, D., Guasch, S., Puiggalí, J.: 2015 Neuchâtel's cast-as-intended verification mechanism. In: Haenni, R., Koenig, R.E., Wikström, D. (eds.) VOTELID 2015. LNCS, vol. 9269, pp. 3–18. Springer, Heidelberg (2015). doi:10.1007/978-3-319-22270-7_1

[Gjø10] Gjøsteen, K.: Analysis of an internet voting protocol. IACR Cryptology ePrint Archive, 2010/380 (2010)

[Gjø11] Gjøsteen, K.: The Norwegian internet voting protocol. In: Kiayias, A., Lipmaa, H. (eds.) Vote-ID 2011. LNCS, vol. 7187, pp. 1–18. Springer, Heidelberg (2012). doi:10.1007/978-3-642-32747-6_1

[HLv10] Heiberg, S., Lipmaa, H., Laenen, F.: On E-vote integrity in the case of malicious voter computers. In: Gritzalis, D., Preneel, B., Theoharidou, M. (eds.) ESORICS 2010. LNCS, vol. 6345, pp. 373–388. Springer, Heidelberg (2010). doi:10.1007/978-3-642-15497-3_23

[Lip11] Lipmaa, H.: Two simple code-verification voting protocols. IACR Cryptology ePrint Archive, 2011/317 (2011)

[Mau09] Maurer, U.: Unifying zero-knowledge proofs of knowledge. In: Preneel, B. (ed.) AFRICACRYPT 2009. LNCS, vol. 5580, pp. 272–286. Springer, Heidelberg (2009). doi:10.1007/978-3-642-02384-2_17

[Ped91] Pedersen, T.P.: A threshold cryptosystem without a trusted party. In: Davies, D.W. (ed.) EUROCRYPT 1991. LNCS, vol. 547, pp. 522–526. Springer, Heidelberg (1991). doi:10.1007/3-540-46416-6_47

[PG11] Allepuz, J.P., Castelló, S.G.: Internet voting system with cast as intended verification. In: Kiayias, A., Lipmaa, H. (eds.) Vote-ID 2011. LNCS, vol. 7187, pp. 36–52. Springer, Heidelberg (2012). doi:10.1007/978-3-642-32747-6_3

[PG12] Puiggalí, J., Guasch, S.: Cast-as-intended verification in Norway. In: Kripp, M., Volkamer, M., Grimm, R. (eds.) EVOTE 2012, 5th International Workshop on Electronic Voting, Bregenz, Austria. Lecture Notes in Informatics, vol. P-205, pp. 49–63 (2012)

[SV12] Schläpfer, M., Volkamer, M.: The secure platform problem: taxonomy and analysis of existing proposals to address this problem. In: ICEGOV 2012, 6th International Conference on Theory and Practice of Electronic Governance, Albany, USA (2012)

Improving the Verifiability of the Estonian Internet Voting Scheme

Sven Heiberg[1,2(✉)], Tarvi Martens[2], Priit Vinkel[3], and Jan Willemson[4,5]

[1] Smartmatic-Cybernetica Centre of Excellence for Internet Voting,
Ülikooli 2, Tartu, Estonia
sven.heiberg@ivotingcentre.ee
[2] Electronic Voting Committee, Lossi Plats 1a, Tallinn, Estonia
[3] Chancellery of Riigikogu, Secretariat of National Electoral Committee,
Lossi Plats 1a, Tallinn, Estonia
[4] Cybernetica, Ülikooli 2, Tartu, Estonia
[5] Software Technology and Applications Competence Centre, Ülikooli 2,
Tartu, Estonia

Abstract. We describe an update of the Estonian Internet Voting scheme targeted towards adding verification capabilities to the central system. We propose measures to ensure the auditability of the correctness of vote decryption and i-ballot box integrity. The latter will be improved to a level where it would be possible to outsource the vote collection process to an untrusted party and later fully verify the correctness of its operations.

1 Introduction

In 2005, Estonia became the first country in the world to cast votes over the Internet for state-wide legally binding general elections. In the 2014 and 2015 elections, more than 30% [3] of all the votes were cast this way, making online voting the second most popular means of vote-casting after paper voting in polling stations on election Sunday.

The scheme used in 2015 was still more or less the same as designed for the first Internet-enabled elections in 2005. It mimics double-envelope postal voting, where the inner, privacy-providing envelope is replaced by encrypting the vote using the central system's public key, and the outer authenticity and integrity layer is provided by signing the vote cryptogram with the voter's ID card [6].

While it is straightforward to understand and sufficiently simple to actually implement in practice, the resulting system relies on several external assumptions. In the early days of implementation, the voter's computer was explicitly trusted. By 2011 it had become apparent that this assumption could not be relied upon any longer [6]. As a solution, the scheme was augmented with the option of individual verifiability using an independent mobile computing device [8].

However, individual verifiability alone is not sufficient to mitigate all the risks. For example, the Estonian system has recently been criticized by Springall *et al.* for its excessive reliance on physical and organisational measures [13].

© Springer International Publishing AG 2017
R. Krimmer et al. (Eds.): E-Vote-ID 2016, LNCS 10141, pp. 92–107, 2017.
DOI: 10.1007/978-3-319-52240-1_6

Even though these measures have worked well in practice, auditing them is a non-trivial task that can only be performed by a limited set of trustees.

Even more importantly, both the process and outcome of such an audit are defined in a way that leaves a lot of room for human interpretation, and consequently also errors. The possibility of such errors can be used to raise doubts and these doubts can in turn be used against Internet voting in political debates.

The aim of this paper is to describe the second major update of the Estonian Internet Voting scheme that is targeted towards adding verification capabilities to the parts of the central system that have so far been the most difficult to audit. More precisely, we will propose and discuss measures to ensure third-party auditability of the correctness of vote decryption and i-ballot box integrity. The latter will be improved to a level where it, in principle, becomes possible to outsource the vote collection process to an untrusted party and later fully verify the correctness of its operations.

2 Estonian Internet Voting Scheme

On the conceptual level, the Estonian Internet Voting scheme used in 2005–2015 mimics double envelope postal voting [6]. The core system consists of the Voting Application ($VoteApp$), the Vote Forwarding Server (VFS), the Vote Storage Server (VSS) and the Tabulation Application (TA) with the Hardware Security Module (HSM) for private key protection. The online components log to the Log Monitor (LOG), and there is a OCSP responder ($OCSP$) that provides both certificate validation and time-marking services.

The central voting system generates an RSA keypair with the HSM and publishes the public part ek_{pub}^{elec}. The voter v uses the $VoteApp$ and authenticates herself for the VFS using her smart-card-based digital identity tool, and receives the candidate list. She then makes her choice c_v and encrypts it with the systems's public key.

For encryption, RSA-OAEP is used and a random number r_v is generated for encryption. Hence the anonymous ballot ("inner envelope") is computed as $ballot_{c_v,r_v} = Enc(c_v, r_v, ek_{pub}^{elec})$. The effect of the "outer envelope" is achieved by signing the ballot using the voter's digital identity tool, and the resulting vote $vote_v = Sign(sk_{priv}^v, ballot_{c_v,r_v})$ is sent to the VSS for storage.

Electronic ballots are stored in the signed and encrypted form until the voting period is over. The signatures are then dropped in VSS and anonymous ballots are tallied in TA. For that, they are decrypted with the server's private key stored in a HSM.

In 2013, the scheme was augmented with the option of individual verifiability [8]. The randomness r_v and the unique vote identifier vid generated by the central system are made available by $VoteApp$ to a mobile device running a Verification Application ($VerApp$) in the form of a QR code. The identifier is used by the $VerApp$ to request the inner envelope $ballot_{c_v,r_v}$ from the VSS. The process then uses the list of candidates C and the randomness r_v to find a $c' \in C$ such that

$$Enc(c', r_v, ek_{pub}^{elec}) = ballot_{c_v, r_v}.$$

It is up to the voter to decide if the outcome of this process was expected or not.

3 Shortcomings of the Current Scheme

The security analysis [1] of the Internet voting concept described in Sect. 2 identified security requirements broadly divided into the categories of integrity, confidentiality, transparency and coercion-resistance. A set of measures to mitigate the identified risks was provided under assumptions about the operating environment – the existence of a reliable PKI, the supremacy of paper-voting, the trustworthiness of the Internet voting system and its operations, and the trustworthiness of the voters' computers.

Some of these assumptions – the trustworthiness of the voters' computers – are not considered valid anymore. These new considerations have led to system improvements, e.g. the addition of individual verifiability [8]. Other assumptions – the existence of a reliable PKI – still hold in Estonia.

Assumptions about the trustworthiness of the central system lie somewhere in between. On the one hand, there are a number of physical and organizational measures to ensure them, but on the other hand, such measures can always be questioned [13]. The current nature of these measures increases the involvement of the National Electoral Committee in organizing online voting to the point where it needs to perform the technical tasks of hosting that could normally be outsourced to an external online service provider. Thus, the general goal of this paper is to redesign the Estonian Internet Voting system to become less dependent on the human factor, allow more independent verifiability and a better separation of duties between different organizations.

In the rest of this Section, we will review the main challenges of the current system that will need to be addressed. As a starting point of our analysis, we will use the attack tree presented by Heiberg and Willemson in [7]. We will exclude the availability-related attacks from the discussion and assume the existence of an individual verification tool to detect manipulations on the voters' computers.

3.1 I-Ballot Box Integrity

Three direct attacks on the i-ballot box integrity can be identified: adding votes to the box, removing votes from the box, and modifying votes already in the box [7].

The process of vote storage takes advantage of the Estonian PKI with digital signature capabilities and private keys stored on secure hardware tokens.

– *VoteApp* creates the digitally signed vote and sends it to the *VFS*.
– *VFS* verifies the signature of the vote and forwards the vote to the *VSS*.
– *VSS* verifies the signature and acquires confirmation about the validity of the certificate to the signature from *OCSP*.
– *VFS* and *VSS* log the stages of processing both locally and to the *LOG*.

PKI usage allows us to assume that the stored votes are secured from the manipulations and that the eligibility of voters can be verified by the system. Unauthorized addition or modification of the votes would effectively require forging digital signatures. Estonia has relied on its digital signature infrastructure since 2002, and we can argue that potential weaknesses leading to signature forgery have been mitigated.

However, there are no comparable measures against the unauthorized removal of votes from the i-ballot box. An attacker who wants to remove a vote from the system has to compromise the VSS in a way that it would be possible to delete the corresponding file from storage. The attacker must take the following risks into account:

- There is a certain window of time during which a vote can be verified by the individual verification tool. If the vote is removed before the end of this window, there is a risk of detection.
- There are traces of vote storage in the log files on VFS, VSS, LOG and $OCSP$. If these traces are not removed and the logs are later correlated with the actual list of stored votes, there is a risk of detection.

Potential detection by the individual verification tool can be easily prevented by deleting the vote after the verification window (30 or 60 min) has closed.

Tampering with the log files requires control – such as administrator access – over multiple components. The remaining risk for the attacker is that the $OCSP$ is hosted completely independently from the Internet voting system. Currently the consistency of the VSS and $OCSP$ views is not rigorously audited, which leaves the unauthorized removal of the votes from the i-ballot box a theoretical possibility.

3.2   Tabulation Integrity

The following attacks on tabulation can be identified: i-ballot box replacement, tabulation tool compromise, and forgery of the voting result [7].

There are several steps in the process of tabulating votes.

- VSS verifies the signatures of the stored votes and extracts a set of encrypted votes sent to the tabulation.
- TA takes the set of encrypted votes and decrypts them with the private key stored in the HSM.
- TA aggregates and digitally signs the voting result.
- Both VSS and TA log the status of each encrypted vote. These logs are later audited.

We argue that the threat of actual forgery of the voting result has a valid countermeasure as there exists an audit procedure, which involves retabulating the votes and comparing the result with the published one.

An attacker wishing to replace the i-ballot box before tabulation would have to compromise the VSS. Although the VSS is offline in this stage of the election, the same system is online during the voting period. This makes a remote compromise possible as well. A malicious VSS would simply replace the set of encrypted votes sent to tabulation. It would also use the forged set of encrypted votes as basis for audit log forgery. There is a risk of detection for the attacker – it is possible to repeat the process of anonymization on the original set of signed votes using a different combination of hardware and software. Currently this kind of audit has not been implemented.

An attacker who has compromised the tabulation tool can take advantage of the fact that right now, there is no way to either verify or audit if the encrypted ballots are decrypted correctly. A flaw in the tabulation tool – TA together with HSM – could change the result without anyone noticing.

In the current scheme, the integrity of tabulation relies on the correctness of the software and hardware together with the integrity of the operating personnel. If we want to weaken the assumption that the central system is trustworthy and outsource aspects such as online vote collection to a third party, additional countermeasures are required for both i-ballot box replacement and tabulation tool compromise.

4   Towards the Solution

It is possible to make statements about the integrity of the voting result; the question is how can we prove these statements in a non-disputable manner. Take the example of traditional paper-based systems that can be audited by a full or random-sample recount. Out of the two, a full recount has been established as the common ground for resolving such disputes. Unfortunately, a full recount of all paper ballots is resource-intensive and error-prone due to human inaccuracy in both marking and counting the ballots. Recent research by Goggin *et al.* shows that the margin of error of paper ballot counting can be reduced to about $1 \ldots 2\%$, but not much lower [5].

In the era of computer technology we can actually do better. The corresponding solutions are generally known as providing *end-to-end verifiability*, i.e. allowing to check that certain properties regarding the relationship of the stored ballots and the voting result actually hold.

In our development, we will use the definition of end-to-end verifiability given by Popoveniuc *et al.* [11]. They define end-to-end verifiability through the performance requirements set for the voting system. An end-to-end verifiable voting system should provide the following properties:

1. *Cast as intended:* The voter is able to check that her ballot represents a vote for the candidate to whom she intended to give the vote.
2. *Well-formedness:* Anyone is able to check that valid ballots do not contain over-votes or negative votes.
3. *Recorded as cast:* The voter can check that her ballot is recorded as she cast it.
4. *Tallied as recorded:* Anyone is able to check that all the recorded ballots have been tallied correctly.
5. *Consistency:* Anyone is able to check that the voters and the general public have the same view of the election records.

6. *Authenticity/eligibility:* Anyone can check that any cast ballot has a corresponding voter who can perform check No. 3.

Introducing an individual verifiability tool addressed items 1 and 3 above [8]. These are also the two requirements that are targeted towards the voter herself and are hence relatively straightforward to implement.

The remaining four requirements (often referred to as *universal verifiability*) refer to *Anyone* as a potential verifier. The exact meaning of this term is left somewhat vague by Popoveniuc *et al.*, and thus we need to make it clearer before actual implementation.

4.1 From Observation to Verification

The analogue of universal verification in the case of paper voting is the observation. We design the paper voting methods such as voting in polling stations to protect the integrity of the voting result. With the help of building blocks such as securely sealable ballot boxes, we implement a procedure that makes it possible to claim integrity. As this procedure is carried out by human beings, there is room for mistakes – so as to convince the general public in actual integrity, the observation is applied as a method. Outsiders are allowed to participate and to observe the election procedures – accepting ballots to a ballot box, tabulating the votes, etc. The observers help us to assure the general public that the secure procedure developed for the voting method was correctly put into practice. This assurance makes us trust the integrity of the voting result more.

Following the spirit of universal verifiability, we would like to think that observation is accessible to anybody. This is true in principle, but there are some limitations.

The first obstacle is technical. In case of paper voting, the number of ballots may reach millions and it would be physically inconceivable to recount them all by hand. Instead, the general public relies on a number of designated verifiers (anyone can become one) to check the counting statements to the best of their ability (e.g. partially).

Similarly, verifying statements concerning a digital ballot box or tally integrity assumes proficiency in cryptographic techniques. In principle, anyone can achieve this, but in practice, not everyone does.

The second obstacle involves the threat of coercion. If everyone can get easy access to strong proof that her vote was tallied, this proof can be used to facilitate vote-selling.

The voting legislation in Estonia allows the election organizer to regulate the observation if not all observers can have equal conditions. There is also no universal access to the election data for the observers – for example, lists of voters are out of bounds, only data about the observer herself can be viewed, and the actual tabulation of the votes can only be observed.

The EVIV framework recently proposed by Joaquim *et al.* [9] takes a very pragmatic approach towards universal verifiability. In the election setup, vote-casting and verification phases it explicitly relies on a set of designated trustees, e.g. for distributed key management and homomorphic tally computation.

For the latter task, the EVIV framework introduces a set of trustees (called *Independent Verification Service(s)*). There can be an unlimited number of these services with independent implementations based on the public and verified specifications, the only restriction being the technical/mathematical capability of running the verification. We note that [9] does not specify any conflict resolution mechanisms for cases where some of the services disagree, but at least in principle this task is more feasible compared to agreeing on the count of a pile of paper ballots with possibly millions of ballots.

We shall proceed to present our proposal in the similar trust model as the EVIV. The EVIV uses homomorphic tallying, which has a remarkable performance overhead for large elections (orders of magnitude in Estonia are up to hundreds of candidates in one district and hundreds of thousands of Internet voters). Thus, we will be using provable decryption with mixing to provide vote privacy. However, the problem of verifying the proofs of decryption and mixing still remains, and we will solve it similarly to the EVIV by introducing the Data Auditor role and providing it with cryptographic integrity statements to verify.

This role can be filled by trusted representatives of political parties, foreign research groups or even local civil activists. As is the case with the EVIV, dispute resolution procedures will need to be established in addition to the actual proof-creating software applications.

As with virtually all voting systems with an online component, the Estonian system also features a bulletin board. So far, the functionality of this bulletin board (called *Vote Storage Server*) has been quite restricted, only allowing for limited-time individual verifiability. The second major goal of the current effort is to extend this functionality to also allow the Data Auditor to issue statements about the i-ballot box integrity.

5   IVXV Scheme

This Section describes new mechanisms proposed for the Estonian Internet Voting scheme that provide additional mitigation to the threats related to voting result integrity.

Until 2015, external parties were able to observe various organizational procedures during the tabulation process. In the upcoming system (codename IVXV), additional means will be added to verify that the voting result was tabulated correctly based on the votes that were collected and stored during the voting period.

To perform this verification, a new role – the *Data Auditor* – will be introduced. Technically, the party fulfilling this role will verify the decryption proofs exported during the vote decryption phase. Of course, this process must not violate the secrecy of the votes.

To enable flexible decryption proofs, we replace the current RSA-OAEP cryptosystem used for vote encryption by a randomized homomorphic public-key algorithm, e.g. the ElGamal cryptosystem. This makes it possible to prove correct decryption while preserving privacy, using re-encryption mixnets such as [4,14] or [2].

To address i-ballot box integrity issues, an extra commitment step will be added. This step will be implemented by a new party called the *Registration Service* that will essentially keep a ledger of the stored i-votes. This makes it, in principle, possible to outsource the duty of collecting votes to a third party, as there is a way to ensure that the integrity of the i-ballot box is maintained.

5.1   Setting

We take advantage of standard cryptographic primitives such as the signature scheme $\sigma = (Gen_{sig}, Sign, Verify)$ with its key-generation, signing and verification functions; the randomized homomorphic public-key cryptosystem $\epsilon = (Gen_{enc}, Enc, Dec)$ with its key-generation, encryption and decryption functions, and the cryptographic hash-function $Hash$.

The Estonian Internet Voting scheme has been using three major components: the Vote Forwarding Server, the Vote Storage Server and the Tabulation Application. In the IVXV, the division is different and signifies an opportunity for the organizational separation of duties. The Voting System is divided between the Election Organizer, the Vote Collector, the I-Ballot Box Processor, the Mixing Service and the Tallier. Additional external parties – the Certification Authority, the Time-marking Service, the Registration Service, the Data Auditor(s) and Voters – interact with the system.

The core requirement for the scheme is the existence of a PKI – there is a Certification Authority CA with the keypair $(sk_{pub}^{CA}, sk_{priv}^{CA})$ and the corresponding certificate $Cert_{CA}^{CA}$.

Eligible voters come from a set of persons where each person has a unique identifier $i \in I$, and everybody is in possession of a signature keypair certified by the CA.

$$\forall i \in I, (sk_{pub}^{i}, sk_{priv}^{i}) \leftarrow Gen_{sig}, Cert_{CA}^{i} = Sign(sk_{priv}^{CA}, (i, sk_{pub}^{i}))$$

The CA maintains the time-marking service TMS that for any certificate and bitstring pair $(Cert_{CA}^{i}, b)$ responds with a $Sign(sk_{priv}^{TMS}, (Cert_{CA}^{i}, b, utc))$ iff the certificate was valid at the time of the request. utc is the time of the request.

There is a Registration Service RS with the keypair $(sk_{pub}^{RS}, sk_{priv}^{RS})$ and the corresponding certificate $Cert_{CA}^{RS}$.

The Election Organizer EO has the duty to determine the voting result. EO approves the election configuration – the PKI and CA, RS, the list of choices C and the list of eligible voters $V \subseteq I$.

The EO selects the encryption system ϵ and generates an election keypair that is used for encrypting and decrypting the votes.

$$(ek_{pub}^{elec}, ek_{priv}^{elec}) \leftarrow Gen_{enc}$$

It is the responsibility of the EO to perform the role of Tallier – to protect the election private key and to tabulate the voting result.

EO provides a Voter with a Voting Application ($VoteApp$) and a Verification Application ($VerApp$). It is assumed that these applications are used on independent devices. The public key ek_{pub}^{elec} is made available to everybody.

EO delegates the handling of the online voting phase to the Vote Collector VC and the handling of the post-voting/pre-tabulation offline phase to the I-Ballot Box Processor $IBBP$. Both VC and $IBBP$ can be independent organizations. EO can nominate a Mixing Service MS.

All voting system components have certified signature keypairs.

We now specify the actions of all roles in the voting process.

5.2   Voting Stage

Voting. An eligible voter $v \in V$ who wants to vote for a candidate $c_v \in C$ uses $VoteApp$ to create a double envelope.

- The inner envelope is the encrypted choice $ballot_{c,r} = Enc(c_v, r_v, ek_{pub}^{elec})$, where $r_v \leftarrow R$ is a random number.
- The double envelope is acquired by signing the inner envelope digitally with the voter's private key: $vote_v = Sign(sk_{priv}^v, ballot_{c,r})$.
- Voter identifier v, certificate $Cert_{CA}^v$ and double envelope $vote_v$ are sent to the VC.
- VC responds with an unique identifier vid and the RS confirmation reg_{vid}.
- $VoteApp$ verifies the digitally signed reg_{vid} with respect to $Hash(vote_v)$.
- The identifier vid and the randomness used in encryption r_v are presented by the $VoteApp$ in a form that allows them to later be captured by $VerApp$.

Storing the Vote. In order to store a vote, the VC needs to verify and register the vote.

- VC verifies the eligibility of the voter v and the signature of the vote $vote_v$.
- VC generates a unique random vote identifier vid and stores it together with the vote.
- VC acquires a time-mark $ts_{vid} = Sign(sk_{priv}^{TMS}, (Cert_{CA}^v, Hash(ballot_{c,r}), utc_{vid}))$ from the TMS to show that the data $Hash(ballot_{c,r})$ existed at the time utc_{vid} when the voter's certificate was valid. The time-mark is stored together with the vote.
- VC sends a registration request $req_{vid} = Sign(sk_{priv}^{VC}, (vid, Hash(vote_v))$ to the RS.
- RS verifies the registration request, stores it and returns a signed confirmation $reg_{vid} = Sign(sk_{priv}^{RS}, Hash(req_{vid}))$ to the VC.
- VC stores the RS confirmation reg_{vid} together with the vote.
- VC sends the identifier vid and the confirmation reg_{vid} to the $VoteApp$.

If the procedure is a success, the VC stores the following data for a vote: $stored_{vid} = (v, Cert_{CA}^v, vote_v, vid, ts_{vid}, reg_{vid})$.

RS stores the $registered_{vid} = (req_{vid}, reg_{vid})$ for each vote.

Note that a voter can cast an i-vote as many times as she likes. All i-votes have to be stored in this phase without removal.

Verifying the Vote. The voter uses $VerApp$ to check the cast-as-intended and recorded-as-cast properties.

– Voter captures the identifier vid and randomness r_v with $VerApp$.
– $VerApp$ establishes an authenticated TLS channel with VC and sends vid to the VC.
– VC responds to $VerApp$ with a double envelope $vote_v$ and reg_{vid} corresponding to the vid. In case of an unknown vid or exceeded verification timeframe, an error is returned.
– $VerApp$ verifies both the double envelope and RS confirmation. The identity v determined through the verification is displayed to the voter.
– $VerApp$ uses the list of candidates C and the randomness r_v to find a $c' \in C$ such that $Enc(c', r_v, ek_{pub}^{elec}) = ballot_{c,r}$. The result of this process – either the c' or an error message – is displayed to the voter who has to decide if the result represents her will.

The voter is now assured that her vote is both stored and registered correctly.

5.3   Preparing the Votes for Tabulation

After the online voting phase, the VC contains a set of digitally signed votes D_{VC}, and RS contains a set of registration queries and responses D_{RS}. Both of these sets are transferred to the $IBBP$ responsible for auditing the voting phase and pre-processing the votes for tabulation – revoking superfluous votes, anonymizing votes.

– $IBBP$ verifies all double envelopes, checks eligibility and verifies RS confirmations.
– $IBBP$ compares D_{VC} and D_{RS} for consistency and composes a new list of double envelopes D_{IBBP}^1. This list only contains the latest vote $vote_v$ for each voter v and all entries must have a corresponding registration confirmation linked to the $Hash(vote_v)$.
– $IBBP$ provides EO with the list of people who have i-voted and receives a list of people whose i-vote needs to be revoked, because there is also a corresponding paper vote. $IBBP$ removes those votes from D_{IBBP}^1 and gets a new list D_{IBBP}^2 as a result.
– $IBBP$ anonymizes the double envelopes in the list D_{IBBP}^2, i.e. extracts the list B_1 of encrypted ballots to be tabulated.

$IBBP$ may pass the list B_1 to EO for tabulation. This is equivalent to the current Estonian Internet Voting. Optionally, $IBBP$ can pass B_1 to the re-encryption mixnet MS in order to cryptographically anonymize the votes. The mixnet shuffles and re-encrypts the input votes B_1 and provides the output set of votes B_2 together with the proof of correct operation P_{mix}.

5.4   Tabulating the Voting Result

One of the two lists of encrypted ballots – B_1 or B_2 – is passed to the EO for tabulation. The EO uses the election private key to decrypt each choice c' and to calculate the voting result $result$. The EO must also provide a proof of correct decryption P_{dec} together with the plaintext. In case of the ElGamal cryptosystem, a Schnorr identification proof could be used [12].

5.5   Auditing the Election

In order to claim the integrity of the voting result, we need to audit the processes that led to that result. We will now show step by step, how an election can be audited in the IVXV scheme.

Auditing VC. We rely on digital signatures for vote integrity and on individual verification to ensure the cast-as-intended and recorded-as-cast properties. Note that both voting and individual verification steps also check for the correct registration of the vote by RS. Given that the RS and VC are not compromised in a synchronised manner, we can detect the unauthorized removal of votes from the i-ballot box using the following procedure. We define step $AuditVC$ for verifying the integrity of the i-ballot box as it is retrieved from the VC.

$AuditVC$ takes D_{VC}, D_{RS} and D^1_{IBBP} as inputs. $AuditVC$ accepts iff

- All votes in D_{VC} belong to eligible voters and verify successfully.
- All votes are consistent with the rules of well-formedness.
- All confirmations in D_{RS} verify successfully.
- The views D_{VC} and D_{RS} are consistent.
- The removal of double votes yields D^1_{IBBP}.

Note that due to e.g. network errors there may be votes that are in D_{VC}, but not D_{RS}. The inconsistencies in this step do not mean an immediate problem, but call for further clarification based on e.g. technical logs.

The step $AuditVC$ is part of the routine operation by $IBBP$, as the honest operation of the possibly outsourced VC needs to be verified at all times.

Auditing IBBP. The $IBBP$ makes changes to the contents of the i-ballot box retrieved from the VC – it revokes any votes for a voter v who has voted also on paper, and it only adds to the tally the last i-vote cast by the voter. $IBBP$ also provides a list of encrypted ballots for tabulation.

The $IBBP$ procedure is well-defined and repeatable – the process must always produce the same outputs on the same inputs regardless of implementation. In addition to a complete re-execution of the $IBBP$ procedure, it is possible to perform simple risk-limiting audits – for any vote excluded from the list of votes sent to the tally the $IBBP$ must be capable of providing both VC and RS data together with the reason for revocation.

We refer to the complete auditing step of $IBBP$ as $AuditIBBP$.

Auditing Tabulation. The optional mixing step performed by the MS and the decryption performed by the EO are verifiable by definition. Given a verifiable re-encryption mixnet and proof of correct decryption, the following sets of data give assurance as to the correctness of the voting result: $(B_1, B_2, P_{mix}, P_{dec}, result)$.

We refer to the auditing step of the MS as $AuditMix$ and the auditing step of tabulation as $AuditTally$.

Complete Audit of an Election. The complete audit of an election that would fulfil the criteria of universal verifiability would consist of all steps: $AuditVC$, $AuditIBBP$, $AuditMix$ and $AuditTally$. Informally, the Data Auditor can be assured of the following properties.

- The integrity of the i-ballot box was preserved.
- The contents of the i-ballot box were processed according to the rules.
- The decryption of a list of encrypted ballots B_2 that is equivalent to the original list of encrypted ballots B_1 was done correctly.

These audit steps achieve the verifiability criteria of [11] as follows.

- *Well-formedness* of the double envelope is verified by the $AuditVC$ and the inner envelope is verified by the $AuditTally$. As we do not apply any proof-technique to show that the encrypted data identified an existing candidate, we may have invalid votes that are only detected during the decryption. We do not consider this to be a problem, as we are not implementing homomorphic tally.
- *Tallied as recorded* is achieved by verifying the i-ballot-box integrity and correct post-processing in the $AuditVC$ and $AuditIBBP$, and verifying the correct tabulation in the $AuditMix$ and $AuditTally$.
- *Consistency* is verified by performing the $AuditVC$ and $AuditIBBP$, and checking that the output of the $IBBP$ process is sent to the MS as input.
- *Authenticity/eligibility* is verified by performing the $AuditVC$ and checking that all the double envelopes were signed by eligible voters.

All these checks have to be performed in a holistic manner – in order to be convinced about e.g. consistency, one has to actually perform the complete audit. This way the Data Auditor can verify the integrity of the voting result without breaking ballot secrecy.

6 Discussion

6.1 Levels of Auditing

We described auditing steps that are necessary for the Data Auditor to carry out in order to be convinced about the integrity of the voting result. Different stakeholders could nominate different Data Auditors in order to delegate the verification.

The problem with the complete audit as described above is that the Data Auditor gets access to the complete time-marked set of votes. A malicious Data

Auditor could find out whether somebody has re-voted either on paper or online. The information could be abused for coercion. Due to the re-encryption mixnet used, the malicious auditor could not break the ballot secrecy, but we still have to trust the auditor. This implies that we have to define the audit ceremony that mitigates the risk of data abuse by additional means.

A more contained version of the audit would require more trust in the system components. We define a partial audit as consisting of the steps $AuditMix$, $AuditTally$ based on the list of original encrypted ballots B_1 as committed to by $IBBP$. The audit step $AuditVC$ has already been performed by the $IBBP$. This means that the $IBBP$ becomes a trusted party. Due to the well-defined procedure, the actions of $IBBP$ can be double-checked. It is an open question if such a ceremony is feasible that would allow the Data Auditor to trust a partial audit based on the data given by the $IBBP$ – it is basically stating that "there is a set of encrypted ballots that yield the election result, we have to trust the $IBBP$ for authenticity".

It would be possible to implement both partial audits and complete audits in parallel – this would enlarge the set of parties who could commit to the authenticity of the inputs to the partial audit, and the partial audits could be carried out by a much wider audience.

We note that the bar of observation for electronic voting is higher than in the case of paper voting. In case of paper voting, the observer has to be capable of understanding and following the organizational procedures. However, observation of electronic voting requires both computational capabilities and understanding of the cryptographic protocol. Also, the capability to either produce a correct implementation of auditing application or to verify the correctness of an existing one is necessary.

Given these relatively high entry-level requirements, the election organizer cannot rely on the general public providing a reasonable number of protocol participants, but has to give access to verification together with the open specifications and reference implementations. For the sake of completeness a more capable auditor should have the opportunity to implement its own tools based on the aforementioned specifications.

6.2 The Role of Mixing

The mixnet in the IVXV scheme is only necessary for ensuring ballot secrecy in the case of a third-party Data Auditor. By mixing the encrypted ballots and tabulating the mixed set of encrypted ballots, we assure that two sets are equivalent from the perspective of the voting result, but the one-to-one mapping between two sets is obfuscated. This allows us to give access to the data to an external auditor.

In case of a complete audit, the mixing clearly simplifies the audit ceremony – without mixing, the auditor would have access to both digitally signed encrypted ballots and corresponding plaintexts. Hence, without mixing, the different steps of an audit would have to be separated by other means. In case of a partial audit, the mixing can be considered a safety measure – unless there is a way for the auditor to get the original double envelopes, the plaintexts could not be linked to identities.

There is one party – namely the EO – who by definition has access to the original double envelopes and the election private key. In principle, the EO is capable of breaking ballot secrecy completely. This means that the organizational integrity and private key management are crucial for ballot secrecy – this calls for the threshold scheme – either for the hardware security module activation or threshold decryption.

6.3 Outsourcing the Vote Collection

The assurance of the voting result integrity and ballot secrecy at the same time under the trust assumptions of the Estonian Internet Voting scheme has required the election organizer to become a technical expert in hosting an online service. The IVXV scheme allows to outsource the vote collection task to a third party, as the correct operation of this party is verifiable by voters, third-party auditors and auditors nominated by the election organizer itself.

The IVXV scheme is designed in a way that the *VoteApp* should not accept the session unless the VC has responded with the registration confirmation reg_{vid}. Also, the step of individual verification shall verify the correct registration of the vote by RS.

A malicious RS can perform a service denial attack, but in case of other components not co-operating, this attack will be discovered. It is important that the VC stores the RS confirmation – otherwise the RS could drop those confirmations.

A malicious VC could attempt to drop votes after the end of the individual verification time-window, but this would be discovered with the help of the RS that stores the digitally signed requests by the VC. This means that we need to get both the VC and RS datasets for auditing completeness.

6.4 End-to-end Verifiability

The IVXV scheme provides mechanisms for both individual and universal verifiability. The individual verifiability tools are available for any voter to use. Access to the data available for central system auditing has to be restricted, though. Only properly anonymized (e.g. cryptographically mixed) data can be given to anyone, whereas the data that links voter identities with other parameters (such as the time of vote-casting or specific encrypted ballots) has to be audited in a controlled environment by designated trustees.

All criteria required by [11] are fulfilled with respect to the aforementioned restriction: well-formedness, consistency, tallied-as-recorded and authenticity/eligibility can be checked by a designated trustee; cast-as-intended and recorded-as-cast can be checked by any voter.

Note that due to the verification of the digital signature in the individual verification tool, the clash-attack [10] is not possible. However, this means that now the *VerApp* has access to the voter's identity. This assumes that the verification devices are personalized and cannot be shared among untrusting voters. This is a change with respect to the original verification scheme [8]. We argue that this is a reasonable trade-off, since in 2017 personal mobile devices will be much more widespread than they were in 2013.

Hence, we can conclude that the IVXV scheme achieves all the requirements set in [11] to be called end-to-end verifiable.

7   Conclusions and Further Work

This paper proposed several improvements to achieve the end-to-end verifiability of Estonian Internet voting. In particular, i-ballot box and tabulation integrity have been addressed. Previously, both of these aspects have relied heavily on human control and organizational measures. In the light of the new proposals, it will be possible to offload a lot of this responsibility onto independent external auditors. In principle, it will even be possible to outsource the vote collection part of the central system to a completely untrusted party.

The implementer of the proposed IVXV framework has already been selected and the target is to roll out the system update in time for the local municipal elections due in October 2017.

It is certain that the system development will not end in 2017. The practical try-outs will give us a lot of information about the open issues, e.g. what kinds of conflicts may arise in practice between independent auditor organizations. Resolving these issues will give us a lot of work in future iterations.

A clear separation of roles and their duties opens up the opportunity to apply IVXV also in other elections, not just national elections in Estonia. Implementing this vision also remains a subject for future development.

Acknowledgements. This research has been supported by the Estonian Research Council under grant No. IUT27-1.

References

1. Ansper, A., Buldas, A., Jürgenson, A., Oruaas, M., Priisalu, J., Raiend, K., Veldre, A., Willemson, J., Virunurm, K.: E-voting concept security: analysis and measures (2010). http://www.vvk.ee/public/dok/General_Description_E-Voting_2010.pdf
2. Bayer, S., Groth, J.: Efficient zero-knowledge argument for correctness of a shuffle. In: Pointcheval, D., Johansson, T. (eds.) EUROCRYPT 2012. LNCS, vol. 7237, pp. 263–280. Springer, Heidelberg (2012). doi:10.1007/978-3-642-29011-4_17
3. Estonian National Electoral Committee. Statistics about Internet Voting in Estonia. http://vvk.ee/voting-methods-in-estonia/engindex/statistics
4. Fauzi, P., Lipmaa, H.: Efficient culpably sound NIZK shuffle argument without random oracles. In: Sako, K. (ed.) CT-RSA 2016. LNCS, vol. 9610, pp. 200–216. Springer, Heidelberg (2016). doi:10.1007/978-3-319-29485-8_12
5. Goggin, S.N., Byrne, M.D., Gilbert, J.E.: Post-election auditing: effects of procedure and ballot type on manual counting accuracy, efficiency, and auditor satisfaction and confidence. Election Law J. 11(1), 36–51 (2012)

6. Heiberg, S., Laud, P., Willemson, J.: The application of i-voting for Estonian parliamentary elections of 2011. In: Kiayias, A., Lipmaa, H. (eds.) Vote-ID 2011. LNCS, vol. 7187, pp. 208–223. Springer, Heidelberg (2012). doi:10.1007/978-3-642-32747-6_13

7. Heiberg, S., Willemson, J.: Modeling threats of a voting method. In: Zissis, D., Lekkas, D. (eds.) Design, Development, and Use of Secure Electronic Voting Systems, pp. 128–148. IGI Global, Hershey (2014)

8. Heiberg, S., Willemson, J.: Verifiable Internet voting in Estonia. In: Krimmer, R., Volkamer, M. (eds.) 6th International Conference on Electronic Voting 2014, (EVOTE 2014), Bregenz, Austria, 28–31 October 2014, pp. 23–29. TUT Press (2014)

9. Joaquim, R., Ferreira, P., Ribeiro, C.: EVIV: an end-to-end verifiable Internet voting system. Comput. Secur. **32**, 170–191 (2013)

10. Küsters, R., Truderung, T., Vogt, A.: Clash attacks on the verifiability of e-voting systems. In: IEEE Symposium on Security and Privacy, SP 2012, San Francisco, California, USA, 21–23 May 2012, pp. 395–409. IEEE Computer Society (2012)

11. Popoveniuc, S., Kelsey, J., Regenscheid, A., Vora, P.L.: Performance requirements for end-to-end verifiable elections. In: Jones, D.W., Quisquater, J.-J., Rescorla, E. (eds.) In: Proceeding of the 2010 International Conference on Electronic Voting Technology Workshop/Workshop on Trustworthy Elections, EVT/WOTE 2010, Washington, D.C., USA, 9–10 August 2010. USENIX Association (2010)

12. Schnorr, C.P.: Efficient identification and signatures for smart cards. In: Quisquater, J.-J., Vandewalle, J. (eds.) EUROCRYPT 1989. LNCS, vol. 434, pp. 688–689. Springer, Heidelberg (1990). doi:10.1007/3-540-46885-4_68

13. Springall, D., Finkenauer, T., Durumeric, Z., Kitcat, J., Hursti, H., MacAlpine, M., Halderman, J.A.: Security analysis of the Estonian Internet voting system. In Proceedings of the 2014 ACM SIGSAC Conference on Computer and Communications Security, pp. 703–715. ACM (2014)

14. Terelius, B., Wikström, D.: Proofs of restricted shuffles. In: Bernstein, D.J., Lange, T. (eds.) AFRICACRYPT 2010. LNCS, vol. 6055, pp. 100–113. Springer, Heidelberg (2010). doi:10.1007/978-3-642-12678-9_7

Breaching the Privacy of Israel's Paper Ballot Voting System

Tomer Ashur[1]([⊠]), Orr Dunkelman[2], and Nimrod Talmon[3]

[1] ESAT/COSIC, KU Leuven and imec, Leuven, Belgium
tomer.ashur@esat.kuleuven.be
[2] University of Haifa, Haifa, Israel
orrd@cs.haifa.ac.il
[3] Weizmann Institute of Science, Rehovot, Israel
nimrodtalmon77@gmail.com

Abstract. An election is a process through which citizens in liberal democracies select their governing bodies, usually through voting. For elections to be truly honest, people must be able to vote freely without being subject to coercion; that is why voting is usually done in a private manner. In this paper we analyze the security offered by a paper-ballot voting system that is used in Israel, as well as several other countries around the world. We provide an algorithm which, based on publicly-available information, breaks the privacy of the voters participating in such elections. Simulations based on real data collected in Israel show that our algorithm performs well, and can correctly recover the vote of up to 96% of the voters.

1 Introduction

One of the fundamental mechanisms that allow for democracy is the notion of free elections. In free elections, eligible voters express their opinions on important matters via voting. In liberal democracies, periodical elections (which we refer to as "election cycles") are held for electing the members of the governing bodies. For people to freely express their opinions (that is, without being coerced to external pressure), voting is usually done in a private manner. In other words, the elections allow voters to maintain their privacy regarding their specific vote within a large anonymity set.

One can learn about the importance of secrecy in election processes from the *Declaration on Criteria for Free and Fair Elections*, published by the *Inter-Parliamentary Union* in 1994,[1] and which states [9]:

"2. Voting and Elections Rights:
(7) The right to vote in <u>secret</u> is absolute and shall not be restricted in any manner whatsoever."

---

[1] The Inter-Parliamentary Union (IPU) is an international organization of 162 state parliaments and 10 regional parliaments. This union, which was established in 1889, has a permanent observer status at the United Nations and general consultative status with the Economic and Social Council.

© Springer International Publishing AG 2017
R. Krimmer et al. (Eds.): E-Vote-ID 2016, LNCS 10141, pp. 108–124, 2017.
DOI: 10.1007/978-3-319-52240-1_7

Similarly in spirit, the state of Israel have recognized the importance of secret voting and determined in its *Basic Law: The Knesset*[2] [4], in Sect. 4 that:

"The Knesset shall be elected by general, national, direct, equal, <u>secret</u>, and proportional elections, in accordance with the Knesset Elections Law."

In this paper, we demonstrate that only a few observations are required to breach the privacy of the voters in the Israeli general elections. Our attack uses only the following information: (1) the results of the elections per ballot box (which are published at the end of the election cycle by the general elections committee); (2) the time of vote for each voter (which is collected by the various political parties); and (3) a periodical count of the ballots left in the tray (which can be collected by the members of the local elections committee who are continuously manning the ballot box). It turns out that, by collecting the above information over several election cycles and using it to intersect the anonymity sets, it is possible to recover most votes.

In what follows we report on simulations performed on real data from the 2013 Israeli general elections. We consider variable number of election cycles which the adversary is acting upon and consider different time intervals by which the adversary is able to count the ballots left in the tray. We mention that an attack does not have to be global, and that the adversary can focus on specific polling stations that are of interest.

We do use some assumptions in our simulations. First, we assume that an adversary can periodically count the ballots; we elaborate on this assumption in Sect. 3.1. Second, in the specific simulations reported here, we assume that voters do not switch parties between election cycles; while this assumption is not true for all voters, it is true for most of them (as is apparent by studying recent election surveys [2,19]). While this assumption somewhat weakens the results, it is being used in the absence of sufficient real-world data about specific voters. We further discuss our assumptions in Sect. 5.

Expectedly, the success of our attack increases with the number of election cycles considered and decreases (though not dramatically) when the frequency of the count is reduced. Our simulations demonstrate that, for example, with only three election cycles, it is sufficient to count the ballots once in half an hour, to recover as much as 63% of the voters. Moreover, it turns out that we can correctly recover almost all votes, reaching 100% success in most polling stations, and reaching 93% on the average, using six election cycles and counting once in half an hour. Further, by counting only once in an hour, this number remains as high as 69%.

1.1 Related Work

We briefly discuss several definitions for privacy in elections. Then, we show how the Israeli election system can be modeled as a timed-mix, and mention several known attacks on mixes. Our attack, described in Sect. 3, is different from these attacks, mainly since we use a significantly smaller number of observations.

---

[2] The *Knesset* is the name of the Israeli parliament.

Much of the discussion around e-voting systems evolves around their security. However, the security is hardly ever compared to the alternative system "that was always used". Interestingly, although the underlying crypto is often well understood by specialists, e-voting systems are perceived as insecure by the layman, including decision makers. In this paper we use cryptographic tools to study the behavior of a paper-based system, allowing to compare them on the same field. We believe that adopting ideas from computer science and cryptography to verify desirable properties of real-world paper-based elections is an interesting research direction.

Privacy in Elections. There are several definitions for privacy in elections, most of which borrow ideas from differential privacy. In short, a voting system is said to preserve privacy if it is impossible to distinguish between two scenarios, differentiated by the behavior of several voters; the idea is that, if such events are indistinguishable, then an adversary cannot infer which of them occurred in reality. We mention several papers [6,11,16,17] in this context. In this paper we simply quantify the number of voters whose vote we could correctly de-anonymize. We view our definition as being more natural, and, contrasted with the available definitions—which are specifically tailored for e-voting, more suited to the context of the current paper.

Attacks on Mixes. Mixes are widely used to model private communications. Proposed by Chaum in 1981 [7], a mix is a means for delivering messages anonymously between senders and receivers. Communication in a mix is split into rounds, such that in each round n senders send messages which are then sent to n receivers in an arbitrary or random order.

Each ballot box in the Israeli voting system can be modeled as a certain kind of a mix, namely a timed-mix. In such a mix, a buffer of messages is mixed once in each time period. The set of voters in each polling station corresponds to the set of senders, while the set of parties contesting in an election corresponds to the set of receivers. There are various known attacks on mixes [1,10,14,15,22] and we refer the interested reader to a recent survey [18].

Most of the above-mentioned papers de-anonymize single receivers and assume either a uniform distribution of the other receivers or try to approximate that distribution. In our case, the overall tally is given, and we aim to de-anonymize the whole electorate.

1.2   Paper Organization

The paper is organized as follows: Sect. 2 gives a brief description of the Israeli voting system. Section 3 describes our attack. In Sect. 4, we evaluate our attack through simulations and discuss its tightness. In Sect. 5, we discuss some of the limitations of the attack, suggest ways to overcome these limitations, discuss possible countermeasures, and present future research directions. We conclude the paper in Sect. 6.

2 The Israeli Voting System

The Israeli voting system is described in the *Knesset Elections law - 1969* [21]. In a nutshell, every eligible citizen is assigned to a polling station. In order to vote, each voter arrives to her assigned polling station and identifies herself to the local elections committee. The committee then crosses the voter's name from the list of assigned voters, and hands her a special envelope.

The voter walks behind a curtain and chooses a ballot (a piece of paper with the name of her selected party on it) from a tray, representing her preferred party. The tray (which can be viewed in Fig. 1) includes a stack of ballots for each candidate party (34 parties contested in the 2013 elections). The voter puts the ballot into the envelope, seals, and casts it into the ballot box, where it mixes with all the other envelopes. The members of the local elections committee are all, except for the chairperson, appointed by the political parties. As part of their role these representatives periodically check behind the curtain that all ballots are available to voters. Another informal role of the committee members is to send the time of vote of every voter to the parties, so that the parties can stimulate their support base who did not show up yet, for example, via phone calls or SMS.

At the end of the elections day, the local elections committee breaks the ballot box's seal, opens it, extracts the ballots from each envelope, and counts them.[3] The results of the tally are then sent to the general elections committee, which aggregates and publishes the results (including per-ballot-box statistics). The key observation in this research is the following.

Observation 1. *The size of the stack of leftover ballots "echos" the choices made by previous voters.*

Fig. 1. An example of the tray for the 2013 elections.

---

[3] We stress that the count is done locally, and the votes of each ballot box are not mixed with other boxes.

For example, if 300 ballots are placed in the tray for each of the parties at the beginning of the election day, and 20 are missing from one stack after 20 voters have voted (and no other ballots are missing), then an observer can conclude that all of them voted for the party represented by this stack.

3   The Attack

In this section, we describe our attack, whose goal is to reveal the votes in Israel's general elections.

3.1   Collecting Observations

The adversary collects observations over several election cycles $u = [1, \ldots, U]$. For each election cycle, in order to collect the required observations, the adversary counts all the ballots in the tray at the beginning of the elections day. We define this count to be in time $t = 0$.

Then, the adversary starts counting the ballots in the tray periodically, in times $t = [1, \ldots, T]$. The technical question of *how* the adversary can count the stack of ballots is discussed in Sect. 5.1; we only mention that one might use, for example, accurate weight scales, laser based measurement equipment, or banknote counters. The adversary also collects the time of vote for each voter. This information is already collected by the local elections committee, and is sent to the parties via a dedicated form called "Tofes-1000" (which translates to "1000-Form").

We define a *frame* to be the time period between two consecutive counts. Through their voting times, we can divide the voters into frames, and assign a probability distribution to their vote according to the count of the respective frame. We refer to the set of voters between the count in time $t - 1$ and the count in t, in election cycle u, as $V^{u,t}$, and refer to the probability distribution associated with this time frame as $C^{u,t}$. Notice that we have t frames: frame 1 to frame t. The probability distribution $C^{u,t}$ can be represented as a vector, such that each element in it corresponds to a party p, and each value in it is equal to the number of ballots of party p which are missing from the stack in this frame, normalized by the total number of voters in the frame. For example, if in the second elections Alice voted for the party named *Meretz* between time $t = 5$ and time $t = 6$, then we have that the set $V^{2,5}$ contains Alice and $C^{2,5}[Meretz] > 0$. It follows that, initially, the size of the anonymity set of every voter $v \in V^{u,t}$ is at most the number of non-zero items in $C^{u,t}$ (and not the number of non-zero items in the tally of the whole polling station).

Notice that using these frames, the adversary can recreate the real tally of each polling station. However, the adversary can also directly collect the real tally of each polling station, since this information is published by the central elections.

Indeed, from the perspective of each voter, every election cycle is composed of exactly one frame to which she belongs and an arbitrary number of frames to which she does not belong.

3.2   The Attack Algorithm

Our algorithm is composed of the following three functions.

- The **Find_Homogeneous_Frames** function iterates over all frames, searching for homogeneous ones, i.e., frames in which all voters voted for the same party. If such a frame is found, then all voters in it are assigned to this party, the size of the frame is subtracted from the tally of that party, and the voters in the frame are removed from all other frames they participate in.
- The **Find_Single_Option_Voters** function iterates over all voters. For each voter, it intersects the frames in which it participates, to find which parties are shared by all involved frames. If only a single party is shared between all frames in which a voter participates, then it assigns this party to the voter. The tally for this party is then reduced by 1 and the corresponding frame counts are updated.
- The **Likelihood_Estimation** function iterates over tuples of (voter, party, frame). For each such tuple, it estimates, independently for each frame, the likelihood that a voter in the frame voted for each of the parties involved in that frame. The likelihood is calculated as the number of votes which the party got in this frame over the number of voters in this frame. The likelihood for a voter to vote for a certain party is the product of the respective probabilities in all frames she participated in. The output of this function is a matrix L where each row v is a voter, and each column p is a party. An element $L_{v,p}$ in this table is the likelihood that a voter v voted for a party p. We search for the pair (v, p) giving the largest value $L_{v,p}$ and assign the voter v to the party p. The tally is then decreased by one for that party p and the corresponding frame counts are updated.

The attack algorithm is composed of two phases: the *safe phase* and the *unsafe phase*. In the safe phase we call Find_Homogeneous_Frames and Find_Single_Option_Voters over and over until no new assignments can be made. This phase is safe in the sense that whenever the algorithm assigns a party to a voter, this assignment is necessarily correct. In other words, it can either return the right party for a voter, or output a symbol indicating that it was unable to de-anonymize her. In Sect. 4, we present the success rate of the algorithm when only this phase is being used.

In the unsafe phase, which we invoke after no more voters can be de-anonymized through the safe phase, the Likelihood_Estimation procedure is used for making a probabilistic decision, assigning a party to a single voter for which we are most certain about. We then start over the process of calling to Find_Homogeneous_Frames and Find_Single_Option_Voters until they can no longer de-anonymize voters, in which case we call Likelihood_Estimation again. The algorithm halts when all voters have been assigned to parties. Note that during the course of this phase, Find_Homogeneous_Frames and Find_Single_Option_Voters can err due to previous wrong guesses made by Likelihood_Estimation. However, as we will see in Sect. 4, although the unsafe phase can make wrong guesses, its success probability is much higher than that of safe phase, suggesting that it usually does not. A pseudocode of the attack is given in Algorithm 1.

Algorithm 1. Pseudocode of the attack for a certain polling station.

Input: List of voters $V^{u,t}$ for $t \in [T]$ and $u \in [U]$ (list of voters)
Input: Normalized frame counts $C^{u,t}$ for $t \in [T]$ and $u \in [U]$ (one value per party; sums to 1)

  {Safe phase}
  while progress is made **do**
    {**Find_Homogeneous_Frames**}
    for $u \in [U]$; $t \in [T]$; party p **do**
      if $C^{u,t}[p] = 1$ (and thus, for each $p' \neq p$, we have $C^{u,t}[p'] = 0$) **then**
        assign all voters in $V^{u,t}$ to p and decrease the tally of p by $|V^{u,t}|$
      end if
    end for
    {**Find_Single_Option_Voters**}
    for voter v **do**
      if $\cap_{u \in [U], t \in [T], v \in V^{u,t}} \{p : C^{u,t} > 0\} = \{p\}$ **then**
        assign v to p, decrease the tally for p by one, and update $C^{u,t}$
      end if
    end for
  end while
  {Unsafe phase}
  while not all votes have been extracted **do**
    {**Likelihood_Estimation**}
    for voter v; party p **do**
      compute likelihood of v voting for p as $L^{v,p} = \Pi_{u \in [U], t \in [T], v \in V^{u,t}} C^{u,t}[p]$
    end for
    let v' and p' be the pair for which the likelihood value $L^{v',p'}$ is maximal
    assign v' to p', decrease the tally for p by one, and update $C^{u,t}$
    while progress is made **do** {**Find_Homogeneous_Frames**}
      for $u \in [U]$; $t \in [T]$; party p **do**
        if $C^{u,t}[p] = 1$ (and thus, for each $p' \neq p$, we have $C^{u,t}[p'] = 0$) **then**
          assign all voters in $V^{u,t}$ to p and decrease the tally of p by $|V^{u,t}|$
        end if
      end for{**Find_Single_Option_Voters**}
      for voter v **do**
        if $\cap_{u \in [U], t \in [T], v \in V^{u,t}} \{p : C^{u,t} > 0\} = \{p\}$ **then**
          assign v to p, decrease the tally for p by one, and update $C^{u,t}$
        end if
      end for
    end while
  end while

---

4   Evaluation of the Attack

In this section we evaluate, through simulations, the success rate of the attack proposed in Sect. 3. The model considered here assumes that voters do not change their minds between election cycles. We defer the justification of this assumption to Sect. 5. We also assume, for the sake of simplicity, that voters always vote in the same polling station, and that no new voters join or leave the registry.

4.1   Simulations

To calculate the success rate of the attack, we ran simulations based on the results of the 2013 general elections in Israel as published by the general elections committee [20]. In these elections, Israel's eligible voters were divided into 9879 polling stations. The law upper-bounds the maximal number of eligible voters assigned to a polling station at 900; in practice, the maximal number of voters assigned to a polling station was 894, and the median number of voters assigned to each polling station was 590. The voting turnout was low, and out of the 5,654,842 eligible voters only 3,617,857 (64%) actually voted; as a result, the median number of actual voters per polling station was 366. Out of these, a total number of 3,579,793 votes were counted as legitimate votes.[4]

We model each polling station independently of all other polling stations, as we see no dependencies between different polling stations.[5] The published results include, per polling station, the number of assigned voters, the number of voters who arrived, the number of legitimate votes, the number of votes received by each party per polling station, and an accumulated turnout rate per two hours.

Due to obvious reasons we do not have the real data needed to actually run the attack, although we do use real data from the tallies of the various polling stations. We therefore resort to the "second-best" option and use a simulation of the elections process. We denote the number of voters in the attacked polling station by n and set the number of frames T to be either 30, 15, or 7: for the vast majority of the polling stations, this corresponds to counting the ballots once in half an hour, an hour, or two hours.[6] We created n "virtual" voters, and split them randomly over the frames according to the turnout rate. For each frame we "counted" the number of missing ballots, and built the voting distribution for it. This procedure is repeated U times, corresponding to U consecutive election cycles; we chose $U = \{2, 3, 4, 5, 6, 7\}$.

4.2   Results

We begin by reporting and analyzing our results, where we set T to be 30. Later we report on simulations done with $T = 15$ and $T = 7$.

Average Success Rate. The average success rate of the attack (over the polling stations) is provided in Table 1. The baseline is the success rate had the adversary always assigned the largest party or political group to all voters of the ballot box.

---

[4] Absentee votes (that is, voters who do not vote in their assigned ballot, such as diplomats, soldiers, and seamen), which account to about 5% of the votes, are excluded for simplicity.

[5] This independence implies that an adversary can focus their effort on subsets of polling stations which are of interest, or where they expect to achieve a high success rate.

[6] When $T = 7$ the first count is done after 3 h.

Table 1. Average success rate of the attack, for $T = 30$, for extracting the exact party that the voters voted for, and the political group that the voters belong to. The baseline is 38% for extracting the party and 54% for extracting the group.

Election cycles	Safe phase	Unsafe phase, party	Unsafe phase, group
2	7%	46%	59%
3	19%	63%	73%
4	35%	76%	83%
5	50%	84%	89%
6	62%	90%	93%
7	71%	93%	96%

When trying to recover the political group that a voter voted for we first let the algorithm assign a party to the voter and count it as a success if this party is part of the correct group. Since the safe phase cannot output incorrect assignments, the success rates do not change for that phase. In contrast, we can see in the table that for the unsafe phase, the success rate increases in all cases.

The more natural course, where we first merge the parties into political groups and then run the algorithm with 6 "virtual" parties, was tried but offered inferior results compared with the selected approach. Consider the following scenario: a voter v_1 voted for party 1 and shares a frame in $u = 2$ with a voter v_2 who voted for party 2 and in $u = 3$ with a voter v_3 who voted for party 3. Assume that parties 2 and 3 are of the same political group. Now, before merging them we could exclude parties 2 and 3 as possible parties for v_1. This is no longer possible after the merge as v_2 and v_3 are indistinguishable.

Size and Homogeneity. For a more detailed understanding of the factors which affect our success rate, we provide further results. Specifically, We show the success rate of the attack as a function of the polling station size, and the homogeneity of the polling station (the homogeneity of a polling station is defined to be the standard deviation of its normalized tally with respect to the unanimous vector, i.e., the squared root of the squared difference between the frame and a frame where all parties got the same number of votes, normalized by the number of voters), both for the safe phase of the algorithm and for the unsafe phase of the algorithm, for $U = \{2, 3, 4, 5, 6, 7\}$ election cycles.

Further, we consider the attack as trying to reveal either (1) the exact party for which the voters voted for, or (2) the political group for which the voters voted for. Specifically, the political parties in Israel, as of 2013, can be grouped into six almost distinct groups: left (Meretz and HaAvoda), right (Habait Hayehudi, Likud, and Otzma Leisrael), center[7] (Eretz Chadasha, Kadima, Or, Yesh-Atid, and Hatnuaa), ultra orthodox Jews (Yahadut Hatora, Am Shalem, and Shas),

---

[7] Sometimes referred to as "secular".

Arabs (Balad, Hatikva-Leshinui, Chadash, Raam, and Daam), and MISC (all the other parties, all of which do not meet the election threshold for representation).

The corresponding figures are given in Figs. 2, 3, and 4. In those graphs, we show results for $U = \{2, 3, 4, 5\}$, and do not visualize the results for $U = \{6, 7\}$, to not clutter the image too much, and since the point is already clear with those values.

Results Analysis. There are several important variables which affect our success rate. First, as one might expect, using more election cycles (that is, increasing U), or aiming at finding only the political group for which the voters voted for, increases the success rate of the algorithm. Second, the unsafe phase indeed increases the success rate of the attack, however at the cost of sometimes making wrong decisions and assigning wrong parties to some voters.

The other two important variables are the size of the polling station and the homogeneity of the polling station. Specifically, it is apparent that the strongest factor on our success rate is the size of the polling station. Indeed, we see that the polling station's size and the success rate are highly correlated; concretely, the smaller the polling station is, the higher the success rate.

Less strong than the size of the polling station, the homogeneity of the polling station is an important factor on the success rate of the algorithm. (Recall that we measure the homogeneity of a polling station as the standard deviation of its

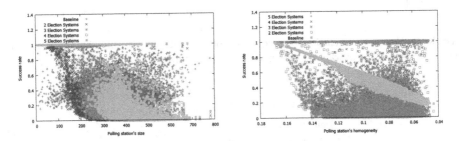

Fig. 2. Results for the safe phase, showing the success rate as a function of the size (left) and the party (right), when extracting each voter's party.

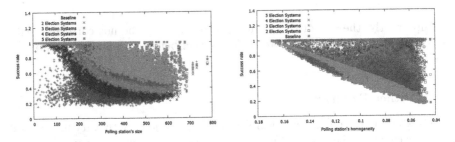

Fig. 3. Results for the unsafe phase, showing the success rate as a function of the size (left) and the party (right), when extracting each voter's party.

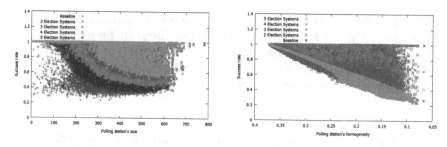

Fig. 4. Results for the unsafe phase, showing the success rate as a function of the size (left) and the political group (right), when extracting each voter's political group.

normalized tally.) Specifically, it seems that the more homogeneous the polling station is, the better the attack performs. Interestingly, the correlation is decreasing as we consider more election cycles.

The opposing trends of these correlations suggest that, as the number of considered election cycles grow, the importance of the homogeneity decreases in favor of the size of the polling station which becomes more prominent.

For validation, the Pearson correlation between the polling station's size and the success rate, and the polling station's homogeneity and the success rate, are given in Tables 2 and 3 when considering the safe phase, the unsafe phase when the exact party is extracted, and the unsafe phase when the political group is extracted.

Table 2. Pearson correlation between the polling station's size and homogeneity to the success rate for extracting the exact party of voters, using the safe phase.

	Size	Homogeneity
2 election cycles	−0.56	0.29
3 election cycles	−0.70	0.17
4 election cycles	−0.76	0.09
5 election cycles	−0.76	0.01

Importantly, the size of the polling station seems to be not correlated with its homogeneity (in fact, the Pearson correlation between these two variables is as low as 0.04).

4.3   Further Experiments

In this section, we report on results of our simulations with varying interval times for counting the ballots. Specifically, the results from the previous section were for $T = 30$, corresponding (for almost all polling stations) to counting the ballots once in half an hour. Next, in Table 4, we report the average success rate

Table 3. Pearson correlation between the polling station's size and homogeneity to the success rate for extracting the exact party of voters and the political group, using the unsafe phase. Each cell contains two numbers, the first of which corresponds to the exact party while the second corresponds to the political group.

	Size	Homogeneity
2 election cycles	−0.64, −0.36	0.57, 0.81
3 election cycles	−0.81, −0.62	0.30, 0.56
4 election cycles	−0.83, −0.70	0.16, 0.38
5 election cycles	−0.80, −0.70	0.05, 0.27

of the attack (over the polling stations) for $T = 15$ and $T = 7$, corresponding (for almost all polling stations) to counting the ballots once in an hour and once in two hours.

Table 4. Average success rate of the attack, for extracting the exact party that the voters voted for, and the political group that the voters belong to, for $T = 15$ and $T = 7$, that is, when counting 15 times a day and 7 times a day.

Election cycles	Safe phase	Unsafe phase, party	Unsafe phase, group
	$T = 15, T = 7$	$T = 15, T = 7$	$T = 15, T = 7$
3	3%, 0.6%	41%, 30%	55%, 46%
4	5%, 0.9%	47%, 33%	60%, 49%
5	7%, 1.2%	53%, 36%	65%, 51%
6	9%, 1.4%	59%, 38%	69%, 53%
7	12%, 1.6%	63%, 41%	72%, 54%

5   Discussion

In this section, we begin by briefly discussing various methods for counting the ballots and the time intervals by which an adversary is able to perform those counts. We continue by discussing some consequences of our research. Then, we discuss countermeasures which can be taken in order to guard the system against attacks as the one described in this paper. Finally, we discuss possible ways of extending our attack when we allow voters to change their minds between election cycles.

5.1   Counting the Ballots

The question of how exactly to count the ballots is somehow beyond the scope of the current paper, however, we do mention some methods bellow, which seem to be sufficient for our needs. As examples, one might use accurate weight scales; one might use laser-based measurement equipment; or one might use banknote counters.

Notice that, during election day, members of the polling station committee are allowed, and encouraged, to go behind the curtains once in a while to check that all parties have sufficient ballots.

We remark also that there is no need for a nation-wide systematic attack, as the polling stations are independent of each other, and it is sufficient to perform the attack on each polling station on its own, thus allowing to focus the efforts on high priority polling stations.

5.2   Putting the Results in Context

We now give examples for countries where a similar voting system is being used and discuss possible consequences in their context.

Our first example is Algeria [13] where the young democracy is still struggling with conducting free elections. During the elections there have been numerous reports about voting-related violence and it is not unreasonable to believe that voting for the "wrong" candidate may put someone under physical danger.

Even in less extreme cases such as Israel, there may be unwanted repercussions such as government-led investments made to prefer some voters over others. This has been more prominent in the early years of Israel, where better rations where given to members of Mapai, the ruling party at the time. Such blunt favoritism has been long abolished now but even today the phenomenon of voting-contractors still exists; a voting-contractor is a person having the power to tell a large group of people how to vote. The power of a voting-contractor is determined by the number of people they can enlist. It is very hard nowadays for a party to contest without soliciting such voting-contractors and this activity is not even being conducted in secret anymore.

Finally, even in countries where the government is unlikely to act dubiously such as Sweden [5] there may still be social consequences for not voting as everybody else in the village. Finally, we mention Spain [12] and France [8] as two further countries where similar voting systems are used.

5.3   Countermeasures

In this section, we briefly present possible countermeasures for the attack. The most obvious countermeasure is switching to cryptographically secure voting systems. Such systems are not only better understood than traditional ones, but they also allow to quantify the security loss in various scenarios.

Should a paper based system is still desired, we note that the weakness of the system comes from the fact that the stack of tickets available to the voters "remembers" all previous choices. This weakness can be avoided by changing the ballot to a one that requires the voter to choose an item from a closed list printed beforehand; consider, for example, the ballots used in most countries of the EU. An additional advantage of such a ballot is that it allows the voters to rely a more complex decision (for example, reordering the members of the list as done in Europe, or moving the vote to another party as done in Australia).

Another improvement that can be introduced into the system is to not allow any information to leave the polling station. The current law in Israel already disallows any form of radio communication. Extending the law to prevent any transfer of information but the tally outside the polling station (both during and after the elections), would make processing such information illegal for third parties, moving our attack from the "gray area" to the black.

Finally, as the obligation to conduct fair elections is the role of the government, it may be useful to develop a mathematical model that will take both heterogeneity and polling stations' sizes to help decision makers to reassign voters to voting precincts.

5.4   Allowing Voters to Switch Parties Between Election Cycles

The whole purpose of holding elections is to allow people to change the composition of the governing bodies. The reason we assume that voters do not change their behavior is made for the sake of simplicity. We can loosen this restriction completely and allow each voter to choose the party she votes for in every election cycle, even uniformly at random. This would be, however, too extreme, since most voters do not tend to change their viewpoints dramatically between election cycles.

Intuitively, in a multi-partied system, a voter who voted for party p in one elections cycle will probably vote for a party ideologically close to p in the successive cycles. There is actually some concrete evidence supporting the above intuition, as we discuss next.

Indeed, by analyzing election surveys provided by the *Israel National Election Studies* [2,19], we found out that roughly 50% of the voters did not change their vote between the 2009 and the 2013 elections (this number becomes roughly 60% if we count the successor of a party as not necessarily the one which inherited its name, but the one which is ideologically closest[8].

Moreover, when groups of parties are being considered, the change is insignificant. In fact, the change in the political map between the 2015 and the 2013 elections was that only a one seat (corresponding to 0.83% of the elected seats) moved between the groups. These numbers mean that we can simply run our attack without accounting for voters which change their minds, and we expect to preserve a fairly high success rate. Moreover, one could take such information into account; we next discuss one possible way of doing so.

In our attack, instead of computing the likelihood of each voter to vote for a specific party in all election cycles, we can compute the likelihood of each voter

---

[8] Due to the somewhat unstable political system of Israel, a large amount of people cannot find their political home in any of the existing parties, and tend to vote in every elections cycle to a newly "trending" party. Moreover, parties often split, merge, or change their names.

to vote for a list of different parties (one element per each election cycle); then, given the information encoded in the transition matrices, we can multiply each likelihood by the 'global' likelihood of such a vote.

We were not able to perform simulations for such scenarios since we do not have the real votes of voters across election cycles. That is, while we have the tallies for each election cycle, we can not infer the real turnover, i.e., which votes correspond to which voters in different election systems.

6   Conclusion and Future Work

Free elections are an essential element in modern liberal democracies. In this paper, we presented a way to attack the Israeli voting system (as well as several other similar systems), showing that it is possible to recover the votes of voters in this system. Specifically, this is possible using a very small amount of additional public information, which includes the results of the elections, the time of vote per voter, and a periodical count of the ballots from the tray.

We would like to end with some ideas for future research and extensions of this attack. First, since the attack assigns voters to the parties they voted for, it sounds reasonable that, using flow techniques (which are successfully being used for assignment problems), we might improve the success rate of the attack. Second, since the safe phase of the attack is based on evaluating constraints on the possible parties for which each voter might have voted for, it sounds reasonable that using constraint satisfaction techniques might improve the success rate of the attack.

Acknowledgment. The authors would like to thank Aviad Stier for bringing into our attention the fact that the parties collect the time of vote of all voters, Adv. Jonathan J. Klinger for assisting us with our petition to the Israeli general elections committee, Amihai Bannett for permitting us to use hit photos in this paper and in a poster that presented preliminary results of this work [3]. We thank Dubi Kanengisser for pointing us to good resources in the field of political studies. Special thanks are to colleagues with which the authors discussed this research, specifically to Gustavo Mesch, Claudia Diaz, Tamar Zondiner, Yair Goldberg, Atul Luykx, Alan Szepieniec, Shir Peled, as well as to the anonymous referees.

The first author was partially supported by the Research Fund KU Leuven, OT/13/071 and by European Union's Horizon 2020 research and innovation programme under grant agreement No. 644052 HECTOR and grant agreement No. H2020-MSCA-ITN-2014-643161 ECRYPT-NET. The second author was supported in part by the Israeli Science Foundation through grant No. 827/12 and by the Commission of the European Communities through the Horizon 2020 program under project number 645622 PQCRYPTO. The third author is supported by a postdoctoral fellowship from I-CORE ALGO.

References

1. Agrawal, D., Kesdogan, D.: Measuring anonymity: the disclosure attack. IEEE Secur. Priv. **1**(6), 27–34 (2003)
2. Arian, A., Shamir, M.: The 2009 Israel National Elections Data (2009). http://www.ines.tau.ac.il/2009.html
3. Ashur, T., Dunkelman, O.: On the anonymity of Israel's general elections. In: Sadeghi, A.-R., Gligor, V.D., Yung, M. (eds.) 2013 ACM SIGSAC Conference on Computer and Communications Security, CCS 2013, Berlin, Germany, 4–8 November 2013, pp. 1399–1402. ACM, New York (2013)
4. Basic Law. The Knesset - 1958. https://www.knesset.gov.il/laws/special/eng/basic2_eng.htm
5. Nyman, B.: Valsedlar För Europaparlamentet 2009. https://commons.wikimedia.org/wiki/Category:Ballot_papers_in_Sweden#mediaviewer/File:Valsedlar_Europaparlamentet_2009.jpg
6. Bernhard, D., Cortier, V., Pereira, O., Warinschi, B.: Measuring vote privacy, revisited. In: Proceedings of the 2012 ACM Conference on Computer and Communications Security, pp. 941–952. ACM (2012)
7. Chaum, D.: Untraceable electronic mail, return addresses, and digital pseudonyms. Commun. ACM **24**(2), 84–88 (1981)
8. Claude Truong-Ngoc. France Présidentielles 6 Mai 2012 Bulletins de Vote Second Tour. https://commons.wikimedia.org/wiki/File:France_%C3%A9lections_pr%C3%A9sidentielles_6_mai_2012_bulletins_de_vote_second_tour.JPG
9. The Inter-Parliamentary Council. Declaration on criteria for free and fair elections. Unanimously adopted by the Inter-Parliamentary Council at its 154th session, March 1994. http://www.ipu.org/cnl-e/154-free.htm
10. Danezis, G.: Statistical disclosure attacks. In: Gritzalis, D., Capitani di Vimercati, S., Samarati, P., Katsikas, S. (eds.) SEC 2003. IFIP, vol. 122, pp. 421–426. Springer, Heidelberg (2003). doi:10.1007/978-0-387-35691-4_40
11. Delaune, S., Kremer, S., Ryan, M.: Verifying privacy-type properties of electronic voting protocols: a taster. In: Chaum, D., Jakobsson, M., Rivest, R.L., Ryan, P.Y.A., Benaloh, J., Kutylowski, M., Adida, B. (eds.) Towards Trustworthy Elections. LNCS, vol. 6000, pp. 289–309. Springer, Heidelberg (2010). doi:10.1007/978-3-642-12980-3_18
12. Correo, E.: Las Papeletas de Bildu, Protagonistas de la Jornada de Reflexión. http://www.elcorreo.com/especiales/elecciones/vizcaya/2011/noticias/papeletas-bildu-protagonistas-jornada-201105211924.html
13. Facebook TV. Le président algérien Abdelaziz Bouteflika Élections en Algérie 17 Avril 2014. https://www.youtube.com/watch?v=FXVXtIdTz7w&t=1m07s
14. Kesdogan, D., Agrawal, D., Penz, S.: Limits of anonymity in open environments. Inf. Hiding, 53–69 (2002)
15. Kesdogan, D., Pimenidis, L.: The hitting set attack on anonymity protocols. Inf. Hiding, 326–339 (2004)
16. Küsters, R., Truderung, T., Vogt, A.: A game-based definition of coercion-resistance and its applications. In: 2010 23rd IEEE Computer Security Foundations Symposium, pp. 122–136. IEEE (2010)
17. Küsters, R., Truderung, T., Vogt, A.: Verifiability, privacy, and coercion-resistance: new insights from a case study. In: 2011 IEEE Symposium on Security and Privacy (SP), pp. 538–553. IEEE (2011)

18. Tianbo, L., Yao, P., Zhao, L., Li, Y., Xie, F., Xia, Y.: Towards attacks and defenses of anonymous communication systems. Int. J. Secur. Appl. **9**(1), 313–328 (2015)
19. Shamir, M.: The 2013 Israel National Elections Data (2013). http://www.ines.tau.ac.il/2013.html
20. The Central Elections Committee. Final Results of the Vote to the 19th Knesset, January 2013. http://www.votes-19.gov.il/nationalresults
21. The Knesset. Knesset Elections Law (1969). http://www.knesset.gov.il/elections16/heb/laws/elections/law.htm (Hebrew)
22. Troncoso, C., Gierlichs, B., Preneel, B., Verbauwhede, I.: Perfect matching disclosure attacks. Priv. Enhanc. Technol., 2–23 (2008)

Apollo – End-to-End Verifiable Internet Voting with Recovery from Vote Manipulation

Dawid Gaweł[2], Maciej Kosarzecki[2], Poorvi L. Vora[1], Hua Wu[1], and Filip Zagórski[2(✉)]

[1] Department of Computer Science, The George Washington University, Washington, D.C., USA
[2] Department of Computer Science, Wroclaw University of Science and Technology, Wrocław, Poland
filip.zagorski@pwr.edu.pl

Abstract. We present security vulnerabilities in the remote voting system Helios. We propose Apollo, a modified version of Helios, which addresses these vulnerabilities and could improve the feasibility of internet voting.

In particular, we note that Apollo does not possess Helios' major known vulnerability, where a dishonest voting terminal can change the vote after it obtains the voter's credential. With Apollo-lite, votes not authorized by the voter are detected by the public and prevented from being included in the tally.

The full version of Apollo enables a voter to prove that her vote was changed. We also describe a very simple protocol for the voter to interact with any devices she employs to check on the voting system, to enable frequent and easy auditing of encryptions and checking of the bulletin board.

1 Introduction

With the perceived security of internet banking and electronic commerce, there has been a lot of interest in voting on the internet. The internet voting system Helios is a prominent end-to-end verifiable (E2E-V) system that has been used for multiple non-governmental elections. In this paper we present attacks to the Helios voting system and propose voting protocol Apollo to address these.

Attempts at voting on the internet in governmental elections have been demonstrated to be vulnerable to client-and/or-server-side adversaries [13,15, 23,25]. An E2E-V system would allow the detection of such attacks. However, the E2E-V property, while necessary, is not sufficient for secure elections. For example, a voting terminal may behave honestly throughout the E2E-V voting protocol, until the voter enters her credential. The terminal could then cast a

This material is based upon work supported in part by the Maryland Procurement Office under contract H98230-14-C-0127 and NSF Award CNS 1421373.

Authors were partially supported by Polish National Science Centre contract number DEC-2013/09/D/ST6/03927.

© Springer International Publishing AG 2017
R. Krimmer et al. (Eds.): E-Vote-ID 2016, LNCS 10141, pp. 125–143, 2017.
DOI: 10.1007/978-3-319-52240-1_8

vote of its choice. Or the election server could replace the vote with another one. An alert voter will notice that there is a problem and may complain; however, she has no evidence to back her complaint. It is well-known that Helios possesses this vulnerability. The inability to resolve multiple such three-way disputes among the voter, her terminal and the election server could result in undesirable uncertainty about an election outcome. Additionally, while voters can audit encryptions and check the bulletin board for the correct vote encryption, it is well-known that they rarely do so. In the 2009 elections of the City of Takoma Park, MD, fewer than 4% of cast ballots were subject to the voter verification [7]. A recent study [20] examined the frequency and conditions under which voters check their receipts, reporting that only about 7.5% of voters performed receipt checks (and just 0.5% filed a dispute when shown an incorrect receipt).

Benaloh's SVE. Benaloh's *Simple Verifiable Elections (SVE)* protocol [3] for in-person voting enables the voter to detect a dishonest terminal (voting machine). After the voter tells the machine her choice, the machine prints an encryption of the choice on a piece of paper. The voter can either take the printout and cast it as her ballot or she can challenge the printed encryption. In the second case, the machine reveals (prints) the randomness used for the encryption; the voter can use another computer, or many computers, she trusts to check that the printed string is indeed an encryption of her vote. In this way, the voter is able check if the voting machine cheats while encrypting votes. One implementation of this protocol is the STAR-Vote system [4].

Helios. The Helios [1] protocol is an online voting protocol inspired by *SVE*. The role of the machine in *SVE* is played by the voter's web browser in Helios. After the voter communicates her choices, the browser encrypts it and displays a commitment to the ballot encryption (called a *ballot tracker*), which plays the role of the printed encryption in *SVE*. The voter chooses whether to audit or cast the encrypted votes. If she audits, the randomness used for encryption is displayed. Else she authenticates herself and the browser sends the encrypted ballot to the server, which performs a verifiable tally of all encrypted ballots sent in with valid credentials.

1.1   Our Contributions

Our contributions are as follow: we present a set of vulnerabilities we discovered in the Helios code (Cross-Site Scripting, Cross-Site Request Forgery and other attacks); we have informed Helios developers about our findings and the currently available version is patched. The main contribution is a voting protocol Apollo which addresses some of the problems with Helios. In addition Apollo explicitly describes an auditing protocol to be used by the voter's computational voting assistant(s), allowing the voter to focus only on checking what the voting assistant says and whether multiple voting assistants agree.

Apollo as an Extension of Helios. Apollo uses the same approach for verification as *SVE*. In contrast with Helios, a machine commits to the ballot encryption on the public bulletin board instead of on the machine's screen. This change has positive security consequences. The posting of the encryption on the bulletin board does not imply that all information necessary to check an audited ballot is also on the bulletin board. We describe a protocol for auditing the vote and checking the bulletin board which allows the voter to choose who obtains this information. This allows the voter to protect not only her true vote, but also the audited vote, which is not displayed on the bulletin board.

The voter is encouraged to use *voting assistants* (*e.g.,* tablet, smart watch, phone) that enable her to check if the voting terminal is behaving honestly. If a voter chooses not to use any voting assistants, her voting experience is exactly the same as in the original Helios system, but she is still better protected than in the original Helios. Additionally, if a voter chooses to use one or more voting assistants, we present a real-time protocol for auditing and checking. We have attempted to keep the voter experience as simple as appears possible for these tasks. If the voter uses a single voting assistant, she needs to only check what the voting assistant says. If she uses multiple assistants, she needs to additionally check if they agree. The insertion of all voter tasks into the voting process, in a minimal fashion will, we hope, increase the frequency and ease of the audits and checks, improving the overall confidence in the election outcome. An experimental study of the usability of the protocol is outside the scope of this paper.

In contrast with the single casting credential used by each Helios voter, an Apollo voter is issued multiple credentials: multiple *casting codes* to change a vote if an incorrect one is posted, and a *lock-in code* allowing the voter to communicate to the public that she believes her vote is correctly represented on the bulletin board (similarly to Remotegrity [26]).

Apollo: Assumptions and Properties. We present two versions of Apollo that address the problems of credential stealing and the attacks described above. Like Helios and all other E2E-V systems, both versions assume a secure bulletin board with authenticated append-only write access and public read access. Both versions explicitly address the audit process as carried out by one or more voting assistants, making it part of the main protocol.

- Making the same assumptions as Helios—of an honest credential authority and a second channel for electronic delivery of credentials—Apollo-lite prevents the inclusion of votes not authorized by the voter by enabling public detection of the problem.
- When an honest registrar may not be assumed, the full version of Apollo allows an incorrect vote to be counted only if the registrar has been dishonest. It enables the voter to prove that she did not cast it. The full version requires that the voter have the ability to provide a final irrepudiable instruction; this can be achieved through the use of scratch-off authentication cards as with

Remotegrity [26], or a special computational device trusted only to digitally sign a single instruction, such as described in [14].

While a rigorous demonstration of the above properties is outside the scope of this paper, we provide a non-rigorous security analysis with respect to common attacks in the paper.

We assume that the voter has access to at least one honest terminal and that there are at most $k-1$ dishonest terminals. When the assumption regarding terminals is not met, the voter encounters a denial of service attack; unlike in Helios, when her vote may be replaced. A denial of service attack may be targeted towards a particular vote or type of voter, preventing the casting of a particular type of vote. However, the voter can prove that her vote is not among those being counted. She can then obtain the opportunity to cast a vote using another channel, such as the postal mail system or in-person voting. Note that any system which receives the plaintext vote is capable of launching a targeted DoS attack of this sort. While coded voting can make targeted DoS harder, coded voting protocols pose usability challenges. Further, a voting terminal, especially one the voter uses for other purposes as well, might be able to profile a voter and guess her vote with considerable accuracy without seeing it.

We assume that at least one of the voting assistants is honest. The assumption of a less powerful adversary (e.g., a majority of the assistants is honest) results in a small modification of the audit protocol. Note that any E2E system used by human voters will need to make an assumption about the computer(s) used to check the audits and/or the bulletin board.

1.2   Organization of This Paper

Section 2 presents related work in remote voting systems, Sect. 3 presents the Apollo protocol, Sect. 4 its security properties, Sect. 5 the vulnerabilities in Helios code and Sect. 6 our conclusions.

2   Related Work

The Helios voting system [1] has been used in several binding elections, including those for office in the ACM and IACR. Main attacks on the system include those that exploit client-side vulnerabilities [11,16] and those where two voters are issued the same receipt ("clash attacks") [19].

To protect against the attacks described in [11,16], a modification of Helios [21] presents to the voter a QR-code with which a mobile application can check whether the ballot is correctly encrypted. But the app does not checke if a ballot is correctly posted.

The idea behind clash attacks [19] on end-to-end verifiable schemes is that an attacker provides two distinct voters with the same cryptographic receipt and casts an additional vote. As described in [19], the original version of Helios—where the name of the voter is published next to her ballot—is immune to the clash attack. However, the variant of Helios proposed in [2] (and used in, for example, IACR elections)—where voters obtain aliases from the election authority in a registration phase—is vulnerable. The browser (Helios client), the bulletin board and the authority in charge of issuing aliases to voters need to collude to carry out the attack.

Online voting using the Smartmatic voting system in the state of Utah to choose the Republican nominee for the Presidential election in the US drew considerable attention recently (the website providing information on the voting process is no longer available). From the information provided, and in the absence of any ability to audit the tally, the system is vulnerable to client and server side attacks.

New South Wales, Australia, used iVote in 2015. iVote was demonstrably vulnerable to attacks on the server side, and to clientside attacks when the voter either did not verify her vote, or was misdirected about where to verify her vote [15].

The Estonian internet voting system is vulnerable to several attacks [23], including client-side attacks that change the ballot without being noticed during the voting phase. The voter will notice the malfunction or cheating if she decides to verify the ballot, but she is not able to prove there is a problem. The system also possesses several server-side vulnerabilities.

The internet voting pilot in Washington, DC, did not provide any means for the voter to verify any aspect of the election, and was demonstrated to be vulnerable to server-side attacks [25].

The Norwegian internet voting system used in 2011 [13] has the voter using a computer to encrypt the vote, and receiving a receipt from the receipt generator. Voter verification requires trusting the receipt generator, and there is no evidence released to enable the public verification of tally correctness.

3   Apollo

In this section we present Apollo, which provides evidence of vote manipulation that can be verified by a third party.

3.1   Participants and Threat Model

We first explain the Apollo contribution in the context of the Helios threat model, which is also standard for other E2E-V voting protocols and systems. We term this the threat model for Apollo-lite, or the *lite threat model*. All except the last assumption below are also assumptions made by Helios.

- The voter, V, is a human and is able to:
  - read and compare short strings;
  - choose a candidate to vote for;
  - choose at random whether to cast or audit an encryption (Benaloh's challenge);

- choose a random short string (this is required to secure the protocol against clash-attacks, but low-entropy strings are sufficient—selected strings need to be unique only across voting sessions active at that time). V need not be honest. In particular, V may make false complaints.
- An honest registrar, R, issues valid credentials, which are securely delivered to the voter through a channel that is not accessible to the voting terminal. The registrar does not share a voter's credentials with anyone other than the voter, and correctly identifies all purported credentials as being valid or not during and after the election, as necessary.
- A secure bulletin board—with append-only-authenticated-write and public-read access—is available to all participants.
- The voting terminal (including any software on it, referred to as *Voting Booth* (*VB*) in Helios) and the election authority (*EA*) (including servers and election officials, any software deployed by the election authority) are not assumed honest for the integrity properties, and may collude. This assumption takes into account the possibility of implementation vulnerabilities (like those described in Sect. 5).
- The protocol is not expected to provide privacy of the vote with respect to *VB* or *EA*, but the *EA* may be split to provide some privacy.
- The voter may have access to one computational device other than the voting terminal (we refer to such a device as a voting assistant, *VA*) which helps her check on *VB* and *EA*. This device should not learn the vote.
- The voter may have access to n such devices, denoted $VA_1, VA_2, \ldots, VA_n$, which she uses to make the checks required by the protocol. The probability with which she makes an incorrect estimate of the correctness of a check using these devices is small. We explicitly include multiple devices here to allow for the possibility of dishonest devices, though our protocol works for $n = 1$.

The full version of the Apollo protocol assumes a threat model exactly like the above, except R may share valid credentials with an adversary, or try to use them to cast a vote. We term this the *full threat model*.

3.2 Voter Experience

In this section we present the voter experience.

Credentials: V receives her credentials from R: a set of k *casting codes* and a *lock-in code*.

Pre-Voting Phase: Before beginning the voting session, V chooses n voting assistants $VA_1, VA_2, \ldots VA_n$. She chooses n based on the maximum acceptable probability of not detecting a cheating *EA* or *VB*. If she chooses $n = 0$, her ability to detect cheating will be limited (just as in the case of Helios)[1].

Role of Voting Assistants: After each protocol step, each *VA* checks *BB* and provides feedback to V. If V is satisfied with the outcome of the check, she moves

---

[1] Apollo is designed so that the terminal cannot tell whether $n = 0$ or $n > 0$.

to the next step. *V* may choose to require that a majority of the *VA* present the same information, or she may require that they all do, or she may choose another rule to determine whether the check demonstrates a problem. If she determines that there is a problem, she should immediately abort the protocol, change the computer running *VB* and try to vote again. She should always (reuse) an old credential unless she hears back from the *EA* that it has been used.

Voting Phase:

1. *V* opens the voting application on *VB*, which asks her to provide a short string for the session title. She enters the string. *VB* displays the (voting) session ID and a *QR*-code. *BB* displays the (voting) session ID, see Fig. 1 and Step 5 on Fig. 2.

2. *V* scans the *QR*-code into all the other voting assistants, and checks that they display the session ID and Title is displayed on *VB* (step 8 on Fig. 2).

Fig. 1. Voter initializes session

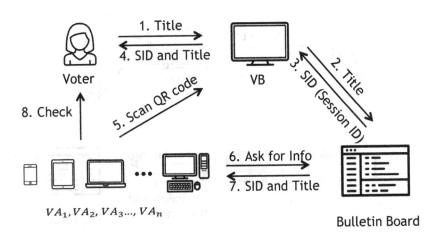

Fig. 2. Voting assistants check bulletin board and inform a voter about the SID and the title.

3. *V* enters a vote for candidate *X*. *BB* displays the encrypted vote and *VB* and each *VA* inform her that the encrypted vote is displayed, and she should now enter an audit or cast request (see Fig. 3).

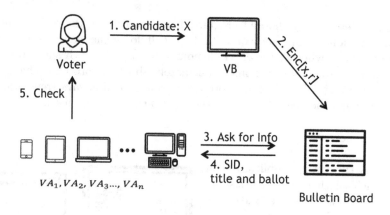

Fig. 3. Encryption is posted

4. If the voter enters a cast code, each VA displays the code she entered and informs her that her vote is ready for locking.
5. If the voter enters an audit request, each VA informs her that the encrypted string has been audited and shows a vote for candidate X (see Fig. 4). The voter may repeat the audit step as many times as she wishes.

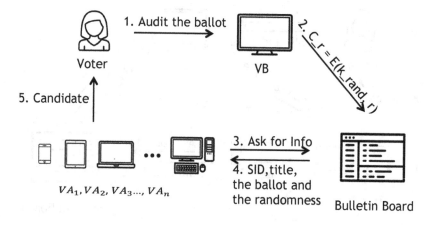

Fig. 4. Voter chooses to audit the vote

Lock-in Phase. The voter may return at any time to lock-in her vote, and she may do so from any computer by identifying her session ID and adding her lock-in code (see Fig. 5). She may check that the code has been posted, again, from any (other) computer.

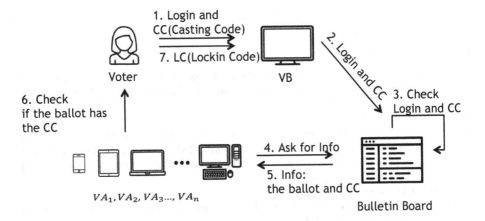

Fig. 5. Voter chooses to cast the vote

3.3   Informal Protocol Description

All interactions among voting assistants and the voting system are digitally signed and posted on the BB. The voter may only post instructions on the BB through a voting assistant. The protocol proceeds as follows.

V interacts with VB to generate an encrypted ballot; this ballot is posted on BB. VB displays a QR-code containing a session ID and a session symmetric key, and a human-readable version of session ID. The voter scans the QR-code onto all n VAs, which each display the session ID. The voter compares it with the one on VB.

Each VA checks BB and indicates to V whether a string is posted for the session. Once V is satisfied that it is, she enters a cast code or audit instruction into VB, which is posted on the BB.

If the code is a cast code, the registrar signs the encrypted ballot with the signing key for cast ballots and posts it on the BB. Each VA checks BB and displays the cast code posted for the session, as well as the fact that a signed encrypted ballot has been posted against the cast code which has been accepted as valid by the registrar. The voting session ends. When a voting session ends with the submission of a cast code accepted as valid, a confirmation email containing: sessionID, session title, cast code and a list of identifiers of audited and cast ballots (together with time stamps of arrival) is sent to V.

If the code is an audit code, VB opens the encryption by posting the randomness encrypted with the session key. Each VA checks BB and displays the plaintext value. V may repeat this audit process as often as she wishes.

After casting her vote and receiving the conformation email, if V is satisfied, she supplies the lock code from any computer by using the session ID. She should then check that it has been correctly posted, from any (other) computer. If not, she attempts to lock-in again.

All locked votes are tallied in a verifiable manner.

The Apollo casting and lock-in procedures are described in detail in Protocol 1.1.

Apollo: casting

1. *VB* generates a key pair, publishes this on *BB* before the voting session begins.
2. *V* initiates the voting session on *VB*, and is asked to enter a short string, *MyTitle*.
3. *VB* displays:
   (a) A qr-code which contains: k_{rand} (a secret key for symmetric encryption), *sessionID* (a string with *MyTitle* appended), signed with its key. This qr-code is intended as communication between *VB* and any *VAs* the voter chooses; it may be stored and/or printed.
   (b) Human-readable *sessionID*
4. *V* checks that *MyString* forms the last part of *sessionID*. She scans the qr-code with multiple *VAs*.
5. *VAs* check the *BB* and look for the *sessionID*, obtain the public key of *VB*, display *sessionID*.
6. *V* verifies whether *sessionID* presented by *VB* and *VAs* is the same.
7. *V* sends vote choices to *VB*: $V \xrightarrow{x} VB$
8. *VB* does the following:
   (a) computes the encryption of the ballot: $c \leftarrow \mathsf{Enc}(x, r)$, where r is the randomness used during encryption,
   (b) sends the encrypted vote to *BB*: $VB \xrightarrow{c} BB$
9. *VAs* inform the voter that c is posted on *BB* in the transcript of her *sessionID*
10. *V* makes a decision about cast/audit:
    Audit is selected:
    (a) *VB* sends randomness $c_r = E(k_{rand}, r)$ used for encrypting c to *BB*
    (b) The *VAs* decrypt c_r and present the vote x' to *V*
    (c) *V* accepts or not based on what the other *VAs* say the vote decrypted to:
    $x = x'$ Prepares new encryption; goto step (7).
    $x \neq x'$ Begins again with new *VB* and, if necessary, *VAs*
    Cast is selected:
    (a) *V* is asked to enter: *Login* and *CastCode* (these can be combined to be a single long string)
    (b) *VAs* display the *Login/CastCode* pair; *V* checks if they are as expected.

Apollo: lock-in

1. *V* chooses a terminal and accesses the election website.
2. *V* enters her *sessionID* and lock-in code.
3. *V* checks *BB* from another terminal. If *V* does not see the lock-in code, she attempts to lock-in again.

Protocol 1.1. The casting and lock-in procedures for Apollo.

4   Security Analysis

In this section, we analyze the security properties of Apollo with respect to common attacks.

4.1   Privacy

In Apollo, voters may lose ballot privacy through information that is (a) posted to the bulletin board, (b) provided to the voting terminal, (c) obtained by the voting assistants.

Bulletin Board (BB). Apollo uses two different encryption schemes for posting vote-related information on the bulletin board: an asymmetric-key encryption scheme for encrypting ballots (*e.g.*, the same scheme as in Helios) and a symmetric-key encryption scheme for encrypting randomness. We follow a series of works [2,5,6,9] suggesting the correct choice of ballot encryption and ZKP-proofs, so that these do not leak the vote to the public; the symmetric-key encryption proposed for use is the authenticated mode of operation of AES.

The privacy of data on the bulletin board thus depends on the security of the symmetric and asymmetric-key encryption schemes used, which depends on the splitting of the EA into trustees (there is no privacy with respect to the combined EA), on the secrecy of the keys of trustees and on whether the collusion among trustees is within the limits of the secret-sharing scheme used.

Note here that the public does not learn the audited vote as the encryption randomness is not posted in the clear when the vote is audited. Through the qr-code, the voter controls the VAs with access to the symmetric-key used to encrypt the encryption randomness.

Voting Booth (VB). VB is the only party of the system that directly learns the voter's choice. It also knows the randomness that is used to encrypt the ballot. VB may reveal the vote to anyone; with the presented version of Apollo, as with Helios, this is inevitable.

Voting Assistant (VA). If we assume that the cast and audited votes are independent, any VA used by the voter learns nothing about the cast vote, because it gets all its information about it from the BB. It learns only the audited votes.

4.2   Integrity

We define three levels of security with respect to different attacks.

Level 1 E2E-V – the voter is able to detect an attack (but cannot prove it to a third party),

Level 2 Evidence of an attack – the voter is able to detect an attack and prove that the attack took place.

Level 3 Recovery: the voter is able to prevent or recover from the attack.

Level 1 corresponds to the end-to-end verifiability approach – the voter can detect that some of her directions were not followed but is unable to transfer this knowledge to a third party.

Level 2 lets the voter detect an attack and provide evidence to a third party that the protocol was not followed. We would like to say that this level corresponds to dispute-resolution [17, 22] or accountability [18] but in the Internet voting setting it is almost impossible to assign blame. For many attacks, it may not be possible to determine whether they result from a dishonest election server or a malicious terminal, which is malicious because of a flaw in the lower-level library (like TLS/SSL allowing an attacker to subvert a terminal's code).

With Apollo, an adversary attempting to change a vote would have to do so before it was locked-in, in which case the voter would not lock it. If a dishonest voting system attempts to count a vote that is not locked-in, this will be detected by the public, and there is evidence (a non-locked-in-vote that is tallied) that the protocol was not followed. There is no other way to include a vote in the tally that is not authorized by the voter. Any errors in the vote tallying process also result in evidence through the tally-correctness proof.

There is always the question of what to do when one discovers that a voting system was the subject of a successful attack during the election (rerunning the election may be difficult, costly or impossible). When a system allows voters not only to detect that the protocol was not followed but also to recover from the "error" we obtain a robust, Level-3 solution. In the case of Apollo, a non-locked-in vote is not final, and can be replaced by the voter using another channel, perhaps by voting in person. Errors in the tally process can only be recovered from if the tallying server(s) cooperate.

4.3 Terminal Misbehaviour

Changing the Vote. Benaloh's challenge protects the voter from *VB*'s attempts to change the vote before she submits her credentials. By itself, as implemented in Helios, it provides Level-1 security against *VB* stealing her credentials to cast another vote.

Stealing Credentials. In Apollo, too, *VB* may attempt to steal the credential (cast code) and post it against a new encryption of its own, either within the same voting session, or in a new session it begins for this purpose.

In the first case, if the voter is using a *VA*, it will inform her of a new encryption posted in her session, and of it being cast. If the voter does not use any *VAs*, she can detect that more encryptions were posted within her session by checking the bulletin board or by checking the confirmation email.

In the second case, if she is using a *VA*, it will not report the correct posting of the cast code. Additionally, the voter will not receive a confirmation email, and the *BB* will not display a successful cast vote, both of which can be detected without the use of a *VA*.

Thus, in either case, whether she uses a *VA* or not, she will notice that the cast session is not successful. She will then use a new terminal and new *VAs* if so indicated (maybe if they don't agree on the outcomes of the checks) to start the voting process again. She should use the same cast code, in general, (in case it was not used by the terminal). If it is rejected because it was used by the malicious previous terminal, she should then use a new cast code.

The voter's ability to successfully complete the cast session is limited by the number of cast codes issued. However, unlike Helios, the lack of access to an honest terminal results in a denial of service and not a change of vote.

4.4 Clash-Attack Resistance

Because voters choose part of the session ID of their own sessions and it is displayed by the VAs, each voter is able to detect the situation when two terminals attempt to generate the same receipt for her and another voter. While the quality of randomness used by voters to generate a session-title can be poor, this should be sufficient to protect against clash attacks that need to happen at about the same time (during the active voting session) when voters are using VAs. This helps protect those voters who do not use VAs as well, because VB does not know if a voter is using a VA or not.

A clash attack can be successful only when: (a) (at least) two voters, who begin their voting sessions at about the same time, pick the same session title (while their terminals collude) and (b) the voter who enters her *cast code* later does not notice that it was not correctly displayed on her VA.

From the birthday paradox the probability of such an event is $\geq 1/2$ when at least $\sqrt{2^l}$ voters start their sessions "at the same time" and l is min-entropy for their session-titles. It hence depends on the size of the alphabet and the length of the session-title (and the ability of voters to compare strings).

Even voters who do not use voting assistants are able to detect the attack by checking session titles and cast codes, and/or by verifying if the(signed) confirmation email contains the correct information.

4.5 Credential Distribution

Apollo does not restrict the format of credentials. Here we describe the security benefits of using ways of distributing credentials other than by email (which is the default in Helios).

Credentials in the form of printed codes hidden under a scratch-off layer provide security against a dishonest Registrar, who might post a vote against a voter's credential. In such a case, the voter has evidence of vote manipulation because she can display an unscratched surface over her lock-in or cast codes.

If one may assume the ability of the voter to sign commands (in a manner similar to [8]) then digital signatures under commands "cast" and "lock in" can be used instead of codes generated by the authority.

5 Evaluation of Helios Implementation

In this section we describe our findings of security-related problems in the Helios implementation (*i.e.*, in `helios-server/heliosbooth`, source code which we refer to was used between May 1, 2014 and December 21, 2015). A description of our findings together with proposed solutions was sent to the Helios team who patched the code in January 2016 (pull requests #111 and #112) and May 2016 (pull request #110).

5.1   Cross-Site Scripting

Description. Helios Booth takes a parameter named `election_url` whose value is a link to a micro-service that sends data in JSON format for the election given an identifier. Based on that data, it builds a form.

Let us take a look at the code responsible for initialization, see Listing 1.1.

```
                              /heliosbooth/vote.html
403  BOOTH.so_lets_go = function () {
404      BOOTH.hide_progress();
405      BOOTH.setup_templates();
406      // election URL
407      var election_url = $.query.get('election_url');
408      BOOTH.load_and_setup_election(election_url);
409  };
```

Listing 1.1: A fragment of Helios Booth responsible for initialization of app modules.

Function `so_lets_go` is executed just after the HTML is loaded. After templates are initialized the GET variable `election_url` is passed to a function `load_and_setup_election`.

To obtain the GET a jQuery method `$.query.get` was used. At this step the obtained parameter is not checked/verified, but is treated as a trusted one – this opens up the possibility for an XSS attack. The parameter is is not checked in any further step, see Listing 1.2.

```
                              /heliosbooth/vote.html
368  BOOTH.load_and_setup_election = function(election_url) {
369      // the hash will be computed within the setup function call now
370      $.get(election_url, function(raw_json) {
371          // let's also get the metadata
372          $.getJSON(election_url + "/meta", {}, function(election_metadata) {
373              BOOTH.election_metadata = election_metadata;
374              BOOTH.setup_election(raw_json, election_metadata);
375              BOOTH.show_election();
376              BOOTH.election_url = election_url;
377          });
378      });
```

Listing 1.2: A code of Helios Booth responsible for retrieving election information data.

The `election_url` variable is treated as an election URL (see lines 370 and 372). In these lines AJAX queries are sent to the URL defined in `election_url`.

All data received is in JSON format and contains: keys, election questions, etc. The problem is that `election_url` may point to a service which is under the control of an attacker.

If this is the case then this malicious service has full control over the data that is passed to the Helios Booth. It, for instance, can play the role of a proxy.

The security vulnerability is caused by the method `$.getJSON` (line 372) – which is a part of jQuery library and is similar to `$.get` method: it performs asynchronous HTTP GET but unlike `$.get` it treats the response as data in JSON or JSONP format (default: JSON) and on receiving it parses it into a JavaScript object. In jQuery library before the version 1.2.3 there was a bug which had the following result: upon querying non-relative URL each response was treated as JSONP (executable JavaScript). Helios Booth was using version 1.2.2 which was vulnerable to this.

The parameter `election_url` was supposed to contain a relative URL but if an attacker used a modified URL leading to the attacker's proxy it would result in the attacker's ability to execute any arbitrary JavaScript code in the voter's browser. It was enough that proxy would answer to a query of `/meta` resource with a JavaScript code.

So the vulnerability can be treated as non-persistent Cross-Site Scripting (A3 from OWASP Top 10).

Exploiting Vulnerability. In order to take advantage of non-persistent Cross-Site Scripting, an attacker needs to make a victim start a voting app with a modified URL.

Then one possibility would be to correctly encrypt every voter choice (to pass each of the Cast/Audit steps) but when the voter decides to submit a ballot, the attacker prepares a new ballot and casts it instead of voter's ballot.

This vector of the attack is impossible to be detected from the server's side. It can still be detected by the voter but only in the situation when the voter: (1) remembers the tracker of the cast ballot and (2) checks the bulletin board later. Various experiences and studies suggest that the (2) check is not performed often enough [7,20], and what is even worse the fraction of voters who discover the discrepancies and report them can be as low as 0.5%.

Remedy. We suggested to (1) replace jQuery library with a newer version and (2) to introduce filtering the `election_url` not to allow non-relative URLs.

Another, more general, suggestion to make the system immune against Cross-Site Scripting we suggest is to introduce Content Security Policy [24] in the most rigorous form `default: self-src`. This would require changes in HTML, CSS and JavaScript.

5.2   Cross-Site Request Forgery

We found that some of the key functions of the system are not secured against the CSRF. This could easily lead to the situation when an election admin (logged in) can be tricked to perform an action that was not intended.

Vulnerability Description. We found a few methods which are executed (both GET and POST) without necessary checks. Actions not immune to CSRF attacks are listed in the Table 1 (This type of attack is at position 8 in OWASP Top 10).

Table 1. List of methods in Helios vulnerable to Cross-Site Request Forgery attacks.

Action	Query type	Relative url of the method
Election creation	POST	/helios/elections/new
Election edition	POST	/helios/elections/:election_id/edit
Archiving elections	GET	/helios/elections/:election_id/archive?archive_p=1
Canceling archiving elections	GET	/helios/elections/:election_id/archive?archive_p=0
Featuring elections	GET	/helios/elections/:election_id/set_featured?featured_p=1
Canceling featuring elections	GET	/helios/elections/:election_id/set_featured?featured_p=0
Adding a trustee	POST	/helios/elections/:election_id/trustees/new

Exploiting CSRF. To exploit a vulnerability, an attacker would need to (1) create a website with self-sending POST or GET query to one of the unsecured methods (2) make a user with admin privileges visit the site.

Lifetime of Helios cookies are set to 14 days so the attack would have been successful if a victim was logged into an admin console within this period of time.

Most of the vulnerable methods cannot do much more than a denial of service. Methods that allow the addition of trustees to given elections, however, can lead to loss of ballot privacy.

5.3   Framework Exploits

Framework exploits is the vector of attacks that lets one attempt to use a vulnerability of the method of the underlying library to attack a given system. Helios relies on the Django framework, so any vulnerable Django method used in Helios can also create a vulnerability.

Description. Helios used Django 1.6 till October 4, 2015 while the support for this branch ended on April 1, 2015. Thus, for about 186 days Helios was not protected by the patches applied to Django. Beginning October 4, 2015, Helios has been using Django 1.7.10 but this version has not been supported since December 1, 2015. Just in 2015 there were 14 vulnerabilities discovered in Django [10].

Exploiting. At the time of our audit no publicly open vulnerability of Django was known. But taking into account the types of security weaknesses, about one third of the discovered issues allowed for the performance of a denial of service attack. An attacker could have selectively disallowed voters to cast their ballots by blocking the server.

5.4   Clickjacking

Clickjacking is an attack that takes advantage of a user who thinks she clicks on an element (*e.g.*, button, link) of an app, while, thanks to the use of invisible layers, the action is linked with an element provided by an attacker.

Description. Every page of the Helios app can be placed in `<iframe>` which can lead to clickjacking attacks.

Exploiting. As with other attacks, one needs to use socio-engineering techniques to convince a voter to visit the site prepared by the attacker. This can be used, for instance, for early-finishing of the elections (if an attacked person has admin privileges).

Remedy. In order to exclude the possibility of clickjacking attacks on Helios we suggested to use HTTP Header `X-Frame-Options: SAMEORIGIN` which disallows the embedding of an app within iframes that are hosted on a different server. Django has a built in middleware `XFrameOptionsMiddleware` that takes care of sending the correct header [12].

6   Conclusions

We presented possible consequences of attacks on Helios. We also proposed an end-to-end verifiable Internet voting scheme Apollo which enables the voter to detect and correct problems in the representation of her vote. Apollo can also be used to provide evidence of vote manipulation. Additionally, Apollo offers a higher level of protection against a number of attacks (*e.g.*, clash-attacks, credentials stealing) than does, for example, Helios. We proposed an easier way to integrate the use of voting assistants, requiring the scanning of a single QR-code. Other proposals require the scanning of $2k$ codes for k audited ballots (a scan each for reading the commitment and checking encryption-correctness).

Interesting future directions include usability testing of the protocol, and an open problem is whether the credential stealing problem can be addressed with simpler protocols.

References

1. Adida, B.: Helios: web-based open-audit voting. In: USENIX Security Symposium, pp. 335–348 (2008)
2. Adida, B., De Marneffe, O., Pereira, O., Quisquater, J.-J., et al.: Electing a university president using open-audit voting: analysis of real-world use of helios. EVT/-WOTE **9**, 10 (2009)
3. Benaloh, J.: Simple verifiable elections. In: EVT (2006)

4. Benaloh, J., Byrne, M., Kortum, P.T., McBurnett, N., Pereira, O., Stark, P.B., Wallach, D.S.: STAR-vote: a secure, transparent, auditable, and reliable voting system. CoRR, abs/1211.1904 (2012)
5. Bernhard, D., Cortier, V., Pereira, O., Smyth, B., Warinschi, B.: Adapting Helios for provable ballot privacy. In: Atluri, V., Diaz, C. (eds.) ESORICS 2011. LNCS, vol. 6879, pp. 335–354. Springer, Heidelberg (2011). doi:10.1007/978-3-642-23822-2_19
6. Bernhard, D., Pereira, O., Warinschi, B.: How not to prove yourself: pitfalls of the Fiat-Shamir heuristic and applications to Helios. In: Wang, X., Sako, K. (eds.) ASIACRYPT 2012. LNCS, vol. 7658, pp. 626–643. Springer, Heidelberg (2012). doi:10.1007/978-3-642-34961-4_38
7. Carback, R.T., Chaum, D., Clark, J., Conway, J., Essex, A., Hernson, P.S., Mayberry, T., Popoveniuc, S., Rivest, R.L., Shen, E., Sherman, A.T., Vora, P.L.: Scantegrity II municipal election at Takoma Park: the first E2E binding governmental election with ballot privacy. In: USENIX Security Symposium (2010)
8. Cortier, V., Galindo, D., Glondu, S., Izabachène, M.: Election verifiability for Helios under weaker trust assumptions. In: Kutyłowski, M., Vaidya, J. (eds.) ESORICS 2014. LNCS, vol. 8713, pp. 327–344. Springer, Heidelberg (2014). doi:10.1007/978-3-319-11212-1_19
9. Cortier, V., Smyth, B.: Attacking and fixing Helios: an analysis of ballot secrecy. J. Comput. Secur. **21**(1), 89–148 (2013)
10. Details, C.: Django: list of security vulnerabilities. MITRE's CVE web site, Technical report (2015)
11. Estehghari, S., Desmedt, Y.: Exploiting the client vulnerabilities in internet e-voting systems: hacking Helios 2.0 as an example. In: EVT/WOTE (2010)
12. D. Foundation. Clickjacking protection in django. Technical report, Django Software Foundation (2015)
13. Gjosteen, K.: Analysis of an internet voting protocol. Technical report, IACR Eprint report 2010/380 (2010)
14. Grewal, G.S., Ryan, M.D., Chen, L., Clarkson, M.R.: Du-vote: remote electronic voting with untrusted computers. In: IEEE 28th Computer Security Foundations Symposium, CSF 2015, Verona, Italy, 13–17 July 2015, pp. 155–169 (2015)
15. Halderman, J.A., Teague, V.: The New South Wales iVote system: security failures and verification flaws in a live online election. In: Haenni, R., Koenig, R.E., Wikström, D. (eds.) VOTELID 2015. LNCS, vol. 9269, pp. 35–53. Springer, Heidelberg (2015). doi:10.1007/978-3-319-22270-7_3
16. Heiderich, M., Frosch, T., Niemietz, M., Schwenk, J.: The bug that made me president a browser- and web-security case study on Helios voting. In: Kiayias, A., Lipmaa, H. (eds.) Vote-ID 2011. LNCS, vol. 7187, pp. 89–103. Springer, Heidelberg (2012). doi:10.1007/978-3-642-32747-6_6
17. Kiayias, A., Yung, M.: The vector-ballot e-voting approach. In: Juels, A. (ed.) FC 2004. LNCS, vol. 3110, pp. 72–89. Springer, Heidelberg (2004). doi:10.1007/978-3-540-27809-2_9
18. Kusters, R., Truderung, T., Vogt, A.: Accountability: definition and relationship to verifiability. In: CCS (2010)
19. Kusters, R., Truderung, T., Vogt, A.: Clash attacks on the verifiability of e-voting systems. In: 2012 IEEE Symposium on Security and Privacy (SP), pp. 395–409. IEEE (2012)
20. Moher, E., Clark, J., Essex, A.: Diffusion of voter responsibility: potential failings in E2E voter receipt checking. USENIX J. Election Technol. Syst. (JETS) **1**, 1–17 (2014)

21. Neumann, S., Olembo, M.M., Renaud, K., Volkamer, M.: Helios verification: to alleviate, or to nominate: is that the question, or shall we have both? In: Kő, A., Francesconi, E. (eds.) EGOVIS 2014. LNCS, vol. 8650, pp. 246–260. Springer, Heidelberg (2014). doi:10.1007/978-3-319-10178-1_20

22. Popoveniuc, S., Kelsey, J., Regenscheid, A., Vora, P.: Performance requirements for end-to-end verifiable elections. In: Proceedings of the 2010 International Conference on Electronic Voting Technology/Workshop on Trustworthy Elections, pp. 1–16. USENIX Association (2010)

23. Springall, D., Finkenauer, T., Durumeric, Z., Kitcat, J., Hursti, H., MacAlpine, M., Halderman, J.A.: Security analysis of the Estonian internet voting system. In: Proceedings of the 2014 ACM SIGSAC Conference on Computer and Communications Security, CCS 2014, pp. 703–715. ACM, New York (2014)

24. West, M., Barth, A., Veditz, D.: Content security policy level 2. Last call WD, W3C, July 2014

25. Wolchok, S., Wustrow, E., Isabel, D., Halderman, J.A.: Attacking the Washington, D.C. Internet voting system. In: Keromytis, A.D. (ed.) FC 2012. LNCS, vol. 7397, pp. 114–128. Springer, Heidelberg (2012). doi:10.1007/978-3-642-32946-3_10

26. Zagórski, F., Carback, R.T., Chaum, D., Clark, J., Essex, A., Vora, P.L.: Remotegrity: design and use of an end-to-end verifiable remote voting system. In: Jacobson, M., Locasto, M., Mohassel, P., Safavi-Naini, R. (eds.) ACNS 2013. LNCS, vol. 7954, pp. 441–457. Springer, Heidelberg (2013). doi:10.1007/978-3-642-38980-1_28

Simulating STV Hand-Counting by Computers Considered Harmful: A.C.T.

Rajeev Goré[✉] and Ekaterina Lebedeva

Research School of Computer Science, The Australian National University,
Canberra, Australia
{rajeev.gore,ekaterina.lebedeva}@anu.edu.au

Abstract. We outline various ways in which the single transferable vote-counting (STV) algorithm used by the Australian Capital Territory (ACT) differs from the basic STV algorithm as well-known from social choice theory. Most of these differences were instituted to make it easier and faster to determine the result of counting around 300,000 ballots by hand. We give small examples to show how such "simplifications" can lead to counter-intuitive results. We also argue that these "simplifications" significantly complicate computer implementation and general understanding of the counting procedure, especially in a mathematical sense. We then demonstrate the strange effects of these "simplifications" in real-world computer counted election results which were published by ACT Elections. It is imperative that electoral commissions begin the legislative processes required to replace their existing "simplified" STV with "unsimplified" STV.

1 Introduction

Complex vote-counting schemes such as proportional representation single transferable voting (PR-STV) are used in many jurisdictions around the world. There are many variants, but the core algorithm is well-known [6]. For want of a better term, we use the appellation "VanillaSTV" to refer to such methods.

The parliamentary legislation that governs STV elections typically dates back to when counting was done by hand. Hand-counting STV elections is notoriously error-prone so most jurisdictions use a significantly "simplified" version of the VanillaSTV method that is easier to count manually. Again, for want of a better term, we use the appellation "ManualSTV" to describe such versions.

Computers are increasingly being used for electronic vote-casting and vote-counting because they have the potential to be cheaper, faster and more accurate than hand-counting. When moving to e-counting, electoral commissions invariably choose to implement some versions of ManualSTV for three main reasons: (i) it is mandated by the legislation and any changes require the passage of new

---

E. Lebedeva—Supported by Australian Research Council Grant DP140101540.
Author order is alphabetical by surname.

R. Krimmer et al. (Eds.): E-Vote-ID 2016, LNCS 10141, pp. 144–163, 2017.
DOI: 10.1007/978-3-319-52240-1_9

legislation; (ii) doing so allows them to transfer the considerable in-house experience in hand-counting to the software vendor during design and testing; and (iii) hand-counting remains as an acceptable back-up if the software fails.

For example, the Australian Capital Territory (ACT) has used an electronic vote-casting system and electronic vote-counting system called eVACS in the past four elections. In 2001 and 2004, e-casting collected approximately 10% of the ballots, rising to 25% in 2012. The eVACS system e-counted all ballots since 2001, with the paper ballots either manually entered (2001 and 2004) or digitally scanned (2008 and 2012). The counting module of this system is publicly available for scrutiny [4]. The official legislation which it attempts to capture is also publicly available [3], and is quite algorithmic. Compared to VanillaSTV, the legislation, and hence eVACS, contains various "simplifications" which make it easier to count votes by hand. Thus, eVACS implements a significantly "simplified" hand-counting version of VanillaSTV, which we call ManualACT.

Here, we analyse the effects of the numerous "simplifications" that are included in ManualACT. We give small examples to show how these "simplifications" lead to counter-intuitive results. We then highlight where these "simplifications" have played a role in previous ACT elections to prove that they are not just theoretical possibilities. Our hope is that election commissions will cease to use computers to simulate STV hand-counting and instead recommend that Parliament changes the legislation to allow them to implement the appropriate variant of VanillaSTV.

2   Notations and Definitions for STV

We first begin with an informal description of STV counting. As usual, we first tally the first preferences for all candidates. All candidates that obtain a pre-defined quota of votes are elected and the votes that are surplus to requirements (i.e. above the quota) are distributed to their next preference. If no candidates obtain the quota then some candidate is selected as the weakest candidate for exclusion and the votes for the excluded candidate are distributed to their next preference. Thus a conventional STV algorithm contains the following two important mutually exclusive operations that distribute votes:

Exclusion: distribution of votes of excluded candidate c;
Surplus distribution: distribution of surplus votes of elected candidate c.

Informally, each of these operations corresponds to a "count" of the scrutiny. That is, given a multi-set of input ballots, $\mathcal{E}$, each of these mutually exclusive operations returns a different multi-set of ballots $\mathcal{E}'$. Each ballot in $\mathcal{E}$ appears in $\mathcal{E}'$ except that c is deleted from its position in that ballot, if it appears in that ballot, and the "weight" of that ballot may change. Of course, if c is the only candidate on the ballot in $\mathcal{E}$ then this ballot becomes "exhausted". We say that ballot papers from $\mathcal{E}$ in which c is the first preference are *pruned* in $\mathcal{E}'$ because candidates that follow immediately after c *receive, in* $\mathcal{E}'$, *(a fraction of the) votes from* c under various conditions of the particular STV version. In VanillaSTV, exclusion is one operation, but in ManualACT, an exclusion may consist of many "partial exclusions" [3].

More formally, let $\mathcal{C} = \{c_1, \ldots, c_k\}$ be a set of $k \geq 1$ distinct candidates. A preference pref $= [p_1, p_2, \ldots, p_l]$ is a list of $l \leq k$ distinct candidates from $\mathcal{C}$: that is, $p_i \neq p_j$ for all $i \neq j$. In some versions of STV, l must equal k in each ballot, meaning that "partial preferences" are forbidden. Here, we allow partial preferences. A weight is a rational number between 0 and 1 (inclusive). A ballot $b = \langle \text{pref}, \text{weight} \rangle$ is a pair consisting of a preference (list) and weight. The initial weight in every ballot is 1. If a ballot $b = \langle \text{pref}, \text{weight} \rangle$, then $b.\text{pref}$ is pref and $b.\text{weight}$ is weight. An *election* $\mathcal{E} = \{b_1, \ldots, b_m\}$ is a set of $m > 0$ ballots.

We write the list $[p_1, p_2, \ldots, p_l]$ of preferences as $p_1 > p_2 > \cdots > p_l$ to capture the intuition that it is a linear order of preferences from most preferred to least. If we want to specify only the head of the preference list then we write the list as $p_1 :: ps$ where $::$ is the operation on lists that adds the element p_1 to the front of the list $ps = [p_2, \ldots, p_l]$. Candidate p_i has a *higher preference* than candidate p_j in $b.\text{pref}$ if $i < j$. The candidate p_1 has the highest preference in ballot b in election $\mathcal{E}$ and is called *the first preference of b in $\mathcal{E}$*. In this case, ballot b *favours* candidate p_1 in $\mathcal{E}$. A *continuing ballot* is one whose preference (list) is of length greater than 1. For ballots, the appellations "exhausted" and "continuing" are opposites, hence an exhausted ballot is non-continuing and *vice-versa*.

For an election $\mathcal{E}$, the *total* $tt(c, \mathcal{E})$ of a candidate c is the sum of the weights of those ballots of $\mathcal{E}$ that favour c: that is,

$$tt(c, \mathcal{E}) = \sum \{b.\text{weight} \mid b \in \mathcal{E} \text{ and } b.\text{pref} = c :: ps \text{ for some } ps\}.$$

The *quota* q is the minimum total a candidate is required to reach in order to be elected. There are numerous ways to compute a quota and it is calculated to ensure that the number of elected candidates cannot exceed the number of vacant seats. In the versions of STV that we consider, a candidate can be elected without a quota when the number of remaining candidates equals the number of vacant seats because all other candidates have been elected or excluded. Here, we use the Droop quota which is defined as the greatest integer less than the number:

(total number of initial ballots/(number of vacant seats + 1)) + 1.

The *surplus* $sp(c, \mathcal{E})$ of an elected candidate c is the difference between c's total and the quota q:

$$sp(c, \mathcal{E}) = tt(c, \mathcal{E}) - q.$$

If c is elected, each ballot $b = \langle [c, p_2, \ldots, p_l], wt \rangle$ that favours c is "pruned" so it favours the next continuing candidate p_i with some new weight as described below: thus p_i is not necessarily p_2.

Different versions of STV declare candidates to be elected at different moments in the scrutiny. As soon as some candidate c is *declared a winner*, c stops receiving surplus votes from other winners since c is no longer a continuing candidate. Declared winners whose surpluses are not yet distributed are called *pending winners*.

The candidates with the lowest total are the *weakest* candidates and one of them is selected for exclusion if no candidate reaches the quota. There are many different ways to select such a weakest candidate.

Therefore, at certain moments of scrutiny, that depend upon the vote counting method, each candidate's total is compared with the quota to determine whether the candidate is *a winner* (elected), is *excluded* or is a *continuing candidate* who has neither been elected nor excluded.

To distribute the surplus of an elected candidate c, we compute the *transfer value* $tv(c, \mathcal{E}) = sp(c, \mathcal{E})/denom$, where the value of *denom* depends on the vote counting method. Although *denom* can be 0 in both `VanillaSTV` and `ManualACT`, the transfer value $tv(c, \mathcal{E}) \neq 0$ in both. However, as we shall see, for all c and all elections $\mathcal{E}$, $tv(c, \mathcal{E}) \leq 1$ in `VanillaSTV`, but not in `ManualACT`.

In `VanillaSTV`, a *count* is any one of the two fundamental operations that distribute votes: that is, either the surplus distribution of a winner or the distribution of votes of an excluded (weakest) candidate. In `ManualACT`, although each surplus distribution is one count, the exclusion of the weakest candidate consists of multiple "partial exclusions", and each of these is a count, as described next.

2.1 Vote Distribution in `VanillaSTV`

We now describe formally how each of these operations transforms an election $\mathcal{E}$ into an election $\mathcal{E}'$ for `VanillaSTV`. We first define how to distribute the votes of some candidate c (who may be either a winner or the weakest candidate):

If ballot b favours c, then "prune" the preference $b.\mathsf{pref} = [c, p_2, \ldots, p_l]$ in $\mathcal{E}$ into $b.\mathsf{pref} = [p_i, \ldots, p_l]$ in $\mathcal{E}'$, where p_i is the next continuing candidate of $[c, p_2, \ldots, p_l]$ and let $b.\mathsf{weight} = w$ in $\mathcal{E}$ become $b.\mathsf{weight} = w \times x$ in $\mathcal{E}'$, where x is determined by whether c is a winner or the weakest candidate in $\mathcal{E}$, as explained shortly.

If ballot b does not favour c, but c appears in $b.\mathsf{pref}$, then delete c from $b.\mathsf{pref}$.

Surplus distribution of a winner c is the distribution of the votes of c but with $x = tv(c, \mathcal{E})$ where *denom* is the *sum of the weights* of all continuing ballots that favour c. Thus, in `VanillaSTV`, a ballot cannot gain weight. Exclusion of the weakest candidate c is the same but with $x = 1$. Thus, in `VanillaSTV`, the next preferred candidate gets the full current weight of ballot b.

2.2 Vote Distribution in `ManualACT`

We now describe formally how each of these operations transforms an election $\mathcal{E}$ into an election $\mathcal{E}'$ for `ManualACT`.

In `ManualACT`, *denom* is the *number* of all continuing ballots in the "last parcel" of c, as described next. For an elected candidate c, the ballots whose votes are distributed to c in the count that resulted in c reaching quota and being declared elected, constitute c's last parcel. That is, for all candidates c and d, if distributing d's votes in $\mathcal{E}$ results in $\mathcal{E}'$ and c reaches quota (and is therefore declared elected) in $\mathcal{E}'$, the last parcel of c in $\mathcal{E}'$ contains any ballot $\langle[d, d_1, \ldots, d_m, c, c_1, \ldots, c_{l-m-2}], wt\rangle$ in $\mathcal{E}$ where $d_1, \ldots d_m$ are winners with pending surplus distributions who all met quota in $\mathcal{E}$ (with d). In $\mathcal{E}'$ this ballot appears as the ballot $\langle[c, c_1, \ldots, c_{l-m-2}], wt'\rangle$. If c reaches quota when $\mathcal{E}'$ is the first count, there is no such $\mathcal{E}$, so all ballots that favour c constitute c's last parcel.

We first define how to distribute the votes of some elected candidate c:

If ballot b favours c, then "prune" the preference $b.\mathsf{pref} = [c, p_2, \ldots, p_l]$ in $\mathcal{E}$ into $b.\mathsf{pref} = [p_i, \ldots, p_l]$ in $\mathcal{E}'$, where p_i is the next continuing candidate of $[c, p_2, \ldots, p_l]$ and update the weight $b.\mathsf{weight}$ to be $min(b.\mathsf{weight}, tv(c, \mathcal{E}))$, where $tv(c, \mathcal{E}) = sp(c, \mathcal{E})/denom$ and $denom$ is the number of continuing ballots in the last parcel of c.
If ballot b does not favour c, but c appears in $b.\mathsf{pref}$, then delete c from $b.\mathsf{pref}$.

The partial distribution of the votes of the weakest candidate c is defined as:

If ballot b favours c, and $b.\mathsf{weight} = x$ then "prune" the preference $b.\mathsf{pref} = c::ps$ to $b.\mathsf{pref} = ps$ (even if ps is the empty list) and do not change $b.\mathsf{weight}$, where the parameter x is defined below.
If ballot b does not favour c, but c appears in $b.\mathsf{pref}$, then delete c from $b.\mathsf{pref}$.

To exclude the weakest candidate c, distribute the votes of c as follows: for every different value w of **weight** that appears in the ballots that favour c, apply partial distribution with $x = w$ to all ballots.

Finally, given an election $\mathcal{E}$·with n vacancies and a set $\mathcal{C}$ of at least n distinct candidates, a *vote counting algorithm* returns from $\mathcal{C}$ a set $\mathcal{W}$ of n distinct *winners*.

2.3   Illustrative Example of VanillaSTV to Highlight Notation

Example 1. Table 1 shows two elections: $\mathcal{E}$ and $\mathcal{E}'$. The set of candidates of both $\mathcal{E}$ and $\mathcal{E}'$ is $\mathcal{C} = \{A, B, C\}$. Election $\mathcal{E}$ consists of four ballots and the quota is $q = 2$. Ballots $b_1 - b_3$ are continuing ballots. Ballot b_1 has preferences $A > B > C$ (favouring A) and weight 1. Ballot b_2 has preferences $B > C > A$ (favouring B) and weight $1/2$. Ballot b_3 has preferences $C > B$ (favouring C) and weight 1. Ballot b_4 favours C and C is the only preference of b_4. Therefore, b_4 is not continuing. The weight of b_4 is $1/3$. The total $tt(A, \mathcal{E})$ of candidate A in $\mathcal{E}$ is 1 since the only ballot that favours A has weight 1. The total $tt(B, \mathcal{E})$ is $1/2$ since the only ballot that favours B has weight $1/1$. Since b_3 and b_4 both favour C, the total $tt(C, \mathcal{E})$ is the sum of their weights $b_3.\mathsf{weight} = 1$ and $b_4.\mathsf{weight} = 1/3$: that is, $tt(C, \mathcal{E}) = 1/3 + 3/3 = 4/3$.

Nobody is elected in $\mathcal{E}$ because the totals of all candidates are below the quota $q = 2$. The weakest candidate in $\mathcal{E}$ is B because it has the smallest total $1/2$. Therefore, B is excluded. The double vertical line denotes the count that distributes votes of B. By distributing votes of B this count converts $\mathcal{E}$ to $\mathcal{E}'$.

Table 1. Example of an STV exclusion of the weakest candidate

	$\mathcal{E}$, q = 2			$\mathcal{E}'$, q = 2	
ID	pref	weight		pref	weight
b_1	A > B > C	1		A > C	1
b_2	B > C > A	1/2		C > A	1/2
b_3	C > B	1		C	1
b_4	C	1/3		C	1/3

$\mathcal{E}$	A	B	C
tt	1	1/2	4/3

$\mathcal{E}'$	A	C
tt	1	11/6

3   Comparison of VanillaSTV and Variations of ManualACT

We now present examples of counting votes with the methods VanillaSTV, ManualACT and ManualACT modified in certain ways. Each example is accompanied by a table that shows distributions of votes. When using ManualACT, the column marked LP shows whether a ballot is or not in the last parcel of the winning candidate. If an election is obtained from an election $\mathcal{E}_i$ by distributing the surplus of candidate c but there is still a candidate whose surplus distribution is pending, it is called a *quasi-election* and marked as $\mathcal{E}_i^c$. All quasi-elections are elections. Initially all ballots have weight 1.

Figures 1 and 2 summarise, respectively, the differences between VanillaSTV and ManualACT regarding surplus distribution and candidate exclusion.

3.1   Example of VanillaSTV

Example 2. We begin with an example that helps to highlight the differences in the distribution of votes between VanillaSTV and ManualACT. We analyse each election of Table 2 in turn.

Election $\mathcal{E}_1$. In election $\mathcal{E}_1$, two candidates, A and B, with $tt(A, \mathcal{E}_1) = 8$ and $tt(B, \mathcal{E}_1) = 6$, reach quota $q = 4$, with surpluses 4 and 2 respectively. Their respective transfer values are therefore $4/8 = 1/2$ and $2/6 = 1/3$. The surplus of the winner with the highest surplus, i.e. A, is distributed first leading to $\mathcal{E}_1^A$.

Election $\mathcal{E}_1^A$. Although candidate C has a total $tt(C, \mathcal{E}_1^A)$ of $8 * 1/2 + 3 * 1 = 7$ votes and thus $tt(C, \mathcal{E}_1^A) > q$, C is not yet declared elected because candidate B has a pending surplus (hence, $\mathcal{E}_1^A$ is a quasi-election).

Election $\mathcal{E}_2$. In election $\mathcal{E}_2$ surplus $sp(B, \mathcal{E}_1)$ is distributed and ballots b_9 to b_{14} are pruned as the result of this distribution. Their weight is attenuated by the transfer value $tv(B, \mathcal{E}_1) = 1/3$ and their first preference is C. Tallying C's ballots, we find that C's total is now $8 * 1/2 + 6 * 1/3 + 3 * 1 = 9$. There are no pending candidates and C is therefore declared a winner. Its surplus is $9 - 4 = 5$, giving us a transfer value of $5/9$.

Property	VanillaSTV	ManualACT
Declare new winners from surplus distribution	after surpluses of all pending winners are distributed.	after distribution of every surplus.
Denominator $denom$ of transfer value $tv(c,\mathcal{E}) = sp(c,\mathcal{E})/denom$ is	the sum of the weights of the continuing ballots that favour c.	the number of continuing ballots from the last parcel of c that favour c.
Can we have transfer value $tv(c,\mathcal{E}) > 1$?	No.	Yes, but eVACS fixes it via $$tv(c,\mathcal{E}) = \begin{cases} 1 & \text{if } denom = 0 \\ 1 & \text{if } \dfrac{sp(c,\mathcal{E})}{denom} > 1, \\ \dfrac{sp(c,\mathcal{E})}{denom} & \text{otherwise.} \end{cases}$$
Which ballot papers are considered for distribution of the surplus of c?	All ballot continuing papers that favour c.	Only continuing ballot papers from the last parcel of c.
Are any continuing ballot papers ignored when a surplus is distributed?	No.	Yes. Ballots that favour the winner but do not belong to the last parcel are ignored even if they are continuing.
How are ballot weights updated when distributing $sp(c,\mathcal{E})$?	By multiplying their current weights in $\mathcal{E}$ by transfer value $tv(c,\mathcal{E})$.	By replacing a ballot weight in $\mathcal{E}$ with $tv(c,\mathcal{E})$, if tv is smaller than the ballot weight else keeping the weight from $\mathcal{E}$ unchanged.
Can votes disappear during scrutiny?	No.	Yes.

Fig. 1. Differences in VanillaSTV and ManualACT related to distribution of surpluses.

Property	VanillaSTV	ManualACT
Number n of steps in exclusion of c is	1.	equal to the number of different weights associated with ballots that favour c.
Quota check and winner declaration during exclusion happens	once, after exclusion is fully completed.	n times, i.e. after every (partial exclusion) step.

Fig. 2. Differences in VanillaSTV and ManualACT related to exclusion.

Election $\mathcal{E}_3$. In election $\mathcal{E}_3$, C's surplus is distributed. Ballots b_9 to b_{14} now get their previous weight $1/3$ attenuated by the transfer value $5/9$ of C, giving them a weight of $5/27$. Ballots b_{15} to b_{17} now get their previous weight 1 attenuated similarly, giving them a weight of $5/9$. The total of D is $20/27 + 27/27 = 47/27 < 4$ and the total of E is $10/27 + 15/9 + 1 = 10/27 + 45/27 + 27/27 = 82/27 < 4$. Thus D is the weakest candidate and is excluded.

Table 2. Example 2: Distribution of votes according to `VanillaSTV`

	$\mathcal{E}_1$, q = 4		$\mathcal{E}_1^A$, q = 4		$\mathcal{E}_2$, q = 4		$\mathcal{E}_3$, q = 4	
ID	pref	weight	pref	weight	pref	weight	pref	weight
b_1	**A** > C	1	C	1/2	**C**	1/2		
b_2	**A** > C	1	C	1/2	**C**	1/2		
b_3	**A** > C	1	C	1/2	**C**	1/2		
b_4	**A** > C	1	C	1/2	**C**	1/2		
b_5	**A** > C	1	C	1/2	**C**	1/2		
b_6	**A** > C	1	C	1/2	**C**	1/2		
b_7	**A** > C	1	C	1/2	**C**	1/2		
b_8	**A** > C	1	C	1/2	**C**	1/2		
b_9	**B** > C > D	1	B > C > D	1	**C** > D	1/3	D	5/27
b_{10}	**B** > C > D	1	B > C > D	1	**C** > D	1/3	D	5/27
b_{11}	**B** > C > D	1	B > C > D	1	**C** > D	1/3	D	5/27
b_{12}	**B** > C > D	1	B > C > D	1	**C** > D	1/3	D	5/27
b_{13}	**B** > C > E	1	B > C > E	1	**C** > E	1/3	**E**	5/27
b_{14}	**B** > C > E	1	B > C > E	1	**C** > E	1/3	**E**	5/27
b_{15}	C > E	1	C > E	1	**C** > E	1	**E**	5/9
b_{16}	C > E	1	C > E	1	**C** > E	1	**E**	5/9
b_{17}	C > E	1	C > E	1	**C** > E	1	**E**	5/9
b_{18}	D	1	D	1	D	1	D	1
b_{19}	E	1	E	1	E	1	**E**	1

$\mathcal{E}_1$	$\mathcal{E}_1^A$	$\mathcal{E}_2$	$\mathcal{E}_3$
A B C D E	B C D E	C D E	D E
tt 8 6 3 1 1	*tt* 6 7 1 1	*tt* 9 1 1	*tt* 47/27 82/27
sp 4 2		*sp* 5	
tv 1/2 1/3	$sp(A, \mathcal{E}_1)$ distributed	*tv* 5/9	$sp(C, \mathcal{E}_2)$ distributed
A elected **B** elected	$sp(B, \mathcal{E}_1)$ pending	$sp(B, \mathcal{E}_1)$ distributed **C** elected	D excluded **E** elected

Since E is the only continuing candidate, and there is only one vacancy left, E is elected automatically. Thus the set $\mathcal{W}$ of winners is $\{A, B, C, E\}$.

3.2 Effects of the Last Parcel Simplification

In Example 3, we apply `ManualACT` to the same ballots as in Example 2. Table 3 illustrates this. For each ballot paper, a mark in form of a tick ✓ next to it signifies that this ballot paper was pruned in the previous count and therefore belongs to the last parcel of a candidate that wins in the current election as the result of the count. In the initial election $\mathcal{E}_1$, all ballots are marked by definition.

Example 3. We describe each column in turn.

Election $\mathcal{E}_1$. Two candidates, A and B, with $tt(A, \mathcal{E}_1) = 8$ and $tt(B, \mathcal{E}_1) = 6$, reach quota $q = 4$, with surpluses 4 and 2 respectively. The surplus of the winner A with the highest surplus is distributed first, giving $\mathcal{E}_1^A$.

Table 3. Example 3: Distribution of votes according to `ManualACT`

ID	$\mathcal{E}_1$, q = 4 LP pref	weight	$\mathcal{E}_1^A$, q = 4 LP pref	weight	$\mathcal{E}_2$, q = 4 LP pref	weight	$\mathcal{E}_3$, q = 4 LP pref	weight
b_1	✓ A > C	1	✓ C	1/2	C	1/2		
b_2	✓ A > C	1	✓ C	1/2	C	1/2		
b_3	✓ A > C	1	✓ C	1/2	C	1/2		
b_4	✓ A > C	1	✓ C	1/2	C	1/2		
b_5	✓ A > C	1	✓ C	1/2	C	1/2		
b_6	✓ A > C	1	✓ C	1/2	C	1/2		
b_7	✓ A > C	1	✓ C	1/2	C	1/2		
b_8	✓ A > C	1	✓ C	1/2	C	1/2		
b_9	✓ B > C > D	1	B > C > D	1	✓ D	1/3	D	1/3
b_{10}	✓ B > C > D	1	B > C > D	1	✓ D	1/3	D	1/3
b_{11}	✓ B > C > D	1	B > C > D	1	✓ D	1/3	D	1/3
b_{12}	✓ B > C > D	1	B > C > D	1	✓ D	1/3	D	1/3
b_{13}	✓ B > C > E	1	B > C > E	1	✓ E	1/3	E	1/3
b_{14}	✓ B > C > E	1	B > C > E	1	✓ E	1/3	E	1/3
b_{15}	✓ C > E	1	C > E	1	C > E	1		
b_{16}	✓ C > E	1	C > E	1	C > E	1		
b_{17}	✓ C > E	1	C > E	1	C > E	1		
b_{18}	✓ D	1	D	1	D	1	D	1
b_{19}	✓ E	1	E	1	E	1	E	1

	A	B	C	D	E
tt	8	6	3	1	1
sp	4	2			
tv	1/2	1/3			

A elected
B elected

	B	C	D	E
tt	6	7	1	1
sp	3			
tv	1			

$sp(A, \mathcal{E}_1)$
distributed
$sp(B, \mathcal{E}_1)$
pending
C elected

	C	D	E
tt	7	2	1

$sp(B, \mathcal{E}_1)$
distributed

	D	E
tt	2	1

$sp(C, \mathcal{E}_1^A)$
distributed
E excluded
D elected

Election $\mathcal{E}_1^A$. Since all (continuing) ballots are marked with a ✓ in $\mathcal{E}_1$, all of them that favour the winner A are involved in the distribution of the surplus of A. The denominator *denom* of the transfer value is the number of continuing ballot papers that favour A and is equal to 8: thus $tv(A, \mathcal{E}_1) = 4/8 = 1/2$. The old weights of ballots involved in the surplus distribution are replaced with the transfer value $tv(A, \mathcal{E}_1)$. Therefore, the weights of the ballots b_1 to b_{14} in $\mathcal{E}_1^A$ are equal to 1/2.

For all continuing candidates in $\mathcal{E}_1^A$, the weights of the ballots that favour these candidates sum to integers. Thus, there is no rounding down and their totals are equal to these sums.

Note that although weights of ballots in elections $\mathcal{E}_1^A$ in Tables 2 and 3 happen to be the same, they are obtained differently. In Table 2, they are obtained not by simply assigning $tv(A, \mathcal{E}_1)$ to them, but by multiplying their weights in $\mathcal{E}_1$, which are equal to 1, by $tv(A, \mathcal{E}_1)$.

After every count, `ManualACT` checks for new winners and declares them. Candidate C's total $tt(C, \mathcal{E}_1^A) = 8 * 1/2 + 3 * 1 = 7$ reaches quota 4 in $\mathcal{E}_1^A$. C is immediately declared elected and therefore stops receiving votes. The surplus of C is distributed only after the distribution of the surplus of B because B was elected earlier.

Election $\mathcal{E}_2$. The distribution of $sp(B, \mathcal{E}_1)$ leads to $\mathcal{E}_2$. Ballots b_9 to b_{14} are marked ✓ in $\mathcal{E}_2$, because they are the pruned ballots. But notice that C has disappeared from these ballots because C was elected in $\mathcal{E}_1^A$, is not a continuing candidate any more and cannot receive votes. The sum of the weights of the ballots $b_1 - b_8$, that favour C, is an integer 7. Thus, $tt(C, \mathcal{E}_2) = 7$. However, the sum of the ballots $b_9 - b_{12}$, that favour D, is $4/3 + 1 = 7/3$. Rounding this down gives us $tt(D, \mathcal{E}_2) = 2$.

Election $\mathcal{E}_3$. Only ballots $b_1 - b_8$ are marked in $\mathcal{E}_1^A$, the election where C became a winner, because these ballots form the last parcel for C. Thus only these eight ballots are involved the distribution of surplus $sp(C, \mathcal{E}_1^A) = 3$ and computing the denominator of the transfer value of C. Continuing ballots $b_{15} - b_{17}$, highlighted with red, are no longer involved in the scrutiny, although they favour C. Their next preferences are never considered in further counting, thus robbing E of some votes.

Since the number of continuing ballots in the last parcel of C is equal to 0, $denom = 0$ and cannot be used in the formula $tv(C, \mathcal{E}_2) = sp(C, \mathcal{E}_2)/denom$. Nevertheless, the transfer value does not play a role in further scrutiny because no ballot receives (a fraction of) $s(C, \mathcal{E}_2)$ anyway, since there are no continuing ballots in the last parcel of C. Three ballots $b_{15} - b_{17}$ of the true surplus of C are lost.

No candidate reaches the quota in $\mathcal{E}_3$, the weakest candidate (with the smallest total) E is excluded and the only remaining candidate D wins the last vacant seat.

The set of winners $\{A, B, C, D\}$ according to `ManualACT` is different from the set $\{A, B, C, E\}$ of winners according to `VanillaSTV`.

3.3   `ManualACT`$^{\neg LP}$: `ManualACT` Without the Last Parcel

Example 4. Table 4 shows totals and distribution of the votes of the same initial election $\mathcal{E}_1$, as in Examples 3 and 2, but this time using method `ManualACT`$^{\neg LP}$. `ManualACT`$^{\neg LP}$ is identical to `ManualACT` with the only exception that there is no notion of "Last Parcel" in `ManualACT`$^{\neg LP}$. That is, when a candidate wins with a surplus, all continuing ballots which favour this candidate are taken into consideration in `ManualACT`$^{\neg LP}$ for computing the transfer value and distributing the surplus of this candidate. Therefore, ballots do not need to be marked with a ✓ in Table 4.

Table 4. Example 4: Distribution of votes according to $\texttt{ManualACT}^{\neg LP}$

ID	$\mathcal{E}_1$, q = 4 pref	weight	$\mathcal{E}_1^A$, q = 4 pref	weight	$\mathcal{E}_2$, q = 4 pref	weight	$\mathcal{E}_3$, q = 4 pref	weight
b_1	A > C	1	C	1/2	C	1/2		
b_2	A > C	1	C	1/2	C	1/2		
b_3	A > C	1	C	1/2	C	1/2		
b_4	A > C	1	C	1/2	C	1/2		
b_5	A > C	1	C	1/2	C	1/2		
b_6	A > C	1	C	1/2	C	1/2		
b_7	A > C	1	C	1/2	C	1/2		
b_8	A > C	1	C	1/2	C	1/2		
b_9	B > C > D	1	B > C > D	1	D	1/3	D	1/3
b_{10}	B > C > D	1	B > C > D	1	D	1/3	D	1/3
b_{11}	B > C > D	1	B > C > D	1	D	1/3	D	1/3
b_{12}	B > C > D	1	B > C > D	1	D	1/3	D	1/3
b_{13}	B > C > E	1	B > C > E	1	E	1/3	E	1/3
b_{14}	B > C > E	1	B > C > E	1	E	1/3	E	1/3
b_{15}	C > E	1	C > E	1	C > E	1	E	1
b_{16}	C > E	1	C > E	1	C > E	1	E	1
b_{17}	C > E	1	C > E	1	C > E	1	E	1
b_{18}	D	1	D	1	D	1	D	1
b_{19}	E	1	E	1	E	1	E	1

	A B C D E	B C D E	C D E	D E
tt	8 6 3 1 1	6 7 1 1	7 2 1	2 4
sp	4 2	2 3		
tv	1/2 1/3	1		
		$sp(A, \mathcal{E}_1)$	$sp(B, \mathcal{E}_1)$	$sp(C, \mathcal{E}_1^A)$
	A elected	distributed	distributed	distributed
	B elected	**C** elected		**E** elected
		$sp(B, \mathcal{E}_1)$		
		pending		

As before, there are 19 ballot papers, 4 vacancies and the Droop quota is equal to 4. In $\texttt{ManualACT}^{\neg LP}$, elections $\mathcal{E}_1^A$ and $\mathcal{E}_2$ are identical to those in $\texttt{ManualACT}$. They diverge when the surplus of C is distributed. Since all continuing ballots that favour C are considered, ballots $b_{15} - b_{17}$ in green are involved in $\texttt{ManualACT}^{\neg LP}$ in computing $tv(C, \mathcal{E}_1^A)$ and distributing $sp(C, \mathcal{E}_1^A)$.

The denominator $denom = 3$ of the transfer value $tv(C, \mathcal{E}_1^A)$ is equal to the number of continuing ballots ($b_{15} - b_{17}$), and the transfer value $tv(C, \mathcal{E}_1^A)$ is therefore equal to $3/3 = 1$. Consequently, E, being the next preference after C in ballots $b_{15} - b_{17}$, gains 3 surplus votes of C in $\mathcal{E}_3$, reaches the quota and becomes the fourth winner.

Because ballots $b_{15} - b_{17}$ remain in scrutiny according to $\texttt{ManualACT}^{\neg LP}$, their second preferences are taken into consideration and lead to the victory of E.

Summary of VanillaSTV Versus ManualACT Last Parcel Variants

Example	Table	Algorithm	Election	Winners	Comment
2	2	VanillaSTV	$\mathcal{E}_1$	A, B, C, E	E wins
3	3	ManualACT	$\mathcal{E}_1$	A, B, C, D	E loses
4	4	ManualACT$^{\neg LP}$	$\mathcal{E}_1$	A, B, C, E	E wins

3.4   Effects of Declaring Winners at Different Moments in ManualACT

In ManualACT, candidates are declared winners as soon as their totals reach the quota as a result of a count (i.e. either surplus distribution or partial exclusion), even if there are still candidates pending for surplus distribution. If the newly declared winners have surpluses, they are placed at the end of the queue of pending candidates. ManualACT declares winners as soon as they meet the quota to prevent them from receiving further votes. In the case of exclusion, this, however, leads to an unbalanced distribution of votes of the excluded candidate. In the case of surplus distribution, this leads to an unbalanced distribution of surpluses of candidates that were declared winners in the same election. Examples 5 and 6 illustrate this situation.

ManualACT: Declaring Winners After Every Count

Example 5. This example applies ManualACT to an election consisting of 21 ballot papers. There are 4 vacant seats and the Droop quota is equal to 5. Table 5 shows the initial election $\mathcal{E}_1$, as well as totals and distribution of votes.

In $\mathcal{E}_1$, candidates A and B reach quota with totals 10 and 9 respectively. First the algorithm distributes the surplus of the candidate A with the most votes. In $\mathcal{E}_1^A$, total $tt(C, \mathcal{E}_1^A)$ is above the quota, so C is declared elected. Thus C no longer receives surplus votes, including those from B.

Distributing the surplus of B leads to $\mathcal{E}_2$. Ballots $b_{11} - b_{19}$ in $\mathcal{E}_2$ have C as the next preference after B. Since C is declared elected in $\mathcal{E}_1^A$, surplus votes from B in these ballots go to the next continuing preference D.

In $\mathcal{E}_3$, the surplus of C is distributed. No candidate reaches the quota in $\mathcal{E}_3$. The candidate E with the lowest total gets excluded and D gets elected as the only remaining candidate for the only remaining seat.

The distribution of surplus votes of B to D instead of C in election $\mathcal{E}_2$ deserves special attention. Both A and B simultaneously reach the quota in the initial election $\mathcal{E}_1$. The next preference on all of their ballots is C. Therefore, the distribution of surplus votes from A to C and the distribution of surplus votes from B to C should be treated equally. However, this is not the case in ManualACT. By skipping the second preference C (marked in red) in ballots $b_{11} - b_{19}$ when $sp(B, \mathcal{E}_1)$ is distributed, candidate D obtains a higher total in election $\mathcal{E}_2$ than it would obtain if C were not skipped when distributing the surplus votes of B.

Table 5. Example 5: Declaring winners after every count i.e. `ManualACT`

		$\mathcal{E}_1$, q = 5		$\mathcal{E}_1^A$, q = 5		$\mathcal{E}_2$, q = 5		$\mathcal{E}_3$, q = 5	
ID	LP	pref	weight	pref	weight	pref	weight	pref	weight
b_1	✓	A > C > E	1	✓ C > E	1/2	C > E	1/2	✓ E	1/5
b_2	✓	A > C > E	1	✓ C > E	1/2	C > E	1/2	✓ E	1/5
b_3	✓	A > C > E	1	✓ C > E	1/2	C > E	1/2	✓ E	1/5
b_4	✓	A > C > E	1	✓ C > E	1/2	C > E	1/2	✓ E	1/5
b_5	✓	A > C > E	1	✓ C > E	1/2	C > E	1/2	✓ E	1/5
b_6	✓	A > C > E	1	✓ C > E	1/2	C > E	1/2	✓ E	1/5
b_7	✓	A > C > E	1	✓ C > E	1/2	C > E	1/2	✓ E	1/5
b_8	✓	A > C > E	1	✓ C > E	1/2	C > E	1/2	✓ E	1/5
b_9	✓	A > C > E	1	✓ C > E	1/2	C > E	1/2	✓ E	1/5
b_{10}	✓	A > C > E	1	✓ C > E	1/2	C > E	1/2	✓ E	1/5
b_{11}	✓	B > C > D	1	B > C > D	1	✓ D	4/9	D	4/9
b_{12}	✓	B > C > D	1	B > C > D	1	✓ D	4/9	D	4/9
b_{13}	✓	B > C > D	1	B > C > D	1	✓ D	4/9	D	4/9
b_{14}	✓	B > C > D	1	B > C > D	1	✓ D	4/9	D	4/9
b_{15}	✓	B > C > D	1	B > C > D	1	✓ D	4/9	D	4/9
b_{16}	✓	B > C > D	1	B > C > D	1	✓ D	4/9	D	4/9
b_{17}	✓	B > C > D	1	B > C > D	1	✓ D	4/9	D	4/9
b_{18}	✓	B > C > D	1	B > C > D	1	✓ D	4/9	D	4/9
b_{19}	✓	B > C > D	1	B > C > D	1	✓ D	4/9	D	4/9
b_{20}	✓	C > E	1	C > E	1	C > E	1		
b_{21}	✓	C > E	1	C > E	1	C > E	1		

A B C D E	B C D E	C D E	D E
tt 10 9 2 0 0	tt 9 7 0 0	tt 7 4 0	tt 4 2
sp 5 4	sp 4 3		
tv 1/2 4/9	tv 4/9 1/5	$sp(B, \mathcal{E}_1)$	$sp(C, \mathcal{E}_1^A)$
	$sp(A, \mathcal{E}_1)$	distributed	distributed
A elected	distributed		E excluded
B elected	$sp(B, \mathcal{E}_1)$		**D** elected
	pending		
	C elected		

If C received this missing fraction of the surplus of B in $\mathcal{E}_2$, the fourth winner would be E. Example 6 shows this in detail.

`ManualACT` ^{DWD}: Declaring Winners after all surpluses are Distributed

Example 6. `ManualACT`^{DWD} is identical to `ManualACT` except that new winners are declared only after all pending surpluses are distributed. Table 6 shows totals and preference distributions using the initial election $\mathcal{E}_1$ from Example 5.

Elections $\mathcal{E}_1^A$ are identical in Tables 5 and 6. But C is not declared elected in $\mathcal{E}_1^A$ in Table 6, because there is still a pending winner, B.

Ballots $b_{11} - b_{19}$ are involved in distributing $sp(B, \mathcal{E}_1)$ and B's surplus votes go to candidate C in $\mathcal{E}_2$. There are no more pending winners, therefore candidates that have reached the quota can be declared winners in $\mathcal{E}_2$. Thus, C gets elected in $\mathcal{E}_2$ and C's surplus is distributed in the next count. Since A and B are declared

Table 6. Example 6: ManualACT^{DWD}: ManualACT but declaring winners after all surpluses are distributed

ID	$\mathcal{E}_1$, q = 5			$\mathcal{E}_1^A$, q = 5			$\mathcal{E}_2$, q = 5			$\mathcal{E}_3$, q = 5		
	LP	pref	weight	LP	pref	weight	LP	pref	weight	LP	pref	weight
b_1	✓	A > C > E	1	✓	C > E	1/2		C > E	1/2	✓	E	6/19
b_2	✓	A > C > E	1	✓	C > E	1/2		C > E	1/2	✓	E	6/19
b_3	✓	A > C > E	1	✓	C > E	1/2		C > E	1/2	✓	E	6/19
b_4	✓	A > C > E	1	✓	C > E	1/2		C > E	1/2	✓	E	6/19
b_5	✓	A > C > E	1	✓	C > E	1/2		C > E	1/2	✓	E	6/19
b_6	✓	A > C > E	1	✓	C > E	1/2		C > E	1/2	✓	E	6/19
b_7	✓	A > C > E	1	✓	C > E	1/2		C > E	1/2	✓	E	6/19
b_8	✓	A > C > E	1	✓	C > E	1/2		C > E	1/2	✓	E	6/19
b_9	✓	A > C > E	1	✓	C > E	1/2		C > E	1/2	✓	E	6/19
b_{10}	✓	A > C > E	1	✓	C > E	1/2		C > E	1/2	✓	E	6/19
b_{11}	✓	B > C > D	1		B > C > D	1	✓	C > D	4/9	✓	D	6/19
b_{12}	✓	B > C > D	1		B > C > D	1	✓	C > D	4/9	✓	D	6/19
b_{13}	✓	B > C > D	1		B > C > D	1	✓	C > D	4/9	✓	D	6/19
b_{14}	✓	B > C > D	1		B > C > D	1	✓	C > D	4/9	✓	D	6/19
b_{15}	✓	B > C > D	1		B > C > D	1	✓	C > D	4/9	✓	D	6/19
b_{16}	✓	B > C > D	1		B > C > D	1	✓	C > D	4/9	✓	D	6/19
b_{17}	✓	B > C > D	1		B > C > D	1	✓	C > D	4/9	✓	D	6/19
b_{18}	✓	B > C > D	1		B > C > D	1	✓	C > D	4/9	✓	D	6/19
b_{19}	✓	B > C > D	1		B > C > D	1	✓	C > D	4/9	✓	D	6/19
b_{20}	✓	C > E	1		C > E	1		C > E	1			
b_{21}	✓	C > E	1		C > E	1		C > E	1			

	A	B	C	D	E			B	C	D	E			C	D	E			D	E
tt	10	9	2	0	0		tt	9	7	0	0		tt	11	0	0		tt	2	3
sp	5	4					sp	4					sp	6						
tv	1/2	4/9					tv	4/9					tv	6/19						

A elected
B elected

$sp(A, \mathcal{E}_1)$
distributed
$sp(B, \mathcal{E}_1)$
pending

$sp(B, \mathcal{E}_2)$, q = 5
distributed
C elected

$sp(C, \mathcal{E}_2)$
distributed
D excluded
E elected

winners simultaneously, the last parcel of C contains ballots from both A and B that contribute votes to C's victory. Thus, the last parcel of C consists of ballots $b_1 - b_{19}$. $\mathcal{E}_3$ is the result of distributing $sp(C, \mathcal{E}_2)$.

No candidate reaches the quota in election $\mathcal{E}_3$. Since D has a lower total, it is excluded, and E becomes the fourth winner.

Note that D's total is lower than E's total in this example, because they both were equally regarded as the third preferences in ballots $b_1 - b_{19}$, taking into consideration that the first preferences of these ballots were declared winners in the same election $\mathcal{E}_1$ and their second preferences are identical. D appears in a smaller number of ballots than E and therefore eventually loses to E.

Note that although ballots $b_1 - b_{10}$ and $b_{11} - b_{19}$ had different weights in $\mathcal{E}_2$, their weights become identical in $\mathcal{E}_3$ and are equal to 6/19. This happens because in ManualACT, and hence in ManualACT^{DWD}, the new weights of ballots involved in the surplus distribution of C all become equal to the transfer value of C (unless the current weight is smaller than the transfer value, the weight remains unchanged then).

Summary of `ManualACT` Versus `ManualACT`^{DWD}

Example	Table	Algorithm	Election	Winners	Comment
5	5	`ManualACT`	$\mathcal{E}_1$	A, B, C, D	E loses
6	6	`ManualACT`^{DWD}	$\mathcal{E}_1$	A, B, C, E	E wins

4   Examples from Real ACT Elections

We now show that the issues that we have raised so far do manifest themselves in real elections in the ACT using our own independent implementation of `ManualACT`.

4.1   Last Parcel Anomalies

We now illustrate three inter-related anomalies which arise because of the use of the notion of the last parcel, which does not exist in `VanillaSTV`.

As Fig. 1 shows, `VanillaSTV` and `ManualACT` consider different sets of ballot papers when distributing the surplus of an elected candidate c: while `VanillaSTV` considers all continuing ballot papers that favour c, `ManualACT` considers only continuing ballot papers from the last parcel of c. If there is a large difference between the cardinality of these sets, then `ManualACT` can disenfranchise voters whose ballots favour c without being in the last parcel of c. Effectively, these ballots are mistakenly deemed to be exhausted as shown in Example 3.

A real instance of this phenomenon happens in Count 36 of the Brindabella scrutiny of the ACT Legislative Election 2012 [1] where Mick Gentelman's total is 12522 and the quota is 10594. This means that Mick Gentleman's surplus is $1928 = 12522 - 10594$. The number of continuing ballot papers from his last parcel is equal to 955, so they remain in scrutiny and are allowed to contribute to their next preference with a certain transfer value. But there were 2470 *other* continuing ballot papers that contributed to the total of Mick Gentleman (i.e. had Mick Gentleman as the first preference) but which were not in his last parcel. Thus 2470 voters were denied their next preference even though their ballot was not actually exhausted.

As we pointed out in Sect. 2, for an elected candidate c, each ballot that favours c is given a *transfer value* $tv(c, \mathcal{E}) = sp(c, \mathcal{E})/denom$ where *denom* is a function that depends on the vote counting approach. In `ManualACT`, *denom* is the number of the continuing ballots in the last parcel of c. Thus $s(c, \mathcal{E})/denom$ may be greater than 1. Moreover, if *denom* $= 0$, we get a "division by zero" error. The ACT Electoral Act is silent about the division by zero error but to handle both situations, the Electoral Act [3] (subclause 1C(4)) says: *"However, if the transfer value of a ballot paper ⟨...⟩ would be greater than the transfer value of the ballot paper when counted for the successful candidate, the **transfer value** *of that ballot paper is the transfer value of the ballot paper when counted for the successful candidate."* eVACS attempts to handle this situation by assigning 1 to the transfer value of c instead of $s(c, \mathcal{E})/denom$, if $denom = 0$ or if $s(c, \mathcal{E})/denom > 1$ [4]. Without further action, the next preferred candidate on the ballot papers that favour c would effectively receive a full vote, so eVACS resets the transfer value of these ballot papers to their original value rather than 1, thereby implementing subclause 1C(4).

In the Mick Gentleman example mentioned above, since 1928/955 is greater than 1, the transfer value of Mick Gentleman is assigned value 1. That is, without further action, the 955 ballots from Mick Gentleman's last parcel would suddenly increase in weight from some fraction $n/m < 1$ to 1. As stated above, eVACS detects this event and resets the transfer value of these 955 ballots to n/m, leading to the following two oddities:

1. These 955 voters contributed n/m of a vote to elect Mick Gentleman and can now contribute to their next preferred candidate without any reduction in their weight n/m;
2. Of Mick Gentleman's 1928 surplus votes, at least $1928 - 955 = 973$ were lost simply because their corresponding ballots do not belong to the last parcel for Mick Gentleman. That is, votes can "disappear" during scrutiny.

Another real instance of this phenomenon happens in Count 43 of preferences distribution of electorate Molonglo of the ACT Legislative Assembly Election 2012 [2]. In this count, the surplus votes of Simon Corbell are distributed. His surplus is equal to 1278 and there are 648 continuing ballot papers from his last parcel. Since 1278/648 > 1, the transfer value of Simon Corbell becomes 1. All 648 ballots of Simon Corbell that are considered for the distribution have weight 12554/23872. This weight is smaller than 1, therefore the weight of these ballots remains 12554/23872. Therefore, only $648 * (12554/23872) \approx 340.775$ of the surplus votes were distributed. The remaining $1278 - 648 * (12554/23872) \approx 937.22$ surplus votes were lost. Moreover, 648 voters were allowed to "double dip" by contributing 12554/23872 of a vote to Simon Corbell, and also to their next preferred candidate.

4.2   Loss by Fraction

According to the ACT Legislation [3], each candidate is associated with a number, called "total votes", that changes as the scrutiny proceeds. The "total votes" of a candidate is defined in the Legislation as *"the sum of all votes allotted to the candidate"*. However, as we show below, the manner of computing "total votes" in `ManualACT` means they do not equal the sum of all votes allotted to the candidate.

The following two statements from the Legislation seem to instruct us to use "count votes" of a candidate for computing his or her "total votes", although it is not stated precisely. *"6(3) The count votes for each continuing candidate shall be determined and allotted to him or her. 6(4) After the allotment under subclause (3), the continuing candidates' total votes shall be calculated and, if the total votes of a candidate equal or exceed the quota, the candidate is successful."*

Section 1A of Schedule 4 of the Legislation defines the notion of "count votes" as the result of multiplying *"the number of ballot papers to be dealt with at a count that record the next available preference for the candidate"* and *"the transfer value of those ballots"* and disregarding any fraction. The fraction is disregarded because it is easier to deal with natural numbers when counting by hand.

Indeed, eVACS computes totals of candidates in the following way that interprets the above mentioned statements 6(3) and 6(4) of the Legislation. Here is an extract from [4]: *"25) ⟨...⟩ Calculate the sum of the Vote Values of all ballots in the candidate's Pile for this Count, and truncate it to an integer (i.e. 700.9999 becomes 700). Set the candidate's Total for this Count to the candidate's Total for the last Count plus the truncated sum."*

More mathematically: let $\lfloor CV^c \rfloor$ denote "count votes" of candidate c. Assume candidate A obtained initially N votes and then obtained his or her part of surpluses of candidates $c_1, \ldots, c_k$. Then "total votes" of A is equal to $N + \lfloor CV^{c_1} \rfloor + \cdots + \lfloor CV^{c_k} \rfloor$. Because of all the truncations, "total votes" of a candidate defined by statements 6(3) and 6(4) is in fact lower than the sum of the weights of the ballots allotted to the candidate.

In other words, the numbers that appear in the ACT scrutiny tables do not correspond exactly to the actual distribution of votes.

The impact of this truncation of "total values" can be substantial as demonstrated below by running a variant of the `ManualACT` that does not round down the "count votes" on the Brindabella Legislative Assembly Election 2012.

Example 7. Using `ManualACT`, consider the Brindabella Distribution of Preferences [1, Table 2]. After Brendan Smyth's surplus votes are distributed, no candidate reaches quota $q = 10594$ and Rebecca Cody is chosen for exclusion with the lowest "total votes": 6257. Amanda Bresnan has a slightly higher value of "total votes" of 6261 so she continues in the scrutiny. In the first partial exclusion of Rebecca Cody's votes, Mick Gentleman reaches quota with "total votes" 12522. Eventually, after fully excluding Rebecca Cody, distributing the surplus votes of Mick Gentleman and excluding Amanda Bresnan, Andrew Wall becomes the final winner as the only continuing candidate in the scrutiny with "total votes" 10541.

Applying `ManualACT` without truncation of totals to the same election, Amanda Bresnan has a *fractionally* lower total ($48855454926329/7794085572 = 6268.27284292$) than Rebecca Cody ($87405572581/13942908 = 6268.81942999$) after the distribution of Brendan Smyth's votes and is therefore selected for exclusion. About 1830.5 votes from Amanda Bresnan go to Mick Gentleman, giving him a total $39279302005211/3897042786 = 10079.2585974$ after Amanda Bresnan's full distribution. Then Rebecca Cody is excluded and her first partial exclusion brings 5566 votes to Mick Gentleman and Mick Gentleman becomes the winner with $60970242152087/3897042786 = 15645.2585974$ votes.

Table 7. Winner totals in Brindabella 2012 ACT Legislative Assembly Election

Winner	ManualACT	ManualACT without truncation
Zed Seselja	18566	18566
Joy Burch	11671	11676.7267256 (215353871/18443)
Brendan Smyth	11470	11477.1555854 (63713627319/5551343)
Mick Gentleman	12522	15645.2585974 (60970242152087/3897042786)
Andrew Wall	10541	9089.16365112 (70841719274717/7794085572)

Thus, in ManualACT, the truncation of totals causes Mick Gentleman to obtain $15645.2585974 - 10541 = 5104.2585974$ fewer votes than if totals are not truncated. The totals of other winners are also reduced due to truncation. Table 7 shows the number of votes of all winners in both approaches.

Note also that, in this example, the rounding of totals has an effect on the order of exclusion of candidates Rebecca Cody and Amanda Bresnan. In another election this may lead to different winners.

4.3 Effects of Rounding

We now describe another important observation about numbers that appear in the ACT scrutiny sheets. As explained in Sect. 2, ManualACT excludes a candidate not at once, but in several partial exclusions. The number of such partial exclusions is equal to the number of different weights that exist in the continuing ballots that favour the candidate. Each partial exclusion of a candidate reduces his or her total. The legislation does not define how the total of this candidate should be recomputed. But it is reasonable to expect that the sum of the weights of the remaining ballots in favour of this candidate should be equal to the candidate's total after the partial exclusion. This is not the case in the ACT scrutiny tables produced by eVACS [4]. eVACS classifies ballots that favour the candidate to be excluded into groups/piles according to weights of these ballots. Then eVACS performs partial exclusions of the candidate in a consecutive order starting with the pile with the highest weight. After each partial exclusion eVACS recalculates the candidate's total in the following way: *"36) Set Group Sum to 0. For each pile forming the Group: Multiply the number of Ballots in this pile by their vote value and truncate to an integer (i.e. 700.9999 becomes 700). Add this value to the Group Sum. 36b) Subtract this Group Sum from the excluding candidate's Total for previous Count to give the excluding candidate's Total for this Count."* Note that "candidate's Total for previous Count" is a truncated value.

Example 8. In Count 7 of the Brindabella 2012 ACT Election, Ben Murphy who has the lowest (truncated) number of votes 754 is chosen to be excluded. There are 825 ballot papers in scrutiny that favour Ben Murphy at that election. Of these papers 702 papers have weight 1 and 123 papers have weight 7972/18443.

Since some ballots for Ben Murphy have one weight, and other ballots for Ben Murphy have a different weight, his full exclusion takes two counts. The first partial exclusion transfers votes of Ben Murphy to the next continuing candidates in the ballots with weight 1. According to statements 36) and 36b) of eVACS, the "Group Sum" of these ballots is equal to $\lfloor 702 * 1 \rfloor = \lfloor 702 \rfloor = 702$ (*"Multiply the number of Ballots in this pile by their vote value and truncate to an integer"*). Then the "Total" of Ben Murphy after the first partial exclusion is $754 - 702 = 52$ (*"Subtract this Group Sum from the excluding candidate's Total for previous Count"*).

The second partial exclusion deals with ballots that have transfer value $7972/18443$. The "Group Sum" of these ballots is equal to $\lfloor 123 * (7972/18443) \rfloor = \lfloor 53.166838367 \rfloor = 53$. Then the "Total" of Ben Murphy after the second and final partial exclusion is $52 - 53 = -1$. A negative number!

Analogously, other excluded candidates end up with negative "Totals" in the Scrutiny. For example, Rebecca Cody ends up with total -8, Val Jeffrey with -5, Karl Maftoum with -7, Nicole Lawder with -4.

These negative numbers of excluded candidates do not appear in ACT's scrutiny tables because eVACS does not print totals of candidates that are fully excluded, as can be seen from the following extract of void report_votes_transferred from [5], where static void draw_empty draws an empty cell.

```
/* No box if they're excluded */
if (status == CAND_EXCLUDED) {
 draw_empty(distribution.out, count-1, candpos,"", 0);
 return;
}
```

The discrepancy between "Totals" which appear on the ACT's scrutiny tables and the actual sum of weights of ballots that still remain in scrutiny as these candidates are partially excluded does not influence the outcome. However, this discrepancy is yet another example of mathematical imprecision that happens when the hand counting approach is implemented literally.

5   Further Work and Conclusion

There are many other variations of STV in use in Australia and around the world. Many of them have their own "simplifications". For example, the province of New South Wales uses a version of STV where the surplus votes are sampled randomly to obtain the votes to transfer. All these versions require further analysis. Regardless, we have hopefully shown that the legislation governing ACT elections needs to be thoroughly revised to eliminate the "simplifications" that pander to hand-counting since ACT Elections now use full e-counting.

Acknowledgements. We are grateful to the ACT Electoral Commissioner, Phillip Green, for his numerous comments on a previous draft. Any errors that remain are ours.

References

1. ACT Elections. ACT Legislative Assembly Election 2012 - Interim Distribution of Preferences: Brindabella Table 2 - Votes. http://www.elections.act.gov.au/__data/assets/pdf_file/0008/836063/table2.Brindabella.pdf
2. ACT Elections. ACT Legislative Assembly Election 2012 - Interim Distribution of Preferences: Molonglo Table 2 - Votes. http://www.elections.act.gov.au/__data/assets/pdf_file/0004/836068/table2.Molonglo.pdf
3. ACT Elections. Australian Capital Territory Electoral Act 1992. Republication No 51. Effective, 27 April 2016. Authorised by the ACT Parliamentary Counsel, March 2016. http://www.legislation.act.gov.au/a/1992-71/20160302-62977/pdf/1992-71.pdf
4. Software Improvements Pty Ltd. Documentation of the eVACS® source code: 2012. File: /evacs/counting/hare_clark.txt. http://www.elections.act.gov.au/__data/assets/file/0003/835509/evacs2012.zip
5. Software Improvements Pty Ltd. Source code 2012 of eVACS®. File: /evacs/counting/report.c. http://www.elections.act.gov.au/__data/assets/file/0003/835509/evacs2012.zip
6. Wikipedia. Single transferable vote. https://en.wikipedia.org/wiki/Single_transferable_vote. Accessed 26 Aug 2016

Internet Voting in Sub-national Elections: Policy Learning in Canada and Australia

Nicole Goodman[1] and Rodney Smith[2(✉)]

[1] Munk School of Global Affairs, University of Toronto, Toronto, Canada
nicole.goodman@utoronto.ca
[2] Department of Government and International Relations, University of Sydney,
Sydney, Australia
rodney.smith@sydney.edu.au

Abstract. In advanced democracies, the expansion of internet voting in national elections appears to have stalled. New announcements by governments of online voting initiatives seem to be matched by announcements elsewhere that trials will not proceed, or that completed trials will not result in wider deployment. Debates between proponents and opponents of internet voting in advanced democracies now run along well-worn lines. The same examples are endlessly recycled. This apparent inertia at the national level masks the gradual increase in examples of deployment at the sub-national level. These sub-national cases provide a growing stock of evidence about more and less successful ways of managing transitions to voting by internet. This article draws upon advocacy coalition theory to analyse some of these sub-national developments, focusing on remote online voting in Australia and Canada.

Keywords: Internet voting · Sub-national elections · Policy · Canada · Australia

1 E-Voting: No Movement?

In July 2014, the Norwegian government announced that it was ending its internet voting trials, following concerns about privacy and the failure of internet voting to increase turnout, especially among young voters. The trials had been judged by many to be popular and successful, with the most recent pilots in 12 municipalities resulting in 38% uptake among 250,000 eligible voters [5, 39]. At around the same time, the United Kingdom's Electoral Commissioner, Jenny Watson, and the Speaker of the UK House of Commons, John Bercow, separately announced their support for the UK to move to remote online voting in order, among other things, to increase youth turnout [4, 5]. The UK government had ended its own internet voting pilots a decade earlier, due to criticisms about the insecurity of online voting and its failure to raise turnout, criticisms that were eerily similar to the conclusions now being drawn in Norway [28, 40].

These synchronous examples are typical of the lack of progress toward internet voting in advanced democracies over the past decade. While the use of internet and computer technology for other electoral tasks such as voter registration, voter identification and electoral roll mark-off at polling places, and electronic counting of scanned

© Springer International Publishing AG 2017
R. Krimmer et al. (Eds.): E-Vote-ID 2016, LNCS 10141, pp. 164–177, 2017.
DOI: 10.1007/978-3-319-52240-1_10

paper ballots has increased, the initial expansion of remote online voting appears to have stalled. Every new announcement by a government that e-voting should be trialled or introduced seems to be matched by an announcement elsewhere that trials will not proceed, or that completed trials will not result in wider use.

The voting technology that is the subject of this article, remote online voting is presently used for binding elections in ten countries: Australia, Armenia, Canada, Estonia, France, India, Mexico, Panama, Switzerland and the United States. While there was a flurry of adoption in the early 2000s, many pilots were terminated because hoped-for effects on turnout were not realized or due to technical considerations. Today only Estonia permits voting by internet in national elections for all electors. Armenia, France, Mexico, Panama and the United States have also used the technology in national elections but only as an option for citizens or military living abroad. Internet voting is deployed sub-national or local elections in all the other countries listed above. This change in the pace of development is the result of several factors. First, online voting did not deliver 'magic bullet' improvements to waning voter participation as was hoped in places such as the UK and Norway. These assessments, however, were often based on one or two elections and did not consider other contextual variables that may have affected the rate of voter participation. Second, concerns about security, fraud, and new pressures to create verification tools to ensure votes were cast as intended slowed i-voting developments in Estonia and Switzerland. Finally, in Europe in particular, budget crises and declining trust in the internet contributed to the halting or stalling of voting technology purchases and trials.

Perhaps as a result of this stasis, public debates over remote online voting in advanced democracies now run along well-worn lines. Proponents argue that internet voting will bring modernisation, efficiency, improved access to the voting process and increased turnout, especially among targeted populations such as young people. Opponents warn of threats to electoral integrity wherever online voting is introduced or expanded, citing issues of security and privacy (see Table 1). In these debates, the same examples of success and failure are endlessly recycled.

Table 1. The well-established remote online voting debate

Arguments in favour	Arguments against
Modernisation	Caution (let others take the risk)
Accessibility (for remote voters, immobile voters, busy voters, persons with disabilities etc.)	Accessibility (the 'digital divide', variable internet coverage and quality, and computer literacy etc.)
Engagement, participation and turnout (especially for the young)	Erosion of social rituals of voting (the death of the 'sausage sizzle' etc.)
Reduction in voter error and accidentally spoiled ballots	Security threats (hacking, viruses, denial of service attacks etc.)
Secrecy (for voters with disabilities etc.)	Secrecy (family members voting together, coercion, vote-buying, intercepted votes etc.)
Faster and more accurate ballot counts.	Loss of scrutiny of the ballot count
Reduced expense (over time)	Expense of setting up system, voter education, etc.
Environmentally friendly	Voting occurs without full information (since people vote early)

2   Internet Voting and Advocacy Coalition Theory

One way of understanding this apparent impasse can be found in the advocacy coalition framework developed by Paul Sabatier and other public policy scholars [23]. Adopting this approach, we can view the remote online voting debate as mostly occurring in a policy sub-system, well away from the everyday cut and thrust of policy debates that attract the attention of the news media and the general public. As a specialised issue, internet voting policy involves established, small and relatively closed groups of expert participants, including electoral officials, members of parliamentary committees on electoral issues, political party officials, online voting system vendors, computer scientists, internet security specialists, political scientists, and advocacy groups for people with disabilities, people living in remote areas and the like. These participants form competing advocacy coalitions that use technical expertise and other resources to try to influence public policy via strategies such as submissions to policy-makers, media campaigns and specialist conference presentations [23].

As Table 1 suggests, the contest between supporters and opponents of online voting has become stable both with regards to opposed core normative beliefs (participation versus security) and opposed specific policy preferences. The advocacy coalition framework suggests three general pathways by which an impasse between competing coalitions can be broken. One is a shock or crisis that provides an advantage to one side of the policy argument. These shocks might be external to the policy sub-system (e.g., a fiscal crisis that causes governments to cut funding for innovations in electoral management) or internal to it (e.g., a major failure of paper or electronic voting processes). A second pathway is policy-oriented learning from the accumulation of new information and examples over time, which favour the position of one coalition over another. A third pathway of compromise occurs when the competing advocacy coalitions recognise that the policy status quo is unacceptable to each of their positions [23].

The first or second pathways to policy change appear more likely than the third in the field of remote online voting policy. The fear of electoral shock or crisis is seen in the reluctance of governments in advanced democracies with well-run elections to introduce internet voting, in case its use results in a failed election that they are forced to invalidate. The continued decline in electoral turnout represents a countervailing set of repeated shocks or crises facing political elites in these countries, which internet voting may potentially counter. A less dramatic policy-learning path is provided by the accumulation of examples of internet voting at the sub-national level. These sub-national cases provide a growing stock of under-examined evidence about more and less successful ways of managing any transition to the use of internet voting and the effects that the technology has on elections. The following sections of this paper explore these developments at the sub-national level, focusing on Canada and Australia. Our analysis draws upon a review of sub-national electoral commission reports and other government documents, news media reports, and survey, interview and focus group data. The Australian survey and interview results presented are based on secondary analysis of research originally conducted for the New South Wales Electoral Commission. The Canadian survey data was collected as part of the Internet

Voting Project; a study focused on understanding the effects of online voting on local elections in the province of Ontario.

3   The Canadian Municipal Experience

Since 2003, 192 municipal elections with a remote online component have taken place in Canada. The number of municipalities using online voting has nearly doubled with each election (see Table 2). There have been more than 4.5 million online 'voting opportunities' in these municipalities since 2003, although the actual number of online

Table 2. Remote online voting in Canadian municipal elections

Year	Number of Municipalities	All electronic elections	Pre-registration	Online voting period	Number and proportion of online voters[a]
2003	12 (including Markham) in Ontario	10 (83%)	1 Yes; 11 No	1 advance; 12 in full election	Markham: 7,210 (16.7%)
2006	20 (including Markham and Peterborough) in Ontario	13 (65%)	2 Yes; 18 No	2 advance; 19 in full election	Markham: 10,639 (17.7%); Peterborough: 3,473 (14%)
2008	4 (including Halifax) in Nova Scotia	0	No	3 advance; 4 in full election	Nova Scotia: 29,918 (10.85%)
2009	Halifax, Nova Scotia by-election	0	No	1 in full election	Halifax: 9,259 (74.2%)
2010	43 (including Markham) in Ontario[b]	24 (54.5%)	6 Yes; 37 No	6 advance; 37 in full election	
2012	14 of 54 (including Halifax) in Nova Scotia[c]	5 (35.7%)	No	10 advance; 4 in full election	Nova Scotia: 490,535 (67.1%)
2014	97 of 444 (including Markham) in Ontario	59 (61%)	12 Yes; 85 No	6 advance; 91 in full election	Ontario: 335,257 (51.5%)

Sources: [12, 14, 15, 29]. Additional data collected by the Internet Voting Project and provided by Intelivote Inc.

[a]The proportion of online voters is calculated based on the number of votes cast in communities that offered internet voting.

[b]Forty-four municipalities planned to use internet voting, however all seats were acclaimed in the Town of Hawkesbury and so elections took place in 43 of them.

[c]Online voting was approved for 16 communities, but all seats were acclaimed in the Town of Middleton and the Municipality of East Hants determined that it could not afford implementation.

votes is much lower. In the 2014 Ontario municipal elections for example, about 2.2 million electors had the option to vote online, with 335,257 online ballots cast. Presently municipal online voting is limited to the provinces of Ontario and Nova Scotia, where communities have the option of passing by-laws to introduce alternative voting modes. The provinces write municipal election legislation in Canada. To date six provinces (Alberta, British Columbia, New Brunswick, Nova Scotia, Ontario and Saskatchewan) have passed legislative provisions that allow for the use of alternative voting methods by municipalities [15]. Despite a supportive legislative framework, however, and a great deal of local interest, provinces such as Alberta and British Columbia have not permitted municipalities to proceed with internet voting trials primarily because of security concerns. In Alberta in particular, a group of municipalities planned to adopt internet voting in 2013 when the Minister of Municipal Affairs issued a moratorium. Many of these communities have since argued for more autonomy and it appears as though online voting will be used in select Alberta municipalities in 2017.

Rationales for the introduction of internet voting in Canadian municipalities vary, but there are common themes. A 2013 Elections Canada research report found that anticipated improvements in accessibility, voter turnout, and leadership in e-government were the most popular reasons for adopting, or considering deployment of, internet voting [31]. In a 2014 survey of election administrators in Ontario, the three top cited reasons for the use of internet voting in elections were accessibility (25%), increasing voter turnout (22%), and voter convenience (17%) [13, 16]. Apart from the desire to be a modernising leader in e-government, these reasons focus on making it easier for electors to vote and promote their participation. They do not include efficiency goals such as improving counting processes or reducing election costs. For Canadian election administrators, improvements in voter participation and retention of current voters motivate shifts to online voting.

Many municipalities in Ontario and Nova Scotia have used, or continue to offer, remote voting channels such as postal voting, and in some cases proxy voting [8, 30]. Remote online voting is typically offered as one of multiple voting modes including some combination of paper, telephone, and postal ballots. Many communities, however, have opted for all electronic elections. In 2014, 59 of 97 Ontario municipalities that used internet voting eliminated paper voting altogether. Fifty-eight of these used a combination of internet and telephone ballots, while the Municipality of Leamington ran the first all internet election in Canada [9].

Beyond differences in voting modes, municipal internet voting deployment varies in two important ways. One is the time period in which internet voting is made available. Smaller communities (populations less than 25,000 persons) or those with large seasonal populations (e.g., in areas where there are a lot of cottages) typically offer internet voting for the full election (during the advance voting period and on Election Day). By comparison, larger places with populations greater than 100,000 inhabitants generally have online voting in the advance vote period only. Another difference is whether pre-registration is required to vote online. Most small communities do not require registration beforehand and also use fewer credentials to authenticate voters' identities (e.g., items such as a PIN, date of birth, security question, and password). A municipal association survey of 38 municipalities that used internet voting in 2014 asked which credentials were used. In 92% of cases, a PIN was required to cast a ballot online, 42% required date of birth be filled in, and in 16% the creation of a security question was necessary. Most large cities require registration ahead of time. This latter approach customarily involves the successful completion of multiple credentials [16].

The examples of remote online voting in Canadian municipalities since 2003 offer considerable scope for policy learning, since they vary across key dimensions, including the size, demographics and geographic location of the municipalities involved, the combination of voting modes, the online voting vendors, online voting process requirements (e.g., registration or no registration) and the online voting period [14, 16]. Policy learning has been important for growing uptake amongst Canadian municipalities and has influenced the type of models adopted.

The fact that communities with populations greater than 100,000 have opted for a registration requirement, for example, is largely a consequence of the City of Markham initially adopting that approach in 2003. Markham's process meant that electors received a letter with instructions for registering to vote online, with those who registered receiving their voting credentials in a second letter. A risk assessment conducted by Professor Henry M. Kim from York University found that Markham's two-step approach reduced the chances of fraudulent internet voting [25]. All large municipalities followed suit, although some amended the Markham approach slightly by using email instead of paper mailing for the second 'mail-out'.

In a further step, policy-makers in the Town of Ajax decided that using email to communicate voting credentials to electors was not necessarily secure, given that creating a fake email account was easier than intercepting mail. At the same time, Ajax officials determined that the initial registration requirement increased the perceived costs of internet voting for electors and thus worked against their goal of increasing turnout. For these reasons, Ajax retired paper voting altogether in 2014 and ran an all-electronic election in which the 75,000 eligible voters could gain access to internet or telephone ballots using a mailed out PIN and additional personal details [1, 11, 22]. The Ajax experience may change the patterns of online voting implementation by encouraging other mid-sized and large municipalities to adopt a similar approach to deployment.

Policy learning has also influenced the period in which municipalities make online voting available. Some communities, such as Halifax Regional Municipality and the Town of Whitby, first trialled remote online voting in a by-election before deploying it in a regular election. In addition, steady growth in municipal uptake with each election can be attributed to the fact that early adopters have reported successful deployment of the voting method. Hearing positive testimonials from voters, candidates and election administrators has encouraged other communities across the provinces of Ontario and Nova Scotia to modernise voting.

Generally, online voting experiences have been positive for stakeholders. Reported technical and security issues have been limited [15]. Technical issues in 2014 Ontario municipal elections concerned the accuracy of voters' lists, delays in the postal delivery of voting instructions and credentials to households, and a two and a half hour election night delay in the posting of results for about 44 municipalities [3, 16, 34]. The latter problem prompted the online voting provider to reduce its fee to the affected municipalities by 25% [2]. One mayoral contest in Napanee involving a three-vote margin resulted in a recount of internet ballots, after which the original result was confirmed [3, 38].

Canadians that have used online voting report positive experiences. The 2014 Ontario local elections provide evidence that internet voting is popular, even where paper and telephone options are also available. In the 23 municipalities that offered all three voting modes, 55.6% of votes were cast by internet, 31.6% by paper and 12.8% by telephone [16]. Similarly in the 2010 elections in the 12 municipalities that used all three voting options, internet ballots were more popular than telephone and paper combined in eight municipalities, more popular than either of the other two channels in three municipalities, and less popular than both the other channels in just one municipality (calculated from [12]). Satisfaction levels among surveyed internet voters have consistently been over 90%, with similarly high proportions of users claiming they would use internet voting again and recommending its expansion into provincial and federal elections [12, 16].

The primary rationale voters cite for using internet voting is convenience, however access also appears to be a factor. Among Ontario voters surveyed in 2014, 14% claimed that they would probably or definitely not have voted without the internet option. Fifty-eight percent of people who voted in 2014 and had not done so in 2010 identified the accessibility of internet voting in 2014 as the factor that made the difference to their behaviour [12, 15, 16]. Canadian studies find a 3% increase in municipal election turnout following the adoption of the voting reform [17]. Goodman and Pyman conclude that internet voting has a 'modest potential to engage non-voters' [16]. Notably, the voting mode does not appear to have met the goal of engaging young voters, as the most common users are middle–aged or older. The average internet voter in the 2014 Ontario municipal elections was 53 years old [16].

Despite the issues mentioned earlier, most municipal electoral officials involved in the 2014 Ontario election had positive views about internet voting deployment. Over 90% of those surveyed would recommend using online voting in the next municipal elections, and for future provincial and federal elections. Officials cited accessibility, turnout and convenience as the primary benefits of the voting reform. When considering risks, they tended to rate internet voting as involving more risks than paper ballots cast at a polling place but as less risky than the other remote options of telephone or postal voting. For officials, the greatest challenges posed by internet voting adoption were public education and countering negative news media [16]. Internet voting policy learning has occurred in Canada and this is likely continue, since a record number of about 200 Ontario municipalities anticipate adopting voting reform in the 2018 election.

Election candidates were perhaps the group most affected by the adoption of internet voting. With increasing numbers of voters casting an early ballot, candidates had to work harder to get campaign messages to voters at the start of the election period [12]. Many candidates in 2014 believed that remote online voting had improved turnout and interest in the election. Eighty-nine percent supported its use as an additional voting channel, although 64% opposed the use of the internet ballots as the only voting channel [16].

Finally, it is worth noting that internet voting was halted municipally in the province of Alberta because of an internal policy shock. In 2012 the City of Edmonton invested in a public consultation process to evaluate the possibility of using internet voting in future municipal elections. This included carrying out public opinion surveys, a mock online election to test the technology, a series of citizen roundtables and the creation and implementation of a Citizens' Jury. After hearing expert testimony and careful deliberation the Jury voted in favour of proceeding with internet voting in the 2013 elections, 16 to 1. The negative juror eventually changed his vote to support the policy change [24].

Although the Jury supported the change and compiled a list of recommendations for adoption, the voting reform had to be approved by City Council before implementation. As the issue came before Council, a local computer programmer and public opponent of internet voting, Mr. Chris Cates, requested to speak to Council. During his presentation to an Executive Committee of six councillors on 28 January 2013, Cates explained that he had voted twice in the mock election and argued that the system security was therefore unsafe. He would not explain how he had cast two ballots. (Officials wanted persons from anywhere in the world to be able to vote in the mock election and test the technology so registration was not tightly controlled. It is thought that Cates registered twice to vote). Cates' testimony cast doubt upon the security of internet voting and echoed concerns raised by computer scientists during the Jury process. While councillors had other concerns about proceeding with internet voting, Cates' allegation of voting twice has been suggested as a reason for their rejection of the proposal in a vote of 11 to 2 [24].

The rejection of internet voting by Edmonton City Council led the office of Alberta's Minister of Municipal Affairs to place a moratorium on internet voting for the 2013 elections, preventing other municipalities that had planned to use the technology from proceeding. The 'shock' of a potential security compromise, even in a mock election, is a key reason why internet voting has experienced a standstill in Alberta. Although some municipalities have revisited the issue and lobbied to use online ballots in 2017, this case illustrates the way shocks can shift internet voting policy debates.

4 The Australian Experience

Remote online voting is currently offered in only one jurisdiction in Australia. Certain groups of voters in New South Wales (NSW), the most populous of Australia's six states, are able to cast their votes via the internet or telephone using the iVote® system. Since 2011, NSW voters have cast nearly 339,000 votes across nine elections (see Table 3).

The development of remote online voting in Canada and NSW has differed in two ways. First, while remote online voting in the Canadian municipalities is now available to all voters and is the only way to vote in some municipalities, only certain categories of NSW voters are eligible to vote via the internet. Registration and voting are compulsory for almost all adult citizens in NSW elections, as they are in national, state and territory elections across Australia. Thus the goals of the policy-makers who introduced remote online voting were not to boost overall voter turnout but instead to improve access to the ballot for citizens who would otherwise find it difficult to cast a vote. Division 12A of the NSW *Parliamentary Electorates and Elections Act 1912* specifies that 'technology assisted voting' such as remote online voting is intended only for use

Table 3. Elections using internet voting in New South Wales

Election	Number of internet voters	Total number of voters	Percentage of internet voters
2011 State Election	46,862	4,290,595	1.09%
2011 Clarence By-election	1,246	44,412	2.08%
2012 Heffron By-election	798	36,724	2.17%
2012 Sydney By-election	2,192	38,457	5.70%
2013 Northern Tablelands By-election	1,859	44,393	4.19%
2013 Miranda By-election	679	41,289	1.64%
2014 Charleston By-election	763	42,592	1.79%
2014 Newcastle By-election	836	43,645	1.91%
2015 State Election	283,669	4,561,234	6.22%
Total Votes Cast	338,904	9,143,341	3.70%

Source: Figures from the New South Wales Electoral Commission.

by voters who are vision impaired, illiterate or have another disability that prevents them from voting without assistance or makes voting a challenge, as well as voters who live 20 kilometres or more from a polling place, or who will be out of the state during polling day. Many NSW voters using internet voting would otherwise not have voted, would have voted by postal ballot, or would have been unable to cast a secret ballot [21].

As with most online voting in Canadian municipalities, the NSW iVote is offered as part of a suite of voting channels. In the NSW case, these include paper ballots at polling places on or before polling day, postal voting and some mobile voting services. In contrast to some Canadian municipalities, the NSW government currently has no plans to make internet voting the only available voting channel, or to expand the categories of voters that are eligible to vote online. At the same time, the NSW Electoral Commission has little incentive to take action against the significant minority of voters who actually use the iVote system but are officially ineligible to do so because they do not fit the categories of voter specified in the *Act* (see above). These ineligible voters mainly vote online for reasons of convenience. Survey research suggests that ineligible voters comprised around one-quarter of voters using the iVote system in the 2015 NSW election, a figure that is likely to increase as these voters recommend online voting to others and it becomes better known (IPSOS 2015: 73–74; 83–84).

The second difference between Canada and Australia with respect to online voting has to do with number of significant organisations involved in its authorisation and administration. The introduction of internet voting in NSW has occurred under the oversight of a single legislative body, the NSW Parliament, has been managed by a single electoral management body, with a technical system provided by a single electronic elections company (Scytl). Canadian developments, by contrast, have involved a growing number of municipal governments and about six competing technology vendors. The relatively low initial uptake of online voting at the 2011 NSW state election (just over 1% of voters), was followed by a series of seven by-elections involving limited numbers of voters, which allowed the NSW Electoral Commission to test and refine the iVote system before it was used by a much larger group of voters (over 6%) in the 2015 state election [7]. By contrast, 54 Canadian municipalities used remote online voting for the first time in 2014, although as shown earlier, many of them drew upon the experiences of earlier adopters.

The different ways in which the growth of remote internet voting has occurred in Canada and Australia mean that the risks of internal shocks and the patterns of policy learning are likely to vary to some degree. A critical technology failure in one Canadian municipal election, for example, may not affect the commitment of other municipalities to deploy online voting, while a critical failure in a NSW election might cause a complete suspension of the voting method.

Similarly, Canadian municipalities can learn from each other's experiences of different online voting systems, while NSW policy-makers will primarily learn lessons from the performance of the iVote® system in light of the specific context and demands of NSW elections. Some of this policy learning is directed by the NSW Electoral Commission, which undertakes internal and external testing of the iVote® system and reports the results [27]. Other aspects of this policy learning are more open-ended. The most important forum for this type of policy learning is the parliamentary inquiry into the conduct of each NSW state election undertaken by the Joint Standing Committee on Electoral Matters (JSCEM). JSCEM is a cross-party committee, whose members are drawn from the NSW Parliament's two houses, the Legislative Assembly and the Legislative Council. It receives submissions and takes evidence from interested individuals and organisations, including supporters and opponents of internet voting in NSW. JSCEM's recommendations on internet voting following the 2011 NSW election led to some modification of remote online voting for the 2015 election, particularly through provision of a new process whereby internet voters could verify their votes [26, 33].

Almost all of the nine NSW elections using internet voting have been uncontroversial. At the 2015 state election, however, two contentious issues developed soon after online voting began on 16 March. First, for the initial 36 h of voting, an administrative error led to the names of two minor parties being omitted from the online ballot paper for the state's upper house, the Legislative Council. During this period, about 19,000 votes were cast online [19]. Voting by internet was briefly suspended while the mistake was corrected. Nonetheless, the error raised the possibility that the Legislative Council election result might be challenged in the NSW Court of Disputed Returns and the outcome altered by the Court or the election rerun, if either of the affected parties narrowly missed out on winning a seat [18]. Ultimately, one of the parties—the Animal Justice Party—won the last seat in the contest, while the Outdoor Recreation Party fell short of gaining a seat and did not launch a legal challenge [20].

The second issue involved a public intervention on 21 March by two university computer scientists, one from the United States and one from Australia, who had previously opposed internet voting internationally on security and privacy grounds. They advised NSW voters that vulnerability in the system meant that 'your vote could have been exposed or changed without you knowing' and 'recommend[ed] you stick with an old-fashioned paper ballot' [37]. The NSW Electoral Commission disputed the seriousness of the problem and criticised the two academics for the way in which they publicised their claims [10].

If the two controversies had any affect on voters, they appeared to pique interest in voting online. Daily registrations to use the iVote reached 10,000 on 17 March and then began to decline, falling to around 7,000 on 21 March, two days after the missing party name controversy and the day of the computer scientists' media intervention. Over the next few days, daily registrations increased sharply to 20,000, eventually reaching 50,000 new registrations on 27 March, the day before the close of online voting [6].

Surveys of online voters in 2011 and 2015 indicate they like the convenience of the voting mode [21, 35]. As in Canada, almost all NSW voters that voted online in 2015 (96%) were satisfied with the overall process, while satisfaction levels with more specific elements of the process—registration, receiving an iVote PIN number, and the time and ease of remote voting—all also exceeded 90% [21]. Although iVote users who reported being aware of iVote news during the 2015 election campaign were more likely to remember negative news items than positive ones, almost two-thirds of users remained 'very confident' that their votes had been recorded securely and accurately and a further third were 'fairly confident' [21]. These findings about confidence in the system are supported by the fact that only 1.7% of online voters used the iVote verification tool to check their votes after casting them at the 2015 NSW election [7]. Trust in online voting among non-users in NSW is likely to be lower; however, national survey research following the 2013 federal election found that over half (57%) of Australian voters were confident that a vote cast remotely via the internet would be recorded and counted accurately [36].

The nine NSW elections conducted using remote online voting have been considered a success by officials. The two potential internal shocks that occurred during voting in 2015 had little apparent impact on growing community acceptance in NSW of the internet as a trustworthy and convenient voting channel. The NSW Electoral Commission responded to these incidents by further modifying its remote online voting systems. The policy lessons other Australian jurisdictions draw from the NSW experience are mixed. In November 2014, the Commonwealth Parliament's Joint Standing Committee on Electoral Matters produced a report reviewing Australian experiences. It rejected internet voting for national elections, invoking familiar concerns about security, hacking, fraud, vote-buying, and voter coercion [32]. By contrast, the Western Australian Parliament recently drew on the NSW iVote® experience to pass the *Electoral Amendment Act 2016*. This *Act* will result in the adoption of limited remote online voting at the March 2017 Western Australian state election.

5 Conclusion

This article presents a comparative analysis of remote online voting adoption at sub-national level. Together, Canada and Australia provide nearly 200 examples of internet voting deployment in sub-national elections from which policy-makers can draw valuable lessons. This accumulation of cases carries the potential to inform expansion of remote online voting developments both horizontally (to other sub-national elections) or vertically (to national or supra-national elections) via a process of careful policy learning. The evidence may show policy-makers, for example, that with proper planning the integrity of elections can be maintained or improved with internet voting adoption. Alternatively, it may show them that it does not achieve hoped-for goals such as increased turnout, or that it is too costly or risky. Internet voting adoption at sub-national levels may also create new informal forces for retention and expansion. Citizens who have experienced the convenience of remote online voting, for example, may be reluctant to give it up. The cases discussed here suggest that policy learning can be an iterative process involving fixed policy actors within a single jurisdiction, as in the NSW case, or it can be a policy borrowing process in which new policy actors adopt and adapt practices developed and tested by others, as has been common among the Canadian municipalities.

Coalition advocacy theory has proven useful in understanding the development of policy in both sub-national contexts and is likely to provide guidance for future developments. Given the high rates of reported satisfaction with remote online voting in both contexts, the trend to more government and non-government services moving online, and increased internet penetration, there is good reason to believe that voters themselves will support policy shifts toward online voting. Deciding whether or not to make such shifts is likely to be a consequence of policy learning and political will. The strengths of the competing narratives advanced by coalitions of supporters and opponents about each new case of internet voting will be important in determining the direction of online voting policy.

Internal and external policy shocks will also play a part. As the 2014 Alberta and 2015 NSW experiences suggest, even well-prepared policy development and implementation of remote online voting may be struck by an internal shocks that force policymakers to decide whether they have the willpower to continue with its use.

One way or another, the growing number of sub-national cases adds an important dimension to the current policy impasse between competing advocacy coalitions that marks national and international debates on the issue. As more jurisdictions investigate the possibility of deploying internet voting, or develop plans for adoption, looking to these cases and modelling the policy learning they have experienced will be important. As governments and election management bodies increasingly modernise other parts of the voting process, such as voter registration, voters' lists, and ballot tabulation, it is only a matter of time before they reconsider the possibility of digital voting. When that time comes, the sub-national remote online voting laboratories of Canada and Australia will provide valuable lessons.

Acknowledgement. The authors thank Social Science and Humanities Research Council of Canada for financial support of the research.

References

1. Ajax News Advertiser: Votes Piling Up in Ajax, 22 October 2014
2. Baker, L.: Scytl Offers 25% Discount Over Election Problems. Cornwall Standard Freeholder, 28 November 2014

3. Baloch, M.: Council Moves to Recount Election Result. Kingston Whig Standard, 12 November 2014

4. BBC News: Bercow: E-voting would not be 'earth-shattering' step, 10 June 2014. http://www.bbc.com/news/uk-politics-27783329

5. BBC News: E-voting experiments end in Norway amid security fears, 27 June 2014. http://www.bbc.com/news/technology-28055678

6. Brightwell, I.: Administration of elections in NSW. In: Presentation to VoteID 2015: The Fifth International Conference on E-Voting and Identity, Bern, 3 September 2015

7. Brightwell, I., Cucurull, J., Galindo, D., Guasch, S.: An overview of the iVote 2015 voting system. http://www.office.elections.nsw.gov.au/__data/assets/pdf_file/0019/204058/An_overview_of_the_iVote_2015_voting_system_v4.pdf

8. Canada-Europe Transatlantic Dialogue: A Comparative Assessment of Electronic Voting, February 2010. https://elections.virginia.gov/Files/Media/SB11Workgroup/Comparative AssessmentElectronicVotingElectionsCanada.pdf

9. CBC News: Online Voting Only for Leamington, Ont. Municipal Election, 2 April 2014. http://www.cbc.ca/news/canada/windsor/online-voting-only-for-leamington-ont-municipal-election-1.2595300

10. Easton, S.: Electoral Commission Goes to the Home of Direct Democracy to Defend iVote. The Mandarin, 9 October 2015. http://www.themandarin.com.au/55543-nsw-electoral-commission-goes-switzerland-defend-ivote/?pgnc=1

11. Gilligan, K.: Ajax Plugged into Electronic Voting in Municipal Election. Ajax News Advertiser, 29 September 2014. http://www.durhamregion.com/news-story/4884507-ajax-plugged-into-electronic-voting-in-municipal-election/

12. Goodman, N.: Internet voting in a local election in Canada. In: Grofman, B., Trechsel, A., Franklin, M. (eds.) The Internet and Democracy in Global Perspective, pp. 7–24. Springer, Berlin (2014)

13. Goodman, N.: Will E-Voting Boost Turnout in Ontario's Municipal Elections? The Globe and Mail, 21 October 2014

14. Goodman, N., Pammett, J.: The patchwork of internet voting in Canada. In: Krimmer, R., Volkamer, M. (eds.) Proceedings of Electronic Voting 2014 (EVOTE2014), pp. 13–18. TUT Press, Tallinn (2014)

15. Goodman, N., Pammett, J., DeBardeleben, J.: Internet voting: the Canadian experience. Can. Parliam. Rev. **33**(3), 13–21 (2010). Autumn

16. Goodman, N., Pyman, H.: Understanding the Effects of Internet Voting on Elections: Results from the 2014 Ontario Municipal Elections. Centre for e-Democracy, Toronto (2016)

17. Goodman, N., Stokes, L.C.: Internet Voting's Effect on Voter Turnout: An Empirical Examination of Local Elections, unpublished manuscript

18. Green, A.: Could NSW be Facing a Second Legislative Council Election? 8 April 2015. http://blogs.abc.net.au/antonygreen/2015/04/could-nsw-be-facing-a-second-legislative-council-election.html#more

19. Hasham, N.: 19,000 Electronic Votes Valid Despite Error on Ballot Paper. The Sydney Morning Herald, p. 9, 19 March 2015

20. Hasham, N.: iVote Glitch Raises Prospect of Legal Bid and Return to Polls. The Sydney Morning Herald, p. 4, 31 March 2015

21. IPSOS: 2015 NSW State General Election Research. Prepared for the NSW Electoral Commission, IPSOS, North Sydney, June 2015

22. Javed, N.: Ajax Ditches Paper Ballots for Online Municipal Election. The Toronto Star, 6 October 2014

23. Jenkins-Smith, H., Nohrstedt, D., Weible, C., Sabatier, P.: The advocacy coalition framework: foundations, evolution, and ongoing research. In: Sabatier, P., Weible, C. (eds.) Theories of the Policy Process, 3rd edn, pp. 183–223. Westview, Boulder (2014)

24. Kamenova, K., Goodman, N.: Public engagement with internet voting in Edmonton: design, outcomes, and challenges to deliberative models. J. Public Deliberation, 11/2: Article 4 (2015)

25. Kim, H.: Risk Analysis of Traditional, Internet, and Other Types of Voting Alternatives for Town of Markham. A Study Prepared for the Chief Electoral Officer, Town of Markham (2005)

26. New South Wales Electoral Commission. Voting with iVote®, 15 March 2015. http://www.elections.nsw.gov.au/voting/ivote/overview

27. New South Wales Electoral Commission. iVote Reports, 15 July 2016. http://www.elections.nsw.gov.au/about_us/plans_and_reports/ivote_reports

28. Norris, P.: E-voting as the magic bullet for european parliamentary elections? Evaluating E-voting in the light of experiments in UK local elections. In: Trechsel, A., Mendez, F. (eds.) The European Union and E-Voting: Addressing the European Parliament's Internet Voting Challenge, pp. 60–90. Routledge, London (2005)

29. Nova Scotia: 2012 Nova Scotia Municipal Elections Highlights. http://novascotia.ca/dma/pdf/mun-2012-nova-scotia-municipal-elections-highlights.pdf

30. Nova Scotia: Municipal Elections Handbook 2012. http://novascotia.ca/dma/pdf/mun-municipal-elections-handbook.pdf

31. Pammett, J., Goodman, N.: Consultation and evaluation practives in the implementation of internet voting in Canada and Europe. Elections Canada, November 2013. http://www.elections.ca/res/rec/tech/consult/pdf/consult_e.pdf

32. Parliament of Australia: Joint Standing Committee on Electoral Matters: Second Interim Report on the Inquiry into the Conduct of the 2013 Federal Election: An Assessment of Electronic Voting Options, Parliament of Australia, Canberra (2014)

33. Parliament of New South Wales: Joint Standing Committee on Electoral Matters: Administration of the 2011 NSW Election and Related Matters, Parliament of New South Wales, Sydney (2012)

34. Sacheli, S.: Angry Towns Consider Withholding Payment to Internet Voting Company. Canwest News Service, 28 October 2014

35. Smith, R.: Internet Voting and Voter Interference: A report prepared for the New South Wales Electoral Commission, March 2013. https://www.elections.nsw.gov.au/__data/assets/pdf_file/0003/118380/NSWEC_2013_Report_V2.0.pdf

36. Smith, R.: Confidence in paper-based and electronic voting channels: evidence from Australia. Aust. J. Polit. Sci. 51(1), 68–85 (2016)

37. Teague, V., Halderman, A.: Thousands of NSW Election Online Votes Open to Tampering. The Conversation, 23 March 2015. https://theconversation.com/thousands-of-nsw-election-online-votes-open-to-tampering-39164

38. The Canadian Press: Napanee Recount, 16 November 2014

39. The Carter Center: Internet Voting Pilot: Norway's 2013 Parliamentary Elections. Expert Study Mission Report, 19 March 2014. https://www.regjeringen.no/globalassets/upload/krd/kampanjer/valgportal/valgobservatorer/2013/rapport_cartersenteret2013.pdf

40. The Electoral Commission: Electronic Voting: May 2007 Electoral Pilot Schemes, The Electoral Commission, London (2007)

The How and Why to Internet Voting an Attempt to Explain E-Stonia

Priit Vinkel[1(✉)] and Robert Krimmer[2]

[1] Estonian National Electoral Committee, Tallinn, Estonia
Priit.Vinkel@riigikogu.ee
[2] Ragnar Nurkse School of Innovation and Governance,
Tallinn University of Technology, Tallinn, Estonia
Robert.Krimmer@ttu.ee

Abstract. The introduction of remote electoral methods (also, e.g., postal voting) serves the citizen in providing an easily accessible and comfortable means of voting. In addition, remote voting is also considered a viable alternative for disenfranchised voters whose participation in elections has always been dependent on the methods they are offered – voters living or residing permanently abroad, voters who are living in conditions which make it difficult for them to attend elections for geographical reasons and voters with disabilities. All these voters need to make extra efforts in participating in the democratic process, and in all these cases, the principle of universality (or general elections) prevails over the possible concerns connected with the way of voting.

Still, Estonia is the only country in the world providing remote electronic means to its citizens in all elections countrywide. In this article we try to explain the reasons and modalities how Estonia could retain this service where other countries failed.

1 Introduction

We live in a time where information and the development of information and communication technologies (ICT) – most importantly the Internet – have shaped the understanding of communication. As Manuel Castells has put it "The diffusion of Internet, mobile communication, digital media, and a variety of tools of social software have prompted the development of horizontal networks of interactive communication that connect local and global in chosen time." [1] These networks build connections among persons and enhance the communication with the public as Internet-based transactions have grown to be a part of both private and public conduct. We see this tendency in commerce, where online business is growing stronger [2]; likewise in online banking where the usage numbers in Europe reach up to 91% [3], and in the public sector where ICT-enabled services have also found growing acceptance [4].

The nature of one country's democratic processes takes many influences from the development of the country and its democratic and legal culture [5]. Therefore, the conduct of elections has many unique features in every country – e.g. the choice of voting channels or the time of voting. However, democratic elections have to adhere to a set of core principles – universality, freedom, equality (uniformity) and secrecy

© Springer International Publishing AG 2017
R. Krimmer et al. (Eds.): E-Vote-ID 2016, LNCS 10141, pp. 178–191, 2017.
DOI: 10.1007/978-3-319-52240-1_11

[6, Art 25b]. Guaranteeing these principles in all different electoral procedures (including electronic ones) is the challenge that is important to uphold the legitimacy of elections.

The transformation of electoral procedures has been seen as a part of the development of e-democracy, which has gained considerable interest since the dawn of the 21st century. According to Krimmer circumstances like decreasing voter turnout, continuing disconnection of the citizen and the representative and general implications of globalization have driven the process [7].

Introducing remote electoral methods (also, e.g., postal voting) serves the citizen in providing an easily accessible and comfortable means of voting. In addition, remote voting is also considered a viable alternative for disenfranchised voters whose participation in elections has always been dependent on the methods they are offered – voters living or residing permanently abroad, voters who are living in conditions which make it difficult for them to attend elections for geographical reasons and voters with disabilities. All these voters need to make extra efforts in participating in the democratic process, and in all these cases, the principle of universality (or general elections) prevails over the possible concerns connected with the way of voting [8].

The core assumption of this paper is that in order to establish the principle of universal elections (ultimately freedom of vote), additional complementary methods of voting should be offered for the citizens in addition to Election Day voting. Therefore, an experience-based approach on Internet Voting has been presented. Moreover, especially in a small country like Estonia, it is commonly understood that as many voters as possible (and feasible) are to be engaged in voting. Therefore, innovative, comfortable and attractive ways of voting are created. However, the catch for the lawmaker is to find a suitable balance between the principle of universal elections and the rest of the core principles.

The main question this paper aims to answer is how has Estonia managed to implement remote electronic voting as an established and credible voting channel? In order to answer the main question it is necessary to further look at how has the Estonian Internet Voting system developed over the course of its implementation and what impact did it have?

2 Theoretical Background

Remote state-citizen communication has been implemented in many communities, but Estonia has been one of the most eager countries to actively pursue electronic services and procedures [9, 10]. Estonia has featured a remote online voting method since 2005, and has been the only country in Europe (not to say the world) to have it without limitations in all types of elections. However, despite the widespread acceptance of ICT in the Estonian society, the constant development of the system has to guarantee the accordance with up-to-date security and usability recommendations.

Researchers all over the world have early on tried to find suitable solutions to fit the criteria set by universal electoral principles and tackle the questions posed by different fields of interest. The research fields could be divided into four categories – computer science, legal science, social science and political science [11].

Theoretical literature in the computer science is often related to voting from an uncontrolled environment and connected technical risks (e.g. security of the voting device and voting channel). Most of the papers and new scientific thought are being channeled to the vision of finding the safest, tamper-proof, mathematically sound system currently possible [e.g. 12, 13]. This field of study looks for the ideal solution to answer all possible theoretical risks and practical acceptance. The theoretical literature, however, is by and large explored and tested in laboratory conditions and unfortunately is not often viable or feasible in practical implementations. Nevertheless, all these studies also help the operational researchers (including those in Estonia) to further improve systems that are used in practice [e.g. 14, 15]. Additionally, many articles are devoted to a topic that has been seen as the number one confidence builder in remote Internet Voting systems – verification. In theory, verification can be seen in several categories – individual verification, where only the voter is able to verify the trail of the vote, and universal verification, where any person or institution is able to verify the overall results of the I-voting – and in multiple stages – cast as intended (ballots are well-formed), recorded as cast and tallied as recorded– depending on the level of assurance [16]. Estonia has implemented the recorded as cast level in 2013 [17]; however, discussions about possible additional steps in this field are ongoing. The verification scene is very rich and filled with different ideas to offer credible ways towards higher verifiability [18]. Historically, in the early 2000s, the domain of trust building in (remote) electronic voting solutions was dominated by the concept of certification [19]. Over the years, and with the growing possibilities of different solutions, verifiability has grown to be the main factor in guaranteeing the theoretical trustworthiness of an electronic voting solution.

Legal science discussions form the basis for the implementation of a remote electronic voting system, as the question of constitutionality is the first issue to be answered [20, 21]. Additionally, legal scientists are worried about judicial review of the election results and the legitimization of election outcomes [22, 23].

In social and political sciences, Internet Voting has been researched in wide variety. The main interests are summarized by the effect of Internet Voting on effective turnout [24–26], experiences of various implementations, as in Switzerland or Norway [27, 28], or more general discussions on the democratic implications of novel ideas in the electoral field [29, 30]. However, since most of the papers are bound to the context of the appropriate countries, the field lacks social-science papers about the possible introduction of remote electronic voting in other countries and the implications of their use on a more theoretical level.

Moreover, the international community is looking for the best practices in different countries. The most prominent process being the work of the Organization of Security and Co-operation in Europe (OSCE) and its institution in charge of the human dimension, the Office for Democratic Institutions and Human Rights (ODIHR). The organization has intensified its observation of countries that are using alternative remote-voting methods (see www.osce.org/odihr/elections/). Recently it has published a handbook on observing elections using new voting technologies [31].

Literature about the Estonian Internet Voting experience was more concentrated in the early years, right after its adoption [9, 32–34], with some more specialized articles in the last years [7, 10, 17, 29, 35, 36].

Consequently, a gap in the scientific literature concerning a holistic interdisciplinary approach of a remote electronic-voting experience over a longer period could be seen. This paper aims to address the issue by offering an evidence-based approach with insight from electoral practice into the experience of the Estonian Internet Voting program and explaining how Estonia has managed to implement remote electronic voting as an established and credible voting channel.

The theoretical framework of this paper is built on studies of election and constitutional law, the existing literature on the Estonian implementation and applicable studies in other countries.

3 The Development

3.1 Setup Phase of Estonian I-Voting 2002–2005

The year 2002 marked the start of the setup phase, when a very general principle of remote electronic voting was stipulated in the electoral law, allowing the election authorities to start with the project preparations, find a vendor and prepare for the 2005 local elections. Legal debates on the topic were restarted in 2005 to broaden the regulations in the law. This period also holds the discussions about the constitutionality of the system in the Constitutional Chamber of the Estonian Supreme Court.

The 2005 constitutional debate has maintained its position throughout the years of Internet Voting implementation in Estonia. The principle of the "virtual voting booth" as a guarantee for freedom and the understanding of teleological secrecy of voting have become the cornerstones of the Estonian system and are also adopted in other Internet Voting systems. The electoral complaints hold an important role in surfacing possible challenges with the use of Internet Voting. During the first ten years, complaints on equality, secrecy, technical uniformity, procedural soundness and security of the system have been raised. However, no violations have been found.

The constitutionality of an Internet Voting system can be assessed on levels of the general compliance with the electoral principles and the soundness of the implementation of the system in actual elections. The first-level question in the Estonian case could be answered positively, the system is in general compliance with the constitutional provisions. The answer to the second-level question in Estonia could also be seen in a positive light, but it depends heavily on the processes of verification and auditing. In addition, the appropriate measures need constant upgrading and development.

To test the features of the system a limited pilot was held in Tallinn in January 2005 [34]. The first e-enabled elections (for the local government councils) were held in October 2005.

3.2 Pivotal Discussions in the Parliament and Amendments in Electoral Law 2005–2013

The second phase entails a steady rise in user numbers and diffusion of the solution in elections. The legal stipulations had not been changed between the years 2005 and 2011. However, the technical solution was constantly updated for every implementation; the Mobile-ID support and a new voter-application interface were developed for the 2011 general elections [37]. The end of this phase is marked by a report by OSCE/ODIHR [38], where several key features of the Estonian Internet Voting system and the regulation were revised and recommendations were made. This process was the main engine to launch renewed discussions in the parliament to look over the Internet Voting regulations and amend the procedures to bring more transparency and introduce additional steps on verifiability [39].

After the 2011 general elections, where almost a quarter of all votes were given electronically, the parliament decided to specify the norms of I-voting in electoral law in order to improve the legitimacy and transparency of I-voting. Until 2011, the I-voting procedures had only very brief legislative regulations (despite the discussions in 2005). The parliament established a special working group that, in addition to detailed procedures, had to propose a solution for raising transparency and accountability in the I-voting system [40].

At the same time the technical community, which had been involved by the EMB in discussions about the security and transparency of I-voting, came to the conclusion that a new mechanism for some level of verification was needed in Estonia. The perceived aim was to detect possible malicious attacks on the I-voting system. The EMB has a better chance to discover attacks and react to those if I-voters, even a relatively small amount of them, verify their vote. If somebody finds out and reports that his/her vote is not stored correctly, measures can be taken immediately [37]. In addition, a second channel for executing the verification had to be found, because if voters use the same personal computers for voting and verification, it will only add a limited amount of additional information regarding the voting computers. Therefore, an independent channel, like a mobile phone or a mobile device, was introduced for verification [17].

In 2012, the parliament adopted several amendments to the electoral law, stating that a new electoral committee – the electronic voting committee – was to be created for the technical organization of I-voting.

The first elections where the committee was in charge were the 2013 local elections. The law also regulates that before every implementation the I-voting system must be tested and audited. The most significant change of the law was the statement that, from 2015 on, voters have to have the possibility to verify that their vote has reached and is stored at the central server of the elections and reflects the choice of the voter correctly [39].

The main lesson that can be learnt from this period is that together with the development of the technical environment, also the legal regulation has to be kept up. As Drechsler and Kostakis [41] argue, technology is constantly evolving, but the law is not updated immediately. This allows for a process of consideration where only sustainable and desirable technologies are implemented. Verifiability was not implemented when it was available (years before the actual introduction) but when there was a concrete need due to the recent discussions in the country. Moreover, only the quiet period between elections allowed these discussions to take place where a reasonable system was selected and implemented. Additionally, widely accepted reports and input from the specialists' community have shown to be strong initiators in the 2011–2012 legal processes. Moreover, the timing of possible reforms has to be taken into account, as the election-free period from 2011 to 2013 came after a long period of back-to-back elections and was the only time where EMB and the parliament could take up a larger reform of the system.

3.3   Recent Years 2013–2015

The third phase of development could be defined in the last three elections, where the share of I-voters among all voters has stayed high and additional steps of individual verification – recorded as cast – were implemented [39]. The number of I-voters who verified their vote has grown through the years, reaching 4.3% in the 2015 elections (Table 1). Despite the relatively small number of verifiers, mathematically the absence of any large-scale attacks or manipulations is notable [17].

Table 1. Detailed data on Internet voting in Estonia 2005–2015 (Data: National Electoral Committee)

	2005 Local Elections	2007 Parliamentary Elections	2009 European Parliament Elections	2009 Local Elections	2011 Parliamentary Elections	2013 Local Elections	2014 European Parliament Elections	2015 Parliamentary Elections
Eligible voters	1,059,292	897,243	909,628	1,094,317	913,346	1,086,935	902,873	899,793
Participating voters (voter turnout)	502,504	555,463	399,181	662,813	580,264	630,050	329,766	577,910
General voter turnout	47.4%	61.9%	43.9%	60.6%	63.5%	58.0%	36.5%	64.2%
I-voters	9,317	30,275	58,669	104,413	140,846	133,808	103,151	176,491
I-votes counted	9,287	30,243	58,614	104,313	140,764	133,662	103,105	176,329
I-votes cancelled (replaced with paper ballot)	30	32	55	100	82	146	46	162
I-votes invalid (not valid due to a nonstandard of vote)	n/a	n/a	n/a	n/a	n/a	1	n/a	1
Multiple I-votes (replaced with I-vote)	364	789	910	2,373	4,384	3,045	2,019	4,593
I-voters among eligible voters	0.9%	3.4%	6.5%	9.5%	15.4%	12.3%	11.4%	19.6%
I-voters among participating voters	1.9%	5.5%	14.7%	15.8%	24.3%	21.2%	31.3%	30.5%
I-votes among advance votes	7.2%	17.6%	45.4%	44%	56.4%	50.5%	59.2%	59.6%
I-votes cast abroad among I-votes	n/a	2% 51 countries	3% 66 countries	2.8% 82 countries	3.9% 105 countries	4.2% 105 countries	4.69% 98 countries	5.71% 116 countries
I-voting period	3 days	3 days	7 days	7 days	7 days	7 days	7 days	7 days
Share of I-votes that were verified by the voter	n/a	n/a	n/a	n/a	n/a	3.4%	4.0%	4.3%

The discussion about transparency and verifiability in a remote electronic voting system has clearly defined the general Internet Voting discussion in the past [7, 15, 42] and will define it in the nearer future. The same is true for Estonia, despite introducing the first stages of verification [14, 43].

The OSCE/ODIHR election specialists' report [44] emphasizes the need for added verifiability and transparency in the conduct of electronic elections, and according developments have also been evident in the preparation for the 2017 local municipal elections. According to the plans of the organizers is the voting solution thought to be fitted with added features like universal verifiability or wider auditability. All changes serve the underlying purpose of building the trust into fair and sound conduct of elections.

4 The Impact of Internet Voting

Estonia has implemented Internet Voting in eight consecutive elections. It was the first country, in 2005, to introduce remote electronic voting in pan-national binding elections and was leading a kind of "race" at the beginning of the 2000s for introducing remote electronic methods in elections [34, 45]. The number of Internet Voters has been rising from the beginning, reaching more than 176,000 voters and comprising more than 30% of all given votes in the 2015 parliamentary elections.

Internet Voting started low, with only 9,317 I-voters, but began to grow in the following implementations. The low start and the following step-by-step rise in numbers could be explained by Rodgers' theory on the diffusion of innovation [46]. The number of eligible voters and turnout numbers are distinctively different per election type. For example, European Parliament election turnout is also by general measures [47] lower than in other election types, like local or national elections. Therefore, the absolute numbers as seen in Fig. 1 have fluctuated per election type after reaching the highest level in the 2015 parliamentary elections.

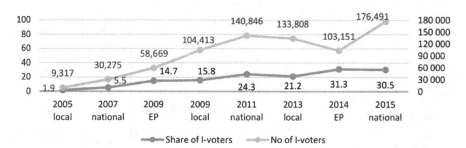

Fig. 1. Number of I-voters and share of I-voters from all voters in 2005–2015

However, the share of Internet Voters among all voters has shown a steady rise despite the absolute number fluctuations, having risen to over 30% in the last two elections. Moreover, Internet Voting is offered for a seven-day period during advance voting, and since 2011, there have been more electronic advance voters compared to paper advance voters [48]. This process has had an impact on the paper-voting organization by putting the local governments under pressure to reduce the number of polling stations, as the attendance numbers have decreased, especially in rural areas. The effect is emphasized by the finding that the relative distance from the polling station has a clear correlation to the use of Internet Voting [49, 50].

When looking at the impact of the Internet Voting results, at least three categories could be distinguished: firstly the impact on the election turnout, whether adding a new voting method raises the turnout; secondly the effect of socio-demographic factors on the use of Internet Voting; and thirdly the relation of Internet Voting and the election results. Scientific reports on Estonian Internet Voting have been compiled after all eight elections [50], and the results have been publicly discussed and are available on the EMB webpage.

One of the most frequent questions with any novelty electoral solution is the impact on turnout. Without a doubt, the hope to have a positive influence on the general turnout was one of the claimed aims in the early discussions of I-voting in Estonia [34]. Nevertheless, it is difficult to assess the actual impact of Internet Voting on turnout because a direct comparison of the same election with and without I-voting is not possible. Perhaps a better question to be asked is what share of the electorate would not have participated in the voting, if the Internet Voting opportunity had not been provided. Unfortunately, only voter survey results can be used here. One exception is the case when Internet Voting is the only possibility for the voter and he/she uses this possibility. In the local elections, Estonia does not provide for voting from abroad by postal ballot or at a diplomatic representation, therefore voting over the Internet is the only voting method abroad [39]. The number of I-voters from abroad has grown after every election (Table 1).

The relation of the absolute number of I-voters and the general turnout has not been a linear one. Scientific surveys [e.g. 49] have shown that most Internet Voters are actually paper voters who decide to switch the voting method; only a relatively small number of voters have started voting because of such a possibility. In 2005, I-voting seems to have had a slight effect on the increase in the turnout of voters who sometimes vote and sometimes do not. In 2007, already approximately ten percent of the questioned I-voters said that they certainly or probably would not have voted without having had the possibility to vote via the Internet [51]. Trechsel and Vassil show [52] (in 2011) that the percentage of the I-voters questioned who certainly or probably would not have voted without having had the possibility to vote via the Internet has risen to 16.3%, which allows for the conclusion that the overall turnout might have been as much as 2.6% lower in the absence of such a method of voting. That is already a significant marker when one looks at the impact of Internet Voting on the overall turnout [39].

Another interesting question is whether Internet-based voting shows any difference of representation within social groups. Remote electronic voting removes physical barriers hindering participation in elections of the aged, disabled or other groups with restricted mobility or ones that have difficulty in attending polling stations (e.g. persons having tight work schedules or working, studying or travelling abroad, parents of small children and persons living in regions with poor infrastructure), assuming, of course, that these people have access to the Internet.

Trechsel et al. and later Vassil and Solvak have concluded in their reports following the experience of Internet Voting from 2005 to 2015 that education and income, as well as type of settlement have been insignificant factors when choosing the Internet instead of other voting channels [50, 52]. One of the most important findings of the studies researching I-voting predictors until the 2009 elections has been that it is not so much the cleavage between the Internet access haves and have-nots, but clearly computing skills and frequency of Internet use. However, since the 2009 local elections, where more than 100,000 voters used Internet Voting, those factors have become non-detectable [52]. Confidence (trust) in the I-voting system and procedure has been the most significant factor throughout the years that directs the voters' choice in using a remote electronic voting method [15, 42]. Vassil et al. [46] have also claimed that based on empirical analysis at least a three-election period has to be studied to have adequate results for assessing the impact of different features on Internet Voting.

The question for political parties is whether the use of I-voting has an influence on the overall election results. Estonian parties that have favored I-voting in their campaigns and supported this voting method, have received more I-votes compared to those parties not supporting the use of I-voting. However, studies have shown that political left-right auto-positioning does not play an important role when choosing a voting channel [52]. In a separate study on the possible bias of I-voting on election results a similar conclusion was drawn – I-voting is politically neutral and does not have a direct impact on the election results [50].

In conclusion, a steady rise in the use of Internet Voting in Estonia was seen until the 2011 general elections; after that, the absolute number of voters has been fluctuating because of the nature of the elections it is used in, but the share of I-voters has kept on rising. Additionally, in advance voting, since 2011 I-voting has been more popular than traditional paper voting. When looking at the impact factors it can be seen that only a small amount of I-voters are completely new voters, the majority of I-voters are converted paper voters. A stronger impact could be made out in local elections, where I-voting is the only voting method from abroad. Additionally, socio-demographic features in determining the use of I-voting have been fading since the 100,000-voter hurdle was broken in 2009. Nevertheless, the factor of confidence (trust) in the system and procedures has stayed the most important determinant of I-voting use. Finally, several studies have looked into the political influence of I-voting and have found that I-voting is politically neutral and does not bring about biased results in elections. However, one should refrain from drawing conclusions on the impact of Internet Voting based solely on one execution of the method. At least three elections have to be analyzed to see the effects unfolding [50].

5   Comparison with Experience from Switzerland and Norway

The Internet Voting landscape has been quite active [53–55]. Remote electronic voting has been utilized on some level in more than twenty countries, and several countries analyze possible implementation. The largest steps in Europe and maybe even worldwide have been made (beside Estonia) in Switzerland and Norway. Therefore, the experience of these two countries is analyzed next.

Switzerland, as a confederation, hosts its online elections in the cantons. With postal voting being a long-time favorite in a country where elections and referendums are held often, the step to online solutions was not far-fetched. Different cantons have had pilots and try-outs since the early 2000s. Currently two different technical voting systems are in use, and less than ten Swiss cantons use Internet Voting on some level of their electoral activity (until 2015 there used to be three different solutions with more than half of the cantons participating in Internet Voting). Identification is based on unique passwords, and individual verification is offered. Since 2008, voting is also offered for Swiss expatriates. Similar to Estonia, the Swiss reached a stable user experience at the beginning of the 2010s and are today looking for possibilities to enhance their (different) systems by making them more transparent, observable and verifiable. The Swiss experience has also been studied by Schweizer Bundesrat [27, 56–61].

Norway started its Internet Voting project with two pilots, the first in the 2011 local elections and the second in the 2013 general elections. Both pilots were held in a small number of local-government units. Norway implemented the system after rigorous constitutional analysis and an international public tender [62]. From the beginning, recorded as cast verifiability was implemented, and a large effort was deployed to ensure public trust with the latest security solutions for the system. Technically and from the public perspective, both pilots were perceived as successful. However, after some evaluation, the Norwegian government decided to discontinue Internet Voting pilots due to possible risks in the system's security with the underlying reasons being the change in political leadership and the lack of trust the politicians held for the system. The Norwegian pilots are discussed in detail by OSCE/ODIHR [28, 63–65].

As seen in Table 2, there is no single working solution for introducing Internet Voting. The compared countries show differences across the board and are/were nevertheless able to implement Internet Voting in their respective countries.

Table 2. Comparison of main features in the Estonian, Swiss and Norwegian I-voting experience.

	Estonia	Switzerland	Norway
Authentication method	eID	Passwords through postal system	Unique ID tied with mobile phones
Implementation style	Snap implementation, nationally	Step-by-step, canton-based	Step-by-step, only limited pilots
Verifiability	Individual	Individual	Individual and universal
Multiple vote casting	Yes	No	Yes

6 Conclusion

In conclusion, what the Estonian experience, so far, has shown is that it has been implemented as a solid voting method. The channel has also become an integral part of the Estonian so-called "e-stonia" narrative. Many news articles about Estonia in the international media define the country by its e-capability in the electoral field. Nevertheless, in order to see beyond the shiny surface presented in the newscasts, questions that are more detailed need to be asked.

The Estonian experience in implementing Internet Voting could be seen in three stages, where firstly constitutional debate and introduction of the novelty system took place, after five elections a refreshment of the legal stipulations was in order and additional measures for more transparency and accountability in the system were debated about, and lastly a three-election period could be distinguished where a new level of verifiability was applied and a gap between elections ushered in a new discussion about additional measures of confidence.

What can be learnt from the Estonian experience to date is that the build-up of Internet Voting turnout takes time, as does looking at the diffusion of any innovative solution. Additionally, the effects and impact of the added voting method will not appear after the first application; it has been claimed that at least three elections have to be taken into account. As for the impact of the Estonian system, it has been found that introducing Internet Voting has had a slightly positive influence on the general turnout, but most Internet Voters are former paper voters who started using a different method of voting. However, in specific groups (like abroad voters) the effect on turnout is present. Different socio-demographic values, like type of settlement or rate of computer use, were important determinants of I-voting before the 2009 elections, but they have become irrelevant since. The principal important factors for voters to choose I-voting through all elections have been trust and confidence in the solution.

When comparing the Estonian experience and solution to Switzerland and Norway, it can be seen that no single characteristic makes up a working system, and verifiability and trustworthiness are features other implementers are investing in as well. Each Internet Voting system has been developed in line with the needs of the actual context it was implemented in. Therefore, this does not allow for generalizing based on individual features; it is the complete solution that needs to be looked at. Additionally, the factor of political will and support in explaining the rise or demise of such a novelty idea should not be easily discarded. What can be learnt from Norway is that the ways of implementation are irrelevant if the politicians are not convinced that the election results would remain the same regardless of the new voting channels.

Acknowledgements. This work was supported by the European Commission (OpenGovIntelligence H2020 grant 693849), Estonian Research Council (grants IUT19-13) and Tallinn University of Technology Project B42.

References

1. Castells, M.: Communication, power and counter-power in the network society. Int. J. Commun. **1**, 29 (2007)
2. Statista: More of the Same from Amazon (2015)
3. Statista: Online Banking Penetration in Selected European Markets in 2014 (2015)
4. World Economic Forum: Sections 10.1 and 10.3. In: Global IT Report 2015, Geneva (2015)

5. Venice Commission: Report CDL-AD on Constitutional Amendment adopted by the Venice Commission at its 81st Plenary Session (Venice, 11–12 December 2009) (2009)
6. United Nations: International Covenant on Civil and Political Rights, 10 August 1966. http:// www2.ohchr.org/english/law/ccpr.htm
7. Krimmer, R.: The evolution of E-voting: why voting technology is used and how it affects democracy. Ph.D. Dissertation, Institute for Public Administration, Tallinn University of Technology, Tallinn (2012)
8. Gronke, P., Galanes-Rosenbaum, E., Miller, P.A., Toffey, D.: Convenience voting. Ann. Rev. Polit. Sci. **11**, 437–455 (2008)
9. Drechsler, W.: The Estonian E-voting laws discourse: paradigmatic benchmarking for central and Eastern Europe. In: NISPAcee Occasional Papers in Public Administration and Public Policy, vol. 5, pp. 11–17 (2006)
10. Madise, Ü.: Legal and political aspects of the internet voting: Estonian case (2007)
11. Prosser, A., Krimmer, R.: The dimensions of electronic voting: technology, law, politics and society. In: Prosser, A., Krimmer, R. (eds.) Electronic Voting in Europe: Technology, Law, Politics and Society. Proceedings of the ESF TED Workshop on Electronic Voting in Europe, vol. 47, pp. 21–28. Gesellschaft für Informatik, Bonn (2004)
12. Joaquim, R., Ferreira, P., Ribeiro, C.: EVIV: an end-to-end verifiable internet voting system. Comput. Secur. **32**, 170–191 (2013)
13. Mohammadpourfard, M., Doostari, M., Bagher Ghaznavi-Ghoushchi, M., Mikaili, H.: Design and implementation of a novel secure internet voting protocol using Java card 3 technology. Int. J. Bus. Inf. Syst. **17**, 414–439 (2014)
14. Halderman, J.A., Hursti, H., Kitcat, J., MacAlpine, M., Finkenauer, T., Springall, D.: Security analysis of the Estonian internet voting system, May 2014
15. Spycher, O., Volkamer, M., Koenig, R.: Transparency and technical measures to establish trust in Norwegian internet voting. In: Kiayias, A., Lipmaa, H. (eds.) Vote-ID 2011. LNCS, vol. 7187, pp. 19–35. Springer, Heidelberg (2012). doi:10.1007/978-3-642-32747-6_2
16. Popoveniuc, S., Kelsey, J., Regenscheid, A., Vora, P.: Performance requirements for end-to-end verifiable elections. In: Jones, D., Quisquater, J.-J., Rescorla, E. (eds.) Proceedings of the 2010 International Conference on Electronic Voting Technology/Workshop on Trustworthy Elections, Berkeley USENIX Association, pp. 1–16 (2010)
17. Heiberg, S., Willemson, J.: Verifiable internet voting in Estonia. In: Krimmer, R., Volkamer, M. (eds.) EVOTE 2014. IEEE (2014)
18. Nestås, L.H., Hole, K.J.: Building and maintaining trust in internet voting. Computer **45**, 74–80 (2012)
19. Council of Europe: Legal, operational and technical standards for E-voting. Recommendation Rec(2004)11 and explanatory memorandum. Council of Europe, Strasbourg (2004)
20. Braun, N.: Stimmgeheimnis. Eine rechtsvergleichende und rechtshistorische Untersuchung unter Einbezug des geltenden Rechts. Stämpfli Verlag, Bern (2006)
21. Mitrou, L., Gritzalis, D.A., Katsikas, S., Quirchmayr, G.: Electronic voting: constitutional and legal requirements, and their technical implications. In: Gritzalis, D.A. (ed.) Secure Electronic Voting, pp. 43–60. Kluwer Academic Publishers, Boston, Dordrecht (2003)
22. Loncke, M., Dumortier, J.: Online voting: a legal perspective. Int. Rev. Law Comput. Technol. **18**(1) (2004)
23. Meagher, S.: When personal computers are transformed into ballot boxes: how internet elections in Estonia comply with the United Nations international covenant on civil and political rights. Am. Univ. Int. Law Rev. **23**(2) (2008)
24. Bochsler, D.: Can the internet increase political participation? An analysis of remote electronic voting's effect on turnout (2009)

25. Vassil, K., Weber, T.: A bottleneck model of E-voting: why technology fails to boost turnout. New Media Soc. **13**, 1336–1354 (2011)
26. Solop, F.I.: Electronic voting in the United States: at the leading edge or lagging behind? In: Kersting, N., Baldersheim, H. (eds.) Electronic Voting and Democracy: A Comparative Analysis, pp. 61–74. Palgrave, London (2004)
27. Driza-Maurer, A., Spycher, O., Taglioni, G., Weber, A.: E-voting for Swiss abroad: a joint project between the confederation and the cantons. In: Electronic Voting EVOTE 2012, vol. 205, pp. 173–187 (2012)
28. Stenerud, I., Bull, C.: When reality comes knocking: Norwegian experiences with verifiable electronic voting. In: Kripp, M., Volkamer, M., Grimm, R. (eds.) Proceedings of the 5th International Conference on Electronic Voting (EVOTE 2012), pp. 21–33 GI, Bonn (2012)
29. Reiners, M.: E-revolution. Actor-centered and structural interdependencies in the realization of Estonia's democratic revolution (2013)
30. Mendez, F.: Elections and the internet: on the difficulties of 'upgrading' elections in the digital era. Representation **46**, 459–469 (2010)
31. OSCE/ODIHR: Handbook for the Observation of New Voting Technologies. OSCE/ODIHR, Warsaw (2013)
32. Drechsler, W., Madise, Ü.: E-voting in Estonia. Trames **6**, 3 (2002)
33. Drechsler, W., Madise, Ü.: Electronic voting in Estonia. In: Kersting, N., Baldersheim, H. (eds.) Electronic Voting and Democracy: A Comparative Analysis, pp. 97–108. Palgrave, London (2004)
34. Madise, Ü., Martens, T.: E-voting in Estonia 2005. The first practice of country-wide binding Internet voting in the world. In: Krimmer, R. (ed.) Electronic Voting 2006, vol. P-87, pp. 27–35. Gesellschaft für Informatik, Bonn (2006)
35. Alvarez, R.M., Hall, T.E., Trechsel, A.H.: Internet voting in comparative perspective: the case of Estonia. PS: Polit. Sci. Polit. **42**, 497–505 (2009)
36. Musiał-Karg, M.: The theory and practice of online voting. The case of Estonia (selected issues). Athenaeum. Polish Polit. Sci. Stud. **29**, 180–198 (2011)
37. Heiberg, S., Laud, P., Willemson, J.: The application of I-voting for Estonian parliamentary elections of 2011. In: Kiayias, A., Lipmaa, H. (eds.) Vote-ID 2011. LNCS, vol. 7187, pp. 208–223. Springer, Heidelberg (2012). doi:10.1007/978-3-642-32747-6_13
38. OSCE/ODIHR: Election Assessment Mission Report on the 6 March 2011 Parliamentary Elections in Estonia. 01 April 2011. http://www.osce.org/odihr/77557
39. Madise, Ü., Vinkel, P.: Internet voting in Estonia: from constitutional debate to evaluation of experience over six elections. In: Kerikmäe, T. (ed.) Regulating eTechnologies in the European Union, pp. 1–19. Springer, Berlin (2014)
40. Madise, Ü., Vinkel, P.: A judicial approach to internet voting in Estonia. In: Barrat, J., Driza Maurer, A. (eds.) E-Voting Case Law: A Comparative Analysis, pp. 1–35. Ashgate, Farnham (2015)
41. Drechsler, W., Kostakis, V.: Should law keep pace with technology? Law as Katechon. Bull. Sci. Technol. Soc. **34**, 128–132 (2015)
42. Volkamer, M., Spycher, O., Dubuis, E.: Measures to establish trust in internet voting. In: Estevez, E., Janssen, M. (eds.) Proceedings of the 5th International Conference on Theory and Practice of Electronic Governance (ICEGOV 2011). ACM (2011)
43. Vinkel, P.: Presentation to the OSCE Human Dimension Committee on 27 March 2012 by the Estonian Delegation on Follow-up to the Recommendations Contained in the 2011 OSCE/ODIHR Election Assessment Mission Report, Vienna (2012)
44. OSCE/ODIHR: Election Expert Team Report on the 1 March 2015 Parliamentary Elections in Estonia, 17 September 2015. http://www.osce.org/odihr/elections/estonia/139571
45. Maaten, E.: Towards remote E-voting: Estonian case. In: Prosser, A., Krimmer, R. (eds.) Electronic Voting in Europe Technology, Law, Politics and Society, vol. P-47, pp. 83–90. GI, Bregenz (2004)

46. Vassil, K., Solvak, M., Vinkel, P.: E-valimiste levik Eesti valijate hulgas. Riigikogu Toimetised (Parliamentary Journal) **30**(2), 116–128 (2014)
47. Ehin, P., Madise, Ü., Solvak, M., Taagepera, R., Vassil, K., Vinkel, P.: Independent candidates in National and European elections: study, Brussels (2013)
48. Heinsalu, A., Koitmäe, A., Pilving, M., Vinkel, P.: Elections in Estonia 1992–2015. National Electoral Committee, Tallinn (2016)
49. Vassil, K., Solvak, M.: Ten years of internet voting in Estonia: overview of research on internet voting in 2005–2014. Seminar on 22 January 2015 (2015)
50. Vassil, K., Solvak, M.: E-voting in Estonia: Technological Diffusion and Other Developments Over Ten Years (2005–2015) (2016)
51. Trechsel, A.: Internet voting in the March 2007 parliamentary elections in Estonia. Report for the council of Europe (2007)
52. Trechsel, A., Vassil, K.: Internet voting in Estonia: a comparative analysis of five elections since 2005 (2011)
53. Krimmer, R.: The 2016 World-Map of E-Voting Activities. Sulz: E-Voting. CC (forthcoming) (2016)
54. Stein, R., Wenda, G.: The council of Europe and E-voting: history and impact of Rec(2004) 11. In: Proceedings of Electronic Voting 2014 (EVOTE 2014). IEEE (2014)
55. Barrat i Esteve, J., Goldsmith, B., Turner, J.: Speed and efficiency of the vote counting process: Norwegian E-vote project, Washington (2012)
56. Bundesrat, S.: Bericht über den Vote électronique. Chancen, Risiken und Machbarkeit elektronischer Ausübung politischer Rechte. In: Bern BBl 2002, p. 645 (2002)
57. Bundesrat, S.: Bericht über die Pilotprojekte zum Vote électronique. In: Bern BBl 2006, p. 5459 (2006)
58. Bundesrat, S.: Bericht des Bundesrates zu Vote électronique. Auswertung der Einführung von Vote électronique (2006–2012) und Grundlagen zur Weiterentwicklung, Bern (2013)
59. Gerlach, J., Gasser, U.: Three case studies from Switzerland: E-voting (2009)
60. OSCE/ODIHR: Election Assessment Mission Report on the 23 October 2011 Elections in Switzerland, 01 April 2011. http://www.osce.org/odihr/87417
61. Serdült, U., Germann, M., Mendez, F., Portenier, A., Wellig, C.: Fifteen years of internet voting in Switzerland (History, Governance and Use). In: Teran, L., Meier, A. (eds.) Proceedings of the Second International Conference on eDemocracy and eGovernment (ICEDEG), pp. 126–132. IEEE, Quito (2015)
62. Ansper, A., Heiberg, S., Lipmaa, H., Øverland, T.A., Laenen, F.: Security and trust for the Norwegian E-voting pilot project *E-valg 2011*. In: Jøsang, A., Maseng, T., Knapskog, S.J. (eds.) NordSec 2009. LNCS, vol. 5838, pp. 207–222. Springer, Heidelberg (2009). doi:10.1007/978-3-642-04766-4_15
63. OSCE/ODIHR: Election Expert Team Report on the 12 September 2011 Local Government Elections in Norway, Warsaw (2012)
64. OSCE/ODIHR: EAM Final Report on the 9.09.13 Parliamentary Elections in Norway (2013). http://www.osce.org/odihr/elections/109517?download=true
65. Markussen, R., Ronquillo, L., Schürmann, C.: Trust in Internet election: observing the Norwegian decryption and counting ceremony. In: EVOTE 2014, pp. 24–31. TUT Press (2014)

A Risk-Limiting Audit in Denmark: A Pilot

Carsten Schürmann[(✉)]

DemTech, IT University of Copenhagen, Copenhagen, Denmark
carsten@itu.dk

Abstract. The theory of risk-limiting audits is well-understood, at least mathematically. Such audits serve to create confidence in the reported election outcome by checking the evidence created during the election. When election officials introduce election technologies into the voting process, it is best to do this after the appropriate auditing framework has been implemented. In this paper, we describe our experiences with piloting a risk-limiting audit of a referendum that was held in Denmark on December 3, 2015. At the time of the publication of this paper, Denmark's election law did not permit electronic voting technologies to be used during voting allowing us to study auditing in isolation.

Our findings are that (1) risk-limiting audits also apply to paper and pencil elections; (2) election officials usually support risk-limiting audits even if no voting technologies are used because these audits can improve the efficiency of the manual count; (3) that practical and organizational challenges must be overcome to keep audits repeatable, in particular it must be possible to identify individual ballots repeatedly and reliably; (4) it is possible to arrange an audit for the result of an earlier stage in a count during a later stage, for example, an audit of the rough count results fine count; and (5) that whenever the electronic voting technologies are considered, auditing should be considered as part of feasibility study.

1 Introduction

A voter verifiable paper audit trail is only as good as its curation and the auditing procedure that uses it to check the validity of the election result. If a voting machine creates a paper audit trail, it is only meaningful when it is inspected in a valid and systematic fashion, for example, by means of a manual recount or a risk-limiting audit. Electronic voting technologies should therefore only be used *after* a suitable auditing framework and the relevant auditing procedures have been defined and implemented.

In 2013, Denmark held an European parliament election, for which we attempted to pilot a first nation-wide risk limiting audit across jurisdictional

C. Schürmann—This publication was made possible in part by the DemTech grant 10-092309 from the Danish Council for Strategic Research, Program Commission on Strategic Growth Technologies and in part by NPRP Grant #7-988-1-178 from the Qatar National Research Fund (a member of Qatar Foundation). The statements made herein are solely the responsibility of the authors.

R. Krimmer et al. (Eds.): E-Vote-ID 2016, LNCS 10141, pp. 192–202, 2017.
DOI: 10.1007/978-3-319-52240-1_12

boundaries with the goal to learn about the requirements and challenges to Danish election processes and procedures. Unfortunately, the pilot failed, because too few constituencies participated in this pilot where participation was voluntary. Audits require that ballot papers are stored in such a way that they can be easily retrieved. This can be challenging, especially for larger constituencies that have to curate large stacks of ballot papers, draw large random samples, and have only limited resources to conduct the audit. The Copenhagen constituency is so big, for example, that they rent extra containers to store all ballot papers. This made us wonder *what are the main challenges for adopting risk-limiting audits in Denmark, and how can election procedures be modified to render them feasible.* In 2013, Denmark held a referendum, where we expected large margins, and so we took a second attempt to undertake a national risk-limiting audit, but this time we only focused only on Copenhagen.

At the time of the publication of this paper, Denmark's election law did not permit electronic voting technologies to be used during voting. None the less, studying auditing in the setting of paper-only based elections is important to understand the implications of auditing frameworks on the electoral process in preparation, for example, for nation states that consider introducing electronic voting technologies. Risk-limiting audits allow auditors to inspect a small sample of ballots to assess the overall quality of the election result. Risk-limiting audits have been developed by Stark and Lindeman [LS12] in the context of US elections, where the use of electronic voting machines with voter verifiable paper audit trails is prevalent. Stark and Lindeman ask, how to audit the election result computed by an electronic vote tabulation system against the paper trail. For our pilot, we audited the election result against manually completed ballot papers and not a computer generated paper audit trail. The hallmark characteristic of our audit is that we audited the election night results during the fine count phase of the election the very next day. In Denmark, votes are counted multiple times. The *rough count* takes place on election night and the results are usually published before midnight. The next morning, the *fine count* determines the official election result. In our pilot, we audited the result of the rough count during the fine count.

We believe that the findings that we describe in this paper provide valuable insights that are applicable beyond the Danish context and might be of interest to any election commission that considers integrating an auditing framework into their respective administrative processes, for example, as a supplementary quality control mechanisms or in preparation for the introduction of electronic voting technologies into their respective electoral processes. The findings pertain to adjusting the legal framework, devising organizational rules with the goal to create confidence among the electorate. This paper is organized as follows. We first revisit the theory of risk-limiting audits in Sect. 2, then we discuss the design and execution of the audit applied the 2015 referendum on in Sect. 3, finally we discuss our findings in Sect. 4 before concluding in Sect. 5.

2   Risk-Limiting Audits

A risk-limiting audit is a statistical method to create confidence in the correctness of an election result by checking samples of paper ballots. Lindeman and Stark [LS12] distinguish *ballot-polling audits*, where they draw a carefully chosen random sample of ballots to check whether the sample gives sufficiently strong evidence for the correctness of the published election result. In contrast, a *comparison audit* checks the ballot interpretation for a random sample during the audit against their respective interpretation in a vote tabulation system.

One of the requirements is that a ballot manifest is available that describes in detail how ballots are organized and stored, including how many stacks there are and how many ballots can be found in each stack. This information establishes a total order among all ballots that is needed for drawing the sample and being able to retrieve individual ballots for inspection. For this pilot, we have chosen a comparison audit, which follows the steps defined in [LS12] and described below and commences only after the election has closed and the election results were published.

1. Entropy is generated, for example by throwing physical dice. The entropy is subsequently used to initialize the random generator. We denote entropy with e.
2. From the election result we compute the smallest margin of the election. There are many different margins to consider, we only focus on one-vote overstatements where ballots were accidentally not counted for a loosing candidate, because they were either invalid, or counted to someone else but the winner and two-vote overstatements, which are ballots that were erroneously counted for the winning candidate instead of the loosing candidate. For more details on margin computation, consult [Sta10].
3. Using some more statistics [Sta10], we determine the number of ballots to be audited. We denote this number with k. Note, that one input to this computation is the total number of ballots cast in the contest to which we refer with n.
4. Using the algorithm depicted in Table 1, we compute a set of ballots to be audited, the random sample, from inputs e, k, n. As the audit needs to be reproducible, we cannot simply apply the random generator provided by an implementation language. Instead, we trust that hashing strings gives us a uniform distribution. In the implementation is done using sha256 (see line 6, in Table 1). The result of the algorithm is a list of random numbers, between the 0 and $n - 1$, each identifies a particular ballot in the total order. Because the computation is parametric only in e, k, and n, the result is reproducible.
5. Using the total order given by the ballot manifest, we can now compute the precise location (in terms of municipality, polling station, party name, candidate name, for example) for each ballot to be audited.

Table 1. Drawing a random sample of ballots

```
 1: function DRAWSAMPLE(string e; int k; int n)
 2:     i = 1
 3:     bs = {}
 4:     while i ≤ k do do
 5:         x = e + "," + intToString(i)
 6:         y = sha256(x)
 7:         z = decimal(y)
 8:         b = z mod (n − 1)
 9:         bs = bs ∪ {b}
10:     end while
11:     return(bs)
12: end function
```

3 Referendum

We conducted a risk-limiting audit for a national referendum in Denmark that took place on December 3, 2015[1]. Elections in Denmark allow for advance voting, where voters can vote form anywhere in the country (and abroad), but their votes will be registered in their respective constituencies. Different from other countries, that allow voters to complete their ballots at home and mail them in, Denmark requires voters to cast their vote in controlled environments using the double envelope technique; officials will then mail the envelopes to the voter's behalf to their respective polling places, where they are registered on the electoral roll before the polling places open in the morning of the election day.

Denmark consists of 92 constituencies, where Copenhagen and Aarhus are the largest. Copenhagen alone organizes 50 polling stations.

Denmark does not offer computer-enabled vote casting. It neither offers internet voting as an alternate voting channel, nor electronic ballot markers. Special rules apply to voters with disabilities, who may take a friend to help complete a ballot but are required to have an election official present to witness that the voter's intent is correctly reflected on the ballot. All ballots are completed by pencil and paper and then hand-counted by elections officials in the evening of election day, which is called *rough count*, and again during the next day which is called *fine count*. This means, in Denmark, ballots are counted several times.

Computers, however, play an important part in other parts of the electoral process. The electoral roll is digitally copied from the public registry of all residents of Denmark a few days prior to the election. Every voter receives a document (*valgkort*) in the mail, allowing them to register to vote on election day. For municipalities that support digital voter lists this document contains also a computer readable barcode. The barcode is read and the voter is then digitally checked off the electoral role. Other municipalities check voters manually of the electoral role.

---

[1] http://www.dst.dk/valg/Valg1664255/valgopg/valgopgHL.htm.

During election night, computers are used to report the results from each polling station to the ministry. To verify that the reporting was ok, the ministry expects a telephone call from each polling station within five minutes of the original reporting, where subsequently all totals are manually checked. The final seat assignment for national parliament, European parliament, or municipal elections is usually computed by a computer program in the ministry using a combination of D'Hondt and Saint Leguë methods. For the referendum that we describe here, the computer program only added the totals from each reporting constituency. The results of the referendum contest are depicted in Table 2. The referendum was rejected by majority.

Table 2. Official results of the 2015 referendum

YES	1.375.862	46,9%
NO	1.558.437	53,1%
Total number of valid votes	2.934.299	
Blank votes	48.216	
Other invalid votes	7.746	
Total number of invalid votes	55.962	
Total number of votes	2.990.261	

3.1 Designing the Audit

The audit we have chosen was a comparison ballot audit [LS12], where we compare the interpretation of ballot in the random sample to how it was recorded. We designed our audit in such a way that we would audit the result of the rough count (on election night) during the fine count, which took place the next day. Fortunate for us, the company that conducts the election night reporting, publishes all results online. Scraping their webpage allowed us to compute the ballot manifest, which we subsequently used to draw the random sample.

This referendum is the kind of election [Sta10] can be applied to directly. We decided for a risk limit of 0.1%, which means that after the audit, we can be 99.9% sure that the published election outcome is correct. Note that the following rough count totals differ from the official elections result described in Table 2.

YES	1.377.678
NO	1.556.761
Total number of votes	2.989.925

As these were the only numbers we had, we used them to compute the margin for our risk limiting audit, using Stark's online resources[2]. A screenshot of our interaction with the tool is depicted in Table 3, with the result, that the margin

---

[2] http://www.stat.berkeley.edu/~stark/Vote/auditTools.htm.

is 179083 votes, the diluted margin is 5.99% and the number of ballots to audit is 249. As the margin is large, it is perhaps not surprising that the sample size is relatively small.

Table 3. Screenshot of Stark's risk limiting audit tool

We derived entropy by rolling the dice and so we could run the algorithm from Table 1 with arguments

$$e = \text{"674987539957481874"}$$
$$k = 249 \tag{1}$$
$$n = 2.989.925$$

to draw the sample. Out of the 249 ballots, 36 fell into the Copenhagen constituency, the other 213 were distributed among the rest of Denmark. We focused the audit exclusively on Copenhagen, because (1) this was only a pilot, where we wanted to learn about the mechanisms behind executing the audit, and not really audit the correctness of the election result. It is worth mentioning that we found no misinterpretation of any of the 36 ballots that we checked. (2) Copenhagen is the biggest municipality in Denmark, which means, that if we can have a successful audit in Copenhagen, then risk-limiting audits could be – at least in principle – be executed anywhere in the country. The list of all ballots that we audited can be found in Table 4.

3.2 Executing the Audit

With the sample computed, we, a team of academic election researchers, went to the fine count center for the constituency of Copenhagen on the morning

Table 4. List of ballots to be audited

Bispebjergkredsen	6. Syd	Ballot 2037 interpreted as NO?
Bispebjergkredsen	6. Øst	Ballot 650 interpreted as YES?
Brønshøjkredsen	7. Kirkebjerg	Ballot 821 interpreted as YES?
Brønshøjkredsen	7. Nordvest	Ballot 864 interpreted as YES?
Brønshøjkredsen	7. Syd	Ballot 1624 interpreted as NO?
Indre Bykredsen	3. Indre By	Ballot 2305 interpreted as YES?
Indre Bykredsen	3. Indre By	Ballot 4434 interpreted as YES?
Indre Bykredsen	3. Syd	Ballot 2243 interpreted as YES?
Indre Bykredsen	3. Øst	Ballot 1750 interpreted as YES?
Indre Bykredsen	3. Øst	Ballot 4926 interpreted as YES?
Indre Bykredsen	3. Øst	Ballot 2390 interpreted as NO?
Nørrebrokredsen	5. Nordvest	Ballot 1925 interpreted as YES?
Nørrebrokredsen	5. Nordvest	Ballot 1124 interpreted as NO?
Nørrebrokredsen	5. Nordvest	Ballot 1238 interpreted as NO?
Nørrebrokredsen	5. Vest	Ballot 463 interpreted as NO?
Sundbyvesterkredsen	2. Nord	Ballot 3496 interpreted as YES?
Sundbyvesterkredsen	2. Nord	Ballot 1890 interpreted as NO?
Sundbyvesterkredsen	2. Nord	Ballot 2630 interpreted as NO?
Sundbyvesterkredsen	2. Nord	Ballot 4275 interpreted as NO?
Sundbyvesterkredsen	2. Sundbyvester	Ballot 2965 interpreted as YES?
Sundbyvesterkredsen	2. Sundbyvester	Ballot 3994 interpreted as NO?
Sundbyvesterkredsen	2. Syd	Ballot 2019 interpreted as YES?
Sundbyvesterkredsen	2. Vest	Ballot 2584 interpreted as NO?
Sundbyøsterkredsen	4. Nord	Ballot 1864 interpreted as NO?
Sundbyøsterkredsen	4. Nord	Ballot 4917 interpreted as NO?
Sundbyøsterkredsen	4. Syd	Ballot 2080 interpreted as YES?
Valbykredsen	8. Midt	Ballot 644 interpreted as YES?
Valbykredsen	8. Nord	Ballot 346 interpreted as YES?
Valbykredsen	8. Sydøst	Ballot 260 interpreted as YES?
Valbykredsen	8. Valby	Ballot 2469 interpreted as YES?
Valbykredsen	8. Valby	Ballot 2642 interpreted as YES?
Vesterbrokredsen	9. Nord	Ballot 2533 interpreted as YES?
Østerbrokredsen	1. Nord	Ballot 196 interpreted as YES?
Østerbrokredsen	1. Syd	Ballot 5465 interpreted as YES?
Østerbrokredsen	1. Østerbro	Ballot 2706 interpreted as NO?
Østerbrokredsen	1. Østerbro	Ballot 3476 interpreted as NO?

after the election. The night before, the ballots from each polling center were transported (by taxi) to the fine counting center under constant surveillance of the election officials who would spend the night there. The fine count commences in the following way. The ballot papers from each polling station are placed on a separate table and counted by civil servants. Each table is numbered. Once the fine count is complete, the results are being entered into a database, and the official in charge of the fine count (*rådhusbetjent*) will forward a piece of paper with the number of table that completed to recount to the quality control office. The paper is important, whoever has the paper, has the right to work on the results of the respective table. During quality control, a team will assess the probability, using statistical tools, if errors were made. In the case that the probability is low, the table is officially done, the piece of paper will be returned to the official in charge of the find count, and the ballots will eventually be packed for further storage. In the case that the probability is deemed unacceptable, civil servants return to the table to recount and find the mistake.

Table 5. Layout of the fine count location

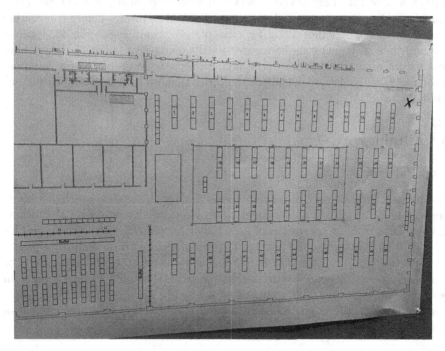

The map of the layout of the different tables can be seen on the map depicted in Table 5. The large white square between table 1 and table 37 is the table of the official in charge of the fine count. The quality control office is to the left of this table and not clearly marked.

The head of elections of Copenhagen municipality gave us permission to conduct the audit. We were permitted to touch the ballot papers of any table that has passed quality control and awaited packing. In preparation for the audit, we determined together with the head of elections, which of tables contained the relevant ballots of our sample described in Table 4. The person in charge of the fine count then kept a stack of the pieces of paper identifying the tables scheduled for auditing and passed them along to us after the table cleared quality control.

On each table, we approached, ballots were packed with rubber bands into stacks of 100, and sometimes 5 such stacks were made into a larger stack, also with rubber bands. On some tables, the stacks were already packed into boxes inducing some kind of order, on other tables, the stacks were placed in no particular order. Advanced votes (which look different in Denmark, because the official ballot form is not yet approved when advanced voting commences) were usually rubber banded and all stacks of a 100 were slipped into one large envelope. It was up to us, the auditors, to fix the order of the ballots.

As depicted in Table 4, some ballot numbers were rather high, 4275 being the highest. From the outset, we decided to assume that all packs of 100 contained a 100 votes, so that finding the correct ballot became feasible in the time frame provided. Also we would consider election day ballots always before considering mail-in ballots. For ballot 4275, for example, we would select the 43. Pack of 100 and then start counting backwards until we arrive at ballot 75. If we could not discern a clear order, we would define one; but because we were handling live ballots, we could not document the order that we have imposed during our audit.

4 Findings

4.1 Paper Elections

Comparison audits do not only apply to elections with an electronic ballot interpretation — they also apply to paper-based elections. We only have to presume that we know the interpretation of each ballot for manual vote tabulation. Our pilot is to our knowledge the first application of a comparison audit to a paper-only election and it shows that it is possible to incorporate the audit into the counting process. A consequence is that countries that plan to transition from pen and paper to electronic elections, can already set up the auditing framework and related processes before even the feasibility study and procurement of election technologies commences.

4.2 Election Officials' Reaction

In our experience, the term *risk-limiting audits* does not sit well with election officials who are not used to the idea of post-election auditing. A few election boards that we interacted with in the past were quite offended by this term. Judging from their reactions, they must have perceived this a sign of distrust that they were informed that their work shall undergo another round of scrutiny. We suspect that a better term is *result-confirming* audits, which is more in line with the interest of most election officials. On the other hand, our pilot was also met with a lot enthusiasm, in particular, it was felt that risk-limiting audits may actually speed up the quality checking and error finding during the fine count. Although this might be true, our pilot shows that there was a noticeable difference between the election results reported after rough count and fine count, respectively, and this difference can only be corrected by a full recount.

4.3 Repeatability

An audit is only then meaningful, if it can be retraced by an independent party of auditors auditing the auditors. In this regards, we noticed, that it is by no means clear if the same set of ballots that we audited could at least in theory be retrieved again. After we left each table, a team of packers arrived, packing the ballots carefully according to the rules, which are clearly specified in Danish election law (*valgloven*). The order we committed to during the audit was likely destroyed when packing the ballots. We conclude that any election that is designed with an audit in mind shall also provide a mechanism for maintaining a particular order for all ballots of each polling station. This order must be preserved when the ballots are stored.

4.4 Integration

A further observation is that of integration of a comparison audit into the larger counting process. We have shown, that it is possible to conduct a risk-limiting audit already one day after the rough count by integrating it into the counting procedures during the fine count. This compares favorably to post-election audits, such as the one conducted in Colorado in 2013 [McB]. This insight suggests that auditing can be an integral part of counting procedures, but it should thought into the process already during the feasibility study.

4.5 Completeness

Our pilot study was not designed as a full scale risk-limiting audit of the Danish referendum. It was more a pilot to understand the changes to the process that occur when conducting such an audit. Were we to scale the audit to all of Denmark, we would need auditors in each fine counting center of which there are 92. Each auditor needs to be properly trained regarding purpose and technicalities. In Copenhagen, counting teams were assigned to the individual tables. Once they finished they were free to leave. We believe it is possible that these teams could also be trained to conduct the audit. And again, such training plans need to be thought carefully into the administrative procedures.

5 Conclusion

In this paper we describe a pilot study for a risk-limiting audit of the 2015 Danish National Referendum. The lessons learned may be of interest to any election managment body that is planning on integrating an auditing framework into their respective electoral processes or that is seeking to introduce electronic voting technology. We conclude that it is advisable to think of auditing as an integral part of the counting activities and to establish clear rules, procedures, and processes for conducting the audit. In the case that the audit is introduced in conjunction with new election technologies, it is best to consider auditing already as part of the feasibility study. The way that paper evidence and ballots are stored is central for the success and the repeatability of the audit. In the case of internet elections, there is no paper trail, and thus standard auditing techniques do not apply.

References

[LS12] Lindeman, M., Stark, P.B.: A gentle introduction to risk-limiting audits. IEEE Secur. Priv. **10**(5), 42–49 (2012)
[McB] McBurnett, N.: State of colorado, risk-limiting audit final report, post-election audit initiative grant no. eac110150e. http://bcn.boulder.co.us/~neal/elections/corla/Risk-Limiting_Audit_Report-Final_20140331.pdf
[Sta10] Stark, P.B.: Super-simple simultaneous single-ballot risk-limiting audits. In: Conference on Electronic Voting Technology/Workshop on Trustworthy Elections (EVT/WOTE), pp. 1–16 (2010)

Legislating for E-Enabled Elections: Dilemmas and Concerns for the Legislator

Leontine Loeber[(✉)]

University of East Anglia, Norwich, UK
leontine_loeber@xs4all.nl

Abstract. The question of the use of new technologies in different aspects of life has been considered in many countries with regard to the electoral process. Since 2000, more and more countries have held experiments with different types of e-voting. A growing body of research has emerged on this topic. However, not much attention so far has been given to the actual choices that legislators have to make when considering the introduction of e-voting. By sketching these issues, this paper aims to help to improve future discussions on this topic by ensuring that all relevant questions are being considered.

Keywords: E-voting · Legislative dilemma's · Election law · Elections · Experiments

1 Introduction

The question of the use of new technologies in different aspects of life has been considered in many countries with regard to the electoral process. Since 2000, more and more countries have held experiments with different types of e-voting. A growing body of research has emerged on this topic. On the one hand, this research is technical in nature, focusing on designing e-voting systems that are safe and can be used in elections. On the other hand, there has been a focus on the implementation and use of e-voting by legislators, electoral management bodies and other relevant actors, such as election observation organizations. This last type of research tends to focus on constitutional and legal demands that e-voting elections have to meet in order to be used. Different authors point towards requirements such as secrecy, transparency, accessibility and so on [1]. However, not much attention so far has been given to the actual choices that legislators have to make when considering the introduction of e-voting. Some of these choices and dilemmas are not limited to e-voting and will have to be considered in every piece of legislation. However, due to the political nature of elections, they might be more pressing when dealing with e-voting.

The goal of the election process is not simply to determine the winners and losers, but also to give legitimacy to the winners, even for those voters who did not vote for them [2]. This stresses the need for free, fair and secret elections to legitimize the outcome [3]. If a part of the election process goes wrong during the actual elections, this could lead to serious doubts on the legitimacy of the final results. It could lead to a major constitutional crisis, if the voters feel that the elected parliamentarians should not

© Springer International Publishing AG 2017
R. Krimmer et al. (Eds.): E-Vote-ID 2016, LNCS 10141, pp. 203–217, 2017.
DOI: 10.1007/978-3-319-52240-1_13

have been elected. Problematic is that political actors each have their own interests to think about when considering the election process [4]. This means that in parliamentary debates over changes is the election law, probably more than in debates over other laws, parliamentarians and political parties look at the effect of the change on their own position [5]. This direct effect has then to compete with the public benefits of a proposed measure. A politician or party may reject even a measure that would be very good for society at large if it will lead to a serious diminishing or even the disappearance of themselves [6]. In order to determine if the legislator is aiming for the public benefits or their own interests when dealing with the issue of e-voting, it is necessary to have better insight in the dilemmas and concerns they have to face with regard to this issue. This paper gives an outline of several of these dilemmas, without trying to answer them. The choices that have to be made will depend on the context of the country in which the introduction of e-voting is discussed. However, the issues that will have to be considered are global in nature. By sketching these issues, this paper aims to help to improve future discussions on this topic by ensuring that all relevant questions are being considered.

2   E-Enabled Elections

2.1   What are E-Enabled Elections?

Often when thinking about e-enabled elections, there is a tendency to think about e-voting and I-voting only. However, there are many phases during the electoral cycle where some form of ICT can be used. An example which became very clear during the 2008 US presidential elections was the use of electoral campaigning through social media. Many countries in the world, including some of the newer democracies use forms of electronic voter registration and identification, for example through the use of biometrics. Tabulation and publishing of results can also be done with the use of ICT, as well as (re)districting. For most of these systems, legislation is necessary in order to allow electoral management bodies and other actors involved in the election process the use of these ICT tools. Although this paper focuses on the use of ICT in the process of the casting of the vote, most of the dilemma's that are mentioned should also be taken into consideration with regard to the use of ICT in other parts of the electoral cycle.

2.2   Reasons for Introduction of E-Enabled Elections

Governments and legislators have expressed various different reasons for the introduction of ICT in the election process. Often, introduction of ICT is seen as a necessary step in the fight against declining turnout. In other cases, improvement of the integrity of the voting process is mentioned. Also, the speedy delivery of results might be a reason to introduce for example electronic counting of ballots [7]. There is a growing body of research on the correctness of the assumptions that are the foundation for these reasons [8–10]. A careful conclusion is that there is yet not enough evidence to state if they are correct or not. However, whatever the outcome of that research will be, one thing should be taken into consideration.

Certain requirements of a free and fair election process can compete with each other. The existing literature on these requirements sometimes briefly mentions this competition, but does not describe how this affects the way a country will have to weigh the different requirements when these requirements call for opposite choices in the election process [11–14]. However, it is very easy to find circumstances where basic requirements on which everybody agrees call for conflicting measures to be taken. For example, to achieve secret ballot elections, both anonymity and integrity of the voting process must be ensured. Anonymity requires that voters cannot be linked to the votes they cast. Integrity guarantees must ensure that all participants can verify that the final tally accurately reflects all legitimate votes cast. Finally, to limit the possibility of vote coercion and selling, it should be impossible for voters to prove to others how they voted. One can see how these requirements can hinder each other. In order to maximize integrity, voters could be given some sort of proof of how they voted so that in case they get the impression that their vote is not counted correctly, they can make a claim based on this evidence. However, giving voters proof of their vote infringes on anonymity. It also increases the risk of vote buying or coercion [15].

This means that however valid the reasons for the introduction of e-enabled elections might be in order to meet a specific requirement for free and fair elections, during the legislative process the possible negative effect this might have on other requirements should be carefully considered in order to find the right balance.

3   General Dilemma's

3.1   Experiments or not?

The first question legislators should face is whether they think it is possible to use the new technology from the start in the whole country or if it would be wise to experiment with it first. Such experiments can take different forms and will be discussed next. The big advantage with going ahead with e-voting right away is that the perceived advantages of introducing it immediately come into effect. Another advantage is that it prevents the often more complicated system where during elections different forms of voting are used parallel. Some countries in recent history have made the decision to implement a new system for the whole country right away, for example Kyrgyzstan in 2015.[1] There are also however considerable disadvantages to approach the question of e-voting in this way. One of the problems is that it forces the legislator to legislate binding general laws for a voting system that has not been used during actual elections. This could be problematic because it might be unclear what issues should be addressed in that legislation. This could have the effect that a lot of amendments to the legislation might be necessary, both during the run up to these first elections and after that one. Another problem could be that if during the elections, a problem arises that, due to the large scale of the use on the technology, causes serious doubts on the correctness of the outcome of the elections, which might mean that a revote might be necessary.

---

[1] See OSCE/ODHIR Kyrgyz Republic, Parliamentary Elections, 4 October 2015: Final Report.

In most cases therefore, it would be the wisest course of action to start with experiments first. Experimental legislation has the advantage that, at least in most countries, it allows the legislator to give the executive a bit of space to deviate on a lower level from provisions in Acts of Parliament, such as the Election Law. However, the legislator should not deviate from constitutional guarantees, such as secret and free elections. This means that the space for experimentation is not unlimited. Experimental legislation should be valid for a fixed period, meaning that they should expire as soon as the underlying motives for holding the experiment cease to exist and enough evidence has been gathered in order to evaluate the experiment and make an informed decision on the question if permanent introduction is a good idea. Experiments should in general be applied to a specific part of the national territory or to a specific group of citizens. Experimental legislation can, when used correctly be an instrument to tackle the uncertainty and lack of information that will exist when considering the introduction of e-voting. However, its use can raise questions as to the compatibility of these rules with the principle of legal certainty [16]. Especially when it comes to the election process, in light of its importance for the functioning of society, uncertainty should be avoided whenever possible.

Politically Binding or Non-Binding Elections. In some countries, the possibilities to hold experiments during binding political elections are limited, but it might be possible to experiment in other elections, such as student or business union elections. An example of such a country is Austria [17]. The advantage of experimenting during these kind of elections is quite clear; there is less of an issue with political pressure and if major problems occur, it might be easier to have new elections than if this would happen during binding political elections. However, there are also some possible negative issues. One of the problems is the representativeness of the group of voters that participate in these elections and the type of organizations running them. Students are in general higher educated than the general population and most likely also better able to use different ICT tools. The fact that they are able to vote with the new technologies therefore might not necessarily mean that this will also be true for other citizens. Another issue is that the organizations involved in these non-political elections are usually not the same as the electoral management bodies involved in political elections. This means that experiences that are obtained with these experiments might be less useful in preparing a change of the election process for political elections because there is no learning curve for the organizations involved that benefit the election process in general. Also, it might be hard to see if the benefits that are expected to be gained with e-voting can be proven with these elections because they are usually held in a completely different environment in terms of closeness of the race, time pressures in getting results etc.

This could lead to the conclusion that it might be better to experiment directly during political binding elections. However, as stated before, the disadvantage of that is that any kind of problems during the experiments could invalid the vote. For political binding elections, this is very problematic. Another downside of experimenting in political elections is that it could potentially cause problems with the equality of the vote, for example if participating in the experiments makes it a lot easier to vote and vote correctly. If this is a problem depends also on other factors, such as the size of the experiment. Finally, there will be a lot more attention for the experiments, probably especially from political parties. This could mean that any minor problems during the experiments might be used by opponents of the experiments to discredit them.

Level of Experiments. Experiment can be held within different levels of elections, from national elections to local elections. Some countries, like the UK, have opted in the past to experiment exclusively in local elections. Other countries, like the Netherlands, Switzerland and Estonia have also allowed e-voting and e-voting experiments during national elections [18, 19]. The reason for not allowing experiments in national elections is in general that national elections are seen as first order elections. The impact of these elections in the constitutional order of a country is seen as too high to risk failures during these elections that can take place when experimenting with new technologies. Experimenting during second or third order elections is therefore seen as better.

However, when only experimenting in lower level elections, problems can occur when dealing with the question of representativeness of the outcome of the elections. It might be hard to compare the experiences in one municipality, where e-voting was used, to that of a municipality where it wasn't used, when the elections that were taken place might differ greatly in for example competitiveness. In such a case, it would be difficult to make informed claims about for example the effect of the use of e-voting on turnout.

This question cannot been seen out of context of the electoral system. For a country like the Netherlands, which uses a nationwide constituency with proportional representation, experimenting in specific municipalities during national elections is quite safe because even if the experiments are not flawless, the overall impact on the outcome of the election will most likely be very small. This is fundamentally different in a country such as the United Kingdom, which uses single-member districts in a First Past the Post system, even for its Parliamentary elections. An experiment gone wrong in one of those districts could very well have an impact on the outcome of the election in that district and therefore on the overall composition of the Parliament.

Specific Target Groups. One option to steer away from the question on level of experiments might be to experiment using not geographical elements, such as a municipality, but specific target groups. One group that is often used to experiment on are voters living abroad. This group often faces problems participating in paper-based elections. Also, in many countries, these voters are allowed to vote by mail. This makes it easier to take the step towards remote voting with the use of the Internet [20]. Experimenting with I-voting for voters living abroad can most definitely be very useful to get a first impression if the chosen system works and what kind of changes will be necessary to implement such a system on a bigger scale. However, there are also some downsides to this kind of experimentation that should be taken into consideration. First, voters living abroad that participate in elections are often a self-selecting group. This means that these voters have gone to a certain amount of trouble to registrate to participate in the first place and often also have the option of participating in the I-voting experiment. It is therefore very likely that the voters participating in the election are already informed and committed voters, who are also comfortable using technology [21]. The question is then how representative this group of voters is compared to the general audience and how well the outcomes of the experiments can be translated into conclusions for the use by other voters. Another issue is that the balance that has to be struck between secrecy of the vote and accessibility of the voting process is different for voters living abroad who in general are not able to participate through voting in the polling station than for voters living in the country. This also means that some risks or concerns regarding voter secrecy and family voting are perhaps acceptable when it comes to this specific group of voters, but not for the general public. When designing experiments for this specific group, these differences have to be taken into account if the desires objective is to in time roll out the technology that is used for the entire voting population.

Number of Experiments. A final question that should be considered is how many experiments should be held before decisions are made about the use of new technology. It is very attractive to hold one successful experiment and then decide to implement this permanently. However, this is risky. Certain issues might not come up during that one election, for example because it was not very competitive and there were no technical problems. However, this does not mean that in future elections, all will go the same. It seems therefore prudent to hold multiple experiments before deciding on the issue at hand. However, since elections in general don't take place very often, this could mean that the timeframe in which experiments have to be held will be quite long [22]. In lieu of wishes of government and Parliament to improve elections through e-voting, there might be a lot of pressure after a first successful experiment to implement this. At the other hand, one failed experiment should also not necessarily lead to the conclusion not to continue with the chosen form of e-voting. Since voting is not an activity that citizens do on a daily basis, it is very likely that it will take them time to adjust to the use of new voting technologies. The same can be said about the people working in election administration. It is therefore wise to carefully evaluate each experiment in order to tweak its weak sides and give it another try. Problems in this process of getting it right might however occur when some geographical units that were experimenting stop using the new technology and others that weren't are starting with experiments. This was for example the case in Switzerland [23]. In such an environment, it might take more experiments and thus more time to gather enough data and information to make an informed decision on the long term use of new voting technologies.

3.2   Level of Legislation

In most countries, there will be some constitutional stipulations on elections. In general, these will be that elections have to be general, direct, free and equal [24]. These rights are also expressed in article 25 of the UN Charter on Human Rights and article 3 of the First Protocol of the European Convention on Human Rights. In most cases, for the introduction of e-voting it will not be necessary to change these articles in the constitution. However, the existing Election law and lower legislation will most likely have to be changed. The question the legislator has to face with regard to these changes is what elements should be regulated by Acts of Parliament and what parts can be delegated to lower levels of legislation. In most legislative systems, the rule is that general and abstract rules will be laid down in Acts of Parliament and administrative and technical issues can be delegated to lower levels of legislation. With regard to e-voting, some authors tend to take this view also [1, 25]. However, as stated before, the election process is a very political one. This means that with regard to legislation concerning elections, it might be necessary to involve Parliament in more elements of the legislative system than with other legislation, to ensure that a ruling party or coalition is not able to change certain legislative elements of the election process to their own advantage.

Problematic in the election process is that details that might seem quite technical and not necessarily political could end up to be used in a political manner [1]. For example, the timeframe in which voters can apply for biometric voter registration can be used to exclude certain groups of voters, for example people who live quite far from places that are used for this registration.[2] If it is known that those groups of voters tend to vote for a certain party or parties, it might be beneficial for the ruling party to set the timeframe either in a way to exclude these voters, if this means weakening the opposition, or to include them if they are their own voters [26]. This would mean that administrative and technical details which would normally be regulated by lower legislation might have to be included in Acts of Parliament when it comes to elections. However, in most countries, changing Acts of Parliament takes more time than changing lower legislation. Since legislation for e-voting will most likely include technical prescriptions that might change quite fast due to new technological improvements, legislating the whole process of e-voting through Acts of Parliament might hinder the legislative process and cause the legislation to be outdated quite fast [27].

Even though it is not possible to give a general rule that would apply to all countries and situations on what to include in Acts of Parliament and what in lower legislation, it should be clear that the normal rules for such a division should not automatically be applied to the voting process. In all cases, it should be avoided to give the executive power the competence to regulate those parts of the election process which could weaken the principles of elections, even when these could be considered to be technical.

3.3 Timeframe

In the literature on implementation of changes in elections, the general assumption is that it is unwise to make major changes in the Election law within one year before Election Day [1]. International bodies concerned with elections, such as the Council of Europe have also stated this rule in their opinions.[3] There is no reason to assume that shouldn't be true for the introduction of e-voting. However, in practice it might not always be easy to follow this rule. Once a decision is made to either implement e-voting or to hold experiments with them, it might not be entirely clear how long it

---

[2] See OSCE/ODHIR Kyrgyz Republic, Parliamentary Elections, 4 October 2015: Final Report.

[3] Code of good practice in electoral matters, Venice Commission of the Council of Europe, Opinion no. 190/2002.

will take from that moment until the implementation process is finished. Also, there might be pressure from political parties to start as soon as possible in light of the expected benefits. In countries where a government can be send home or resign at any given time, it might also not always be very clear what Election Day is going to be and when the year before that day ends. For example, the Dutch government had decided to experiment with I-voting for citizens living abroad during the Parliamentary elections that were supposed to take place in May 2007. However, in July 2006, the government fell and elections were pushed forward to November 2006. This meant that the legislation dealing with the experiment wasn't finished and published until September 2006, only two months before Election Day. The other option would have been to cancel the experiment, but that would have led to a delay of almost three years for the I-voting, namely during the European Parliament elections of 2009. Therefore, although the timeframe is important and it is good to when possible adhere to the one year rule, this can never be guaranteed completely. Legislators should be aware of this, because it stresses the need to start thinking about changes that might have to been made in the election process fairly quickly after the last election was held.

4 Scope of Legislation

The introduction of electronic means for certain steps in the electoral cycle is not just a matter of replacing the articles that dealt with a paper based process for articles describing the electronic means. Issues of transparency, voter secrecy and verifiability will have to be guaranteed, no matter which system you use, but the manner in which these fundamental demands are guaranteed in the process will have to be reconsidered when using e-voting. This means that when a change to e-voting is being considered, this has to involve a complete review of the voting process and most likely, an adaptation of certain rules and procedures [1, 25, 28, 29]. There are three areas in which this is especially necessary that might be overlooked at the start of the legislative process.

4.1 Division of Competences

In countries that have a very decentralized system for running elections, such as the United Kingdom and the Netherlands, a paper based election can very easily be run from this local level of election administration. Although detailed knowledge of the voting procedures is necessary, paper ballot elections do not necessitate very specific technical knowledge. Also chain of command is not really an issue in paper based elections, since election materials are worthless between one election and the next. This means that it does not matter if municipalities and local election management bodies have slightly different procedures for storing materials.

However, when introducing forms of e-voting or e-counting, this changes. First, a greater technical knowledge will be necessary to run elections [22]. EMBs have to be aware of possible technical problems and ways to deal with them. This means that training could not in all cases be left to the local actors, but needs to be done on a central level. Also, a voting computer or a vote scanner in between elections needs to be stored securely in order to prevent outsiders from changing software or other relevant parts of the equipment. Since this chain of custody is of utmost importance in order to guarantee the integrity of elections [30], it might be not best to leave it up to the local authorities to decide how to deal with this, but to have uniform regulations about this for the whole country. This means that the division of competences between national authorities and local authorities operating in the election process will have to be reconsidered [29].

4.2   Judicial Procedures

Within the electoral cycle, there are different stages when courts and judges play a role. In some cases, this involvement will take place in early stages of the cycle, for example in cases concerning the delimitation of boundaries, the registration of parties and certain aspects of campaign finance. A large part of the cases that deal with elections will however deal with the final stages, such as candidate and voter registration, the process of casting ballots and the counting and tabulation of results. Judges delating with conflicts in the earlier stages often have sufficient time to hear the case, study the evidence and give a ruling. This is usually not the case for the later stages where in most instances, judges have at the maximum a couple of days to come to a conclusion. This is why in most countries, there are very strict timelines for filing an appeal in those later stages and for the final ruling [31]. These timelines are usually based on the situation that a paper based election takes place. When introducing e-voting, the legislator will have to rethink this. With e-voting new aspects will be added to the process, such as certification mechanisms, transparency regulations or specific procurement principles. Although these are necessary in order to correctly take care of the later stages of the process, the decisions made within those procedures will take place at an earlier stage. If the strict timelines and rules for evidence in the later stages do not allow people to question these earlier decisions, the process of judicial review might become meaningless. This danger also exist when judges do not have enough technical knowledge to understand the e-voting process that is implemented to an extent where they can make well informed rulings [32]. If special rules exist for the nomination of judges to for example Electoral Courts, the legislator will have to reconsider if the overall making of such a Court includes enough technical experts [33].

4.3   Criminal Law

One thing to consider when introduction e-voting or other forms of electronic usages in the election process is whether the articles in either the Election law or the Criminal Code that deals with election crimes are suitable for offenses committed while using electronics [32, 34]. For example, the Netherlands used DREs in elections, but when a candidate and poll station worker used the DRE to commit election fraud, it was hard to convict him for this crime. This was due to the fact that the articles in the Election law were written for paper based elections and were not rewritten when DREs were introduced. Because there was a general clause in the Criminal Law on computer fraud, it was possible to convict this person, but that might not always be the case. Also, in some countries a conviction for electoral offenses is necessary in order to take away a person's active and passive electoral rights, which might sometimes be desirable, due to the nature of the crime committed. If the Election or Criminal law is not adapted for e-voting, such specific measures might not be available.

Another aspect that should be taken into consideration is the collection of evidence when dealing with election crimes. With paper based elections, it is quite clear which materials can be examined to see if a crime was committed. With e-voting this might be more difficult and could in some cases depend on the vendor or owner of the equipment that is used to cooperate with evidence gathering. It is therefore recommended that the legislator takes into consideration if the inclusion of certain articles dealing with the duty to cooperate is necessary. Finally, the scale of possible election fraud might be larger with e-voting than with paper based voting. To commit outsider fraud, fraud by others than the electoral management bodies, with a paper based election, you might have to get a conspirator in almost every polling station. With e-voting, if an outsider somehow is able to get into the software that is used, this could be done with less people [35]. This makes the risk-benefit analysis for the possible perpetrator different. In order to address this, possible sentences should be higher, to have a higher deterrence.

5 Dilemma's Concerning Other Actors

5.1 Manufacturers and Vendors

A legislator that is interested in the introduction of new technology in the election process faces a difficult question when it comes to the involvement of manufacturers and vendors. On the one hand, it might be very useful to involve these actors very early in the decision making process for several reasons. The first is that these actors are usually very aware of existing systems and can therefore provide valuable information as to what is possible and what not. Manufacturers and vendors can give advice on possible risks and benefits and experiences in other countries. They can give insight in the costs of the system they can provide and they are usually able to advice on the implementation process. A final benefit might be that choosing an existing system might be cheaper than building a new one. However, the risk of this early involvement is that manufacturers and vendors have their own interests and are therefore never completely neutral in their advice. They of course, as any business need to sell their products. This might mean that the legislator might not be able to be completely free in their demands of a system, because they will be pushed towards a specific system. Also, it might not always be clear, especially with large, international companies, who the owners and people in charge are. Given the importance of elections in the allocation of power in a country, this might not be a desirable situation [1, 36]. However, not involving existing companies and for example choosing to build a government owned system has negative sides as well. Besides the cost factor, it might be difficult to maintain a level of expert knowledge that is necessary, not only to build the system, but to keep it running. Also with a new system that has not been used in other countries, there is less knowledge about possible problems. The main thing to keep in mind is that whatever route is taken, even when e-voting is successfully introduced, government cannot step back and let the market and suppliers take over. There should always be enough knowledge of the system within government to make informed decision concerning its use and the possible risks of the system. As was recently confirmed by the Conference of Electoral Management Bodies, the electoral management bodies' choice of new technologies should be guided by the needs of the electoral process and not by the interest of technology providers.[4]

5.2 Other Stakeholders

An important lesson that can be taken away from countries where e-voting has been unsuccessful is that it is not enough for government and the legislator to trust the system and to be content with it. In representative democracies, elections are the number one means for citizens to be involved with the decisions that government will make for them. This means that the way elections are run will always be scrutinized by the general public. It is therefore important that during the introduction of e-voting both supporters and critics of the system will be involved [26, 36]. No e-voting system will ever be completely safe, secure and reliable, just as no paper based system ever is. This means that it will always be possible for critics to find flaws in the system. By including them in the decision making process, their biggest critiques can perhaps be addressed by adding certain features to either the proposed system or the procedures accompanying it [37]. This means that the legislator should have a system in place that ensures that critics have ample time and opportunity to come forward, examine the proposals and give an opinion about it.

It is also necessary to involve the other actors in the election process. If the people that are actually running the elections feel that they were not involved in the changes, they might not perform as well as possible. Research has shown that the way voters feel about the integrity of the elections will be shaped largely by their view of the polling station worker they encountered when casting a vote [38]. Although it will not be possible to include all of these in a legislative process, ways should be found to address questions that election workers might have. Also, the legislator should be aware that the people in the polling stations are usually also very informed about issues within the election process that need to be addressed. They would therefore be a great source of information for the legislator.

6 Technical Issues

Legislators considering the introduction of e-voting will have to face several technical issues. Issues that are well researched are certification procedures and procurement processes. There are however some other issues that are not that well looked into yet.

---

[4] Conclusions of the 13th European Conference of the Electoral Management Bodies, Bucharest 2016.

6.1 Legislating for Emergencies

When using paper ballots, emergency measures might be necessary on Election Day, but usually on a small scale. This would for example be the case if ballot papers are not delivered to a polling station or if there is a case of wrong information printed on them. However, in most of those cases these will be local problems that can quite easily be solved without disrupting the election process too much. However, with e-voting this can be quite different. If a country uses machines and software made by one party, public or private, a problem with that machine or software could be present in all the equipment. This means that the whole election might be compromised. If an I-voting system is used and there are problems with the Internet on Election Day that could also have great consequences for the validity of the elections. The main problem with elections is that they have to happen within a very short timeframe, for the most part on a single day and that there is very little room for do-overs. Legislating for these kinds of emergencies is very difficult. Due to the political nature of elections, it is however also not a good idea not to have any contingency plans in place and make the decisions as problems occur. This could potentially give the executive a lot of room to make politically biased decisions [39]. The legislator should be aware of this dilemma when legislation for e-voting in order to try to find a balance between giving enough direction on how to operate when problems occur, without trying to legislate for every problem that might arise [22].

6.2 Dual Systems

After the discussion in different countries on the 'black box' problem of voting computers, systems have been build that have a paper trail added on the computer. This means that it is possible to compare the results that are given by the computer to the paper trail. This sounds very good in terms of transparency and integrity. However, it also posed difficult questions to the legislator, which will have to be resolved in the law before any election. The main question is which of the systems is leading, the computer results, or the paper trail? If the paper trail is leading, this means that actually in all instances, all the paper printouts have to be counted. This however means that one of the benefits of e-voting, the accuracy and speed of the count is nullified. However, if the legislators chooses to make the computer results leading, the addition of a paper trail is only useful when at least a certain percentage of paper printouts is counted and compared to the computer results. In that case, the legislator does not only have to make rules on that percentage but also on the way polling stations or counting places are assigned to be counted [40]. Most important however is that the law should be clear on what should happen in case there are differences between the computer count and the manual count [32].

7 Conclusions

A well legislated election process is of utmost importance to the legitimacy of the elected representatives and thus to the stability of democracy. Problematic with changes in the election legislation is the fact that those people that have to decide on these changes (parliamentarians and members of the executive) might not be entirely objective since their chances of being reelected can also be directly affected by these changes. This means that it is important that attention if given to the way the legislator deals with the process of introducing changes in the election process, including the decision to use e-voting. As with any type of electoral reform, a balance has to be struck between the different requirements for a free and fair election process. Although there can be very legitimate reasons for introducing e-enabled elections, the benefits thereof should always be weighed against the possible negative effects.

The dilemma's and questions that legislators need to face when thinking about the introduction of e-voting are not easily solved. This is also an understudied field when looking at research about e-voting. The topics mentioned in this paper are by no means an exhaustive list, but can give some insight in important decisions that have to be made during the legislative process. It would be beneficial to legislators if there would be more focus from research on this issues, preferably with a comparative approach. This could give more insight in how different countries have dealt with this questions and if those approaches were successful or not and hopefully lead to some best practices. Such best practices could then be used by countries contemplating a move towards e-voting. Although it will in all likelihood not be possible to give a clear answer to all these issues that is suitable for all countries, a legislator that does take them into consideration during the legislative process will have a better chance to make informed decisions and thus better legislation.

References

1. Maurer, A.D.: Legality, separation of powers, stability of electoral law, the impact of new voting technologies. In: 1st Scientific Electoral Expert Debate, Bucharest (2016)
2. Katz, R.S.: Democracy and Elections. Oxford University Press, New York (1997)
3. Merloe, P.: Human rights- the basis for inclusiveness, transparency, accountability, and public confidence in elections. In: Young, J.H. (ed.) International Election Principles: Democracy and the Rule of Law, pp. 3–39. American Bar Association (2009)
4. Benoit, K.: Models of electoral system change. Elect. Stud. **23**, 363–389 (2004)
5. Gerken, H.K.: The Democracy Index Why our Election System is Failing and How to Fix it, pp. 15–18. Princeton University Press, Princeton (2009)
6. Shorstein, A.: Politicizing the election process: the Katherine Harris effect. Fla. Coast. Law J. **2**, 373–380 (2009)
7. Remmert, M.: Towards European standards on electronic voting. In: Electronic Voting in Europe, pp. 13–16 2004
8. Carter, L., Bélanger, F.: Internet voting and political participation: an empirical comparison of technological and political factors. ACM SIGMIS Database **43**(3), 26–46 (2012)
9. Monnoyer-Smith, L.: How e-voting technology challenges traditional concepts of citizenship: an analysis of French voting rituals. GI-Edition (2006)
10. Boulus-Rødje, N., and Laanggaardsvej, R.: Mapping the literature: socio-cultural, organizational and technological dimensions of e-voting technologies. In: Electronic Voting (2012)
11. Fortier, J.C., Ornstein, N.J.: The absentee ballot and the secret ballot: challenges for election reform. Univ. Mich. J. Law Rev. **36**, 483–516 (2002)

12. Birch, S., Watt, B.: Remote electronic voting: free, fair and secret? Polit Q. **75**(1), 60–72 (2004)
13. Tokaji, D.P., Colker, R.: Absentee voting by people with disabilities: promoting access and integrity. McGeorge Law Rev. **38**, 1015–1064 (2007)
14. Semmel, C.L.: Election reform: alternatives to ensure integrity and increase access. Policy Perspect. **11**, 33–40 (2009)
15. Evans, D., Paul, N.: Elections security perception and reality. IEEE Secur. Priv. **2**, 24–31 (2004). www.computer.org
16. Ranchordás, S.: Sunset clauses and experimental regulations: blessing or curse for legal certainty. Statute Law Rev. **36**(1), 28–45 (2015)
17. Krimmer, R., Ehringfeld, A., Traxl, M.: The use of e-voting in the austrian federation of students elections 2009. Electron. voting **167**, 33–44 (2010)
18. Buchsbaum, T.M.: E-voting: international developments and lessons learnt. In: Electronic Voting in Europe Technology Law, Politics and Society, pp. 31–34 (2004)
19. Stein, R., Wenda, G.: The council of Europe and e-voting: history and impact of Rec (2004) 11. In: Krimmer, R., Volkamer, M. (eds.) Proceeding of Electronic Voting 2014 (EVOTE 2014), pp. 105–110. TUT Press, Tallinn (2014)
20. Chevallier, M., Warynski, M., Sandoz, A.: Success factors of Geneva's e-voting system. Electron. J. e-Gov. **4**(2), 55–62 (2006)
21. Erlach, J., Gasser, Urs.: Three case studies from Switzerland: e-voting. Berkman Center Research Publication (2009)
22. Schwartz, D., Grice, D.: Establishing a legal framework for e-voting in Canada. Elections Canada (2013)
23. Serdult, U., et al.: Fifteen years of internet voting in Switzerland: history, governance and use. In: IEEE 2015 Second International Conference on eDemocracy and eGovernment (ICEDEG), pp. 126–132 (2015)
24. Kersting, N., Baldersheim, H.: Electronic voting and democratic issues an introduction. In: Kersting, N., Baldersheim, H. (eds.) Electronic Voting and Democracy A comparative Analysis, p. 11. Palgrave Macmillan, New York (2004)
25. Caarls, S.: E-Voting Handbook: Key Steps in the Implementation of E-Enabled Elections. Council of Europe, Strasbourg (2010)
26. Hall, T.E., Wang, T.A.: International principles for election integrity. In: Alvarez, R.M., Hall, T.E., Hyde, S.D. (eds.) Election Fraud: Detecting and Deterring Electoral Manipulation, p. 49. Brookings Institution Press, Washington, D.C. (2008)
27. Alvarez, M.R., Hall, T.E.: Electronic Elections: The Perils and Promises of Digital Democracy, p. 184. Princeton University Press, Princeton (2008)
28. Loeber, L.: E-voting in the Netherlands: from general acceptance to general doubt in two years. In: Krimmer, R., Grimm, R. (eds.) Electronic voting 2008, pp. 21–30. GI Lecture Notes in Informatics. Gesellschaft fur Informatik, Bonn (2008)
29. International IDEA: Introducing Electronic Voting: Essential Considerations, Policy Paper, December 2011
30. Hall, T.E., Wang, T.A.: International principles for election integrity. In: Alvarez, R.M., Hall, T.E., Hyde, S.D. (eds.) Election Fraud: Detecting and Deterring Electoral Manipulation, p. 40. Brookings Institution Press, Washington, D.C. (2008)
31. Bickerstaff, S.: Contesting the outcome of elections. In: Young, J.H. (ed.) International Election Principles: Democracy and the Rule of Law, p. 314. ABA Publishing, Chicago (2009)
32. Goldsmith, B., Ruthrauff, H.: Implementing and Overseeing Electronic Voting and Counting Technologies. International Foundation for Electoral Systems and National Democratic Institute, Washington, D.C. (2013)

33. Esteve, J.B.: The role of judiciary in the oversight of electronic aspects of the voting process. In: 1st Scientific Electoral Expert Debate, Bucharest (2016)
34. Electronic Voting: Challenges and Opportunities. Ministry of Local Government and Regional Development (2006)
35. Lauer, T.W.: The risk of e-voting. Electron. J. E-gov. **2**(3), 177–186 (2004)
36. McGaley, M. McCarthy, J.: Transparency and e-voting: democratic vs. commercial interests. In: Electronic Voting in Europe-Technology, Law, Politics and Society, pp. 153–163 (2004)
37. Xenakis, A. MacIntosh, A.: Procedural security and social acceptance in e-voting. In: 2005 IEEE Proceedings of the 38th Annual Hawaii International Conference on System Sciences (HICSS 2005) (2005)
38. Hall, T.E., Monson, J.Q., Patterson, K.D.: The human dimension of elections how poll workers shape public confidence in elections. Polit. Res. Q. **62**(3), 507–522 (2009)
39. Gross, O.: Constitutions and emergency regimes. In: Ginsburg, T., Dixon, R. (eds.) Comparative Constitutional Law, p. 348. Edward Elgar Publishing Limited, Cheltenham (2011)
40. Alvarez, R.M., et al.: Machines versus humans: the counting and recounting of prescored punchcard ballots. In: Alvarez, R.M., Atkeson, L.R., Hall, T.E. (eds.) Confirming Elections, Creating Confidence and Integrity through Election Auditing, p. 83. Palgrave MacMillan, New York (2012)

Electronic Voting as an Additional Method of Participating in Elections. Opinions of Poles

Magdalena Musiał-Karg[✉]

Adam Mickiewicz University, Poznań, Poland
magda.musial@interia.pl

Abstract. The paper discusses Poles' opinions on the adoption of an alternative method of voting i.e. electronic voting (in the context of political preferences). The author focused on analyzing her research results on the adoption of e-voting systems in Poland emphasizing responses to the research question regarding Poles' approval for having Internet-voting available in Polish elections and, whether, given the opportunity, the respondents would make use of this voting mode. In addition to own research findings, reference was made to the results of public opinion polls carried out by the Center for Public Opinion Research and the Ombudsman's Office.

Keywords: Electronic voting · E-voting · Internet voting · Opinions of poles

1 Introduction

Recent years saw electronic voting become the alternative voting method most debated in many countries around the globe. In the wake of the successful adoption and use of this method in countries ranging from Estonia to Switzerland to Norway, political debate ensued not only among politicians and other public officials but also among ordinary citizens eager to gain access to advanced and convenient ways of voting, as offered in addition to the traditional. Poland too has for last years debated e-voting on the occasion of nearly every domestic election[1]. As a consequence, the Polish public has been, as it were, forming opinions on various alternative voting methods which are either in place in Polish political practice or whose adoption is being considered.

This article has been written within the research project: *E-voting as an alternative way of voting procedures in national elections. Experiences of selected countries and prospects for implementation e-voting in Poland (E-voting jako alternatywna procedura głosowania w elekcjach państwowych. Doświadczenia wybranych państw a perspektywy wdrożenia e-głosowania w Polsce)* – financed by the National Science Center in Poland UMO-2014/15/B/HS5/01358.

---

[1] A model enabling Poles to cast their votes in presidential, parliamentary, local and European Parliament elections over the Internet and by correspondence has been prepared by e.g. Palikot's Movement. *Palikot's Movement* (today *Your Move*) is a liberal, anti-clerical, left-wing, and pro-European political party, founded in 2010 by Janusz Palikot – former politician of Civic Platform party. In 2013 *Palikot's Movement* changed its name into *Your Move*.

© Springer International Publishing AG 2017
R. Krimmer et al. (Eds.): E-Vote-ID 2016, LNCS 10141, pp. 218–232, 2017.
DOI: 10.1007/978-3-319-52240-1_14

This paper discusses the opinions of Poles on the adoption of one alternative method of voting in elections and referendums, i.e. electronic voting (or e-voting). The author's primary objective has been to analyze the outcomes of her own research (a quantitative survey of a representative sample of the population)[2]. The research subject of this paper are the opinions of Poles on the implementation of one of the alternative methods of voting in elections - an electronically assisted voting. The main aim of the author is the analysis of the attitudes of Poles towards the idea of introduction of i-voting in Poland. Basing on results of own researches the author will analyze respondents' declarations regarding the use of voting via Internet (if such possibility). The survey's aim was to correlate the given answers with declarations regarding political preferences of the respondents. For the purpose of this survey five political parties have been taken into consideration – each of them has wan a mandate to the European Parliament in the 2014 elections. The own research findings have been backed up by the outcomes of the public opinion polls carried out by the Center for Public Opinion Research and the Ombudsman's Office. Before analyzing the own survey results, some definitional and legal remarks have been presented, as well as attitudes of Polish political parties and politicians toward electronic voting.

2 Electronic Voting – Definitional Remarks

Voting by electronic means is a broad category. ITC technologies are currently employed to:

- collect and process voting data and communicate election results based on input from electoral commissions in a traditional ballot-paper-based vote,
- to receive and tally votes,
- to manage remote online voting [1, 2].

Generally speaking, electronic voting can therefore be defined as the use of ITC tools to gather and count votes as well as to cast votes remotely over the Internet. Simply put, "wherever the electronic medium is the Internet, reference is made to Internet-voting whereas the mode used in voting by mobile telephone is termed mobile voting" [3].

According to the Committee of Ministers of the Council of Europe, electronic voting falls within the two main categories of remote and kiosk voting. In remote electronic voting, use is made of electronic media which allow votes to be cast from any location. In kiosk voting, a voter needs to show up at a polling station or another site indicated by an electoral authority for the purpose of registration. The voter then casts his or her vote electronically, commonly by means of a touch screen. The votes are counted with the so-called DRE machines (Direct Recording Electronic machines) and then forwarded to a central vote register [4]. Specialized literature distinguishes between two types of voting by electronic means: electronic voting (e-voting) and

---

[2] The survey, which relied on a questionnaire, was held in November and December 2014. It involved 930 respondents who made up a representative random sample of adult residents of Poland (the survey was a part of a research "Political Preferences").

internet voting (i-voting). E-voting is the broader term which includes internet voting. As mentioned earlier, electronic voting also refers to the use of such voting technologies as digital television, the telephone and the Internet.

Internet voting comprises the two categories of Internet voting at a polling place and remote Internet voting. In the case of the former, voters cast their votes via the Internet in a specially-designed voting kiosk. Remote Internet voting, in its turn, involves voters casting a vote at either "a voting kiosk" (located outside of a polling station) or a home computer linked to the Internet. The data is then transmitted over the Internet to a central database from a terminal of either type.

Depending on whether a given democratic system is representative or direct, voters engage in either electronic voting (e-voting) or electronic referendums (e-referendums) [5]. In both cases, depending on the medium used in the voting, additional subcategories, i.e. i-voting and i-referendums, can be distinguished (both relying on the use of the Internet).

3   Electronic Voting in the Polish Constitution

The Polish Constitution neither expressly allows nor expressly prohibits providing the option of electronic voting in the national legal system. One can therefore conclude that the Constitution is silent on e-voting, particularly in its elaboration of the rules applicable to general elections.

Therefore, as has rightfully been remarked by Szymanek, the adoption or rejection of e-voting systems in Poland has been left at the discretion of the ordinary legislator whose measures must obviously "comply with any and all electoral standards enshrined in the Constitution" [6].

At this junction, note should be taken of the three electoral rules of universal, direct and secret suffrage, which have been debated in connection with the possible adoption of e-voting.

On the positive side of the issue, universal suffrage requires the legislator to adopt solutions which facilitate and thereby encourage the exercise of voting rights (making elections all the more universal). "As a consequence, (…) viewed as an obligation to create solutions which facilitate the exercise of voting rights, the constitutional rule not only refrains from constraining but in fact encourages the legislator to employ e-voting as a way to incentivize voters" [6].

Applied in connection with e-voting, the direct suffrage principle raises the most serious concerns as it requires that political office holders be elected directly, i.e. not only by having registered voters vote in a single round [7] but also personally (i.e. by showing up at a polling station in person to cast their vote) [8]. Notably, the Electoral Code of 2011 added two options which appear to contradict these principles. These allow proxy and correspondence voting under a changed interpretation of direct suffrage redefined as no longer having to involve voting in person and only retaining the criteria of single-round voting and voter registration [6]. Under the amended rules, electronic voting no longer infringes upon the constitutional principle of direct suffrage as such suffrage no longer requires that voters vote personally, i.e. show up in person at a polling station.

The third principle debated in connection with e-voting is that of secret suffrage. According to Szymanek, despite allowing proxy and correspondence voting (which raise many security concerns), the Electoral Code continues to uphold the principle of secret suffrage. Although electronic voting is bound to raise further concerns of this kind, the biggest challenge will be to establish adequate security safeguards in e-voting systems [6].

Note that the Polish electoral legislation is undergoing an evolution aimed partly at adopting the aforesaid alternative voting methods. The Electoral Code of January 2011 features a host of diverse solutions aimed at facilitating voting in general elections. Designed primarily for disabled and elderly voters, the solutions allow them to use alternative procedures and vote off the premises of polling stations. Furthermore, the Electoral Code provides for mechanisms to keep disabled voters informed about key election issues. In July 2014, an amendment to the Code extended the scope of admissibility for correspondence voting [9]. The amended electoral law allows all citizens to vote by correspondence. The postal service can be used to vote in parliamentary, presidential and European Parliament elections. Correspondence voting is not available to all voters in local elections as it has been reserved for people suffering from serious or moderate disabilities.

Without a doubt, the modifications adopted in the Polish electoral law represent a new quality in upholding the principle of universal suffrage and preventing voter exclusion [10]. Equally significant is the fact that conceptual and legislative work to develop new voting procedures (among them for Internet voting) is now under way (albeit limited in scope). It is clearly essential that Poland consider launching broad-based research into electronic voting procedures which appear to be inevitable in the future. Undoubtedly, the states which have already adopted "electronic models" (such as Switzerland and Estonia) need to be watched closely as a source of valuable insights. The overall public opinion will ultimately reflect the willingness with which voters are prepared to embrace these new voting modes.

4   The Politicians and Political Parties' Stance on E-Voting

In Poland, there is no system that would enable voting in national elections via the Internet. However the topic of implementation of e-voting occurs systematically before every national elections in Poland.

The attitude of politicians and political parties to electronic voting in Poland seemed always to be very pragmatic. Their attitudes of this kind of voting depended primarily on the potential future election benefits in terms of its implementation. Arkadiusz Żukowski points out that "the first serious debate on Internet voting took place only in terms of parliamentary elections in 2005, when voter turnout was one of the lowest [11]" [12]. Donald Tusk – leader of the Civic Platform declared that in next parliamentary elections the electorate would have possibility to vote via the electronic means. Voting on the Internet was also promised by Tusk just after the early parliamentary elections in Poland in 2007.

Jarosław Kaczynski – leader of the Law and Justice Party emphasized that he was against implementation of e-voting in Poland. "He believed that electronic voting trivialized such important act of citizenship as the vote. Moreover, he seemed to be well aware of the fact that among the young electorate and Internet users his party had little electoral support" [12].

One of the biggest supporter of implementation of e-voting in Poland is Wincenty Elsner – former MP of Palikot Movement. He was chairman of Parlamantary Group – Poland 2.0 and he prepared a project of amendment to the Electoral Code. Elsner wanted to introduce Internet voting with the use of the ePUAP (electronic Platform of Public Administration Services). The project was criticized by experts and professionals during a conference in Polish Sejm, and finally nothing was done about it.

One of the most "popular" attempt of implementation of electronic voting in Poland has been conducted in 2010 before the presidential election. Due to the death of President Lech Kaczyński in a plane crash in April, the presidential election that was initially planned to be held in Autumn, had to be brought forward.

It is worth mentioning that after accepting Bronislaw Komorowski and Radoslaw Sikorski as candidates for a candidate for a president's office, the national authority of the Civic Platform decided that the person who would be the party's official candidate for the office is to be elected by the members of the party in primary elections. "This was the first time in Poland that a candidate was chosen in this way. Moreover the party management decided to allow two voting methods: postal and internet voting" [13].

Any of the members of PO could vote either for Bronislaw Komorowski or Radosław Sikorski. There were two methods of voting available - via the Internet or by sending a special form via regular post. Ballot papers were distributed in the all over Poland via the Civic Platform's monthly magazine "POgłos", which is sent to all members of the party. The ballot paper were printed on one of the pages. The election issue of "POgłos" included also two envelopes. One of them contained unique username and password for signing in to a special server. Once the data was entered, the system opened the voting page, where a politician could choose an appropriate candidate. Username and password gave access to the system only once. There was no chance to vote again using the same user's data. Any member of the PO who was registered in the central register of the party's members had the right to vote. Members of the PO, who decided on the traditional method of voting, had to cut the ballot paper from the "POgłos" magazine, insert it into the enclosed envelope and send by post. To prevent double voting, (on-line and traditional) members were advised to attach the envelope with one-time codes to the envelope with the ballot paper. Those, who opened the envelope with the codes, were unable to send a valid vote by post. Hanna Gronkiewicz-Waltz chaired the electoral commission, and on 26 March 2010 she announced that 21246 out of 44759 members of the party had voted in the primary elections. Turnout in presidential primary election in the PO was 47.47%. PO voters definitely preferred the Internet. Over 17 thousand votes were cast in this way. 4 thousand of the party's members sent their votes by post [14]. Members of the Civic Platform have pointed to Bronislaw Komorowski as the party's official candidate for presidential elections in Poland. The Speaker of the Sejm received 68.5% of the votes. 31.5% of the members supported his opponent, Radosław Sikorski [15].

Since then no other serious discussion on e-voting has taken place in Poland. One should remember that in December 2014 huge technical problems occurred by local elections, when the "electronic [counting-M.MK] voting system suffered major technical glitches during local elections, delaying results, and leading to widely unexpected outcomes. (...) Polish courts were flooded with more than a thousand legal challenges contesting election results" [16].

In spite of the fact that the politicians do not discuss implementation of e-voting in Poland, the electorate supports this idea and expects that next to possible voting methods – voting via the Internet will be available in the future. The next part of the paper will give some proofs for it.

5 Public Perception of E-Voting in Poland

Voters in Poland are fairly open to the idea of adopting procedures other than personal voting in polling stations. They may see such modes as ways to vote more conveniently, perhaps in the comfort of their homes. As this paper focuses on the online variety of electronic voting, the findings below will be based on the surveys carried out in 2014 by the Center for Public Opinion Research and the Ombudsman's Office (compared with similar studies by the Center for Public Opinion Research conducted in July 2011). Such a selection of surveys is well suited to help identify trends in public opinion in Poland and compare multiple indicators. Each question put to the respondents in the author's own survey was analyzed threefold by accounting for the constituents of each party participating in the European Parliamentary elections of 2014 as well as the political views declared by the respondents.

5.1 Poles' Views on the Use of E-Voting in State Elections

In view of rapid advances in IT, widespread Internet access and technological progress in nearly every area of human life (e-commerce, e-administration, e-society, e-banking, e-books, etc.), one may presume that voters will want to see "upgrades" also in democratic procedures to make them more accessible and convenient.

A study on the percentage of the voters who approve having Poland adopt Internet voting found that a total of 59.14% of the respondents either "strongly" or "mildly" favor the solution and that 22.90% oppose the option.

Considering who supported each political party (as seen in the EP election), it is evident that the largest share of e-voting supporters in Poland (a total of 65.6%) voted for the Civic Platform party in May 2014 by declaring they were either "strongly" or "mildly" in favor.

Civic Platform voters were followed closely by the supporters of the New Right of Janusz Korwin-Mikke (a total of 64.4%). Internet-based voting was approved by nearly 60% of those voting for the Democratic Left Alliance – the Labor Union. The groups comprising the smallest proportion of electronic voting supporters (and whose members responded with "strong" or "mild" disapproval) could be found among the backers of Law and Justice and the Polish People's Party (49.5% and 45.6% respectively). Supporters of these two parties were also the most likely to oppose this voting mode (33.4% of the Law and Justice supporters and 30.4% of the supporters of the Polish People's Party). The backers of the Democratic Left Alliance – the Labor Union and the New Right of Janusz Korwin-Mikke included respectively 22.3% and 27.2% e-voting opponents. The smallest proportion of such opponents (merely 16%) could be found among the supporters of the Civic Platform (Table 1).

Table 1. Percent distribution of responses to the question: "Do you want the option of electronic voting via the Internet to be available in Polish elections?" by electorate group participating in European Parliament election in 2014

	Strongly opposed	Mildly opposed	Undecided	Mildly in favor	Strongly in favor
New Right of Janusz Korwin Mikke	13.6%	13.6%	8.5%	16.9%	47.5%
Civic Platform	7.3%	8.7%	18.4%	31.1%	34.5%
Polish People's Party	15.2%	15.2%	23.9%	30.4%	15.2%
Law and Justoce	16.3%	17.5%	16.9%	29.4%	20.0%
Democratic Left Alliance-Labor Union	9.3%	13.0%	18.5%	27.8%	31.5%
Other	5.1%	16.9%	8.5%	25.4%	44.1%
Non-voters	7.1%	13.8%	21.6%	19.4%	38.2%
Cannor remember	11.1%	7.9%	15.9%	33.3%	31.7%

Source: own conclusions based on survey findings.

Very interesting results to the question came from the supporters of parties unlisted in the Table, the non-voters and those who could not remember how they voted in the EP election. The vast majority of the above, i.e. 69.5% of other party supporters, 57.6% of the non-voters and 65% of those who could not recall how they had voted, approved of i-voting. An aggregation of all favorable responses suggests that the majority of the participants in the EP election supported the adoption of electronic voting in Poland, which shows that Poles want to see the electoral law modified.

With respect to the ideological inclinations of the surveyed (left/center/right), it is worth noting four issues that distinguish the respondents and that appear to be of significance. An arrangement similar to that performed in the previous part of the findings analysis (of combining all answers that were strongly or mildly in favor as well as all those that were strongly or mildly opposed) revealed the following regularities:

– firstly, the majority of the respondents across all groups would like to see the option of Internet voting made available in Polish elections – this amounts to 69.6% of the centrist voters, 61.8% of the left-wing supporters, 56% of the right-wing supporters as well as 54.5% of those unable to define their political views;

- secondly, the most diverse opinions were noted among the respondents who declared themselves to be centrist as well as those defining themselves as rightist. While 69.6% of the former spoke in favor of e-voting, 56% of the rightist voters shared their opinion. The difference between the two amounted to 13.6 percentage points. Furthermore, 17.1% of centrist voters expressed a reluctance to having e-voting available in Poland. This view was shared by 27.5% of rightist voters (the difference on the issue between the center and right of the political spectrum amounted to 10.4 percentage points) (Table 2):

Table 2. Percent distribution of responses to the question "Do you want the option of electronic voting via the Internet to be available in Polish elections?" relative to declared political views

	Strongly opposed	Mildly opposed	Undecided	Mildly in favor	Strongly in favor
Left	8.7%	14.8%	14.8%	24.6%	37.2%
Center	6.7%	10.4%	13.4%	28.7%	40.9%
Right	13.3%	14.2%	16.5%	26.8%	29.2%
Do not know/cannot say	7.8%	12.3%	25.4%	23.8%	30.7%

Source: own surveys.

- thirdly, the biggest discrepancy in responses in support of e-voting (15.1 percentage points) was recorded between centrist voters (69.6%) and those unable to define their political views (54.5%):
- fourthly, the smallest divergence in the proportions of responses in favor of e-voting (1.5 percentage points) was found between the rightists (56%) and the undecideds. Note that the two groups differed in the distribution of negative responses, which added up to 27.5% and 20.1% respectively (Fig. 1 and Table 2).

In analysis of the average findings for the individual responses suggests that ideological views exceed party preferences as a distinguishing factor for support for i-voting in Poland, although differences between the specific values are minor and fit within the statistical error margin, which renders the finding inconclusive. The only conclusion that can be derived from the data in the Table is that Poles would appreciate an option of using an extra voting mode and that they approve of the adoption of e-voting.

The above has been confirmed by the public opinion polls held in 2011 and 2014 which found that Poles are generally in favor of voting untraditionally outside of polling stations. The most common view is that in support of Internet voting. "The adoption of this procedure in Polish electoral law would be welcome by 76% of the surveyed, 44% of whom believe it should be available to all voters, whereas 32% would rather limit its use to people unable to get to polling stations. 18% of the respondents were staunchly against the procedure. The findings closely reflected those

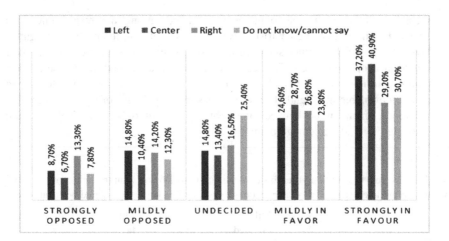

Fig. 1. Percent distribution of responses to the question "Do you want the option of electronic voting via the Internet to be available in Polish elections?" relative to declared political views (Source: own surveys).

Table 3. Average percent distribution of responses to the question "Do you want the option of electronic voting via the Internet to be available in Polish elections?" by the voter groups taking part in the EP elections in 2014 and the regional assembly election in 2014, relative to declared political views.

	Strongly or mildly opposed	Undecided	Strongly or mildly in favor
Electorates in EP election	23.95%	16.53%	59.55%
Political views	22.05%	17.53%	60.48%

Source: own surveys.

of the 2011 study with an only slight shift towards restricting the use of the procedure to persons unable to reach polling stations" [17].

Note that the public opinion poll of 2014 (conducted by the Center for Public Opinion Research and the Ombudsman's Office) found that the strongest support for i-voting could be found in the youngest age groups of 18 to 24 and 25 to 34: "84% of the members of both age groups spoke in favor of such voting. The majority of them (55%) would like the procedure to be available to all voters" [11]. The trend is common in most of the countries which either have adopted or are considering the adoption of the tool. This is due to the fact young people are significantly more likely than the old to use the Internet and that they see it as more convenient than traditional methods (voting without leaving one's home, possible at any location around the world, etc.) (Fig. 2).

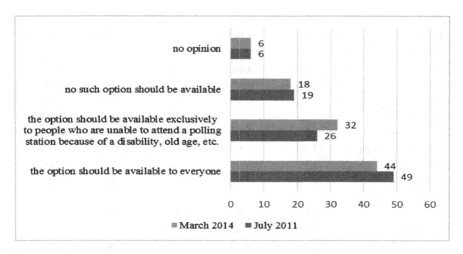

Fig. 2. Should the option of electronic voting (online) be made available? (% of responses) (Source: own study based on: Ułatwienia w głosowaniu. Wiedza, opinie i oczekiwania [Voting facilitation. The knowledge, views and expectations]. Communication 55/2014 of the Center for Public Opinion Research. Warsaw 2014, p. 3)

5.2   Poles' Declarations Regarding the Use of Internet-Voting in Elections

As a consequence of the examination of Poles' views on the adoption of i-voting in elections, a probe has been conducted into their self-declared willingness to make use of the option to vote electronically in an election, were it made available.

A study of the percent distribution of responses to the question of whether, given the opportunity, the respondents (groups voting in the EP election) would make use of the option to vote online, shows that the majority (over 50%) of the members of such groups (other than the supporters of the Polish People's Party) were either strongly or mildly in favor. The largest percent share of the "yes" votes (74.6%) came from persons who voted for parties other than those listed in the study. Ca. 5 percentage points fewer affirmative answers came from the supporters of the New Right of Janusz Korwin-Mikke and the Civic Platform (69.40% each). 50.6% of Law and Justice supporters are prepared to vote online. Meanwhile, only 45.6% of the supporters of the Polish People's Party were willing to take advantage of e-voting (Table 4).

The percent distribution of the "strongly opposed" and "mildly opposed" responses shows that the respondents were significantly more reluctant to engage in e-voting than they were to its mere introduction. The distributors among the individual groups of EP voters ranged from 15.30% (voters for parties unlisted in the table) to 38.2% (supporters of Law and Justice, who included the greatest number of those "strongly opposed"). Of the other parties' supporters, the fewest "against" responses came from those of Janusz Korwin-Mikke's party (17%) and Civic Platform. The voters for the Democratic Left Alliance – the Labor Union, turned out to be fairly disapproving, with nearly 30% declaring they were unwilling to vote via the Internet in an election. An interesting pattern emerged among the supporters of the Polish People's Party who

Table 4. Number and percent distribution of responses to the question "Given the option, would you vote over the Internet in elections?" among electorate groups participating in European Parliament election in 2014

	Strongly opposed	Mildly opposed	Undecided	Mildly in favor	Strongly in favor
New Right of Janusz Korwin Mikke	11.9%	5.1%	13.6%	16.9%	52.5%
Civic Platform	8.3%	11.7%	10.7%	29.1%	40.3%
Polish People's Party	15.2%	19.6%	19.6%	23.9%	21.7%
Law and Justoce	21.3%	16.9%	11.3%	25.0%	25.6%
Democratic Left Alliance-Labor Union	11.1%	18.5%	14.8%	27.8%	27.8%
Other	6.8%	8.5%	10.2%	25.4%	49.2%
Non-voters	12.7%	13.8%	13.1%	20.1%	40.3%
Cannor remember	14.3%	7.9%	14.3%	23.8%	39.7%

Source: own surveys.

comprised the greatest number of "undecideds" (19.6%) alongside 34.8% of "strongly" and "mildly" opposed members (the second largest number of opposed respondents).

The above shows that the supporters of Law and Justice and the Polish People's Party, followed immediately by those of the Democratic Left Alliance, display the most "traditional" approach to elections and are the most reluctant to declare willingness to engage in e-voting in an election.

A confrontation of the above responses with those compared with political views sheds light on a range of issues that appear to be of significance and that help differentiate among the individual respondent groups:

– firstly, across all of the groups, the majority declare willingness to vote electronically in Polish elections given the option: these amounted to 71.9% of the centrist, 61.8% of the leftist, 59.3% of the rightist voters as well as 56.9% of those unable to specify their political affiliations. The data shows an overall approval of the additional voting mode among the surveyed;

– secondly, the smallest proportion (18.9%) of persons unwilling to vote electronically was found among the self-declared centrist voters (the ratio ranged from 25% to 29.8% in the other groups) (Table 5);

Table 5. Percent distribution of responses to the question "Given the option, would you vote over the Internet?" relative to declared political views

	Strongly opposed	Mildly opposed	Undecided	Mildly in favor	Strongly in favor
Left	12.6%	14.2%	11.5%	18.6%	43.2%
Center	7.9%	11.0%	9.1%	27.4%	44.5%
Right	16.2%	13.6%	10.9%	26.3%	33.0%
Do not know/cannot say	11.9%	13.1%	18.0%	22.5%	34.4%

Source: own surveys.

- thirdly, the biggest discrepancies in opinions have been noted between centrist voters and those declaring themselves as right wing. While 71.9% of the former indicated willingness to take advantage of e-voting, only 59.3% of the right-wing voters shared this view. The two groups ended up being 12.6 percentage points apart. On the other hand, 18.9% of the centrist voters compared to 29.8% of the right-wing electorate (a difference of 10.9 percentage points) would rather not vote electronically (Fig. 3);

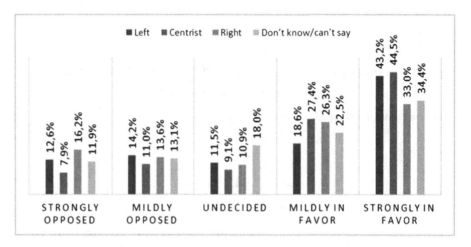

Fig. 3. Percent distribution of responses to the question "Given the option, would you vote over the Internet?" relative to declared political views

- fourthly, the biggest divergence among the persons who declared themselves as willing to vote over the Internet (15 percentage points) arose between centrist voters (71.9%) and those unable to define their political affiliations (56.9%);
- fifthly, the smallest discrepancy (of 2.4 percentage points) in the percent share of persons declared to be willing to vote electronically arose between rightist voters and those unable to define their political affiliations (Table 6).

Table 6. Average percent share of responses to the question "Given the option, would you vote over the Internet in elections?" among the electorate groups taking part in the EP election in 2014 and the regional assembly election in 2014, relative to declared political views

	Strongly or mildly opposed	Undecided	Strongly or mildly in favor
Electorates in EP election	25.45%	13.45%	61.14%
Political views	25.13%	12.38%	62.48%

Source: own surveys

A study of the average findings shows that the discrepancies between the individual values are minor (at ca. 1 percentage point) and that the opinions of persons representing similar party affiliations and political views are comparable. Persons declaring their willingness to use e-voting account for approximately 61% to 62% of the surveyed. The opponents of such instruments make up ca. 24–25% of the respondents. Every 12th or every 13th respondent had no opinion on the matter. The data appears to suggest that, given the opportunity, the majority of the surveyed would vote online. This should inspire a broader debate on adopting an electronic voting system in Poland (Fig. 4).

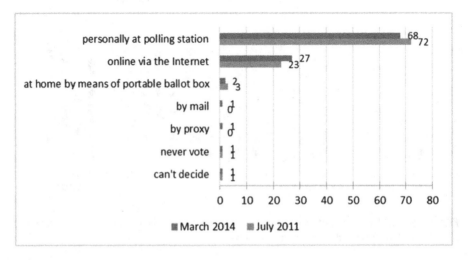

Fig. 4. Given the choice of voting method, I would prefer (% of responses). (Source: own study based on: Ułatwienia w glosowaniu. Wiedza, opinie i oczekiwania (Voting facilitation. The knowledge, views and expectations), Communication 55/2014 of the Center for Public Opinion Research, Warsaw 2014, p. 4)

Despite such unambiguous responses, one is well advised to refer to the findings of the above-mentioned surveys by the Center for Public Opinion Research and the Ombudsman's Office, which show that despite the overall approval of e-voting among Poles, the majority of those entitled to vote are in fact "traditionalists."

The outcomes of the public opinion polls held in March 2014 show that close to two thirds of the surveyed (68%) prefer voting in a polling station over any other available voting mode. Polling station voting slipped in popularity from the 2011 level (72% to 68%). "Meanwhile, a rise was seen in alternative voting procedures, especially in electronic voting, which was named as the preferred voting mode by 27% of the surveyed (up from 23% in 2011). The other procedures (such as correspondence and proxy voting) were only chosen by a small number of respondents" [11].

The aforesaid findings additionally revealed changes in the views of the youngest voters, aged 18 to 24, who were even less likely than in 2011 (49%, down from 60% in

2011) to prefer the traditional polling station voting mode involving a ballot box. As polling stations lost popularity, more respondents supported e-voting (46% in this age bracket, compared to 37–40% in 2011). Note that "the older the voters, the less likely they were to approve of this voting mode with merely 2% of the voters aged above 65 speaking out in its favor" and that "as the voters born in successive years come of age, support for i-voting is bound to rise at the expense of the popularity of polling station voting" [11].

6 Conclusions

A steady increase in the popularity of e-voting has been observed in recent years across many countries of Europe and the rest of the world, including Estonia, Switzerland, the United States and Australia. The adoption of e-voting models in domestic elections and referendums is being widely debated not only among members of parliaments and national government ministers but also the voting population at large. Notably, the new voting technologies provide one benefit of which the voters are aware, that is they eliminate the hurdle of distance between the people entitled to vote and polling stations. Other advantages of e-voting, which are organizational and procedural in nature (e.g. vote tallying), work to the benefit of both administrators and politicians [18].

One must nevertheless bear in mind the drawbacks of e-voting associated in particular with the security of casting and counting votes in elections and referendums. Despite persistent technical issues having to do with election security, etc., the wide range of benefits to be enjoyed by various segments of society such as voters, politicians and administrators as well as the positive experience of many countries, may provide a strong incentive for the adoption of e-voting not only in Europe, including Poland, but also in other parts of the world.

Although much time will certainly be needed before an e-voting model can be put in place, one should not overlook the popular approval for electronic voting that is evidenced by the research carried out in this project. While Poland's electoral law is hardly posed for a revolution, steady change can certainly be noticed. Electronic voting may well one day become a part of this change process. The author believes that this paper is a basic start on analysis on e-voting implementation possibilities in Poland, and it will be incentive for further and more deeper analysis of Polish electorate on this topic.

References

1. Krimmer, R.: Overview. In: Krimmer, R. (ed.) Electronic Voting 2006. 2nd International Workshop Co-organized by Council of Europe, ESF TED, IFIP WG 8.5 and E-Voting.CC, 2–4 August 2006, Castle Hofen, Bregenz, Austria, pp. 9–12. Gesellschaft für Informatik, Bonn (2006)
2. Musiał-Karg, M.: Internetowe głosowanie w Estonii na przykładzie wyborów w latach 2005–2009 [Internet voting in Estonia. The case of the 2005–2009 election]. Przegląd Politologiczny **3**, 99–118 (2011)

3. Maciejewski, A.: E-voting to kwestia czasu [E-voting is a matter of time]. http://www.computerworld.pl/news/83306/E.voting.to.kwestia.czasu.html
4. Recommendation Rec (2004)11 of the Committee of Ministers to member states on legal, operational and technical standards for e-voting, adopted by the Committee of Ministers on 30 September 2004 at the 898th meeting of the Ministers' Deputies
5. Musiał-Karg, M.: Elektroniczne referendum w Szwajcarii. Wybrane kierunki zmian helweckiej demokracji bezpośredniej [Electronic referendum in Switzerland. Selected changes in direct democracy in Switzerland], WNPiD UAM, Poznań (2012)
6. Szymanek, J.: E-voting w świetle przepisów Konstytucji RP [E-voting in the light of the Polish Constitution]. http://www.marketingpolityczny.org/e-voting-w-swietle-przepisow-konstytucji-rp/#.Va_4L_l8mNM
7. Wojtasik, W.: Funkcje wyborów w II Rzeczypospolitej. Teoria i praktyka [The function of elections in the Second Polish Republic. Theory and practice], Wyd. UŚ, Katowice (2012)
8. Zbieranek, J.: W stronę reformy procedur głosowania w Polsce [Towards voting procedure reform in Poland]. Analizy i Opinie 52. Instytut Spraw Publicznych, Warsaw (2005)
9. Act of July 11, 2014 amending the Electoral Code and certain other laws]. The Act was drawn up by the Parliament based on an MP draft tabled in July 2013 (Parliament Journal No. 1786)
10. Zbieranek, J.: Alternatywne procedury głosowania w Polsce na tle państw Unii Europejskiej [Alternative voting procedures in Poland compared with other European Union member states]. Studia BAS 3(27), 126–127 (2011)
11. Bendyk, E.: Elektroniczne głosowanie - lek na całe zło? [Electronic voting – cure for all evil]. "Polityka", 27 March 2008. http://www.polityka.pl/kraj/249743,1,elektroniczne-glosowanie—lek-na-cale-zlo.read#ixzz1x6nrKntz
12. Żukowski, A.: Dispute on Electronic Voting in Poland – Near or Far Future? (Preliminary View). http://paperroom.ipsa.org/papers/paper_14234.pdf
13. Młyńczak, K.: Polish Internet voting – a political tool or a real desire for innovation?. "Modern Democracy the Electronic Voting and Participation Magazine", no 2/2010
14. Szczegółowe informacje dotyczące prawyborów [Details on pre-elections], 27 March 2010. http://www.prawybory.platforma.org/aktualnosci/art40,szczegolowe-informacje-dotyczace-prawyborow.html
15. Platforma Obywatelska wybrała Komorowskiego [Civic Platform has chosen Komorowski], 27 March 2010. http://www.prawybory.platforma.org/aktualnosci/art39,platforma-obywatelska-wybrala-komorowskiego.html
16. Ali, T.: How (not) to deploy an electronic voting system. "The Express Tribune", 21 May 2015. http://tribune.com.pk/story/889594/how-not-to-deploy-an-electronic-voting-system/
17. Ułatwienia w głosowaniu. Wiedza, opinie i oczekiwania [Voting facilitation. The knowledge, opinions and expectations]. Communication on a study by the Center for Public Opinion Research. No. 55/2014, Warsaw (2014)
18. Krimmer, R.: The Evolution of E-voting: Why Voting Technology is Used and How it Affects Democracy. Tallinn University of Technology, TUT Press, Tallinn (2012)

Author Index

Printed in the United States
By Bookmasters